Pointing: Where Language, Culture, and Cognition Meet

Pointing: Where Language, Culture, and Cognition Meet

Edited by

Sotaro Kita

LEA LAWRENCE ERLBAUM ASSOCIATES, PUBLISHERS
2003   Mahwah, New Jersey   London

Lawrence Erlbaum Associates, Inc., Publishers
10 Industrial Avenue
Mahwah, New Jersey 07430

Cover design by Kathryn Houghtaling Lacey
Cover sculpture by Stephen C. Levinson
Cover photography by Sotaro Kita ©

Library of Congress Cataloging-in-Publication Data

Pointing: where language, culture, and cognition meet / edited by Sotaro Kita.
     p. cm.
  Includes bibliographical references and index.
  ISBN 0-8058-4014-1 (cloth : alk. paper)
  1. Pointing (Gesture). 2. Nonverbal communication. 3. Communication and culture.
I. Kita, Sotaro, 1963–

P117.7.P65 2002
302.2′22—dc21

2002070057
CIP

Books published by Lawrence Erlbaum Associates are printed on acid-free paper, and their bindings are chosen for strength and durability.

Printed in the United States of America
10 9 8 7 6 5 4 3 2 1

Contents

Acknowledgments

The origin of this volume is the Max Planck Workshop on Pointing, which was organized by the Max Planck Institute for Psycholinguistics in 1997. The interdisciplinary atmosphere of the workshop engendered exhilarating synergy among ideas and findings presented by the participants. This volume aims to share this excitement with a larger world by putting together the papers written by the participants and some additional contributors in the field into one volume. The chapters are written for this volume and illustrate state-of-the-art findings and ideas from different disciplines.

I thank Pim Levelt and Steve Levinson, two directors of the Max Planck Institute for Psycholinguistics, for their generous support for the workshop and the production of this book. I thank Edith Sjoerdsma and Mark Floris for helping me organize the workshop. I thank Jürgen Streeck and another anonymous reviewer for very helpful suggestions. I thank all the contributors for patiently tolerating delays and requests. I thank Alex Dukers for helping me put together the indexes. I thank also Marianne Gullberg, Nick Enfield, Andrea Krott, and Daan van Exel for their help in the final stage of putting the volume together.

Chapter 1

Pointing: A Foundational Building Block of Human Communication

Sotaro Kita
Max Planck Institute for Psycholinguistics

This volume examines pointing gestures from a multidisciplinary viewpoint. Pointing has captured the interest of scholars from different disciplines who study communication: linguists, semioticians, psychologists, anthropologists, and primatologists. However, ideas and findings have been scattered across diverse journals and books, and researchers are often not aware of results in other disciplines. To date, there have been few opportunities for interdisciplinary exchange of information. The aim of this volume is to provide an arena for such exchange.

The prototypical pointing gesture is a communicative body movement that projects a vector from a body part. This vector indicates a certain direction, location, or object. Why is investigation of pointing gestures important? Because it is a foundational building block of human communication. Pointing is foundational in four respects.

First, it is ubiquitous in our day-to-day interaction with others. When communicating about referents locatable in the speech situation, pointing is almost inevitable. Even when we talk about referents that are distant in space and time, we often point to the seemingly empty space in front of us. Such pointing assigns a certain meaning to the location in the space, and we point back to the same location later in the discourse (see McNeill, chap. 12). The assignment of a meaning to a location by pointing is part of the grammar of signed languages. Pointing in signed languages is equivalent to, and used as frequently as, pronouns in spoken languages ("every

1

four signs in signed discourse is a pointing sign"; see Engberg-Pedersen, chap. 11).

Second, pointing is a uniquely human behavior. In other words, pointing separates humans from primates, just like the use of language does. Primate behaviors that closely resemble pointing lack some of the key components of human pointing (see Povinelli et al., chap. 3; Butterworth, chap. 2). A careful examination sharply delineates the fundamental difference between primate and human communication.

Third, pointing is primordial in ontogeny. Pointing is one of the first versatile communicative devices that an infant acquires. Pointing emerges out of its antecedent behaviors, such as undirected extension of the index finger, several weeks before the first spoken word (see Butterworth, chap. 2; Masataka, chap. 4).[1] Once infants start uttering words, they produce a word and a pointing gesture together. How infants use pointing predicts their later language development to some extent (see Goldin-Meadow & Butcher, chap. 5; Butterworth, chap. 2). In addition, the caregiver's pointing is probably one of the important cues with which infants establish a connection between a word and its referent.

Fourth, pointing does not merely indicate a vector, but it can serve to create further types of signs. For example, a pointing gesture can create an iconic representation by tracing a shape or movement trajectory (see Haviland, chap. 7). It sometimes even leaves a visible mark, "inscribing" a shape on a surface (see Goodwin, chap. 9).

CROSS-CUTTING ISSUES

Because pointing is so ubiquitous and we interpret it with such ease, it might appear that pointing is a trivial phenomenon. On the contrary, as demonstrated by all of the chapters, careful examination reveals that the versatility and interpretability of pointing are based on complex underlying biological, psychological, and semiotic processes. Some issues regarding these processes recur in different chapters in the volume.

One such issue is biological determinism and the putative universality of index finger pointing (see Wilkins, chap. 8; Masataka, chap. 4; Butterworth, chap. 2; Povinelli et al., chap. 3). The question is whether humans are biologically programmed to point with an extended index finger, making index-finger pointing universal across cultures. Although it is anatomically difficult for chimpanzees to extend only the index finger (Povinelli et al.,

---

[1]There seems to be little evidence supporting Vygotsky's (1988) hypothesis that the infant's failed reaching and the caregiver's reaction to it develop into pointing (see the chapters by Masataka and by Butterworth).

chap. 3), human infants produce index-finger pointing from early on in studies conducted in the United States, Europe, and Japan (see Butterworth, chap. 2; Masataka, chap. 4). This might suggest the biological determinism of index-finger pointing. However, in these cultures, adults also frequently use index-finger pointing. Thus, questions still remain. Is infants' index-finger pointing a biologically programmed choice? Or is it due to the input and reinforcement from adults? (See Masataka, chap. 4, for the discussions about the possibility of culture-specific reinforcement.) A more conclusive answer to these questions requires a future study on children's early pointing in a culture where adults do not use index-finger pointing at all or do so only rarely. As noted in Wilkins's chapter, some preliminary reports suggest that such cultures may indeed exist.

Furthermore, Wilkins' chapter notes that even in cultures where index-finger pointing is commonly used among adults, its function vis-à-vis other forms of pointing (e.g., flat-hand pointing) differs from culture to culture. Kendon and Versante's chapter provides a meticulous description of functions associated with different forms of pointing used by Neapolitans. The range of forms used as pointing gestures (i.e., different hand shapes and the choice of other articulators such as the lips[2]) and the form–function mapping in a given culture clearly have to be learned by children.

Another recurring issue in the chapters concerns semiotic processes that underlie interpretation of a pointing gesture. The general problem is that the referent of a pointing gesture can be ambiguous in many ways. Does the pointing indicate a direction (e.g., north)? If so, what is the origo from which the direction should be interpreted: from the location of the gesturer, or from some other reference point? (See Haviland, chap. 7, for discussions on pointing with a "transposed" reference point.) If pointing does not merely indicate a direction, it has a target object or location. If the target is an object, does it simply refer to the object, or does it predicate that the object is located at its location (see Engberg-Pedersen, chap. 11)? Furthermore, which aspect of the object is indicated? To take an example from Clark's chapter (chap. 10), pointing in the direction of a car could be a reference to the car itself, to the color of the car, or to a piece of junk.

There are different suggestions as to how one can narrow down the domain of possible referents. Goodwin (chap. 9) suggests, for example, that an "activity framework" specifies which features of the environment are relevant for the ongoing activity and hence are likely to be the referent of a pointing gesture. In addition, different forms of pointing may correlate with particular types of referents (see Kendon & Versante, chap. 6; Haviland, chap. 7; Engberg-Pedersen, chap. 11; Wilkins, chap. 8; Kita, chap. 13).

---

[2]Lip pointing seems to be more common across cultures than one would suppose from European perspectives. See Wilkins' chapter as well as Sherzer (1973) and Enfield (2002).

Even if one identifies the referent, further pragmatic inferences may be needed to get to the intended interpretation. First, an associative link from the direct referent to the inferred referent may have to be taken into account. For example, a pointing gesture can be directed toward an empty chair (the direct referent) in order to refer to the person who normally sits in the chair (the inferred referent; see Haviland, chap. 7; Clark, chap. 10). Second, a pointing gesture can be interpreted as a social act such as "imperative," which demands a response from the communication partner. For example, an infant may produce a pointing gesture that can be interpreted as a request, "give me that" (see Butterworth, chap. 2; Povinelli et al., chap. 3). Finally, the accompanying speech can narrow down possible interpretations of a pointing gesture (see e.g., Goodwin, chap. 9). Goldin-Meadow and Butcher (chap. 5) note that infants in the one-word stage often combine a word and a pointing gesture, which together comprise a proposition.

To complicate matters further, a pointing gesture may not have a preexisting target, but may be directed toward seemingly empty space. "Abstract deixis" in cospeech gesture (see McNeill, chap. 12) and "indexical signs" in Danish Sign Language (see Engberg-Pedersen, chap. 11) are such cases. In these cases, a physically empty location is assigned a meaning by virtue of being the target of a pointing gesture. Haviland discusses a related case, which involves pointing gestures directed toward a concrete target. In the description of the structure of a sugar-cane press, the speaker points to a wooden post of a house. However, he does not intend to refer to the house post. He uses the house post as a prop. It stands for a supporting post of an imaginary sugar-cane press, which he "builds" with a series of gestures. These are examples of Silverstein's (1976) "creative" function of indexical signs. The interpretation of such creative pointing gestures is constrained not only by the linguistic context, but also by the "deictic field" (see especially McNeill, chap. 12), which is populated by imaginary entities that are also established by other creative pointing gestures. Note the similarity and the difference between activity frameworks and deictic fields. An activity framework imposes a more abstract structure on a cluttered physical environment, whereas a deictic field projects a richer structure on a physically minimal environment.

OVERVIEW OF THE CURRENT VOLUME AND BEYOND

Having laid out some of the issues that cross-cut the chapters, we now turn to the structure of the volume. The first four chapters concern the ontogeny and phylogeny of pointing. The first chapter by Butterworth provides an overview of the literature on developmental and primate studies on pointing and joint attention. He argues that index-finger pointing is a uniquely human behavior (e.g., there has been no report on primates in the wild using index-finger pointing among themselves). He maps out the developmental path of pointing from its antecedent behaviors to the role it plays in early language development.

In the following chapter, Povinelli, Bering, and Giambrone discuss the comprehension of pointing by chimpanzees. The results of their experiments indicate that, unlike young children, chimpanzees lack the understanding that a body part projects a vector toward a particular direction, and, more crucially, they lack the understanding that the communication partner has to mentally represent the direction. The lack of "mentalistic" understanding of pointing by chimpanzees is in sharp contrast to human infants, who check whether the communication partner is attending the same referent (cf. the chapter by Butterworth).

Two chapters on the development of pointing follow. Masataka studies the earliest part of development, namely, the stages that lead up to the emergence of adultlike pointing gestures around the age of 11 months. He proposes that undirected extension of the index finger is one of the key antecedent behaviors for pointing. Index-finger extension tends to be synchronized with speechlike vocalization. In addition, index-finger extensions occur more often when the caregiver reacts to the infant's vocalization in a timely manner and when an infant is confronted with an unfamiliar object. In other words, the situation that leads to index-finger extension is very similar to the situation in which pointing gestures are commonly observed in older infants, namely, verbal communication with a caregiver about a noteworthy object. Furthermore, a longitudinal study has revealed that a sharp drop in the frequency of index-finger extension is immediately followed by a sharp rise in the frequency of pointing.

A later stage of the development is covered by Goldin-Meadow and Butcher, who investigate pointing between the one- and two-word stages. They have found that the onset of utterances in which a word and a pointing gesture refer to two separate entities is a good predictor for the subsequent onset of two-word utterances. In other words, infants package two ideas into a message first in a pointing–word combination and then in a word–word combination.

Four chapters on the ethnography of pointing follow. These chapters examine naturally occurring pointing gestures and contexts of their use, as well as people's meta-knowledge about various types of pointing gestures. Kendon and Versante investigate the relationship between different shape features of pointing and their functions in Neapolitans' gestures. Their analysis of the contexts of use reveals an elaborate system of pointing in this famously gesture-rich culture.

Haviland illustrates various types of semiotic complexity of pointing gestures using data from Tzotzil speakers of Mexico (an 18-month-old child and adults). He discusses relationships between various pointing forms and their functions, relationships to speech, and the influence of spatial and sociocultural contexts on the interpretation of pointing.

Wilkins problematizes what it means to claim universality of index-finger pointing by underscoring the culture specificity of form–function relationships. He examines form–function relationships in the Arrernte community (Central Australia) from a perspective that emphasizes meta-knowledge. He found that some of the hand shape used for pointing in this culture are unusual from Euro-American perspectives. For example, he reports transitional middle-finger pointing by young children.[3]

The last in the series of chapters on the ethnography of pointing is the chapter by Goodwin. He analyzes pointing by archaeologists at an excavation site and by an aphasic patient. He examines various semiotic and interactional structures that support how interactants interpret pointing. Such structures can be exemplified by "activity frameworks," mentioned earlier, and "participation frameworks," which determine how participants of an activity attend to each other and to things in the environment relevant for the activity.

The following chapter by Clark puts pointing in a larger theoretical context. He proposes a general theory of how people indicate. He contrasts semiotic characteristics of two ways in which people indicate: "directing-to," which includes pointing, and "positioning-for" (or "placing"). One of the fundamental differences between the two is what is manipulated for the purpose of indication. In directing-to, one moves the attention of the communication partner to the referent, whereas in positioning-for, one moves the referent to the location of the communication partner's attention.

Engberg-Pedersen investigates different linguistic functions of pointing gestures with both the hand and gaze in Danish Sign Language. She has found that a pointing sign with the hand serves as a pronoun, a determiner indicating specificity of a referent, or a "pro-form" performed simultaneously with another sign. A pro-form adds a spatial component to the concurrent sign when the sign cannot be modulated spatially (e.g., a sign that has to be in contact with the face). Gaze pointing is also multifunctional: checking the recipient's understanding, reference tracking, imitation of the gaze movement by a quoted person, drawing the recipient's attention to iconic depiction. Furthermore, the conditions under which gaze pointing is accompanied by the turning of the head or the torso are also discussed.

In the following chapter, McNeill discusses a frequent type of gesture in conversation, in which the speaker points to seemingly empty space in

---

[3]See also Wilkins (2002).

front. This can be labeled "abstract deixis," in the sense that the gesture points to no concrete target. Such pointing creates an imaginary target at a certain location, which can be revisited later in the discourse. McNeill illustrates how abstract deictic gestures structure the speaker's imaginary space. By virtue of the externalization via pointing, this space is shared with the communication partner. In other words, space becomes personal and public simultaneously. Thus, abstract deixis can be seen as the interface between "interpsychic" and "intrapsychic" processes of meaning creation.

In the last chapter, Kita discusses the cognitive processes that underlie the production of pointing gestures and accompanying spoken utterances through the observation of pointing gestures produced in naturalistic route directions. He argues that pointing helps speaking by facilitating the choice between the notoriously confusing concepts *left* and *right*. He also discusses how torso orientation and gaze movement are systematically coordinated with pointing.

In summary, a wide range of investigations from different disciplines is represented in this volume, although it does not cover fields such as experimental psycholinguistics (de Ruiter, 1998; Feyereisen, 1997; Levelt, Richardson, & La Heij, 1985), neuropsychology (Lausberg, Davis, & Rothenhäusler, 2000; McNeill, 1992), and second language acquisition research (Gullberg, 1998, in press). This is a modest but firm step forward in the synthesis of knowledge from various approaches about pointing—where language, cognition, and culture meet.

REFERENCES

de Ruiter, J. P. (1998). *Gesture and speech production.* Doctoral dissertation, University of Nijmegen.

Enfield, N. J. (2001). "Lip-pointing": A discussion with special reference to data from Laos. *Gesture, 1,* 185–212.

Feyereisen, P. (1997). The competition between gesture and speech production in dual-task paradigms. *Journal of Memory and Language, 36,* 13–33.

Gullberg, M. (1998). *Gesture as a communication strategy in second language discourse. A study of learners of French and Swedish.* Lund: Lund University Press.

Gullberg, M. (in press). Gestures, referents, and anaphoric linkage in learner varieties. In C. Dimroth & M. Starren (Eds.), *Information structure, linguistic structure and the dynamics of language acquisition.* Amsterdam: John Benjamins.

Lausberg, H., Davis, M., & Rothenhäusler, A. (2000). Hemispheric specialization in spontaneous gesticulation in a patient with callosal disconnection. *Neuropsychologia, 38,* 1654–1663.

Levelt, W. J., Richardson, G., & La Heij, W. (1985). Pointing and voicing in deictic expressions. *Journal of Memory and Language, 24,* 133–164.

McNeill, D. (1992). *Hand and mind.* Chicago: University of Chicago Press.

Sherzer, J. (1973). Verbal and nonverbal deixis: The pointed lip gesture among the San Blas Cuna. *Language and Society, 2,* 117–131.

Chapter 2

Pointing Is the Royal Road to Language for Babies[1]

George Butterworth
University of Sussex

Index-finger pointing is a means of making definite reference that is intimately linked to gesture and speech. This chapter examines evidence for its species specificity to humans, considers the development of pointing in babies, and offers some evidence for the universality of the gesture at least in its earliest form. First, it is necessary to describe the typical posture of the hand in pointing to avoid confusion with other indicative gestures and to define it precisely. In pointing, the index finger and arm are extended in the direction of the interesting object, whereas the remaining fingers are curled under the hand, with the thumb held down and to the side (Fig. 2.1). The orientation of the hand, either palm downward or rotated so the palm is vertical with respect to the body midline, may also be significant in further differentiating subtypes of indexical pointing (see also Kendon, chap. 6, this volume).

Deixis is derived from the Greek *deiknunai* meaning "to show" (Collins Softback English Dictionary, 1991). Pointing is a deictic gesture used to reorient the attention of another person so that an object becomes the shared focus for attention. Rolfe (1996) offered three criteria for deictic pointing: (a) It is dialogic in that it requires an audience and is for someone else's benefit, (b) the gesture serves to single something out which the ad-

---

[1] George Butterworth died before the completion of the book production process. The editor took the liberty of updating the references and making minor editorial adjustments in the text.

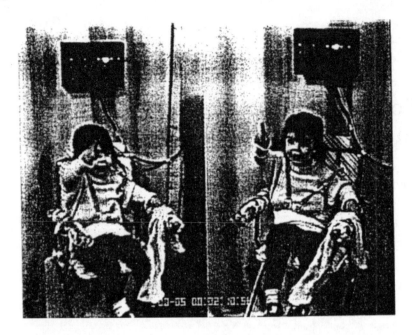

FIG. 2.1. Typical hand posture in infant pointing.

dressee comprehends to be the referent, and (c) the direction of what is being pointed at is seen as away from the pointing hand. These three characteristics constitute the contextual and cognitive requirements for the production of pointing, and they may also be taken as conditions for comprehension of the gesture. In evaluating developmental and comparative evidence, these criteria for deixis need to be borne in mind to differentiate between superficially similar behaviors. We begin by considering when pointing develops in infancy, then turn to some comparative studies to evaluate the claim that pointing is species specific to humans. This gives the background for a new theory of the origins and development of pointing as arising from species-typical human abilities for the precise control of instrumental action.

THE PRODUCTION OF POINTING

A number of studies now agree on the emergence of canonical pointing (as defined earlier) at an average age of 11 months, although babies as young as 8.5 months have been observed to point (Butterworth & Morissette, 1996; Schaffer, 1984). Approximately 33% of parents of 8-month-old babies in the United States say that their babies already point (Fenson et al., 1994). Carpenter, Nagell, and Tomasello (1998), in a longitudinal study of 24 babies also in the United States, found that pointing to nearby objects occurred at 11 months, 2 months before more distal pointing. Butterworth and Morissette (1996), in a similar longitudinal study of 27 babies in England, also found the average age for pointing onset to be in the 11th month (11.2 months for females and 11.7 months for males). Ohama (1984), in a longitudinal study in Japan, reported that 5/9 of her sample pointed by 11 months and 8/9 by 13 months. In the standardization sample for the MacArthur test of early language development, Fenson (personal communication, 1997) found that pointing onset occurred at an accelerated rate for female babies between 9 and 12 months, when the number of boys who have started pointing catches up. Pointing begins rather suddenly, as if the gesture emerges after a stage transition. By 12 months it comprises more than 60% of all gestures made by the infant (Lock, Service, & Chandler, 1990). Pointing is accompanied by checking with the adult (3.4% of points at 12 months according to Lock et al. [1990], rising to about 20% at 18 months in Franco & Butterworth [1996]; Ed. note, see also Franco [1997], Franco & Wishart [1995]). Pointing is also accompanied by vocalization (50% of pointing gestures according to Lock et al. [1990], 76% in Franco & Butterworth [1996], 87% in Leung & Rheingold [1981], all at 12 months).

To establish more precisely for this chapter the actual orientation of the hand around the time of pointing onset, the author checked left- and right-handed examples from video recordings of 10 babies. In 19 cases, the orientation of the pointing hand was palm down; in one case, a left-handed point, the orientation was with the hand rotated at the wrist, through 90 degrees in the horizontal plane, so that the palm was vertical. That is, the canonical pointing gesture, with index finger and arm extended, palm down, is by far the most frequently observed hand orientation in babies at the onset of pointing. We may describe pointing as a universal gesture in babies given the geographical dispersion of the longitudinal studies. Most cross-sectional studies also agree that pointing begins by 12 months (e.g., Leung & Rheingold, 1981; Murphy, 1978).

Wilkins (chap. 8, this volume) observed pointing with the middle finger among three aboriginal children ages 22 to 36 months, a gesture replaced by indexical pointing rather later in development. Such middle finger pointing is occasionally observed in Western infants too. It seems that there is a permissible (but narrow) envelope of variation in the form of the gesture, which during development converges on the canonical indexical form. The questions to be addressed are, why does pointing take this indexical form—is it an aspect of our biological endowment or is it socially derived? If there is evidence for a biological base, is pointing species specific to people?

ANTECEDENTS OF POINTING

It was once widely believed that pointing emerges by the differentiation of in-dex-finger extension from the open-handed waving posture sometime after the seventh month (e.g., Leung & Rheingold, 1981; Murphy & Messer, 1977). Although the canonical form of pointing does emerge toward the end of the first year, there is evidence that antecedents of pointing, in particular the independent extension of the index finger, can be observed much ear-lier. Isolated extension of the index finger, with the other fingers curled in-ward in the pointing posture, has been observed in the 3-month-old baby, in close association with speechlike sounds, when the infant is engaged in social interaction (Fogel & Hannan, 1985; Masataka, 1995; Masataka, chap. 4, this volume). Hannan (1987) found that "pointing" in babies 3 to 9 months old tended to be left-handed when the baby interacted with the mother and right-handed when the mother showed the baby a toy. Hannan and Fogel (1987) in a longitudinal single case study observed pointing movements, pre-dominantly of the right hand, from 18 days. "Pointing" was accompanied by movements of the eyes and mouth that occurred as a cluster of orienting be-haviors. Fogel (1981) observed pointing, sometimes with extended arm and index finger, in babies ranging in age from 18 days to 6 months when in so-cial interaction. These microanalytic studies of babies reveal that embryonic forms of the pointing gesture are already in the repertoire although mothers are not aware that their babies are pointing. The typical pointing posture of the hand does not emerge from a less differentiated form, but shows the typi-cal hand shape soon after birth.

There are also isolated reports that babies can sometimes be observed making pointing movements for themselves before they engage in pointing for others. Tran-Duc Thao (1984), a Vietnamese philosopher, described such behavior as reinforcing for oneself the "sense certainty" of the object. Such phenomena may be involuntary orienting movements or expressions of interest, which are perhaps related to the transitional phenomena ob-served by Franco and Butterworth (1996). These authors found that at 10 months babies sometimes point at an object, then turn to the mother as if to check with her, whereupon they point at the mother. It is as if visual checking and manual pointing are coming together in a new coordinated structure comprising pointing and checking, which is not yet appropriately sequentially organized. Checking is strong evidence both for communica-tive intent and for the deictic nature of the gesture because the audience is being "interrogated" for comprehension of the referent. Thus, it is possible that components of pointing, which are particularly closely linked to syl-labic vocalization, can be observed early in development. The difference between the earlier and later forms is that the gesture is not yet used instru-mentally. The evidence on the antecedents of pointing therefore takes the form of the action comprising the gesture into early human development, again suggesting it is of biological origin.

Once canonical pointing emerges, further changes occur in relation to checking. Franco and Butterworth (1996) found that when babies first point, checking follows the gesture, whereas by 16 months they will first check to establish that they have the attention of the adult and only then do they point. The gesture soon acquires a metacognitive aspect in that the older infant knows that having the attention of the other person is a necessary condition for communication. These observations suggest that pointing has the necessary dialogic aspect to qualify as a deictic gesture from the time the canonical form appears.

Further evidence comes from studies in which the social conditions for pointing were investigated (Franco & Butterworth, 1990; Ed. note, also see Franco, 1997; Franco & Wishart, 1995). Babies were tested alone or with a social partner in the presence of two doll figures that moved their arms and legs in a regular cycle. Pointing occurred only under conditions where a partner was available for communication, which again suggests that the gesture is deictic from its inception. Furthermore, pointing by the baby did not require that the adult also point, nor was the rate of infant pointing a function of the adult rate. That is, infant pointing requires an audience, but the incidence of pointing by the infant was not driven by whether the partner also pointed. This suggests that social influence is limited to the audience effect, rather than social transmission being responsible for creation of the gesture by ritualization or transfer of a conventional act. In another study, infants who had recently begun to point were tested in pairs in the presence of an interesting event. Preverbal babies would point and check with each other, which suggests again that there is no necessity for adults to mediate in the production of the gesture. Such observations argue against any simple theory of transgenerational transmission from adult to baby, although this does not mean that adults do not have an important role in the subsequent elaboration of pointing (Franco, Perucchini, & Butterworth, 1992; Ed. note, also see Franco, 1997; Franco & Wishart, 1995). This evidence also runs against the view that pointing is at first performed primarily for the self because a partner had to be present for pointing to occur at all.

In summary, recent evidence suggests that canonical pointing emerges toward the end of the first year, slightly earlier in females than males. The hand posture observed conforms closely to the description just offered, namely, index-finger extension with palm down, thumb tucked in, and other fingers curled under. Associated phenomena, such as checking (and vocalization), show that pointing already has deictic qualities in requiring an audience and in being performed in order to redirect the attention of others. To determine whether pointing is biological in its origin or species specific to humans requires further comparative evidence.

COMPARATIVE EVIDENCE ON THE
SPECIES SPECIFICITY OF POINTING

The precise definition of the pointing gesture is rather important in evaluating comparative evidence. For example, the pointer dog, according to Hewes (1981), has been associated with humans in hunting for at least 2.5 thousand years. The dog aligns its whole body with the target, from tip of nose to extended tail, sometimes with a front paw raised, in a manner partly analogous to human deictic behavior. The orientation of the dog indicates the general direction of fallen wildfowl, which assists the hunter locate the prey. However, it is not the case that the dog engages in a dialogue with the hunter, and furthermore, whole-body orienting differs in other important ways from indexical pointing. For example, the dog does not see itself orienting toward the prey, whereas sight of the hand and the object in the visual field may be integral to the production and comprehension of pointing in humans. Using a part of the body, the arm and hand, to indicate, in lieu of the whole body, may also require a cognitive analysis of part–whole relations.

Chimpanzees (*Pan troglodytes*) and orangutans (*Pongo pygmaeus*) are capable of signaling with manual indicative gestures, in which the arm, open hand, and extended fingers are oriented in the direction of an interesting sight. The behavior is usually made by captive, trained chimpanzees to their human trainers and is rarely seen between conspecifics. Hewes (1981) described an observational study of a pair of captive bonobos (*Pan paniscus*) in which only 21 indicative gestures were observed in 600 hours of filming. The gestures were described as "completely iconic hand movements" made by the male, which served to indicate to the sexual partner that she should move to another part of the enclosure. The question is, should such open-handed, indicative gestures in chimpanzees be considered equivalent to human pointing? Some authors have argued that it is equivalent and that the function of indicating is more important than the form of the gesture (Krause & Fouts, 1997). For the theory to be proposed here, however, it is important that higher primates generally give no prominence to the index finger in making indicative gestures (Blaschke & Ettlinger, 1987; Call & Tomasello, 1995; Menzel, 1974). One factor that may limit index-finger pointing in apes is the anatomy of the hand. Povinelli and Davis (1994) noted that the resting posture of the index finger in anesthetized humans is slightly proud of the remaining fingers, whereas in chimpanzees all the fingers remain aligned when at rest, which suggests that differences in the insertion of the muscles exist in index-finger control.

However, this need not mean that indexical pointing is impossible for chimpanzees, as the literature used to suggest (Butterworth, 1991a). It has recently been shown that chimpanzees (*Pan troglodytes*) can signal with an index finger (Leavens, Hopkins, & Bard, 1996). The clearest evidence came from a chimpanzee named Clint, age 14 years, who extended the index finger (with left and right hand) apparently as a request to the experimenter for food that had fallen on the ground. Index-finger extension was less frequent (38 occasions) than whole-hand indicative gestures (102 occasions). Indicative gestures were used by Clint as an imperative for food items (i.e., give me that food), and it is possible that his index-finger pointing may have been learned as a particular consequence of social contact with humans. It is interesting that Clint was never observed to use index-finger pointing with conspecifics. Nevertheless, some of his index-finger points were accompanied by checking with the experimenter, suggesting that the gesture required an audience, and he only pointed when the experimenter was facing him. Leavens and Hopkins (1998), in a study of 115 chimpanzees ages 3 to 56 years, found that 47 animals made whole-hand indicative gestures and 6 animals used indexical points with arm extended to single out the location of food for an experimenter. Of 78 chimpanzees who made gestures of any kind, 35% of the gestures were accompanied by vocalization, a figure rather lower than found with babies. High levels of gaze alternation (checking) were observed, however (80% of animals showed checking from 8 years).

Another possibly important factor concerns the species-typical requirements for precision in behavior. Krause (1998) reported indexical pointing, with arm extension, in a 21-year-old captive chimpanzee who was trained to indicate to a naive experimenter which of four possible places contained a hidden object. Under these conditions, which required greater precision than is usually the case for cross-species communication, indexical pointing was used by the chimpanzee. It is possible that the gesture was learned from the human caretakers because the colony contained language-trained animals. Nevertheless, it was perhaps because the testing situation required precision that the chimpanzee used the indexical pointing gesture and not the more common indicative gesture. Feral chimpanzees have not been observed to point indexically, and indeed, whole-body orienting may be sufficiently communicative for the chimpanzee's purposes in the wild (Menzel, 1974). This implies that differential requirements for precision between humans and chimpanzees may be an important factor in determining whether indexical pointing or whole-hand indicative gestures are used.

The contrast in prevalence of pointing in humans is illustrated graphically in a study of congenitally deaf infants by Goldin-Meadow and Feldman (1977). They found that 51% of as many as 5,000 gestures produced by toddlers ages 17 to 47 months were indexical points at things, people, or places (cited in Hewes, 1981). Because the children were being taught language by an oral method and parents avoided signing, the authors concluded that pointing must have been generated spontaneously by the children. Franco and Butterworth (1996) also found that pointing comprised more than 55% of the gestures of babies ages 14 months, whereas other indicative gestures involving the whole hand, or extended arm and closed fist, or isolated index-finger extension accounted for only 18% of gestures in total. Furthermore, whole-hand indicative gestures and index-finger pointing were uncorrelated in development, with indicative gestures remaining at a low constant level between 12 and 18 months, whereas pointing increased exponentially. A similar low correlation between pointing and other indicative gestures was found by Lock, Young, Service, and Chandler (1990). All this evidence suggests that open-hand indicative gestures and pointing are unrelated and therefore may serve different purposes in communication. For babies, indexical pointing is the preferred means of communication; it occurs with great frequency and may well develop spontaneously given the appropriate social context, rather than being taught by parents or otherwise socially transmitted to the infant.

In summary, pointing may have species-typical biological origins in humans. The recent upsurge of research on pointing in chimpanzees suggests that it is not possible to maintain an absolute divide between humans and other higher primate species with respect to the gesture. Some aspects of the capacity for indexical pointing may be shared with other primates, although the possibility that humans taught chimpanzees to point cannot be ruled out. Assuming that indexical pointing is possible in chimpanzees, and that it was not learned from their caretakers or because they were trained in sign language, this makes explaining pointing all the more interesting. On the one hand, continuity with higher primates roots the gesture firmly in our common primate evolutionary heritage. On the other hand, there are many strong contrasts with chimpanzees, including the incidence of the gesture, its precise form, and the preference for pointing in babies over other means of indicating. In particular, indexical pointing in humans is done for conspecifics, whereas it has never been observed to occur between chimpanzees; in humans it is declarative, whereas in chimpanzees almost all examples are imperative. On the evidence to date, by these broader deictic criteria, declarative indexical pointing is species specific to humans.

Perhaps the question of whether chimpanzees point should no longer be expressed simply in terms of presence or absence of the ability. The more appropriate question is, why is index-finger pointing extremely infrequent and difficult to observe in chimpanzees? More progress in understanding the functional significance of index-finger pointing might be made if it could be ascertained why indicative gestures generally take the whole-hand open form in chimpanzees, but generally involve index-finger extension in humans. To examine this question further, we need to consider the relation between pointing and prehension and different theories of the origins of pointing in human ontogeny.

THEORIES OF THE DEVELOPMENT OF POINTING

Traditional views of the origins of pointing are of two types, which stress either that pointing develops out of prehension (e.g., Vygotsky, 1988) or that it is a communicative gesture from the outset. Within the latter type of theory it is often assumed that pointing is initially performed for the self and becomes ritualized through social interaction until it serves purposes of social communication (e.g., Werner & Kaplan, 1963). Vygotsky believed that pointing derives from unsuccessful grasping movements, which are interpreted by the mother as a request. In coming to her infant's aid, the mother converts the movement into a gesture for others, and it acquires an imperative character. No explanation for the specific hand posture is offered except that it is considered somehow transitional with grasping.

Franco and Butterworth (1996) tested both these types of theory in a study that compared the incidence of pointing and reaching gestures in 10- to 14-month-old babies in declarative and imperative communicative contexts. Babies had the opportunity to point at or make grasping gestures to interesting objects that were both in and out of reach. From the onset, pointing was never confused with reaching gestures. It occurred primarily to distal targets (2.7 m away) and was accompanied by vocalization and checking with the partner. Both these accompanying behaviors increased exponentially with age. Reaching gestures were not strongly correlated with checking and remained at a low level. These findings run against the view of the origins of pointing as theorized by Vygotsky (1988) because pointing was not tied in any way to failed grasping, and there was no evidence that the imperative use of the gesture had primacy. Carpenter et al. (1998) in their longitudinal study also found no evidence that the imperative use of pointing emerges before the declarative. That is, on the detailed empirical evidence to date, the pointing gesture in humans initially serves a proto-declarative purpose (i.e., look at that) rather than a proto-imperative purpose (i.e., give me that).

In a recent reinterpretation of the literature on early communicative development, Camaioni (1993) argued that imperative and declarative pointing gestures may differ in their cognitive complexity. The former implies an understanding of others as "agents of action," whereas the latter implies an understanding of others as "agents of contemplation." Exercising a causal effect on the world through physical contact with a person is said to be intellectually less demanding than understanding that interactions can be causally influenced by distal means. Rather than the declarative function of pointing being derived from the imperative function, she suggested that they may be independent. This distinction may partly explain the use of indicative gestures in chimpanzees, where almost all the evidence shows they are used imperatively and not declaratively.

That is not to say that pointing has nothing at all to do with prehension. A clue to the reasons for the morphology of the human pointing gesture comes from the specific adaptations of the hand. The human hand is highly flexible, with a very great capability for precision based on the fully opposable index finger and thumb, which is considered one of the key features differentiating man from other primates. Napier (1970) argued, from rather minimal evidence based on two 2-year-old chimpanzees clutching a grape, that only humans are capable of the pincer grip. The relative size and position of finger and thumb (the opposability index) sets limits on the extent to which the base of the thumb can be abducted against the tip of the index finger. He gave values for the opposability index of 0.65 for humans and 0.43 for chimpanzees, a difference due mainly to the relatively short thumb of the chimpanzee, which is positioned low down the wrist.

Two studies have recently reported that the pincer grip is in fact in the repertoire of the chimpanzee. In one experiment, 80 captive chimpanzees (*Pan troglodytes*) ages 1 to 25 years were observed picking up raisins measuring 1.0 to 1.5 cm from the cage floor. A humanlike pattern of pincer grip was observed at 2 years, which reached a peak of 10% of all responses at 6 years (Tonooka & Matsuzawa, 1995). The same study showed that males were more likely than females to use the pincer grip once they were over 10 years old. A second study of 13 captive chimpanzees (*Pan troglodytes*) ages 2 to 5 years showed that precision grips involving the thumb and index finger at or below the first, distal joint occurred on 25% of trials (Jones-Engel & Bard, 1996). The humanlike pincer grip with thumb pad to finger pad abduction occurred on 2% of trials.

These studies suggest that chimpanzees are capable of a degree of precision but they do not establish how precision grips develop. In human infants the pincer grip and imprecise opposition of the index finger and thumb above the first distal joint (the inferior forefinger grip typically adopted by chimpanzees) can already be observed at 8 months. The pincer grip is systematically selected by 15 months to grip cubes of 0.5 cm. Power grips, where the object is held between flexed fingers and palm, without thumb opposition, are rarely used by human infants with objects of these sizes after 15 months (Butterworth, Verweij, & Hopkins, 1997). To obtain more detailed comparative evidence, Butterworth and Itakura (1998a) studied 11 captive chimpanzees (*Pan troglodytes*) ages 4 to 20 years who were video recorded grasping cubes of apple measuring 0.5, 1.0, and 2.0 cm. This study confirmed that chimpanzees do have precision grips in their repertoire, at least from the age of 2 years, where the object is held between thumb tip and at or below the first joint of the index finger. Precision grips increase in frequency slowly, until chimpanzees are adult, and they are not systematically selected on the basis of object size at any age. Chimpanzees also use a species-typical precision grip, from about 8 years, in which they hold a small object between the index and middle fingers (the so-called *cigarette* grip). Power grips are commonly selected in chimpanzees to the age of 8 years even when grasping small objects. This new developmental evidence shows that chimpanzees, in comparison with human infants, lack strongly systematic selection of precise grips for small objects. Their relative lack of precision extends across the age range from 2 years to full adulthood. Although a humanlike pincer grip is in their repertoire, generally the whole index finger is selected and the exact position of opposition of the thumb is relatively uninfluenced by object size. Furthermore, the pincer grip is more likely to be observed in adult male chimpanzees than in juveniles and may occur simply as a function of changes in hand size, which enable the long index finger more readily to be bent toward the thumb in the male than in the female.

Once again, the contrast with human infants is revealing because the chimpanzee makes a developmental transition from predominance of power to precision grips very much later than is observed in babies. In human infants, there is a transition (between 8 and 15 months) when power grips, which do not involve the thumb, are eliminated and the pincer grip is systematically selected by object size (Butterworth et al., 1997). In human infants, the pincer grip develops earlier in females than in males (Butterworth et al., 1997). Thus, just as for pointing and indicative gestures, the repertoire of precise grips in chimpanzees overlaps that of humans, but the rapid rate of development in humans, especially females, ensures that precision grips and pointing will be used consistently even in infancy. In contrast, precise grips are infrequent, not consistently selected, and more typical of adult male chimpanzees.

The theory to be proposed here is that pointing and the pincer grip are coevolved but different aspects of hand function that are specialized, respectively, for precise instrumental action and precise communication (see Butterworth, 1997b, 1998b). The characteristic hand posture observed in human pointing may be related to the pincer grip but as its "antithesis." Darwin (1904) first proposed the principle of antithesis to explain how animal communication often exploits visual signals to convey information. For example, an animal may signal readiness to attack by making "intention movements" that are preparatory to fighting. After a fight, the subdued posture of the defeated dog signals submission because the muscles are activated in the opposite configuration, or antithesis, to those involved in aggression (Marler, 1959).

In the case of pointing, the opposition of the tip of the index finger and thumb in the pincer grip is postulated to have pointing as its postural antithesis. This also involves a change in the focus of visual attention. In precise manual activities with tools, focal attention is on the hand, the tool, and the object in the service of precise control of manipulation. In pointing, in contrast, attention is outer directed and serves rather precisely to reorient the attention of another person, so that an object at some distance can become a focus for shared experience. On this theory, the emergence of pointing should be related to the development of other precise uses of the hand, and this indeed is what Butterworth and Morissette (1996) established. The pincer grip was invariably in the infant's repertoire, and it was systematically selected by infants approximately 1 month before pointing onset, with females earlier than males. Exploration of objects with the tip of the index finger (tipping) has also been linked to the onset of pointing (Shinn, 1900). Butterworth et al. (1997) showed that tipping and the pincer grip are closely related in development, with the incidence of tipping declining as the pincer grip becomes established.

In summary, the theory that pointing is the antithesis of the pincer grip links precise manual action, pointing onset, and species-specific aspects of hand anatomy and function to the underlying processes governing focused attention. On this argument, precise tool use and precise manual communication through the pointing gesture are coevolved human abilities. Not only do we share some aspects of hand function with other primates, but also there are human species-typical aspects of hand function that harness the human capacity for precision.

POINTING AND JOINT VISUAL ATTENTION

The literature on joint visual attention has been extensively reviewed (Butterworth, 1987, 1995, 1998a, 1998b; Corkum & Moore, 1995; Messer, 1994). Here the discussion focuses on the relation between joint visual attention and the comprehension of manual pointing. Joint visual attention, sometimes called *deictic gaze* or *visual coorientation,* may simply be defined as looking where someone else is looking. There have arisen two contrasting views on the relation between joint attention and pointing. In one account, babies first comprehend signals given by changes in the orientation of another's head and eyes and only then begin to comprehend pointing, whereas in another view, both pointing and head and eye movements are understood simultaneously, relatively late in the first year. Those who favor the hypothesis that joint visual attention is coincident with comprehension of pointing include Moore and Corkum (1994), Corkum and Moore (1995), Morissette, Ricard, and Gouin-Decarie (1995), and Carpenter et al. (1998). Others claim joint visual attention can be observed long before there is evidence for comprehension of pointing (Butterworth & Cochran, 1980; Butterworth & Jarrett, 1991; D'Entremont, Haines, & Muir, 1997; Hood, Willen, & Driver, 1998; Scaife & Bruner, 1975).

Scaife and Bruner (1975) first showed that 2-month-old infants follow a change in the orientation of gaze of an adult. In their study, babies followed the direction of gaze, to left or right, into an empty visual field. In a more recent study, D'Entremont et al. (1997) showed joint attention in babies ages under 4 months. Babies would look in the direction of a change of gaze of the experimenter, toward a doll carefully placed to be within the baby's visual field. Hood et al. (1998) also showed gaze following in babies of 4 months. These results suggest that joint visual attention is possible long before the end of the first year and before the comprehension and production of pointing if the testing conditions are suitable for young babies. An extensive discussion of the methodological factors that may be responsible is published in Butterworth (1998a). To summarize: Some of the important factors are the angular distance of targets from the infant (because joint attention places demands on the ability of the infant to integrate information over space and time); how robust the ability needs to be before it is accepted as "true" joint attention; and whether the infant's response is classified as accurate not only in following the direction of gaze but also in finding the precise location of the object. The infant before 9 months may be able to comprehend a change in a partner's postural orientation as a signal that there is something of interest but may be limited in the capacity to bridge the gap in space between the adult's signal and the object of interest. The baby under 9 months is also limited in the precision with which the correct target is singled out.

At 6 months, for example, the accuracy of the infant's response depends on ecological factors, such as whether the correct target is in motion or somehow differentially salient. The characteristics of the signal (change in head orientation with eye movements or eye movements alone, or pointing plus head and eye movements) also influence the incidence and accuracy of infant responses (Butterworth & Grover, 1988, 1989; Butterworth & Jarrett, 1991). It is relatively difficult to find evidence for eye movements alone being effective in joint attention in large-scale spaces before about 18 months (Butterworth & Jarrett, 1991; Corkum & Moore, 1995). In fact, even among adults, eye movements are not as effective as eye and head movements in allowing an observer to localize a specific target. Itakura and Butterworth (1997) found that adult observers were more accurate in locating a target when the experimenter was wearing sunglasses than when the eyes were visible. Findings such as these suggest that the eyes are not necessarily the primary source of information for singling out the object in joint visual attention tasks and that larger scale postural cues are important for joint attention (this also seems to be true for chimpanzees; see Povinelli & Eddy, 1996a, 1996b; Povinelli et al., chap. 3, this volume). In summary, joint visual attention is possible before the comprehension of pointing.

The fundamental developmental question concerns the mechanisms that operate in joint attention at different ages. The argument to be pursued here is that additional cognitive mechanisms serve joint visual attention after the comprehension and production of pointing. Butterworth and Jarrett (1991) suggested three successive mechanisms of joint visual attention in the age range between 6 and 18 months. At 6 months, babies look to the correct side of the room as if to see what the adult is looking at, but they cannot tell which of the two identical targets on the same side of the room is correct unless it happens to move or in some way be the more salient. The change in the adult's orientation of head and eyes conveys information as to the direction in which to look (i.e., the left or right in the baby's visual field), but the precise location for joint attention is specified by the object itself. This has been called the *ecological* mechanism of joint visual attention (Butterworth & Jarrett, 1991). It depends on the differentiated structure of the natural environment, so that what initially attracts the adult's attention and leads the adult to turn (thus providing the baby with information about *spatial direction* through the change in the adult's postural orientation) is also likely to capture the attention of the infant (thus providing information about *spatial location* through the object's intrinsic properties). The ecological mechanism enables a "meeting of minds" in the self same object.

Between 12 and 18 months the infant begins to localize the target correctly, even when it is further into the periphery than an identical distracter target (Butterworth, 1991b; Butterworth & Jarrett, 1991). This new mechanism was called *geometric* because it appeared to require extrapolation of a vector between the mother's head orientation and the referent of her gaze. The adult's change of gaze then signals both the direction and the location in which to look. The comprehension and production of pointing are more or less coincident in development with the appearance of this "geometric" mechanism. The implication is that a cognitive developmental change has occurred, which leads infants to understand and produce pointing.

Joint visual attention is limited by the boundaries of the babies' visual space even to 18 months of age. The spatial limitation is suggested by the fact that infants only search for targets within their own visual field (Butterworth & Jarrett, 1991). If the mother looks at a target behind the baby, the infant either fixates a target in front or, if the visual field is empty, turns through about 40 degrees and gives up on failing to encounter anything in the periphery of vision (Butterworth & Cochran, 1980). Joint visual attention depends on the infant sharing a visual–spatial frame of reference with others. Furthermore, there are implications for auditory aspects of reference because it seems possible that the space behind the infant is initially specified auditorily. Certainly, babies have no difficulty orienting to a sound behind them, but in joint attention studies, the space behind is silent. Adding pointing to the signal does not help babies search behind them at 12 months, but by 18 months they will search following gaze cues alone as long as the visual field is empty (Butterworth & Jarrett, 1991). Thus, the problem for infants in searching behind them may be to comprehend that the adult's visual signal has made reference to auditory space. The 12-month infant is visually dominated, but by 18 months a representational spatial mechanism becomes available, which serves to integrate the visual space in front of the baby with the auditory space behind. Thus, once the representational mechanism is available, one might theorize that a visual signal, such as pointing, will implicitly carry auditory significance, and this could be an important requirement for the transition to speech.

In summary, as far as the comprehension of gaze is concerned, there is evidence in the first 18 months of life that three successive mechanisms are involved in "looking where someone else is looking." The ecological mechanism is available well before there is comprehension of pointing, but it may encode from the adult's signal only the general spatial direction of a potential target. It requires the intrinsic attention-capturing properties of objects for completion of the reference triangle among infant, adult, and object. At around 12 months, there is evidence for the beginning of a new geometric process, whereby the infant from his or her own position extrapolates, from the orientation of the mother's head or gaze or pointing arm, into the periphery of visual space. This transition has many of the qualities of a stage change within the process of cognitive development. There is a further stage in the development of joint attention to a represented space, which surrounds the infant and other objects like a container. This amodal space serves to link visual signals to the silent auditory space behind the baby. It is interesting to note that children with severe auditory handicaps have difficulty in localizing targets at the periphery of the visual field (Netelenbos & Savelsbergh, 1991), which may support the theory that visual signals become linked to a represented auditory space between 12 and 18 months.

COMPREHENSION OF POINTING IN BABIES

Researchers have distinguished between processes involved in the comprehension and production of manual pointing. Many studies agree that the comprehension of pointing, at about 10 months, slightly precedes its production, but this may simply reflect relative lack of knowledge about the precursors of pointing production (Franco & Butterworth, 1996; Leung & Rheingold, 1981; Messer, 1994). There is evidence that the spatial conditions of testing influence whether infants comprehend pointing. An early study by Lempers (1976, 1979) found that babies of 9 months comprehend pointing to nearby targets and by 12 months they comprehend pointing to more distant targets. Morissette et al. (1995), in a longitudinal study, also found that comprehension of manual pointing to relatively distant targets begins at about 12 months. The most frequent error of babies was to look at the pointing hand rather than at the designated target. Murphy and Messer (1977) found that pointing comprehension was earlier (9 months) for targets on the same side of the room as the pointing hand than when the point was into the contralateral half of the infant's visual space, across the body midline of the adult (12 months). Butterworth and Grover (1989) showed that pointing was understood by 12 months. In contrast, infants at 6 or 9 months were as likely to fixate the pointing hand as the designated target. Carpenter et al. (1998) found that pointing is understood significantly earlier for targets on the baby's right-hand side than on the left, a finding that was replicated in Butterworth and Itakura (1998b). Mothers go to a great deal of trouble, with exaggerated hand movements, to lead the young infant's gaze from the mother's hand onto the target (Murphy & Messer, 1977). Grover (1988) showed that the infant's latency to fixate the correct target significantly decreases between 9 and 12 months, and babies at 12 months were significantly more likely to respond when the signal included a point and to fixate a target further into the periphery of vision. The likelihood of a response to pointing increased from 69% to 80% of trials when the number of targets in the field of view was increased from one to two. When the salience of the targets was experimentally manipulated, by setting them into motion, either singly or in pairs, the infant's response to pointing increased to ceiling level. Target motion was sufficient to eliminate hand fixation in 9-month infants, although babies then went on to fixate only the first target along their scan path from the adult's hand. By 15 months, however, babies did alright on the second, more peripheral target in a sequence of fixations. Thus, infants are not merely fixating the first object they encounter after the adult's hand when they comprehend pointing. Rather, they appear to be extrapolating a vector through space to intersect with a potential target based somehow on the angular orientation of the gesture or the movement of the pointing arm.

Butterworth and Itakura (1998b) reported a series of studies that tested the vector extrapolation hypothesis. Infants were 6 months, 12 months, and 16 months old, and the accuracy with which they could locate one of two identical targets was compared at angular separations between pairs ranging from 25 to 55 degrees. Mother and baby sat *en face*, and one target was always at 10 degrees to the left of the baby's midline (the first target along their scan path from the mother), with the second at a more peripheral leftward position on a semicircular distribution at 2.76 m. The mother either looked at the target (with head and eye movements) or looked and pointed at the target. For all three age groups, there was little evidence that babies could accurately select the more peripheral of the pair just on the basis of head and eye movements. However, from 12 months, manual pointing had a significant effect on the accuracy of the response, and by 15 months, there was a clear advantage to pointing in localizing the more peripheral target at all angular separations. Infants' success following the pointing cue, despite the narrow angular separation between the targets, suggested that they might be solving the problem by vector extrapolation.

In further experiments with 4.5-year-old children and adults, Itakura and Butterworth (1997) and Butterworth and Itakura (1998b) tested the vector extrapolation hypothesis more stringently by presenting targets three at a time on each side of the visual field. The angular separations between targets varied from 4 to 45 degrees for adults and it was held constant at 10 degrees for children, again at 2.7 meters. The task required the participant, who sat next to the experimenter, simply to state the color of the target that was being singled out by a pointing gesture or by combinations of head and eye movements. Children were accurate following pointing but not accurate for head and eye movements. Pointing allowed accuracy only to the inner and outer periphery of each visual hemifield, and children were inaccurate to the intermediate targets. Adults were generally as accurate following head and eye movements as following pointing, but again they were inaccurate for the intermediate targets positioned at separations of 15 degrees or less. That is, the pointing gesture successfully drew attention to the peripheral boundaries of vision, but did not allow precise target localization of intermediate targets either by adults or children.

The results imply that precise linear vector extrapolation is not used in following pointing because there is no reason that a linear vector should be less accurate for intermediate than peripheral positions. Butterworth and Itakura (1998b) explained the added effect of manual pointing in terms of the movement of the lever formed by the arm. For any given spatial separation between a pair of targets, the angular excursion of a long lever, like the arm, will be greater than that of a shorter lever, like the head and nose, or a pair of very short levers, like the eyes. Thus, a part of the body, the arm and pointing hand, may have become specialized for referential communication because it is particularly useful in taking attention further to the extreme periphery (Butterworth, 1997a). The paradoxical finding that adult observers were actually more accurate in following head movement with sunglasses can also be explained by the amplifying effect of the spectacle frames on the observed extent of lateral movement of the head. Thus, following pointing is not completely precise. The mechanism does not operate by extrapolation of linear vectors, and accuracy in a cluttered environment requires supplementary attention to worthy cues from the object of joint attention to help single it out as the referent. Hence, ecological and geometric mechanisms interact even in adults.

Thus, babies may more successfully follow pointing than head and eye movements simply because pointing takes their attention further into the periphery. Their capacity to benefit from the pointing gesture is a function of their ability to bridge progressively larger gaps in space (or time) for which rapid stagelike changes occur between 9 and 12 months that are thought to be linked with maturation of frontal lobe functions. Diamond (1991) reported that babies can successfully search for hidden objects with a delay of 3 sec at 9 months, which increases to 12 sec by 12 months. In these tasks, the infant must keep track of the successive positions of the hidden object across a small spatial gap, typically just a few centimeters, between the hiding locations. Rapid changes in the capacity to integrate attention across successive foci are happening at the stage of development when comprehension and production of pointing begins, and these processes may involve spatial asymmetries in favor of the right visual field (see also Diamond, Werker, & Lalonde, 1994).

In summary, the earliest comprehension of pointing may depend on the infant being able to see the pointing hand and the target simultaneously in visual space, but with development greater angular distances can be bridged. The pointing signal is not only more likely to elicit a response than a simple change of head and eye orientation, but it also allows the baby, once the gesture is understood, to more accurately locate a target in the periphery. There may be an advantage, both in evolution and development, in using the extended arm and index finger to refer to objects for joint attention because it takes attention further into the periphery than a simple change in gaze, head orientation, or whole-body posture.

POINTING PRODUCTION AND ATTENTION

Less research has been done on the relationship between attention and the production of pointing. Manual pointing depends on vision because it is not observed in the congenitally blind (Fraiberg, 1977; Hewes, 1981). As mentioned earlier, pointing is present in the congenitally deaf, which suggests that auditory experience is not necessary for pointing (Feldman, Goldin-Meadow, & Gleitman, 1978). There is other evidence, however, that pointing may be influenced by auditory factors, gender differences, and cerebral asymmetries associated with speech. Pointing favors the right side of visual space when there is a conflict between targets on the left and right (Butterworth, 1997b; Butterworth, Franco, McKenzie, Graupner, & Todd, 2002). When doll-like targets that "speak" and move their arms and legs are used (but not when the targets lack auditory qualities), girls of 15.6 months point right-handed to the right and as far as 15 degrees into the left side of their visual space. Further into the left periphery they are ambidextrous.

Boys at the same age point with the left hand to the left periphery (50 degrees), with the right hand to the right periphery, and they are ambidextrous from 15 degrees right to 15 degrees left of the midline. These sex differences may imply different rates of transition from a bilaterally organized system of communication through the pointing gesture to a species-typical lateralized system favoring speech (Thatcher, Walker, & Giudice, 1987).

In summary, sex differences in age of onset and in the predominance of right-handed pointing may suggest that a transition occurs in the brain mechanisms that control pointing in the second year. Initially (as evidenced by the male pattern) pointing gestures are bilaterally organized, with each hand being responsible for the ipsilateral periphery with shared responsibility for the inner zone stretching approximately 15 degrees to either side of the midline. The transition to a lateralized system occurs in females at 15 months (there is no evidence for whether or when the equivalent change takes place in males). Then the dominant right hand takes responsibility for all locations except those at the extreme left periphery, where pointing is ambidextrous. This effect of hand dominance occurred only when the targets had multimodal auditory and visual properties. This suggests that new patterns of interhemispheric connections are being set up that may be related to the production of speech and language (Witelson & Nowakowski, 1991).

POINTING AND THE TRANSITION TO LANGUAGE

Various studies have linked preverbal referential communication and language acquisition (e.g., Baldwin, 1991, 1993; Baldwin & Moses, 1996). There is evidence that the amount of pointing at 12 months predicts speech production rates at 24 months (Camaioni, Caselli, Longobardi, & Volterra, 1991). Carpenter et al. (1998) showed that maternal language following into the infant's focus of attention is the most important predictor of subsequent speech comprehension and production. The duration of joint attention at around 14 months gave the best prediction of speech development. Pointing onset and comprehension of object names have also been linked, with infants understanding their first categorical object name in the same week as they produce the canonical point (Harris, Barlow-Brown, & Chasin, 1995). This observation, on the relation between pointing and categorization, may allow further interpretation of the significance of the orientation of the hand in the pointing gesture. Kendon and Versante (chap. 6, this volume) noted that adult Italians used the palm-down pointing gesture to single out individual items of fruit in a grocery shop (e.g., "Give me a lemon" accompanied by canonical point) and the palm-vertical posture when referring to categories of objects (e.g., "Give me some lemons"). It is tempting to speculate that the full-hand, open-palm indicative gesture would be applied when even less precision is required, as when the intention is merely to draw attention to the whole scene (e.g., "Look at all the fruit"). On this interpretation, babies use the canonical pointing gesture at the outset of their pointing career to individuate an object within categorical perception. In the individuation posture (palm down), the thumb is out of the way and does not occlude the line of sight. In the categorization posture (with palm vertical), there is less need for precision, and the thumb is allowed to partly occlude the visual field. In the indicative gesture, the scope of the referential action is so broad as to require minimal precision. Furthermore, if pointing is the antithesis of the pincer grip, the indicative gesture would be the antithesis of the power grip. Thus, even the typical, palm-down orientation of the infant's pointing hand brings pointing and language acquisition one step closer in terms of common cognitive characteristics based on individuation and categorization.

Butterworth and Morissette (1996) carried out a longitudinal study of pointing, handedness, and onset of the pincer grip in relation to early verbal and gestural communication. Early language was measured using the MacArthur infant language inventory (Fenson et al., 1994). The earlier the age of onset of pointing, the greater was the number of different gestures and the greater was the amount of speech comprehension at 14.4 months. Girls showed consistent right-handedness before boys in tasks requiring them to use only one hand, and they showed more right-handed pointing than boys. The amount of right-handed pointing and the relative balance of pincer grips between the left and right hands (a measure of lateralized fine motor control) predicted speech comprehension and production at 14.4 months. At this age, boys had relatively few words in production (about 3), whereas girls had on average 12 words. By 16 months, the MacArthur norms show females have 95 words in production and males have 25 words (Fenson et al., 1994). Combinations of pointing and a word are produced consistently by 16 months, just before the child makes the transition to two-word speech. Thus, pointing maximizes communicative effectiveness at a time when vocabulary is still limited (Volterra & Iversen, 1995). Earlier onset of pointing, earlier right-handed pointing, and more rapid development of speech in girls suggest that the link among pointing, gesture, and speech is mediated by species-typical asymmetries in spatial attention and in language mechanisms linked to handedness and cerebral dominance.

CONCLUSION

This chapter began by asking whether human index-finger pointing is biologically based and species specific. Now that the evidence is in, it can be concluded that it is. What is special about pointing is that it is intimately connected with species-typical handedness, precision grip, and acquisition of language. It is one of a set of indicative gestures, some of which overlap with those of the higher primates, but on the evidence to date only humans use the pointing gesture declaratively to share attention with conspecifics. Pointing serves to refer as precisely as possible to objects for joint attention. The precision may arise because pointing makes use of the same anatomical adaptations and attention mechanisms that serve tool use. Pointing connects a visual referent to the concurrent sound stream so that a relation of identity exists between these two aspects of the infant's perceptual experience. That is, pointing serves not only to individuate the object, but also to authorize the link between the object and speech from the baby's perspective. Pointing allows visual objects to take on auditory qualities, and this is the royal road (but not the only route) to language.

ACKNOWLEDGMENTS

I am grateful to the Economic and Social Research Council of Great Britain, which funded many of the studies reviewed here. I acknowledge the generous assistance of Alan Fogel in helping me trace the antecedents of pointing. I have had helpful discussions with Shoji Itakura, David Leavens, Kim Bard, Daniel Povinelli, Michael Tomasello, Tetsuro Matsuzawa, and Mark Krause in introducing me to the flourishing world of research on chimpanzee indicative gestures. Thanks also to the Leverhulme Foundation for the Research Fellowship, which freed the time to write this chapter, and to Sotaro Kita and the Max Planck Institute Nijmegen for taking the initiative to promote an interdisciplinary approach to pointing.

REFERENCES

Baldwin, D. (1991). Infants' contribution to the achievement of joint reference. *Child Development, 62*, 875–890.

Baldwin, D. (1993). Early referential understanding: Infants' ability to recognise referential acts for what they are. *Developmental Psychology, 29*(5), 832–843.

Baldwin, D. A., & Moses, L. J. (1996). The ontogeny of social information gathering. *Child Development, 67*(5), 1913–1915.

Blaschke, M., & Ettlinger, G. (1987). Pointing as an act of social communication by monkeys. *Animal Behaviour, 35*, 1520–1525.

Butterworth, G. E. (1987). Some benefits of egocentrism. In J. S. Bruner & H. Weinreich-Haste (Eds.), *Making sense of the world: The child's construction of reality* (pp. 62–80). London: Methuen.

Butterworth, G. E. (1991a). The ontogeny and phylogeny of joint visual attention. In A. Whiten (Ed.), *Natural theories of mind* (pp. 223–232). Oxford: Blackwell.

Butterworth, G. E. (1991b, April). *Evidence for the "geometric" comprehension of manual pointing.* Paper presented at the SRCD Biennial Meeting, Seattle, WA.

Butterworth, G. E. (1995). Origins of mind in perception and action. In C. Moore & P. Dunham (Eds.), *Joint attention: Its origins and role in development* (pp. 29–40). Hillsdale, NJ: Lawrence Erlbaum Associates.

Butterworth, G. E. (1997a, December). *Did humans evolve pointing because gaze is not enough?* Paper presented at the Conference of the British Psychological Society, London.

Butterworth, G. E. (1997b). Starting point. *Natural History, 1064,* 14–16.

Butterworth, G. E. (1998a). Origins of joint visual attention in human infancy. Commentary on M. Carpenter, K. Nagell, & M. Tomasello, *Social cognition, joint attention and communicative competence from 9 to 15 months of age. Monographs of the Society for Research in Child Development, 63* (Serial No. 255, Vol. 63, No. 4), 144–166.

Butterworth, G. E. (1998b). What is special about pointing in babies? In F. Simion & G. E. Butterworth (Eds.), *The development of sensory, motor and cognitive capacities in early infancy* (pp. 171–190). Hove: Psychology Press.

Butterworth, G. E., & Cochran, E. (1980). Towards a mechanism of joint visual attention in human infancy. *International Journal of Behavioural Development, 3,* 253–272.

Butterworth, G. E., Franco, F., McKenzie, B., Graupner, L., & Todd, B. (2002). Dynamic aspects of visual event perception and the production of pointing by human infants. *British Journal of Developmental Psychology, 20,* 1–24.

Butterworth, G. E., & Grover, L. (1988). The origins of referential communication in human infancy. In L. Weiskrantz (Ed.), *Thought without language* (pp. 5–25). Oxford: Oxford University Press.

Butterworth, G. E., & Grover, L. (1989). Joint visual attention, manual pointing and preverbal communication in human infancy. In M. Jeannerod (Ed.), *Attention and Performance XII* (pp. 605–624). Hillsdale, NJ: Lawrence Erlbaum Associates.

Butterworth, G. E., & Itakura, S. (1998a). Development of precision grips in chimpanzees. *Developmental Science, 1,* 39–43.

Butterworth, G. E., & Itakura, S. (1998b). How the eyes, head and hand serve definite reference for babies, children and adults. *British Journal of Developmental Psychology, 18,* 25–50.

Butterworth, G. E., & Jarrett, N. L. M. (1991). What minds have in common is space: Spatial mechanisms for perspective taking in infancy. *British Journal of Developmental Psychology, 9,* 55–72.

Butterworth, G. E., & Morissette, P. (1996). Onset of pointing and the acquisition of language in infancy. *Journal of Reproductive and Infant Psychology, 14,* 219–231.

Butterworth, G. E., Verweij, E., & Hopkins, B. (1997). The development of prehension in infants. Halverson revisited. *British Journal of Developmental Psychology, 15,* 223–236.

Call, J., & Tomasello, M. (1994). The production and comprehension of referential pointing by orang-utans (*Pongo pygmeaus*). *Journal of Comparative Psychology, 108,* 307–317.

Camaioni, L. (1993). The development of intentional communication: A re-analysis. In J. Nadel & L. Camaioni (Eds.), *New perspectives in early communicative development* (pp. 82–96). London: Routledge.

Camaioni, L., Caselli, M. C., Longobardi, E., & Volterra, V. (1991). A parent report instrument for early language assessment. *First Language, 11,* 345–360.

Carpenter, M., Nagell, K., & Tomasello, M. (1988). Social cognition, joint attention, and communicative competence from 9 to 15 months of age. *Monographs of the Society for Research in Child Development, 63*(4).

Corkum, V., & Moore, C. (1995). The origins of joint visual attention. In C. Moore & P. Dunham (Eds.), *Joint attention: Its origins and role in development* (pp. 61–83). Hillsdale, NJ: Lawrence Erlbaum Associates.

Darwin, C. (1904). *The expression of the emotions in men and animals.* London: John Murray.

D'Entremont, B., Hains, S. M. J., & Muir, D. W. (1997). A demonstration of gaze following in 3 to 6 month olds. *Infant Behaviour and Development, 20*(4), 569–572.

Diamond, A. (1991). Frontal lobe involvement in cognitive changes during the first year of life. In K. R. Gibson & A. C. Petersen (Eds.), *Brain maturation and cognitive development: Comparative and cross-cultural perspectives* (pp. 127–180). New York: Aldine de Gruyter.

Diamond, A., Werker, J. F., & Lalonde, C., (1994). Toward understanding commonalities in the development of object search, detour navigation, categorization and speech perception. In G. Dawson & K. W. Fischer (Eds.), *Human behaviour and the developing brain* (pp. 380–427). New York: Guilford.

Feldman, H., Goldin-Meadow, S., & Gleitman, L. (1978). Beyond Herodotus: The creation of language by linguistically deprived deaf children. In A. Lock (Ed.), *Action, gesture and symbol, the emergence of language* (pp. 351–414). London: Academic Press.

Fenson, L., Dale, P. S., Reznick, L., Bates, E., Thal, D. J., & Pethick, S. J. (1994). Variability in early communicative development. *Monographs of the Society for Research in Child Development, 59*, 5.

Fogel, A. (1981). The ontogeny of gestural communication: The first six months. In R. E. Stark (Ed.), *Language behaviour in infancy and early childhood* (pp. 17–44). Amsterdam: Elsevier.

Fogel, A., & Hannan, T. E. (1985). Manual actions of nine to fifteen week old human infants during face to face interaction with their mothers. *Child Development, 56*, 1271–1279.

Fraiberg, S. (1977). *Insights from the blind.* New York: Basic Books.

Franco, F. (1997). The development of meaning in infancy: Early communication and social understanding. In S. Hala (Ed.), *The development of social cognition* (pp. 95–160). Hove: Psychology Press.

Franco, F., & Butterworth, G. E. (1990, August). *Effects of social variables on the production of infant pointing.* Poster presented at the IVth European Conference on Developmental Psychology, University of Stirling.

Franco, F., & Butterworth, G. E. (1996). Pointing and social awareness: Declaring and requesting in the second year of life. *Journal of Child Language, 23*(2), 307–336.

Franco, F., Perucchini, P., & Butterworth, G. (1992, September). *Pointing for an age mate in 1 to 2 year olds.* Paper presented at the VIth European Conference on Developmental Psychology, Seville, Spain.

Franco, F., & Wishart, J. (1995). The use of pointing and other gestures by young children with Down syndrome. *American Journal of Mental Retardation, 100/2*, 160–182.

Goldin-Meadow, S., & Feldman, H. (1977). The development of language like communication without a language model. *Science, 197*, 401–403.

Grover, L. (1988). *Comprehension of the pointing gesture in human infants.* Unpublished doctoral dissertation, University of Southampton, Southampton, England.

Hannan, T. E. (1987). A cross-sequential assessment of the occurrence of pointing in 3 to 12 month old human infants. *Infant Behavior and Development, 10*, 11–22.

Hannan, T. E., & Fogel, A. (1987). A case study assessment of pointing during the first three months of life. *Perceptual and Motor Skills, 65*, 187–194.

Harris, M., Barlow-Brown, F., & Chasin, J. (1995). The emergence of referential understanding: Pointing and the comprehension of object names. *First Language, 15*, 19–34.

Hewes, G. W. (1981). Pointing and language. In T. Myers, J. Laver, & J. Anderson (Eds.), *The cognitive representation of speech* (pp. 263–269). Amsterdam: North Holland.

Hood, B., Willen, J. D., & Driver, J. (1998). Adult's eyes trigger shifts of visual attention in human infants. *Psychological Science, 9*(2), 131–134.

Itakura, S., & Butterworth, G. E. (1997, April). *The roles of head, eyes and pointing in joint visual attention between adults.* Poster presented at the meeting for the Society for Research in Child Development, Washington, DC.

Jones-Engel, L. E., & Bard, K. A. (1996). Precision grips in young chimpanzees. *American Journal of Primatology, 39*, 1–15.

Krause, M. A. (1998, April). *Comparative perspectives on joint attention in children and apes: Development, functions and the effects of rearing history.* Paper presented at the XIth Biennial conference on Infant Studies, Atlanta, GA.

Krause, M. A., & Fouts, R. S. (1997). Chimpanzee (*Pan troglodytes*) pointing: Hand shapes, accuracy and the role of eye gaze. *Journal of Comparative Psychology, 111*(4), 330–336.

Leavens, D. A., & Hopkins, W. D. (1988). Intentional communication by chimpanzees: A cross-sectional study of the use of referential gestures. *Developmental Psychology, 34*(5), 813–822.

Leavens, D. A., Hopkins, W. D., & Bard, K. A. (1996). Indexical and referential pointing in chimpanzees (*Pan troglodytes*). *Journal of Comparative Psychology, 110*(4), 346–353.

Lempers, J. D. (1976). *Production of pointing, comprehension of pointing and understanding of looking behaviour in young children.* Unpublished doctoral dissertation, University of Minnesota.

Lempers, J. D. (1979). Young children's production and comprehension of nonverbal deictic behaviors. *Journal of Genetic Psychology, 35,* 93–102.

Leung, E. H. L., & Rheingold, H. L. (1981). Development of pointing as a social gesture. *Developmental Psychology, 17*(2), 215–220.

Lock, A., Young, A., Service, V., & Chandler, P. (1990). Some observations on the origins of the pointing gesture. In V. Volterra & C. J. Erting (Eds.), *From gesture to language in hearing and deaf children* (pp. 42–55). Berlin: Springer Verlag.

Marler, P. (1959). Developments in the study of animal communication. In P. R. Bell (Ed.), *Darwin's biological work.* Cambridge: Cambridge University Press.

Masataka, N. (1995). The relation between index-finger extension and the acoustic quality of cooing in three month old infants. *Journal of Child Language, 22,* 247–257.

Menzel, E. W., Jr. (1974). A group of young chimpanzees in a one acre field. In A. Schrier & F. Stollnitz (Eds.), *Behaviour of non-human primates: Modern research trends, 5* (pp. 83–153). New York: Academic Press.

Messer, D. J. (1994). *The development of communication: From social interaction to language.* Chichester: Wiley.

Moore, C., & Corkum, V. (1994). Social understanding at the end of the first year of life. *Developmental Review, 14,* 349–372.

Morissette, P., Ricard, M., & Gouin Decarie, T. (1995). Joint visual attention and pointing in infancy: A longitudinal study of comprehension. *British Journal of Developmental Psychology, 13*(2), 163–177.

Murphy, C. M. (1978). Pointing in the context of shared activity. *Child Development, 49,* 371–380.

Murphy, C. M., & Messer, D. J. (1977). Mothers, infants and pointing: A study of gesture. In H. R. Schaffer (Ed.), *Studies of mother infant interaction* (pp. 325–354). London: Academic Press.

Napier, J. (1960). Studies of the hands of living primates. *Proceedings of the Zoological Society of London, 134,* 647–657.

Napier, J. (1970). *The roots of mankind.* London: George Allen & Unwin.

Netelenbos, J. B., & Savelsbergh, G. (1991). Localization of visual targets inside and outside the field of view: The effect of hearing loss. *Journal of Child Psychology & Psychiatry & Allied Disciplines, 32,* 983–993.

Ohama, K. (1984). Development of pointing behavior in infants and mother's responsive behavior: Longitudinal study of infants from 9 to 30 months. In M. Ogino, K. Ohama, K. Saito, S. Takei, & T. Tatsuno (Eds.), The development of verbal behavior VI. *Bulletin of the Faculty of Education, University of Tokyo.*

Povinelli, D. J., & Davis, D. R. (1994). Differences between chimpanzees (*Pan troglodytes*) and humans (*Homo sapiens*) in the resting state of the index finger. *Journal of Comparative Psychology, 108*(2), 134–139.

Povinelli, D. J., & Eddy, T. J. (1996a). Factors influencing young chimpanzees (*Pan troglodytes*) recognition of attention. *Journal of Comparative Psychology, 110*(4), 336–345.

Povinelli, D. J., & Eddy, T. J. (1996b). What young chimpanzees know about seeing. *Monographs of the Society for Research in Child Development, 61*(2, Serial No. 247).

Rolfe, L. (1996). Theoretical stages in the prehistory of grammar. In A. Lock & C. R. Peters (Eds.), *Handbook of human symbolic evolution* (pp. 776–792). Oxford: Oxford University Press.

Scaife, M., & Bruner, J. S. (1975). The capacity for joint attention in the infant. *Nature, 253,* 265–266.

Schaffer, H. R. (1984). *The child's entry into a social world.* New York: Academic Press.

Shinn, M. (1900). *The biography of a baby.* Boston: Houghton-Mifflin.

Thatcher, R. W., Walker, R. A., & Giudice, W. S. (1987). Human cerebral hemispheres develop at different rates and ages. *Science, 236,* 1110–1113.

Tonooka, R., & Matsuzawa, T. (1995). Hand preferences of captive chimpanzees (*Pan troglodytes*) in simple reaching for food. *International Journal of Primatology, 16*(1), 17–23.

Tran-Duc, T. (1984). *Investigations into the origins of language and consciousness* (D. J. Herman & R. L. Armstrong, Trans.). Dordrecht: Reidel.

Volterra, V., & Iverson, J. M. (1995). When do modality factors affect the course of language acquisition? In K. Emmorey & J. Reilly (Eds.), *Language, gesture, and space* (pp. 371–391). Hillsdale, NJ: Lawrence Erlbaum Associates.

Vygotsky, L. S. (1988). Development of the higher mental functions. In K. Richardson & S. Sheldon (Eds.), *Cognitive development to adolescence* (pp. 61–80). Hove: Lawrence Erlbaum Associates.

Werner, H., & Kaplan, B. (1963). *Symbol formation: An organismic-developmental approach to language and the expression of thought.* New York: Wiley.

Witelson, S. F., & Nowakowski, R. S. (1991). Left out axons make men right: A hypothesis for the origins of handedness and functional asymmetry. *Neuropsychologia, 28,* 327–333.

Chapter 3

Chimpanzees' "Pointing": Another Error of the Argument by Analogy?

Daniel J. Povinelli
Jesse M. Bering
Steve Giambrone
University of Louisiana at Lafayette

DO CHIMPANZEES POINT?

In this chapter, we explore the possibility that chimpanzees do not point. In doing so, it may seem as if we are intentionally exposing ourselves to the ridicule of many comparative psychologists, who find it self-evident that they do. After all, there can be no doubt that chimpanzees engage in behaviors that surely resemble pointing. Figure 3.1 illustrates an example of such a gesture by Megan, a chimpanzee in our own laboratory. How, then, can we seriously entertain the idea that chimpanzees do not point?

If one's interest in "pointing" centers around a particular gestural form, and one is unconcerned with the psychological operations that attend (and perhaps cause) the behavior, then the case is already settled. Indeed, we invite the reader (such as the behaviorist) who is solely interested in a structural or functional analysis of pointing to stop here because we readily concede that chimpanzees perform gestures that structurally resemble pointing. Further, we concede that in captivity they learn to use these gestures to achieve a variety of ends. Yet for the reader whose interest in pointing stems from a desire to understand how language, cognition, and culture intersect (following the subtitle of this volume), we invite a critical evaluation of the assumption that similarity in the spontaneous behavior of two species guarantees psychological similarity. In what follows, we reject this centuries-old "argument by analogy" and, in doing so, show that the conclusion that chimpanzees "point" may just be one in a long line of inferential errors en-

FIG. 3.1. A prototypical instance from our laboratory of a chimpanzee "pointing." Note the discrepancy between the direction of the ape's gesture and her gaze.

couraged by a way of understanding the world that may be unique to our species.

To some extent, the claim that chimpanzees do not "point" is a definitional matter. Indeed, we are far less interested in establishing that chimpanzees do or do not "point" than we are in examining the kinds of psychological representations that are causally bound up with their gestures that look like pointing. To be clear, if it turned out that chimpanzees harbor no second-order intentional states—that is, if they do not see either themselves or others as possessing psychological states (such as attention, desires, knowledge, and belief)—then we would not want to use the term *pointing* to describe any gesture on their part. We recognize that others (such as the behaviorist) might wish to do so in any event. In response, we would merely assert that whatever the similarity in the structural form of their gestures, chimpanzees may mean such gestures in a manner different from us.

THE ARGUMENT BY ANALOGY: A PRIMER

The modern origins of the argument by analogy can be traced to David Hume (1739–1740/1978), who offered the following simple doctrine:

When . . . we see other creatures, in millions of instances, perform like actions, and direct them to like ends, all our principles of reason and probability carry us with an invincible force to believe the existence of a like cause. 'Tis needless in my opinion to illustrate this argument by the enumeration of particulars. The smallest attention will supply us with more than are requisite. The resemblance betwixt the actions of animals and those of men is so entire in this respect, the very first action of the first animal we shall please to pitch on, will afford us an incontestable argument for the present doctrine. (p. 176)

Hume was at least right in believing that his argument was obvious, as a similar line of reasoning persuaded many other theorists as well. Not the least of these was Darwin (1871/1982), who was convinced by behavioral similarities that there "was no fundamental difference between man and the higher mammals in their mental faculties" (p. 446). Unlike Hume, however, Darwin at least felt obliged to present evidence to support this view, and to this end he devoted two chapters of *The Descent of Man* to recounting anecdotes about the intelligent behavior of animals. Near the end of Darwin's life, John George Romanes (1882, 1883) took up his approach, arguing that it could be used to establish a completely new field of science. In exactly the same way that anatomists compared the bodily structures of animals, Romanes reasoned, a new breed of comparative psychologists could compare the mental structures of animals. "Starting from what I know of the operations of my own individual mind," Romanes (1882) noted, "and the activities which in my own organism they prompt, I proceed by analogy to infer from the observable activities of other organisms what are the mental operations that underlie them" (pp. 1–2).

Since Hume, the argument by analogy has (in one form or another) intimately guided the history of our thinking about the psychology of other species.[1] However, there are fundamental errors in the argument—errors that have been explored in detail elsewhere (Povinelli & Giambrone, 1999). Yet because there seemed to be no better explanation available, even Hume was led into believing that the mental states that attend particular behaviors are their direct cause, and therefore that the presence of similar behaviors between two species guarantees the presence of similar mental states. In this chapter, we focus on the case of pointing and show that similar behaviors in humans and chimpanzees may comfortably reside alongside profound differences in the mental states that accompany and/ or cause them.

However, before turning our attention to chimpanzees, we need to detour and consider a number of issues concerning the development of

---

[1]Bertrand Russell (1948) offered a formal version of the argument by analogy to provide a logical basis for believing in the existence of other human minds. For a detailed analysis of his argument, as applied in this context, see Povinelli and Giambrone (1999).

pointing in humans that, if not properly understood, will hopelessly confuse any attempt to understand the case of chimpanzees. First, what do we mean by *pointing*? Second, can we distinguish between the structure of the gesture and the underlying meaning and comprehension of the gesture? Finally, how do both the form and meaning of the gesture develop?

DEVELOPMENT OF THE POINTING GESTURE: IS THE INDEX FINGER PRIVILEGED?

The first issue concerns what structural form we refer to when we discuss pointing. Franco and Butterworth (1996) offered the following definition of *the pointing gesture*: "the simultaneous extension of the arm and index finger towards a target" (p. 308). Throughout the remainder of this essay we are careful to restrict our use of the phrase *the pointing gesture* to this gestural form, whereas other means of indicating are referred to using different terminology. One important behavior that frequently accompanies the pointing gesture is the act of gaze alternation, in which infants look back and forth from the object or event to which they are pointing and their communicative partner.

The separate structural components of the pointing gesture (arm and index-finger extension), as well as behaviors that often accompany it (gaze alternation), do not develop in synchrony. For instance, infants as young as 18 days of age spontaneously extend their index finger from an otherwise closed fist (Hannan & Fogel, 1987). However, at this age, the index finger is not extended in the context of a communicative act, but rather as an ambient, undirected motor activity. By 9 to 12 months of age, the infant has combined the extension of the index finger with object/event-directed arm extensions so that the operational definition for *the pointing gesture* has been met. In addition, during this period, the infant begins to combine the action with gaze alternation (see Desrochers, Morisette, & Ricard, 1995; Franco & Butterworth, 1996; Leung & Rheingold, 1981).

Povinelli and Davis (1994) proposed a morphological constraints model to account for the universality of the pointing gesture in humans. They argued that the gesture may be the result of species-specific morphological features of the human hand (i.e., differential tension of the index finger tendons), which predispose human infants to extend their index fingers relative to the other digits (Fig. 3.2; see Povinelli & Davis, 1994; see also Butterworth, chap. 2, this volume, for a complementary account). Povinelli and Davis speculated that as infants begin to express directed reaches toward objects or events, index-finger extensions initially merely "ride along" with such reaches. If adults within a given culture respond differentially to reaches with such index-finger extensions as opposed to those without such

a

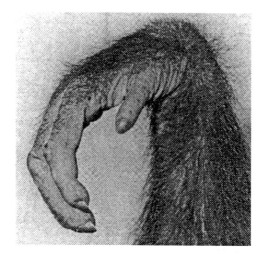

b

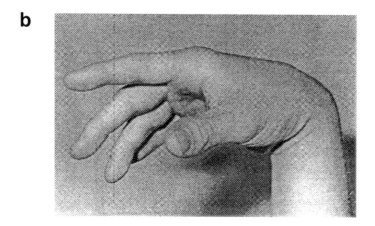

FIG. 3.2.   Differences in the resting state of the index finger in (a) chimpanzees and (b) humans relative to the other fingers of the hand. After Povinelli and Davis (1994).

extensions, infants may detect this contingency and modulate their hand form appropriately. Indeed, there is some evidence that by the time that infants are 9 months of age, parents spontaneously label objects to which infants point more than objects to which they reach. Thus, Povinelli and Davis envisioned that index-finger pointing may emerge from a fairly low-level morphological starting condition, coupled with differential reactions by adults. Furthermore, Povinelli and Davis provided experimental evidence that chimpanzee index fingers do not exhibit this differential action on the

tendons of the index finger (see Fig. 3.2), and suggest that this is why naturally occurring chimpanzee gestures that do involve arm extensions (such
as those used in recruiting allies or food begging) do not typically involve
index-finger extension (see also Itakura, 1996).

Some researchers object to focusing on the role of the index finger in
pointing. Wilkins (chap. 8, this volume), for instance, downplays claims for
the universality of the pointing gesture, noting that in certain cultures
(such as speakers of Arandic languages) the pointing gesture may not be
the only (or, in adults, even the most dominant) form of the indicating act.
To be sure, other forms of indicating, such as using the whole hand, the
lips, the thumb, or other bodily parts, exist within our species (see Wilkins,
chap. 8, this volume). Furthermore, when the pointing gesture is present, it
may possess numerous topographic variants. The model proposed by
Povinelli and Davis explains why the universal pointing gesture is only one
of many kinds of indicating gestures that are used by humans. If early-
emerging morphological constraints tend to channel index-finger extensions into the reaches of young human infants, and if cultural and
attributional influences simultaneously act to reinforce and "pull out" the
pointing gesture, then differing cultural influences may act to broaden the
range of indicating acts, or indeed channel them into other, culturally
dominant forms.[2] Finally, the pointing gesture may (in adults, at least) be
deployed in certain circumstances, but not others (see Wilkins, chap. 8, this
volume). However, to our knowledge, the pointing gesture has been found
in every human culture examined thus far.

DO CHIMPANZEES USE THE POINTING GESTURE?

We have now arrived at the critical crossroads between the form and meaning of the pointing gesture. First, we ask a simple question: Is the pointing
gesture exclusively restricted to the human species, or is it exhibited by
other species such as chimpanzees? For purposes of clarity, we restrict our
focus to chimpanzees—not because they are the only species of interest,
but because any similarities to humans are likely to be greatest in the case of
chimpanzees, and hence it is here that the argument by analogy would
seem to be on its strongest ground.

---

[2]Indeed, if future investigations were to reveal that the ontogeny of reaching in infants in
the speakers of Arandic languages follows the same initial trajectory as infants in Western cultures, but that arm extensions containing index finger extensions are not reinforced (or only
weakly so) relative to other, more culturally dominant gestural forms of indicating, then data
such as those offered by Wilkins (chap. 8, this volume) could be interpreted as prima facie support for the Povinelli and Davis model. It follows from this that even if there were a handful of
cultures in which the gesture were not present, this would not necessarily refute the Povinelli
and Davis (1994) model.

Reports From the "Field"

There is no convincing evidence that natural populations of chimpanzees (i.e., chimpanzees with only marginal contact with humans) display the pointing gesture. Plooij (1978) conducted an analysis of the communicative gestures of young chimpanzees at Gombe and reported no evidence for the appearance of the gesture. Furthermore, neither of the two major long-term studies of the natural history of chimpanzees (which have each spanned nearly 40 years) have reported the presence of the pointing gesture in chimpanzees (Goodall, 1986; Nishida, 1970). Thus, despite intensive observations of the spontaneous interactions of free-ranging chimpanzees, there is no evidence that these animals approach one another and gesture with the arm and/or index finger toward other objects, animals, or events in space. Indeed, the absence of proto-declarative gesturing among wild populations of chimpanzees is simply so striking and overwhelming that the ambiguity of the one published report of what might or might not be a single, isolated instance of pointing (see Vea & Sabater-Pi, 1998), to our minds, simply further highlights the robust nature of this difference in the natural gestural systems of human and chimpanzees.

But what about other gestures that, although not meeting the definition of pointing outlined in the section "Development of the Pointing Gesture," nonetheless appear generally similar in form and/or function? Chimpanzees do exhibit at least one gesture that bears some structural resemblance to the pointing gesture—*holding out a hand* (see Bygott, 1979; de Waal, 1982). The meaning of this gesture appears to be context specific; it can be deployed as a reconciliatory gesture, a food-begging gesture, a solicitation for bodily contact, or a call for support during a conflict (de Waal, 1982; Goodall, 1986). Even here, however, there is little or no evidence that chimpanzees conceptualize this gesture in proto-declarative (or even proto-imperative) fashion, nor has it been interpreted by field researchers as such.

Reports From Captivity

In contrast to free-ranging apes, chimpanzees and other great apes reared and tested in captivity by humans do display arm (or even leg) extensions that structurally (and functionally) resemble the pointing gesture in that they are directed at particular objects, locations, or persons (Call & Tomasello, 1994; Gómez, 1990; Gómez, Sarria, & Tamarit, 1993; Povinelli & Eddy, 1996a; Povinelli, Nelson, & Boysen, 1992; Premack, 1984; Savage-Rumbaugh, 1986; Woodruff & Premack, 1979). Indeed, this similarity has been exploited by a number of researchers who have used such gestures as the dependent measures in studies in which the subjects make a choice between one of several people or locations (see Fig. 3.1). For example, Povinelli, Nelson, and Boysen (1992) trained chimpanzees to extend their arm toward a location where food was hidden. In these contexts, a number of researchers (including ourselves) have frequently glossed such gestures as "pointing."

More recently, several researchers have claimed that the structural similarity is even greater, arguing that captive chimpanzees and orangutans can, in fact, be observed to use the complete pointing gesture in concert with gaze alternation (Krause & Fouts, 1997; Leavens & Hopkins, 1999; Leavens, Hopkins, & Bard, 1996; Miles, 1990). Some researchers have even reported that in their studies the indexical pointing gesture by their subjects was the most common form of the gesture observed (Krause & Fouts, 1997). For some, then, the case can be settled here: Chimpanzees point. If we were behaviorists, we would be forced to agree.

Chimpanzees Use Their Index Fingers!

At this juncture, it is necessary to address the claim that captive chimpanzees display the full pointing gesture (including the index-finger extension). Recall that Povinelli and Davis (1994) proposed that index-finger extension in the pointing gesture is the result of species-specific morphological features of the tendons on the human index finger. It is important not to misinterpret this claim as meaning any of the following: (a) Chimpanzees *cannot* extend their index finger, (b) chimpanzees *do not* extend their index finger, and/or (c) chimpanzees *cannot learn* to extend their index finger in the context of arm extensions and gesturing. None of these claims were made by Povinelli and Davis. Indeed, as we have noted elsewhere, chimpanzees often use their index fingers to probe at objects or to pick at food (see Povinelli, Reaux, Bierschwale, Allain, & Simon, 1997). Figure 3.3 provides an example of this kind of phenomenon from our laboratory.

However, Povinelli and Davis (1994) did argue that pointing with the index finger does not typically emerge in chimpanzees. Indeed, evidence from the wild provides us with no reason to modify this claim. So what do we make of recent demonstrations that chimpanzees gesture with index-finger extensions? Do they falsify Povinelli and Davis's (1994) morphological constraints model, as Krause and Fouts (1997), for example, have maintained? More generally, do such demonstrations imply the presence in chimpanzees of a homologous gestural form, or merely an artificial convergence of form due to the peculiarities of their interactions with humans?

First, the experiments in which indexical pointing has been reported in chimpanzees were typically conducted in enclosures surrounded by cage mesh (e.g., Krause & Fouts, 1997; Leavens & Hopkins, 1998; Leavens et al., 1996). This cage mesh is too small for juvenile and adult subjects to fit their

FIG. 3.3. Chimpanzees frequently (and perhaps preferentially) use the index finger for inspection of objects and bodily parts.

FIG. 3.4. Chimpanzee protruding index finger through wire mesh in the presence of a human offering a banana.

hands through, and thus they must poke one or several fingers through. As far as we are aware, all of the indexical pointing gestures occurred in this manner—with the index finger resting on the mesh (see Fig. 3.4). We do not doubt the occurrence of this kind of phenomenon—we frequently witness such index-finger extensions in precisely this context (see Fig. 3.4). However, Povinelli and Davis accounted for the universal presence of index-finger pointing in humans as emerging from a natural tendency for the index finger to extend—not from some incidental shaping that occurs as the result of wanting to extend the whole hand through a small opening.[3] Second, some of the apes that have been reported to display indexical pointing have been involved in extensive training to produce hand signs used in American Sign Language (chimpanzees: Fouts, Hirsch, & Fouts, 1982; Gardner & Gardner, 1975; Krause & Fouts, 1997; orangutans: Miles, 1990). This training involves many signs in which extension of the index

---

[3]Leavens et al. (1996) maintained that in their study the cage mesh cannot explain why the index finger was shaped over other fingers. Yet this ignores that chimpanzees preferentially use the index finger to touch or pick at objects and that the index finger (independent of the morphological constraints model) is differentially exposed compared to any other fingers (except the thumb, which is truncated; see Fig. 3.3).

finger serves a primary role (i.e., the signs for "me" and "you"). Third, there is no evidence that even these chimpanzees use this gesture (or any other kind of pointing gesture) with each other—a fact consistent with the idea that the pointing-like gestures they learn are tightly connected to a procedural routine that, from their perspective, just so happens to elicit a certain reaction from humans, but not fellow chimpanzees.

Although we are getting ahead of ourselves, it is important to reiterate that the particular form of the pointing gesture may not be a critical issue with respect to the cognitive structures that support and/or attend it. Because we are primarily interested in the underlying cognitive mechanisms engaged by pointing, it is important not to be misled into treating index-finger extension as the issue itself. In this sense, the presence of the extension of the index finger is no better evidence of referential indicating than arm extensions without index finger extensions. As Povinelli and Davis (1994) noted, if chimpanzees were capable of representing the attentional states of others, "more well-developed pointing gestures ought to develop, even if they [did] not exclusively involve the index finger" (p. 135). Thus, although the question of index-finger extension is of interest to the question of the form of the gesture in humans, it is largely irrelevant to the question of whether chimpanzees appreciate the joint-attentional implications of pointing.

DO CHIMPANZEES INDICATE? THE ARGUMENT BY ANALOGY

Having established that chimpanzees display gestures remarkably similar to the pointing gesture (and in certain cases perhaps identical), we now ask whether they understand the gesture in the manner that we do.

First, a comment about humans. Regardless of the exact timing of the development of various aspects of infants' understanding of pointing, one thing seems certain: Humans do come to appreciate pointing as a means of connecting to the inner psychological states of others (for discussions of the timing of this development, see Baldwin, 1991, 1993a, 1993b; Franco & Butterworth, 1996; Franco & Wishart, 1995). This is not to say that pointing is always produced for such reasons by the agent, nor that it is always interpreted in such a manner by the observer. Nonetheless, it appears clear that the pointing gesture becomes intimately bound up with our second-order intentional states. As we show, however, the exact causal role between specific second-order intentional states and the production of the gesture is likely to be complicated (see Povinelli & Giambrone, 1999).

Do chimpanzees also develop this understanding of pointing? Several researchers recently examined captive chimpanzees' use of the gestures just described, and all have concluded that chimpanzees exhibit referential pointing (Krause & Fouts, 1997; Leavens & Hopkins, 1998; Leavens et al., 1996). These researchers stressed that chimpanzee pointing-like gestures serve a communicative function, and therefore they have comfortably assumed that young children and chimpanzees must understand the gesture in a similar manner. In doing so, they have relied heavily on the argument by analogy. Leavens et al. (1996) make the point clearly: "We would not support an interpretation that explained, for example, the pointing behavior of chimpanzees in operant terms and the pointing behavior of human 12-month-olds, or adults, in cognitive terms" (p. 351). Although these alternatives constitute an unnecessarily extreme dichotomy, part of our conclusion (see the section "Toward an Integrated Account of the Form, Function, and Meaning of the Pointing Gesture in Humans and Apes") is that different interpretations may be warranted for the same behavior depending on the species producing it.

Leavens et al. (1996) conducted a retrospective analysis of chimpanzees' reactions when food rewards accidentally spilled out of a testing apparatus beyond their reach. The subjects were observed to protrude their fingers through the mesh toward the food reward, and at least one of the apes looked to the human who was present. The authors note that their data "are amenable to both cognitive and behaviorist interpretations" (p. 351). Similarly, Leavens and Hopkins (1998) placed a banana on the ground in front of a chimpanzee's cage and then left the area. Another experimenter then approached the cage and made eye contact with the chimpanzee. The chimpanzee was given the banana as soon as he or she either (a) gestured (through the mesh), (b) gestured and vocalized, or (c) gestured or vocalized and looked back and forth from the banana to the human. The chimpanzees' gestures and vocalizations were both accompanied by gaze alternation. The authors conclude that "[t]he use of the whole hand in pointing suggests that these chimpanzees . . . may have 'invented' the gesture as part of a problem solving tactic involving the instrumental manipulation of a social agent" (p. 819).

Before critiquing this research, let us note some points of agreement. First, surely these gestures are at least simple communicative acts.[4] Communication minimally involves information being transmitted from one individual to another individual. Thus, the chimpanzee who gestures toward an out-of-reach banana in the presence, but not in the absence, of a human is surely communicating. Likewise, the honeybee whose "waggle dance" informs other bees of the direction and distance of flowering plants is com-

---

[4]We assume a non-Gricean notion of communication. Thus, in this context, communication may be said to occur without reasoning about the psychological states of the communicative partner (or, for that matter, oneself).

municating, as well as the dog snarling at the postman wandering onto its territory. Significantly, note that the bee, or the dog, may neither frequently dance nor snarl in the absence of other individuals. However, insofar as it involves the transmission of information, and influences the behavior of others, communication need not require the sender to understand anything at all about the mental states of the recipients (e.g., their attentional states). Are there any other aspects of these spontaneous acts that might suggest that the chimpanzees are, in fact, reasoning about the psychological states of their communicative partners in this context?

Leavens et al. (1996) believed so. For example, they referred to their chimpanzees' gestures as *referential* pointing (see also Krause & Fouts, 1997) largely because the animals exhibit gaze alternation: "We consider these data to be evidence of perspective-taking in that it seems unlikely that the gaze alternation we observed . . . could be parsimoniously explained without invoking the same functional explanation invoked for gaze alternation in human infant pointing" (p. 351).[5] Leavens et al. (1996) explained their chimpanzees' gaze alternation while pointing to out-of-reach food items by stating that their chimpanzees "recognized the necessity of capturing the attention of human observers in order to achieve desired goals" (p. 350). In other words, by alternating their gaze, the chimpanzees are envisioned to be checking the observers' attentional state in relation to the item of reference, in this case food that had fallen beyond their reach. Leavens and Hopkins (1998) reported that no subject looked at the food item (an out-of-reach banana) without also looking to the experimenter, and that every subject who both vocalized and gestured toward these objects, these authors found, also exhibited gaze alternation. Similarly, Krause and Fouts (1997) reported that two chimpanzees pointed to a bowl containing food while alternating their gaze between the bowl and the observer.

A moment's reflection, however, will reveal that although gaze alternation may signal some sensitivity to the posture of the communicative partner, it may or may not imply an understanding of the psychological aspect of attention. The literature on human development does, indeed, implicate gaze alternation as the mechanism by which an understanding of attentional states emerges. However, we should be wary of such a naked inference. It is not the gaze alternation alone that warrants the conclusion. If it

---

[5]It is unclear the kind of social understanding that Leavens et al. (1996) envisioned as accompanying these acts in chimpanzees. On some occasions they appeared to maintain that these behaviors are simply a form of intentional communication, whereas at other times (as in the cited text) they maintained that the execution of the behavior implies an understanding of the internal visual (attentional) states of others. Indeed, their use of the term *attention* was somewhat ambiguous. At times they appeared to restrict the term to refer to postural or behavioral states, whereas in other cases they appeared to imply the second-order intentional state of attention.

were not for other, independent evidence that slightly older infants do possess the capacity to represent the psychological states of others, we would not seriously entertain the conclusion that gaze alternation alone signifies an understanding of such states (at that younger age). Captive chimpanzees are routinely exposed to situations where desired objects are just out of their reach, and probably initially reach for those objects anyway. On seeing this, human observers are likely to interpret this behavior—and rightly so— as the chimpanzee wanting the object, and therefore observers hand the object to the animal. After several such responses from humans, a gesture resembling pointing with the whole hand might become conventionalized (for evidence concerning this process of gestural development in chimpanzees, see Tomasello, Gust, & Frost, 1989; Tomasello, Call, Nagell, Olguin, & Carpenter, 1994). In this context, gaze alternation may merely reflect the chimpanzee's understanding of this behavioral routine. Thus, the subject alternates looking at the two items of interest: the object the subject wants, and the human whom the subject expects to hand it to him or her.

Yet if such conventionalization processes can account for the presence of pointing-like gestures and gaze alternation, why are Leavens et al. (1996) persuaded that such acts are evidence of "perspective-taking"? The answer is because of their implicit reliance on the argument by analogy: This is how we understand the act of gaze alternation in ourselves as well as young infants. Indeed, most researchers in this area seem to be wary of arguing for one interpretation of the gesture when it is produced by chimpanzees and another when it is produced by human infants. However, as we see, this may be exactly what is required.

"DO CHIMPANZEES INDICATE?" REVISITED

In this section, we attempt to move beyond the argument by analogy by critically examining chimpanzees' use of pointing-like gestures. We ask several questions:

1. Do chimpanzees understand the attentional space that psychologically surrounds their gestures?
2. Do they comprehend pointing gestures when they are used by others?
3. What is the significance of gaze alternation in the context of these gestures—for example, do they understand that their gestures need to be seen in order to be effective?

In short, we examine whether they understand the psychological grounding of the gesture in the manner that humans do. To explore these questions, we review recent empirical research from our laboratory and else-where.

Do Chimpanzees Know That Their Gestures Must Be Seen?

First, although chimpanzees naturally deploy visually based gestures such as those just described, do they understand that these gestures must be seen to be communicatively effective? We have attempted to answer this question through an extensive series of studies with a cohort of seven chimpanzees. We conducted the initial studies when the animals were 5 to 6 years of age, and conducted additional studies when they were 7 and 8 to 9 years of age. Our results suggest that despite their use of such visually based gestures—and despite their simultaneous interest in and sensitivity to the postures, faces, and eyes of others—chimpanzees may know very little (if anything at all) about attention as a psychological state. Indeed, although we do not review this work here, we have obtained evidence that they appear to understand little about any psychological states at all.

How have we reached this conclusion—one that seems to fly in the face of what our intuitions demand? To begin, we examined our chimpanzees' natural inclination to direct a pointing or begging gesture to familiar human caregivers (usually in contexts where they want out-of-reach food or other objects). Initially, we simply created a standardized context in which the subjects could use these gestures. Each subject was separated from the group and placed in an outdoor waiting area (a process with which the subjects were very familiar). The area was connected by a shuttle door to an indoor testing unit. While the subject waited outside, a familiar experimenter inside either sat or stood in front of a Plexiglas partition (that we use to separate the apes from the experimenters). This person positioned him- or herself behind a hole in the Plexiglas on either the right or left side of the partition, just out of reach of the apes. Next, the shuttle door was opened, allowing the subject to enter and freely respond. The apes quickly learned to enter, reach their arm through the correct hole (the one directly in front of the experimenter), and beg for a food reward (see Fig. 3.5). They also frequently glanced back and forth from the food on the floor and the experimenter.

Of course, we already knew that our apes would do this—they had been deploying such gestures since they were infants. As we have seen, some researchers would be content to label this behavior "pointing"; however, we sought to determine whether the subjects understood that their visually based gestures are "seen"—that is, whether they understand the gestures as part of an attentionally based interaction. To do so, we first studied their spontaneous play behavior and from this derived a number of conditions that would allow us to ask this question. For example, we had frequently wit-

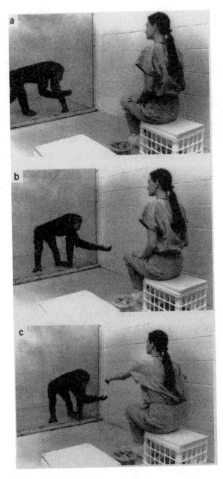

FIG. 3.5.   After shuttle door opens, a chimpanzee (a) enters test unit and approaches a familiar experimenter, (b) deploys species-typical begging gesture through hole toward experimenter, and (c) is given a food reward.

nessed our apes placing their hands over their eyes and wandering about the compound until they bumped into something. Further, we had seen them placing plastic buckets and bowls and burlap sacks over their heads in a similar way, and even occasionally lifting them—to peek, as it were. But did they understand what they were doing in terms of the conceptual notion of "seeing"?

These observations inspired an initial set of experimental conditions to ask the apes what they knew about seeing (see Fig. 3.6a). The idea behind all of these conditions was the same: one person who could see the apes and another person who could not. How did the animals react to confronting

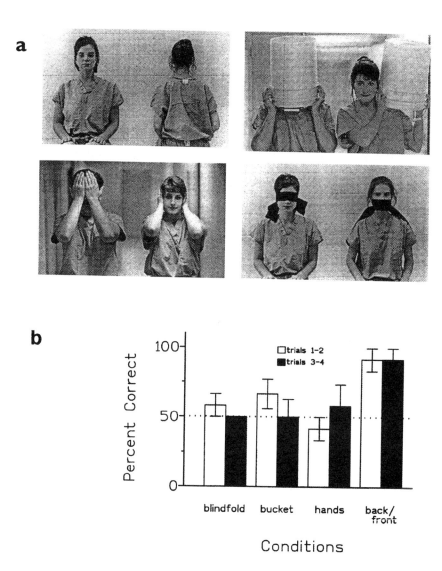

FIG. 3.6.   (a) Conditions (modeled after spontaneous play behavior of the chimpanzee subjects) used to test subjects for their understanding of seeing/ not seeing. (b) Mean percent correct (±SEM) in blocks of two trials. The dotted line indicates levels expected by chance.

these conditions? Before answering this question, however, it is important to note that the animals performed almost perfectly on control trials in which both experimenters could see them, but one was holding out food and the other was offering a block of wood. Here, where no understanding of the internal subjective state of the experimenters was required, the apes performed almost without error. They entered the lab, paused, and then immediately gestured to the experimenter holding out the food. Thus, they were clearly motivated to receive a reward and would look for, and act on, the relevant and observable aspects of the experimenter's location and actions.

In direct contrast, a very different picture emerged on the critical seeing/not seeing trials. On the blindfolds, buckets, and hands-over-the-eyes trials, the subjects were just as likely to gesture to the person who could not see them as to the person who could (Fig. 3.6b). The apes entered the lab, paused, but then went on to deploy their gesture as if unaware that only one person could see them! There was, however, one notable exception—the back-versus-front trials. Here the apes performed correctly from their very first trial forward. We found these initial results difficult to understand. After all, how could the apes not understand such a (seemingly) critical aspect of this interaction? In an initial set of 14 studies, we tested a number of ideas about how our apes were reasoning about this kind of situation. First, we pursued the question of why the apes responded nearly perfectly in the back/front condition, but not in the other conditions. Two possibilities suggested themselves. On the one hand, maybe back/front was simply the instance of seeing/not seeing with which our apes were most familiar—or perhaps it was just the most obvious of the instances that we had selected. On the other hand, perhaps in truth they had no understanding of "seeing" at all, and were merely responding to the general frontal orientation of the experimenter; something they do naturally (see Tomasello et al., 1994) and, indeed, something we had reinforced repeatedly in their initial training. In other words, maybe they just knew a rule that might verbally be described as "Gesture to the person facing forward."

To test this idea we created a new naturalistic condition—one that we felt was just as obvious an instance of seeing/not seeing as the back/front condition, and one that the animals experience many times a day in their natural interactions with each other, as well as with us. This new condition, looking-over-the-shoulder, involved both experimenters with their backs to the apes, but one of them looking over his or her shoulder toward the ape (see Fig. 3.7a). The significance of this condition is that it allowed us to pit the competing interpretations of the back/front performance against each other. After all, if the animals were simply relying on the frontal aspect of the person to solve the back/front problem, they could not do so here. In response to confronting this treatment, the apes entered the lab, paused,

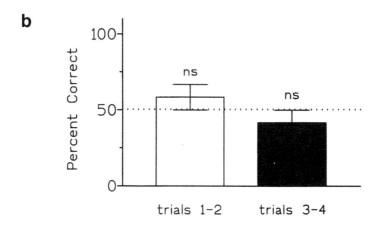

FIG. 3.7. (a) Looking-over-the-shoulder condition along with (b) mean percent correct (±SEM) in blocks of two trials. The dotted line indicates levels expected by chance.

and then proceeded to gesture as often to the person not looking over his or her shoulder as to the person who was (Fig. 3.7b).

We would be remiss if we did not point out that with experience on some additional conditions, such as the screens condition depicted in Fig. 3.8a, the apes did begin to learn to respond correctly—that is, to the person who could see them (Fig. 3.8b). However, there were at least two potential explanations of this learning. First, because the apes were only reinforced (that is, handed the food reward) when they gestured to the person who

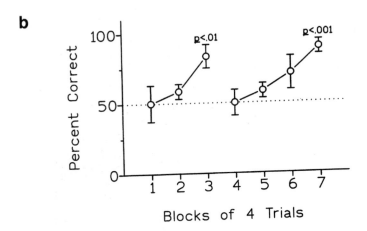

FIG. 3.8. (a) Screens condition along with (b) mean percent correct (±SEM) in blocks of four trials. The dotted line indicates levels expected by chance.

could see them, they may have simply learned a second rule (e.g., "Gesture to the person whose face is visible") when the first rule could not be satisfied. Yet maybe they had just needed more experience to figure out that the problem was about seeing. One way of addressing these competing ideas was to determine if their learned success on the screens conditions would transfer to the other conditions. The low-level model predicted that this understanding would transfer to all of the previous conditions except one—blindfolds. The low-level model envisioned that the subjects had learned another rule about gesturing to the person whose face is visible. The blind-folds condition was the only one of the original conditions in which this rule could not work. Just as the low-level model predicted, this was the only condition in which the apes performed randomly.

Of course, there were many other possible interpretations of these data, many of which we systematically explored and ruled out. In the interest of space, let us just examine one of these possibilities. Perhaps the apes were basing their choices on the global presence or absence of the face simply because they were not carefully monitoring the eyes of the experimenters. We tested this by confronting the apes with the condition depicted in Fig. 3.9. As can be seen, in both options the experimenters' faces (and eyes) are visible. The only difference is that one of them is looking toward the ani-mal, whereas the other is looking away—above and behind the animal. In response to this condition, the apes entered the test unit and, on almost half of the trials, turned and followed the distracted experimenter's gaze up into the corner of the ceiling behind them. Nonetheless, on those same trials, the apes were just as likely to deploy their visually based gesture to this distracted experimenter as to the one who was looking in their direc-tion. (Additional tests with these same animals have now experimentally confirmed and extended this gaze-following ability. Indeed, we now have evidence that chimpanzees will follow gaze in response to head and eye movement in concert, eye movement alone, and will follow gaze into a par-ticular quadrant of space; see Fig. 3.10 [Povinelli, Bierschwale, & Cech, 1999, Experiments 1 & 2; Povinelli & Eddy, 1996a, Experiment 12; Povinelli & Eddy, 1996b, 1997; see also Tomasello, Call, & Hare, 1998].)

Were these results just an indication of the young age of our subjects or did they reflect something intrinsic about the nature of chimpanzee social understanding? To explore this, we conducted several longitudinal follow-up tests with these same animals (see Reaux, Theall, & Povinelli, 1999). Thirteen months after the original tests were completed, when the apes were 7 years of age, we retested them using three of the conditions used previously—screens, eyes open/closed, and back/front. Recall that by the end of the original series of tests the subjects were performing excellently on the screens condition. Yet, to our surprise, the apes initially responded randomly on this condition. Indeed, it was only after 12 trials that the ani-mals began responding significantly above chance (and even this level, 57% correct, was hardly impressive). The subjects had received far fewer of the eyes open/closed trials, and here, despite receiving 48 massed trials of eyes open/closed, the subjects did not learn to respond preferentially to the ex-perimenter with his or her eyes open. In contrast, the animals responded at ceiling levels from trial 1 forward on the back/front trials. Furthermore, a year after this, when the animals were on the cusp of young adulthood (8 to 9 years of age), we returned with a full battery of the original tests. Al-a

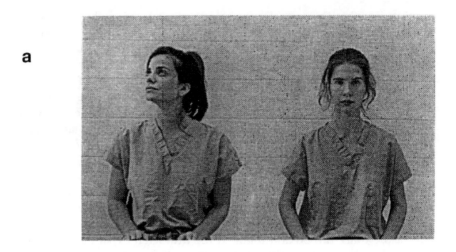

b

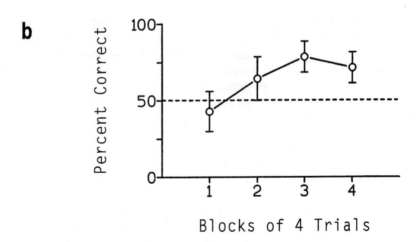

Blocks of 4 Trials

FIG. 3.9.   (a) Attending-versus-distracted condition along with (b) mean percent correct (±SEM) in blocks of two trials. The dotted line indicates levels expected by chance.

though the animals showed some evidence of responding correctly on one of the conditions (buckets) within the first four trials, in general their responses were not impressive (see Fig. 3.11). However, after additional trials, their performance began to improve, at least in some of the conditions.

   This learning raised a familiar, but still troubling, question. To what extent did the apes just need to reorient themselves to the general procedures, having understood "seeing" all along? Although it took many trials, perhaps they now—finally!—grasped what we were asking them. Perhaps

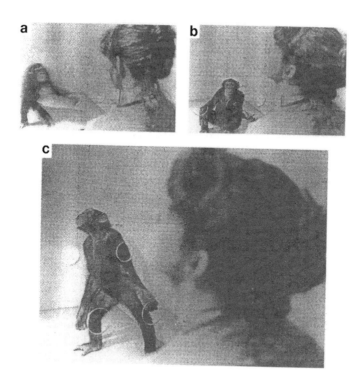

FIG. 3.10. Gaze following in a 6-year-old chimpanzee in response to head and eye movement of a familiar experimenter.

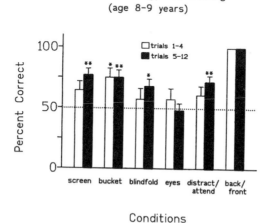

FIG. 3.11. Mean percent correct (±SEM) at third longitudinal assessment (at 8 to 9 years of age) of a cohort of chimpanzees understanding of seeing/not seeing. See Figs. 3.6 to 3.9 for description of some of the conditions.

the most striking results came from an experiment in which we combined two of the conditions to produce the mixed treatment depicted in Fig. 3.12. This condition can be understood as a combination of the *correct* option from the looking-over-the-shoulder condition, and the *incorrect* option from eyes open/closed. The significance of this condition can be understood by hypothesizing that the apes had simply formed a series of rules in descending order of importance—frontal aspect > face > eyes. If so, they could be expected to perform well on looking-over-the-shoulder (neither frontal aspect is visible, so it represents a choice between face and no face). Likewise, in the eyes open/closed condition, both experimenters' frontal aspects were equally visible, and both faces were equally visible; thus, the apes would resort to the eyes rule and perform excellently. However, in the mixed condition, the frontal aspect of the incorrect experimenter (eyes closed) was visible, but not the frontal aspect of the correct experimenter (the one looking over her shoulder with eyes open). Thus, the low-level model predicted they would significantly prefer the *incorrect* experimenter—which is exactly what they did (Reaux et al., 1999, Experiment 4).

The results of this extended series of studies suggested that despite their natural use of the begging gesture, and despite their interest in the eyes and gaze direction of others, chimpanzees do not, in fact, understand a key

FIG. 3.12.   Mixed condition used to assess rules used by chimpanzees to decide to whom they should gesture. Subject preferred the experimenter facing forward with eyes closed.

aspect of these gestures—namely, that the gestures must be seen by the recipients in order for the gesture to function. In contrast, by 2 years of age, young children seem to understand this aspect of seeing (Lempers, Flavell, & Flavell, 1977; Povinelli & Eddy, 1996a, Experiment 15).

Do Chimpanzees Comprehend the Pointing Gestures of Others?

The results discussed previously cast serious doubt on assuming that chimpanzees understand their visually based gestures in a similar manner to the way in which 2- to 3-year-old children do. We now ask whether they comprehend pointing gestures when they are used by others. Although early reports suggested that they might understand the referential significance of pointing acts (e.g., Call & Tomasello, 1994; Povinelli, Nelson, & Boysen, 1992), more controlled research has recently cast serious doubts on such a view.

For example, we trained our apes to respond to our pointing gestures to locate which of several locations contained a hidden treat (see Povinelli et al., 1997). As can be seen from Fig. 3.13a, we used the standard form of the gesture and its natural context of occurrence, with the experimenter's hand closer to the correct location. The apes took varying numbers of trials to learn to exploit this gesture, but none of them did so immediately. This initial difficulty was of interest in its own right, because our apes had been exposed to human pointing since birth. Nonetheless, within several dozen trials the animals were responding in a highly accurate manner.

What did the initial learning signify? Had the apes understood all along (or at least now learned) that the experimenter was intentionally signaling one of the boxes through the pointing gesture, but merely needed a bit of time to orient to the task? Or had they just learned a conditional discrimination of one kind or another? For example, perhaps the apes had either just learned to respond to the local stimulus configuration of the experimenter's hand and the box (a stimulus configuration rule), or to simply select the box closest to the experimenter's hand (a distance cue). Although these two models are distinct, they both differ from the one that posits that the apes understand the referential significance of the gesture.

We conducted two experiments to test these ideas. In the first one, we simply increased the distance between the distal end of the experimenter's pointing gesture and the correct location as shown in Fig. 3.13b. In this new position, the experimenter's pointing hand was still closer to the correct box, and thus this condition could not distinguish between the high-level model and the distance model. However, it did allow us to distinguish between the distance model and the low-level stimulus configuration model. Remarkably, although the apes entered the lab and looked at the experi-

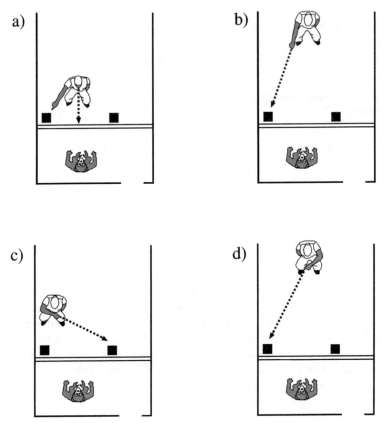

FIG. 3.13. Conditions used to assess chimpanzees' understanding of the pointing gesture. See text for details of the conditions, hypotheses, and results.

menter before responding on every trial, this simple manipulation caused 5 of the 7 subjects' performances to drop from 100% correct to chance levels (50% correct). The implication was clear. Far from understanding the gesture in referential terms, most of the apes were simply focusing on the local configuration of the experimenter's hand and the box. Young 3-year-old children, in contrast, performed at near-perfect levels from Trial 1 forward.

However, two of our chimpanzees (Kara and Apollo) performed quite differently from the others—they continued to respond well even with this increased distance between the experimenter's gesture and the box. Did these apes, then, understand the referential nature of the act? As we explained earlier, the first study was designed to distinguish between the two low-level models; it did not allow us to distinguish between the distance based model and the high-level model. However, Kara and Apollo's performance provided a reason to test the apes in a second experiment, which could distinguish between these accounts. Thus, in a second experiment, the experimenter pointed from several locations and postures. In one case the tip of his pointing finger was equidistant from the two locations (Fig. 3.13d), and in another it was closer to the incorrect location (Fig. 3.13c). As before, we included versions of these treatments in which the experimenter was and was not gazing at the location to which he was pointing (see Povinelli et al., 1997, for a complete description of the conditions).

The results of these tests cast serious doubt on the validity of the referential comprehension model. First, all of the apes continued to perform excellently when the experimenter's pointing hand was near the correct box (within 5 to 10 cm; see Fig. 3.13a). In contrast, most of the apes continued to perform at chance level when the pointing hand was considerably farther away (80 cm) from the correct box, but still closer to it than to the incorrect box (see Fig. 3.13b). Third, the apes actually preferred the *incorrect* box when the experimenter's body was positioned closer to it than to the correct box, even though his pointing gesture was clearly referencing the opposite box (see Fig. 3.13c). Fourth, and perhaps most important, when the experimenter's body with gesture was equidistant from the two boxes, the animals performed randomly—including the two apes who had performed well in the initial experiment. Perhaps most striking of all was that in the cases where the experimenter was closer to one box than the other (see Fig. 3.13c), the subjects performed better when the experimenter gazed at the correct box *without* pointing, as opposed to when he both gazed *and* pointed! In previous studies we had explicitly taught the apes to choose the box to which an experimenter glanced (Povinelli, Bierschwale, & Cech, 1999; Povinelli et al., 2002). However, introducing the pointing hand misled the apes into choosing the incorrect box because the hand was closer to it than to the correct box. In contrast, 26-month-old human toddlers performed excellently on their very first trial with even the most difficult of these conditions (see Povinelli et al., 1997).

It is important to reiterate that these chimpanzees had been exposed to the pointing gesture (and many other indicating gestures) in their spontaneous interactions with their human caregivers (and later trainers) since birth. And it is surely our subjective impression that, in some sense or another, they learned to respond appropriately to these gestures. However, the results of our experiments clearly support the idea that they did not learn about the referential import of the gesture. Although the chimpanzees came to exploit the gesture, whether from trial-and-error learning or by the expression of some innate tendency to be attracted to those objects physically closest to another individual, it seems likely that lower level processes were at work. Indeed, similarities of this with stimulus enhancement are quite striking (e.g., Galef, 1988). The manipulation of an object, for instance, increases its salience, and thus it obtains a higher valence. In the context of our experiments, it seems likely that the experimenter's hand acted in precisely this manner to enhance the salience of the nearest box.[6] Although it was conducted for somewhat different reasons, and therefore lacks important controls, a recent experiment by Tomasello, Call, and Gluckman (1997) supports a simple discrimination model of pointing comprehension.

TOWARD AN INTEGRATED ACCOUNT OF THE FORM, FUNCTION, AND MEANING OF THE POINTING GESTURE IN HUMANS AND APES

The Reinterpretation Model

Although the strands of an alternative to the argument by analogy are already in place, in this section we provide an explanation of how it is that humans and chimpanzees can share so many behavioral patterns in common (including those under examination here) and yet understand them so differently. In short, we propose that social complexity evolved independently of psychological complexity. We speculate that primate social evolution (and the evolution of mammalian social communication in general) was driven by fairly ancient psychological processes, coupled with selection for certain physiological, attentional, behavioral, and morphological structures subserving these communicative acts. Thus, the behavioral forms that primatologists are fond of calling deception, empathy, grudging, reconciliation, and even pointing all evolved and were in full operation long before there were any organisms that could understand them in these terms. They evolved not because these primate ancestors possessed the means of representing the minds of their fellow groupmates, but because such acts became inevitable as selection honed behaviors that maximized each group member's inclusive fitness given the constraints in place. Thus, contrary to the so-called "social intelligence hypothesis" (e.g., Humphrey, 1976; Jolly, 1966), we do not suppose that the psychological demands of living in a so-

---

[6]Call and Tomasello (1994) claimed that an orangutan they tested displayed evidence of referential comprehension of the pointing gesture. However, as in other studies (e.g., Anderson, Sallaberry, & Barbier, 1995; Povinelli, Nelson, & Boysen, 1992), the pointing hand was much closer to the correct location than the incorrect one. If we compare conditions in which distance was not controlled, our subject Kara displayed better evidence for exploiting the gesture than did their subject. However, when the cue distance was neutralized, even Kara's performance plummeted to chance.

cial group required an understanding of others as psychological agents. On the contrary, we suspect that only one lineage—the human one—evolved abilities related to understanding others in mentalistic terms.

The significance of this proposal comes from considering what this means about human behavior. In evolving a cognitive specialization in representing mental states, humans did not (we propose) shed their ancestral behavioral patterns in favor of some dramatically new set of behaviors. We suspect that most of the basic behavioral patterns remained intact. What changed was that for the first time such behaviors became understood in mentalistic terms. In one sense, then, these ancient behaviors were reinterpreted in terms of an explanatory system we now call "theory of mind." Just as the addition of a device to represent the speed of an automobile—a speedometer—does not radically alter the basic propensities of the vehicle, so too can we imagine that humans evolved novel representational systems related to second-order intentional states without dramatically altering their ancient behavioral patterns (see Povinelli & Giambrone, 1999). Indeed, to push the example even further, just as the speedometer does not endow the automobile/driver system with a score of previously impossible behaviors, but rather makes certain behaviors much easier to accomplish, so too might the ability to understand ancient behaviors in explicitly mentalistic terms have made certain complicated behavioral routines much more likely.

The Reinterpretation Model Applied

How does the reinterpretation model help us to understand the similarity between human pointing and structurally similar gestures in chimpanzees? First, we know that chimpanzees and humans (like other nonhuman primates) exhibit visually guided prehension—that is, they reach toward things they want and visually monitor those reaches. Second, as part of a ritualized communicative signal (begging), chimpanzees extend their arms and hands toward things that they cannot take without the tolerance of others. Third, they extend their arms toward others as part of a communicative signal involved in reassurance after a fight or in ambiguous social situations. All three of these behaviors are displayed by chimpanzees in the field and in captivity. We presume many of the structural aspects of these gestures were in place prior to the evolutionary divergence of the human and chimpanzee lineages.

These primitive gestures may have provided the raw behavioral fabric out of which pointing as a referential gesture emerged in humans. We suggest that with the emergence of psychological innovations in social understanding (in particular, second-order intentional states), existing gestures or actions were explicitly reinterpreted as functioning to influence the attentional/mental states of others. Although in one sense these behaviors did in fact function to influence the attentional states of others from their earliest inception, we advance the hypothesis that only the human lineage evolved the psychological faculties that made it possible to understand this fact.[7] As we have argued elsewhere, this need not mean that each occurrence of such acts that *can* be understood in this manner will be so understood. On the contrary, we suspect that frequently such actions are not prompted by second-order intentional states (i.e., the representation of the mental states of self or other), but instead are controlled by lower level psychological processes. Just as the reading on the speedometer of an automobile need not directly cause the speed of the automobile in order to causally interact with it, we conclude that second-order intentional states need not directly cause the behaviors that they represent, or indeed even always causally interact with them.

What about the case of captive chimpanzees? Here we see a degree of functional similarity to human pointing not approximated by wild chimpanzees. It is not difficult to imagine how these ancient behavioral similarities might become shaped during interactions with humans to produce the kinds of gestures described earlier. Let us provide just two examples of how this might operate. First, in captivity, young chimpanzees invariably reach out toward observers who pass their enclosures. Also invariably, these human observers misinterpret this signal as indicating that the ape wants them to touch him or her. Thus, the human observers are usually a bit startled when, far from an enthusiastic reception, the apes withdraw their arms in alarm as the observers reach toward them. Although initially this constitutes an unexpected response, chimpanzees may rapidly learn a new function for this gesture: getting humans to approach them. A second case (mentioned previously) involves a chimpanzee reaching toward an object. Human observers correctly interpret this behavior as the chimpanzee wanting the object. Therefore, they pick up the object and hand it to the ape. Indeed, the more closely the gesture looks like a request (regardless of what the chimpanzee understands about the gesture), the more rapidly it will be interpreted as such by the human. In short order, then, chimpanzees may develop a gesture in the presence of humans that serves to cause the human to hand them what they want. We emphasize that this gesture is *not* reaching—it is a social signal that functions very much like pointing. But, as

---

[7]Call and Tomasello (1996) suggested an alternative to this view, namely, that chimpanzees (and perhaps other great apes) can, and at least some do, possess second-order intentional states but require human culture to shape their cognitive systems in this manner. This intriguing hypothesis suggests that a "theory of mind" is not a tightly canalized system that evolved exclusively in the human lineage. At this point, however, there is little or no direct evidence to support this hypothesis (see Povinelli, 1996).

we have seen, there is good reason to suspect that all of this occurs in the absence of the chimpanzee understanding the psychological states of his or her communicative partner. Indeed, the driving force shaping the chimpanzee's gesture is the human's representation of the chimpanzee's psychological state. This would explain why these gestures are not exhibited by chimpanzees as they interact with each other.

Some researchers find these explanations unlikely, noting that their subjects' "pointing" occurs significantly more often in the presence of an experimenter than in his or her absence (Krause & Fouts, 1997; Leavens & Hopkins, 1999; Leavens et al., 1996; see also Call & Tomasello, 1994, for similar findings with orangutans). Leavens et al. (1996) argued that if the gestures were simply "failed reaching attempts" (which is *not* the explanation offered here), then the apes would produce these gestures with equal frequency in the presence or absence of humans or when the experimenter's back is toward them. However, such findings do not contradict the claim that chimpanzees know little or nothing about attention as a mental state. Not even radical behaviorists would deny that chimpanzees could readily learn the connection between the posture of a person and the effectiveness of a social signal in eliciting a desired behavior from him or her. Given that the presence and forward-facing posture of the human typically covary with chimpanzees' success in using their visually based gestures, their perceptual and attentional systems would have to be extraordinarily different from ours indeed not to uncover this connection. Indeed, regardless of their understanding of the psychological states of others, it is hard to imagine how chimpanzees could not learn to avoid using visually based, social gestures when someone is facing away from them, or absent altogether. Indeed, our experimental work shows exactly how quickly these understandings can develop— and how narrowly restricted these understandings may be.

We end on what may be the central question of all concerning the argument by analogy. The question is best put simply: "Are not processes similar to ones explored here also at work in human infants and children? Are the same processes not responsible for their construction of an understanding of others as psychological agents?" The reinterpretation hypothesis offers a way out of this apparent impasse. If we grant that humans have evolved novel psychological specializations related to social understanding (and perhaps others as well), and if we grant that apes and humans share ancient behavioral patterns that evolved in the absence of these representational systems, then the answer to this question becomes straightforward. On the one hand, it may be that the processes that govern the emergence of gestural forms in humans and chimpanzees (especially those reared with humans) reflect genuine evolutionary homology. But this homology may, at each twist and turn in the developmental process, be associated with profound differences as well. In humans, the old psychological systems may develop alongside the new in such a way that those looking for simple differences between humans and chimpanzees may come away unimpressed. The real differences may lie not in the dramatic appearance of a structurally new behavior per se, or even in old behaviors put to distinctly new functions. Rather, the ability to represent others as possessing internal, attentional states may have allowed existing gestural forms to be woven into a much larger, more efficient and productive system of communication—a system in which understanding the psychological meanings behind the gestures is just as important as the gestures themselves. Both systems involve a description of others, and both provide predictions for how others are likely to behave. But only one can be considered a genuinely psychological description of others. Humans—unlike other animals—appear to have evolved the latter. But in doing so, we did not discard the ancient in favor of the new. Rather, the two systems appear to have been combined in such a way that our efforts to specify the unique role that each plays in causing our behavior may turn out to be an impossible—and perhaps nonsensical—undertaking.

ACKNOWLEDGMENTS

The research described in this chapter was supported by NSF Young Investigator Award SBR-8458111 to D. J. Povinelli. It would not have been possible without the talents of numerous staff and students who have assisted in the training and testing of the chimpanzees over the past 5 years, including Anthony Rideaux, James Reaux, Donna Bierschwale, Laura Theall, and Timothy Eddy. Photographs are by Donna T. Bierschwale and Corey G. Porché.

REFERENCES

Anderson, J. R., Sallaberry, P., & Barbier, H. (1995). Use of experimenter-given cues during object-choice tasks by capuchin monkeys. *Animal Behaviour, 49,* 201–208.

Baldwin, D. A. (1991). Infants' contribution to the achievement of joint reference. *Child Development, 63,* 875–890.

Baldwin, D. A. (1993a). Early referential understanding: Infants' ability to recognize referential acts for what they are. *Developmental Psychology, 29,* 832–843.

Baldwin, D. A. (1993b). Infants' ability to consult the speaker for clues to word reference. *Journal of Child Language, 20,* 395–418.

Bygott, J. D. (1979). Agonistic behavior, dominance, and social structure in wild chimpanzees of the Gombe National Park. In D. A. Hamburg & E. R. McCown (Eds.), *The great apes: Perspectives on human evolution* (Vol. 5, pp. 405–427).

Call, J., & Tomasello, M. (1994). The production and comprehension of referential pointing by orangutans (*Pongo pygmaeus*). *Journal of Comparative Psychology, 108,* 307–317.

Call, J., & Tomasello, M. (1996). The effect of humans on the cognitive development of apes. In A. E. Russon, K. A. Bard, & S. T. Parker (Eds.), *Reaching into thought* (pp. 371–403). Cambridge: Cambridge University Press.

Darwin, C. (1982). *The descent of man.* New York: Modern Library. (Original work published 1871)

de Waal, F. (1982). *Chimpanzee politics: Power and sex among Apes.* New York: Harper & Row.

Desrochers, S., Morisette, P., & Ricard, M. (1995). Two perspectives on pointing in infancy. In C. Moore & P. J. Dunham (Eds.), *Joint attention: Its origins and role in development* (pp. 85–101). Hillsdale, NJ: Lawrence Erlbaum Associates.

Fouts, R. S., Hirsch, A. D., & Fouts, D. H. (1982). Cultural transmission of a human language in a chimpanzee mother–infant relationship. In H. E. Fitzgerald, J. A. Mullins, & P. Gage (Eds.), *Child nurturance series: Vol. 3. Psychobiological perspectives* (pp. 159–193). New York: Plenum.

Franco, F., & Butterworth, G. (1996). Pointing and social awareness: Declaring and requesting in the second year. *Journal of Child Language, 23,* 307–336.

Franco, F., & Wishart, J. G. (1995). Use of pointing and other gestures by young children with Down syndrome. *American Journal of Mental Retardation, 100,* 160–182.

Galef, B. G., Jr. (1988). Imitation in animals: History, definition and interpretation of data from the psychological laboratory. In T. R. Zentall & B. G. Galef, Jr. (Eds.), *Social learning: Psychological and biological perspectives* (pp. 1–28). Hillsdale, NJ: Lawrence Erlbaum Associates.

Gardner, B. T., & Gardner, R. A. (1975). Evidence for sentence constituents in the early utterances of child and chimpanzee. *Journal of Experimental Psychology: General, 104,* 244–267.

Gómez, J. C. (1990). The emergence of intentional communication as a problem-solving strategy in the gorilla. In S. T. Parker & K. R. Gibson (Eds.), *"Language" and intelligence in monkeys and apes: Comparative developmental perspectives* (pp. 333–355). Cambridge, England: Cambridge University Press.

Gómez, J. C., Sarria, E., & Tamarit, J. (1993). The comparative study of early communication and theories of mind: Ontogeny, phylogeny, and pathology. In S. Baron-Cohen, H. Tager-Flusberg, & D. Cohen (Eds.), *Understanding other minds: Perspectives from autism* (pp. 397–426). Oxford, England: Oxford University Press.

Goodall, J. (1986). *The chimpanzees of Gombe: Patterns of behavior.* Cambridge, MA: Belknap, Harvard University Press.

Hannan, T. E., & Fogel, A. (1987). A case-study assessment of "pointing" during the first three months of life. *Perceptual and Motor Skills, 65,* 187–194.

Hume, D. (1978). *A treatise of human nature* (2 Vols., L. A. Selby-Bigge, Ed.). Oxford: Clarendon. (Original work published 1739–1740)

Humphrey, N. K. (1976). The social function of intellect. In P. P. G. Bateson & R. A. Hinde (Eds.), *Growing points in ethology* (pp. 303–317). Cambridge: Cambridge University Press.

Itakura, S. (1996). Manual action in infant chimpanzees: A preliminary study. *Perceptual and Motor Skills, 83,* 611–614.

Jolly, A. (1966). Lemur social intelligence and primate intelligence. *Science, 153,* 501–506.

Krause, M. A., & Fouts, R. S. (1997). Chimpanzees (*Pan troglodytes*) pointing: Hand shapes, accuracy, and the role of eye gaze. *Journal of Comparative Psychology, 111,* 330–336.

Leavens, D. A., & Hopkins, W. D. (1998). Intentional communication by chimpanzees: A cross-sectional study of the use of referential gestures. *Developmental Psychology, 34,* 813–822.

Leavens, D. A., & Hopkins, W. D. (1999). The whole hand point: The structure and function of pointing from a comparative perspective. *Journal of Comparative Psychology, 113,* 417–425.

Leavens, D. A., Hopkins, W. D., & Bard, K. A. (1996). Indexical and referential pointing in chimpanzees (*Pan troglodytes*). *Journal of Comparative Psychology, 110,* 346–353.

Lempers, J. D., Flavell, E. R., & Flavell, J. H. (1977). The development in very young children of tacit knowledge concerning visual perception. *Genetic Psychology Monographs, 95,* 3–53.

Leung, E., & Rheingold, H. (1981). Development of pointing as a social gesture. *Developmental Psychology, 17,* 215–220.

Miles, H. L. (1990). The cognitive foundations for reference in a signing orangutan. In S. T. Parker & K. R. Gibson (Eds.), *"Language" and intelligence in monkeys and apes: Comparative developmental perspectives* (pp. 511–539). Cambridge, England: Cambridge University Press.

Nishida, T. (1970). Social behavior and relationships among wild chimpanzees of the Mahale Mountains. *Journal of Human Evolution, 2,* 357–370.

Plooij, F. X. (1978). Some basic traits of language in wild chimpanzees? In A. Lock (Ed.), *Action, gesture and symbol* (pp. 111–131). London: Academic Press.

Povinelli, D. J. (1996). Growing up ape. *Monographs of the Society for Research in Child Development, 61*(2, Serial No. 247), 174–189.

Povinelli, D. J., Bierschwale, D. T., & Cech, C. G. (1999). Comprehension of seeing as a referential act in young children, but not juvenile chimpanzees. *British Journal of Developmental Psychology, 73,* 37–60.

Povinelli, D. J., & Davis, D. R. (1994). Differences between chimpanzees (*Pan troglodytes*) and humans (*Homo sapiens*) in the resting state of the index finger: Implications for pointing. *Journal of Comparative Psychology, 108,* 134–139.

Povinelli, D. J., Dunphy-Lelii, S., Reaux, J. E., & Mazza, M. P. (2002). Psychological diversity in chimpanzees and humans: New longitudinal assessments of chimpanzees' understanding of attention. *Brain, Behavior, and Evolution, 59,* 33–53.

Povinelli, D. J., & Eddy, T. J. (1996a). What young chimpanzees know about seeing. *Monographs of the Society for Research in Child Development, 61*(2, Serial No. 247).

Povinelli, D. J., & Eddy, T. J. (1996b). Chimpanzees: Joint visual attention. *Psychological Science, 7,* 129–135.

Povinelli, D. J., & Eddy, T. J. (1997). Specificity of gaze-following in young chimpanzees. *British Journal of Developmental Psychology, 15,* 213–222.

Povinelli, D. J., & Giambrone, S. (1999). Inferring other minds: Failure of the argument by analogy. *Philosophical Topics, 27,* 167–201.

Povinelli, D. J., Nelson, K. E., & Boysen, S. T. (1992). Comprehension of social role reversal by chimpanzees: Evidence of empathy? *Animal Behaviour, 43,* 633–640.

Povinelli, D. J., Reaux, J. E., Bierschwale, D. T., Allain, A. D., & Simon, B. B. (1997). Exploitation of pointing as a referential gesture in young children, but not adolescent chimpanzees. *Cognitive Development, 12,* 423–461.

Premack, D. (1984). Pedagogy and aesthetics as sources of culture. In M. S. Gazzaniga (Ed.), *Handbook of cognitive neuroscience* (pp. 15–35). New York: Plenum.

Reaux, J. E., Theall, L. A., & Povinelli, D. J. (1999). A longitudinal investigation of chimpanzees' understanding of visual perception. *Child Development, 70,* 275–290.

Romanes, G. J. (1882). *Animal intelligence.* London: Kegan Paul.

Romanes, G. J. (1883). *Mental evolution in animals.* New York: Appleton.

Russell, B. (1948). *Human knowledge: Its scope and limits.* London: Unwin Hyman.

Savage-Rumbaugh, E. S. (1986). *Ape language: From conditioned response to symbol.* New York: Columbia University Press.

Tomasello, M., Call, J., & Gluckman, A. (1997). Comprehension of novel communicative signs by apes and human children. *Child Development, 68,* 1067–1080.

Tomasello, M., Call, J., & Hare, B. (1998). Five primate species follow the visual gaze of conspecifics. *Animal Behavior, 55,* 1063–1069.

Tomasello, M., Call, J., Nagell, K., Olguin, R., & Carpenter, M. (1994). The learning and use of gestural signals by young chimpanzees: A trans-generational study. *Primates, 35,* 137–154.

Tomasello, M., Gust, D., & Frost, G. T. (1989). A longitudinal investigation of gestural communication in young chimpanzees. *Primates, 30,* 35–50.

Vea, J. J., & Sabater-Pi, J. (1998). Spontaneous pointing behavior in the wild pygmy chimpanzee (*Pan paniscus*). *Folia Primatologica, 69,* 289–290.

Vygotsky, L. (1962). *Thought and language.* Cambridge, MA: MIT Press.

Woodruff, G., & Premack, D. (1979). Intentional communication in the chimpanzee: The development of deception. *Cognition, 7,* 333–362.

Chapter 4

From Index-Finger Extension to Index-Finger Pointing: Ontogenesis of Pointing in Preverbal Infants

Nobuo Masataka
Kyoto University

Pointing with the index finger is a vital part of human communication. Index-finger pointing, which often co-occurs with speech, is characterized by an arm and index finger extended to the direction of an interesting object, with the other fingers curled under the hand and the thumb held down and to the side. We point at things we know and things we have never seen before. Pointing can be a way of declaring, making a point, or asking. The underlying intention is always to draw someone else's attention to an object or event of interest.

Index-finger pointing is apparently unique to humans. No doubt, most animals do not possess fingers to point with, but even apes do not point in their natural state. Although apes sometimes use an extended hand to refer to things after extensive interactions with humans, they practically never extend the index finger separately when making the gesture. In a recent study (Leavens & Hopkins, 1998), a chimpanzee was found to use a form of index-finger pointing to draw his trainer's attention to food that had fallen out of reach. This chimpanzee, however, never pointed for the benefit of other chimpanzees, and even with his trainer, he used his flat hand more often than his index finger. This fact indicates that there is something special about finger pointing in humans.

Developmentally, the pointing gesture is known to first emerge near the end of the first year of life. However, prior to the intentional use of pointing, there is an interval of a month or more in which infants point but do not yet comprehend or follow the pointing of others (Murphy & Messer,

1977). During this period, they learn to turn their heads in response to other signals—head and eye movements, for example, or shifts in body orientation—that indicate a change in others' focus of interest. That indicates the possibility that meaningful pointing—a precursor to speech—has its own motoric precursors in some other manual action. Nevertheless, little has been revealed so far about the ontogenesis of index-finger pointing.

The aim of this chapter is to pursue this issue. Here I present evidence showing the developmental continuity from index-finger extension to index-finger pointing. Index-finger extension here is defined as the manual activity characterized by an extended index finger, with other fingers lightly or tightly curled and the arm not extended and thus not specifically directed at any target object.

PREVIOUS STUDIES OF THE DEVELOPMENT OF POINTING IN INFANTS

Although empirical data about the development of pointing in infants are meager, several hypotheses have been presented about its origin so far. One theory argues that pointing diverges from the movements of reaching and grasping (Leung & Rheingold, 1981). This theory assumes that the movement for reaching and grasping is made more economical in pointing, and pointing replaces reaching and grasping as a referential gesture. Bruner (1983) argued that the gesture does not emerge as modification of reaching, but emerges, at least partly, as a primitive marking system for singling out the noteworthy. Vygotsky (1961) saw pointing as originating in the failed reaching activities of the infant. However, this failure occasionally results in the successful access to the object the infant originally attempted to reach through the intervention of adults around the infant. According to his hypothesis, this occasional success makes the infant realize a communicative utility of the failed reaching.

The arguments developed on the basis of these hypotheses are obviously incompatible with one another. Nevertheless, it may be noticeable that all of them commonly assume that cognitive development around the 1-year-old period—the ability to carry out a plan and signal intentions—induces the child to learn the new behavior of pointing. This was a purely cognitive interpretation based on traditional reports on observations that infants begin to point at the age of 8 months. However, virtually no work has ever addressed the questions of what ontogenetic process is at work during early infancy that leads to the subsequent emergence of pointing gesture, and why index-finger pointing is used predominantly as pointing gesture.

In this regard, two previous observations are noteworthy. First, Bates, Benigni, Bretherton, Camaioni, and Voltera (1979), in their observation of interactions of 9- to 13-month-old infants with their mothers, found that the movement of an outstretched arm with an extended index finger emerges ontogenetically first in order to "poke" or "scratch" proximal objects. This was considered to be an early form of object exploration. Apparently this activity emerges earlier than the pointing gesture, and after the appearance of the pointing gesture it was reported to be no longer observed. Second, Fogel and Hannan (1985) reported the occurrence of index-finger extensions in preverbal infants as young as 2 months. In a sample of 28 three-month-old infants, 64% of the infants performed at least one index-finger extension (sometimes produced as many as six) in a 2-minute session of face-to-face interaction with the mother. Obviously, the manual action was never temporally accompanied with an outstretching movement of the arm, and was never spatially oriented to any distal object. However, the manual action was observed to occur most frequently just before or after a nondistress, comfort-state vocalization, that is, cooing. Thus, although it is most likely not an intentional act of the infant, the manual action is a coordinative structure appearing in nonrandom contexts. Moreover, the emergence of this behavior might have ontogenetic significance because index-finger extension, when it emerged first as an object exploration, is also reported to be frequently accompanied by the infant's vocal utterances (Bates et al., 1979).

The main issue to be addressed in this chapter is whether index-finger extension performed by preverbal infants, which resembles a true pointing gesture, is significantly associated with the emergence of pointing as referential gesture. If so, how does index-finger extension develop during the first year of life? In the following sections, I address the latter question first. I start with the demonstration that index-finger extension is associated more with the infant's speechlike vocalization than with its nonspeechlike vocalization. Further, it is shown that speechlike vocalization occurs more frequently when the adult responds to the vocalization as if holding a conversation. The increase in speechlike vocalization in turn leads to the increase in index-finger extension. Furthermore, the combination of index-finger extension and speechlike vocalization gives the adult a favorable impression of the infant. Thus, presumably adults are more likely to respond to such a combination, thereby further reinforcing the combination. The strength of this reinforcement may be variable across cultures. It may be weaker in some cultures where index-finger pointing is not the predominant form of pointing among adults. This is presumably a part of the mechanism in which cultural diversity of pointing is maintained across generations. In the second part of the chapter, I present evidence from a longitudinal study that index-finger pointing emerges from index-finger extension, but not from reaching. Finally, I discuss a study that shows that index-finger extension indexes the infant's exploration of, and self-regulation of attention toward, an interesting novel object, rather than a desire to bring the object closer to the infant. I argue that when the infant develops the desire to share with others what he or she is exploring and attending to, index-finger extension develops into index-finger pointing.

STRONG CONNECTION BETWEEN SPEECHLIKE
VOCALIZATIONS AND INDEX-FINGER EXTENSION
DURING EARLY INFANCY

As a first step to answering the question just posed, 14 3-month-old first-born male infants were observed when freely interacting with their mothers, and their nonvocal and vocal behaviors were simultaneously recorded (Masataka, 1995). I conducted this observation because Fogel and Hannan (1985) reported a strong tendency of temporal association between cooing and index-finger extension in 3-month-olds, although they did not report any further information on the quality of the infant vocalizations. Because index-finger pointing performed by adults is often accompanied by speech, and pointing can be a way of telling and asking, I hypothesized that a rudimentary form of this association can be seen in the synchronization of speechlike cooing and index-finger extension in 3-month-old infants.

Contrary to the widely assumed notion that language structures should be analyzed only in terms of speech sounds and grammar, and that body movement and postural signals comprise a structured system of their own, which typically expresses affective and unconscious meaning, McNeill (1985) proposed that gesture and speech can be conceived as an integral whole, with gesture as part of the process of speaking. Gesture is produced along with speech, and it is not fundamentally different from speech. On the basis of such a view of language and gesture, I hypothesized that both linguistic production and the production of the precursors of pointing gesture develop ontogenetically together even at a very early stage.

The behaviors of the 14 three-month-old infants were coded by four raters. Nonvocal behaviors and vocal behaviors were coded separately by two different pairs of coders using different sources: videotapes for nonvocal behaviors and audio tapes for vocal behaviors. Concerning nonvocal behaviors, coding categories included: infant's direction of gaze (GAZE AT mother: action of looking at mother's face), infant's facial action (SMILE: friendly facial expression characterized by lip corners retracted up; MOUTHING: movements of the mouth such as chewing, sucking, puckering, etc.; CRY: distress vocalizations or distressed expression including frowning and distress brow—although crying did not occur in this sample), infant's manual action (SPREAD: all fingers extended and held for a period longer than 1.5 sec; INDEX-FINGER EXTEND: index finger extended and held for a period longer than 1.5 sec; GRASP: holding an object, clothes, self, or mother; CURL: any other movements or positions including making a fist, partial spreading, and rhythmical moving of fingers). Concerning vocalizations, each of them was judged whether it was truly speechlike (syllabic) or not (vocalic). Syllabic sounds are those perceived as sounding like "the baby is really talking." They have greater oral resonance and pitch contour, and are produced towards the front of the mouth, frequently with the mouth open and moving and the voice more relaxed. Vocalic sounds are, in contrast, nondistress, nonvegetative, but less speechlike. They have greater nasal resonance, are more often produced toward the back of the mouth, are more uniform in pitch, and seem more effortful.

The codes for vocalizations were compared with the codes for nonvocal behaviors obtained from an independent observation of the videotapes. If any nonvocal behavior was coded during an occurrence of a syllabic sound, this nonvocal behavior was operationally defined as having occurred in a *syllabic context*. Similarly, if a behavior was recorded during an occurrence of a vocalic sound, it was defined as having occurred in a *vocalic context*. Behaviors that fell into neither of these categories were defined as occurring in a *silent context*.

The rate of all the types of nonvocal behaviors was compared across these three contexts. This analysis revealed that occurrences of two categories of manual action were different across the contexts. The two categories were index-finger extension and spread. Index-finger extension occurred more often in a syllabic context than in either a vocalic or silent context (Table 4.1). In contrast, spread was observed more often in a silent context than in a syllabic or a vocalic context. In other words, index-finger extension, but not spread, occurs specifically in association with truly speechlike sounds.

Although noncry vocalizations of 3-month-old infants are anatomically and acoustically immature and quite variable, they can be reliably grouped

TABLE 4.1
Rates per Minute of Nonvocal Behaviors
in Three Types of Vocalization Contexts

	Context		
Behavior	*Syllabic*	*Vocalic*	*Silent*
Index-finger extension	3.8	1.6	1.4
Spread	1.2	0.9	4.2
Curl	3.6	4.9	4.5
Grasp	0.8	1.1	1.0
Smile	1.6	2.1	1.8
Mouthing	3.2	2.6	2.8
Gaze at	6.9	8.4	6.6

into two categories: syllabic and vocalic. Originally this categorization was established on the basis of a number of findings in phonemic, acoustic, anatomical, and neurophyisological investigations on the development of infant vocalizations. These studies have all indicated that the age of 3 months is a marked period as a threshold between the earliest, nasalized sounds of short duration with a small pitch contour and the prebabbling vocalizations of longer duration, which have higher pitch, simple consonant–vowel combinations, and a larger pitch contour. This threshold has been described either as the transition from quasi to fully resonant nuclei (Oller, 1980, 1981), as the transition from comfort sounds to vocal play, partially arising from the development of laughter (Stark, 1978, 1981), or as the transition from the neonate to the "yabbler" (Netsell, 1981). Netsell argued that acquisition of speech-motor control enabled infants to produce speechlike sounds that were initially the result of the infants' accidental opening and closing of the mouth while phonating. Taken together with these findings, the results summarized in Table 4.1 indicate that at the very onset of speechlike vocalization and of index-finger extension, these two behaviors are closely connected. No such relations exist between the other nonvocal activities investigated in this study and the two types of vocalizations.

INADVERTENT CONDITIONING
OF INDEX-FINGER EXTENSION

Next, I examined whether the occurrence of index-finger extension could be socially modulated in an experiment in which infants were provided with some social stimulation. To test this, an experimental methodology based on Bloom, Russell, and Wassenberg (1987) was used, in which the 3-month-old infants experienced either conversational turn-taking (contingent stimulation group) or randomly timed responses (random stimulation group) from their mothers.

Bloom, Russell, and Wassenberg (1987) compared the vocal activity level of the infants between the two groups during a 2-min period before the commencement of stimulation, and they found no significant difference. However, once the stimulation started, a striking difference appeared. When the mother maintained a give-and-take pattern of vocal interaction (i.e., in the contingent stimulation group), the rate of vocalic sounds decreased dramatically and thereby infants produced a greater proportion of speechlike syllabic sounds. However, if infants experienced random stimulation, such a change did not occur.

The adult's contingent vocal stimulation, which apparently was verbal in nature, led to the production of syllabic vocalization by the infant. In other words, the quality of vocalizations by adults influences the quality of infant vocalizations, and the influence is effective only when the adult's vocalizations are delivered contingently to the vocal production of the infant. This finding was replicated by Bloom (1988) and Masataka (1993). Furthermore, in the present study too, the 3-month-old infants produced a higher proportion of syllabic sounds in the interaction period when the adult's stimulation was contingent (Table 4.2).

In addition to the change in the vocalization type after the commencement of stimulation, the rate of index-finger extensions also exhibited a similar change (Table 4.3). The activity level of this manual action did not differ significantly before the onset of stimulation, regardless of whether the infants were to receive contingent stimulation or randomly timed stimulation. However, once the stimulation started, the rate of index-finger extensions showed a significant increase if the infants experienced contingent stimulation. In contrast, no such change occurred if the infants experienced randomly timed stimulation. For other categories of nonvocal behaviors, no significant change was observed before or after the onset of stimulation, regardless of whether the infants were stimulated contingently or randomly.

In this experiment, it was shown that, as a consequence of contingent stimulation by the mothers, the frequency of syllabic sounds increased, and the frequency of index-finger extension increased as well. During circular chains of reactions between the adult and the infant, this manual action was facilitated without itself being contingently stimulated. Because it tended to co-occur with syllabic sounds, the index-finger extension was inadvertently conditioned as infant vocal activity was contingently stimulated. Given the fact that both syllabic sounds and index-finger extension are performed by infants as young as 3 months, the tendency for temporal association between the two should be predispositional. The occurrence of this specific pattern of motor activities must be genetically preprogrammed to be developed with greater ease than other patterns of motor activities.

TABLE 4.2
The Rate and Quality of Sounds Produced by the Infants

Type of Stimulation Received	Vocalization Rate per Minute	Sounds Categorized as Syllabic (%)
Contingent		
During the baseline period	4.1	36.8
During the interaction period	9.3	59.2
Random		
During the baseline period	4.0	37.6
During the interaction period	9.6	39.3

TABLE 4.3
Rates per Minute of Nonvocal Behaviors Produced by the Infants

	Behavioral Category					
Type of Stimulation Received	Index-Finger Extension	Spread	Curl	Grasp	Smile	Mouthing	Gaze At
Contingent							
During the baseline period	2.2	3.7	4.4	1.3	1.4	2.9	6.6
During the interaction period	4.9	3.4	4.6	0.9	1.3	3.2	6.9
Random							
During the baseline period	2.3	3.9	4.8	1.0	1.6	2.9	6.4
During the interaction period	2.5	3.5	4.3	1.2	1.5	3.0	6.6

SELECTIVE REINFORCEMENT OF INDEX-FINGER EXTENSION IN INFANTS BY ADULTS

We now know that the adult's contingent verbal response to the infant's vocalizations affects the quality of manual activities as well as the quality of vocalizations by the infant, although those manual activities and vocalizations are highly restricted by developmental immaturity. The infant's early behavioral responses result from the dynamics of early motor development, which is driven by the temporal and acoustic cues in adult talk. Furthermore, it has been reported that, much like the influence of the adult's talk on the infant, the behavior of the infant in turn influences the adult's favorable perception and attribution of the infant as a communicative partner.

The phenomenon was experimentally demonstrated first by Bloom and Lo (1990). In their study, Canadian adult participants viewed 20-sec video segments from 12 infants producing syllabic sounds and 12 different infants producing vocalic sounds. After viewing each segment, the participants were asked to complete a questionnaire after viewing each infant. The questionnaire, which included 5-point rating scales for cuddliness, likeability, and fun, measured the adults' perception of the favorability of the infants. It was found that the adults gave higher ratings of favorability to those infants who produced syllabic sounds. This finding was confirmed again by another group of adult participants (Bloom, D'Odorico, & Beaumont, 1993).

During vocal communication, 3-month-old infants vocalize roughly the same amount of syllabic and vocalic sounds. Nevertheless, one of them (syllabic) is preferred over the other (vocalic), at least by Canadian adults. It would not be difficult to assume that such a preference for a specific type of vocalization causes higher probability of the adult's contingent stimulation of that vocalization with speech. Given that the contingent stimulation is performed in the form of verbal responses, the adult's preference for speechlike sound serves as a selective reinforcer for the infant's production of speechlike sounds. This reinforcement enhances the development of the infant's phonetic ability.

Because there is already a strong connection between production of syllabic vocalizations and that of index-finger extension in 3-month-old infants, the occurrence of the manual activity might, to some degree, contribute to the caretaker's impression of vocalizing infants. To test this hypothesis, the next experiment was conducted, controlling for the occurrence of index-finger extension as well as for the quality of cooing (Masataka, 1996). In this experiment, like that of Bloom and Lo (1990), a video stimulus, consisting of recordings from 24 infants, was presented to Japanese adults. Half of the 24 infants were producing syllabic sounds, and the other half were vocalizing vocalic sounds. Six of the 12 infants producing syllabic sounds were showing index-finger extension, while the remaining six were not. Similarly, 6 of the 12 infants uttering vocalic sounds were showing index-finger extensions, whereas the other six were not. The total amount of index-finger extensions did not differ in the 12 infants regardless of whether they were vocalizing syllabic or vocalic sounds. Besides the index-finger extension, the total amount of other motor actions (spread, curl, grasp, mouthing, smiling, and gazing at) did not significantly differ among four cohorts of infants, classified according to the quality of vocalization and the absence/presence of index-finger extension.

When preference was measured in 100 adults according to the same procedure as in previous literature (e.g., Bloom et al., 1993), there was a significant main effect of the quality of vocalizations. The infants producing syllabic sounds were preferred over the infants producing vocalic sounds. There was also a significant main effect of index-finger extension, and further, an interaction between the two factors was significant (Table 4.4). As long as the infants in the stimulus tape were uttering vocalic sounds, the preference scores did not differ regardless of whether they were showing index-finger extension or not. However, for the infants who were uttering syllabic sounds, the preference scores for the infants showing index-finger extension significantly exceeded those for the infants who were not showing index-finger extension.

As a result of such selective reinforcement, the temporal connection between speechlike vocalizations and index-finger extension appears to be strengthened from early infancy.

The results of this experiment converges with the ecological theory of the adult's perception on child development proposed by Zebrowitz and McArthur (e.g., McArthur & Baron, 1983; Zebrowitz, 1990). The adult's perception of the infant as a social, communicative partner has adaptive significance for both the adult and infant. This perception emerges from stimulus properties of the infant's voice and visual cues such as manual movements (e.g., index-finger extension). The ecological theory predicts that the degree to which the infant's behavior affects the adult's perception is modulated by characteristics in the adult (e.g., the adult's cultural perspective) and the adult's willingness to overgeneralize various characteristics of

TABLE 4.4
Mean Preference Scores (SDs) in Terms
of the Types of Vocalization and Manual Action

Index-Finger Extension	Vocalization	
	Syllabic	Vocalic
Present	20.6 (5.7)	13.2 (4.9)
Absent	15.7 (3.8)	12.9 (4.4)

his or her own behavior to the infant's behavior. Because adults are likely to use visual cues in evaluating conversations among adults, nonvocal cues to the infant's vocalizations (e.g., manual movements) remain a strong affordance for their impression of the infant as socially favorable and communicatively intentional.

This argument leads us to speculate that if the same stimulus is presented to people living in those cultures in which index-finger pointing is regarded as some sort of taboo, this property as a visual cue to infant vocalizations would merely work as an extremely weak affordance, if any, for their positive impression of the infant. Consequently, this activity would be much less likely to receive selective reinforcement in such a culture, and its development in the infant would not be facilitated.

DISAPPEARANCE OF INDEX-FINGER EXTENSION AND EMERGENCE OF POINTING

As a consequence of inadvertent conditioning by parental verbal responses, which in turn is performed selectively depending on the quality of cooing and manual activities of infants, the overall amount of index-finger extensions increases during development. Masataka (1996) made longitudinal observations of manual activities during interaction with mothers in eight firstborn Japanese infants ages 3 to 16 months.

As presented in Fig. 4.1, the mean number of index-finger extensions per 15 min differed significantly as a function of the infants' age. Initially,

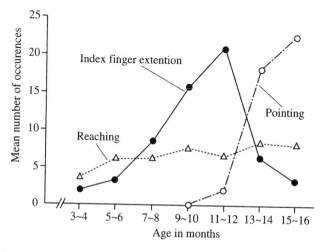

FIG. 4.1. Mean number (per 30 min) of infants' manual activities as a function of their age.

the infants produced an increasing number of index-finger extensions as they got older. The frequency reached its peak when the infants were between 11 and 12 months old. Interestingly, this period exactly coincided with that of the onset of pointing (index-finger pointing). Moreover, once pointing emerged, its frequency showed a dramatic increase, whereas the frequency of index-finger extensions decreased sharply. On the other hand, the number of occurrences of reaching did not differ significantly as a function of the infants' age.

These results could be evidence against the notion that pointing is an abbreviated form of reaching: If the explanation is plausible, the patterns of occurrences of the two activities should ontogenetically change in relation to one another. Rather, the results indicate that the onset of index-finger pointing as a developmental product of having learned, and moving beyond, index-finger extension. Furthermore, the learning should be enhanced presumably only in cultures where pointing with index-finger occurs prevalently, as discussed earlier. It is predicted that the replacement of index-finger extension by index-finger pointing does not occur robustly in cultures where index-finger pointing is regarded as a taboo.

CONTEXT IN WHICH INDEX-FINGER EXTENSION OCCURS

Previous research on the origin of manual pointing has been energized by the enduring debate over the initial function of human communication. So far, two broad alternatives have been articulated. The first proposition is that infants initially communicate because they want and need others to fulfill their demands. The second proposition is that, in addition to pleas for assistance, infants are motivated to communicate by an inherent desire for intersubjective experiences. That is, infants have a desire to share with others what they are attending to and exploring.

The first proposition would be supported if we obtain evidence that pointing emerges from acts such as grasping and reaching, which bring desired objects to the infant. However, in the previous section, we have seen that this is not the case. Rather, there is evidence that the precursor of pointing gesture is index-finger extension. The second proposition would be supported if we obtain evidence that pointing arises from manual acts related to exploration and self-regulation of attention. Based on the results discussed in the previous section, the second proposition predicts that index-finger extension is related to exploration and self-regulation of attention, but not to the infant's desire to bring an object to him or herself.

To test this prediction, Masataka (1996) conducted an experiment in which various objects were presented to 8-month-old infants and their responses were observed. Ten firstborn male infants and their mothers participated in the experiment. Each infant was tested while seated in an infant chair. An experimenter, who was blind to the purpose of the experiment, presented one of the following three types of toys: a familiar toy bear, an unfamiliar toy automobile with one randomly blinking colored light, or an unfamiliar toy automobile with three blinking colored lights. The latter two toys were different from one another only in the number of lights blinking. The toy automobile with three lights is expected to elicit more intense interest in the infant than that with a single light.

Manual action related to exploration and self-regulation of attention is expected to be produced by the infant most frequently in response to the unfamiliar toys, especially to the automobile with three lights, and least often in response to the familiar toy. Furthermore, attempts to bring the object closer to the infant are expected to occur most often in response to the familiar toy and least often in response to the automobile with three lights, which is unfamiliar and in some sense more intimidating.

Each of the three toys was presented to each infant in two different conditions. In one condition, it was presented within reach (approximately 15 cm away from the infant); in the other condition, it was presented beyond reach (approximately 60 cm away from the infant). On the basis of video recording, the infants' behaviors were categorized into the following three types: (a) reaching, (b) failed reaching/indicative gesture, and (c) index-finger extension.

A movement was classified as a "reaching" when the infant reached out to the stimulus, and the infant's hand touched it. A movement was classified as a "failed reaching/indicative gesture" when the arm was extended toward the stimulus with an open hand, without reaching it. This movement was often accompanied by an alternating look between the stimulus and the mother. An index-finger extension was characterized by extension of the index finger and nonextension of the arm. A movement was assigned to this category regardless of whether the finger was directed toward the stimulus or not.

The results are shown in Fig. 4.2. Let us consider the within-reach condition first. Not surprisingly, reaching was observed frequently, and failed reaching/indicative gesture was not observed. The number of occurrences of reaching was greatest when the presented toy was familiar, and was smallest when it was the unfamiliar toy with three blinking lights. The number of occurrences of index-finger extension, in contrast, showed the opposite tendency. It was smallest when the presented toy was familiar, and was greatest when it was the unfamiliar one with three blinking lights.

Let us now turn to the beyond-reach condition. In this case, failed reaching/indicative gesture was observed fairly abundantly. Like reaching in the within-reach condition, it occurred most often when the presented toy was

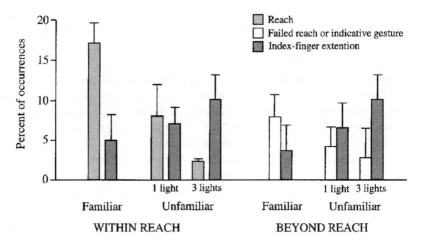

FIG. 4.2. Percentage of three types of infants' manual activities when familiar and unfamiliar toys were presented within reach and beyond reach.

familiar and least frequently when the toy was the unfamiliar one with three blinking lights. Index-finger extension was also observed relatively often, but for different types of stimuli than failed reaching/indicative gesture. Index-finger extension again occurred most frequently when the presented object was the toy with three blinking lights and least often when it was a familiar one.

Index-finger extension occurred more often when the presented object called for exploration more intensely. The pattern of frequency was reversed for the manual acts that were aimed at bringing the object to the infant, namely, reaching and failed reach/indicative gesture. They occurred more often for the objects that were more familiar and less intimidating. This indicates that index-finger extension is related to exploration and self-regulation of attention, and not to the infant's desire to bring the object to him or herself. In other words, index-finger pointing emerges from a manual act related to exploration and self-regulation of attention. When infants develops the desire to share the exploration and attention intersubjectively, index-finger extension develops into index-finger pointing.

CONCLUDING REMARKS

In 1912, Wilhelm Wundt noted in his massive *Vokerpsychologie* that pointing was "nothing but an abbreviated grasp movement" (cited in Werner & Kaplan, 1963, p. 78). Other developmentalists, however, countered this view with reports that the precursors of pointing are rudimentary acts of contemplation that direct attention outward toward an object and thus, in essence, "push it away" rather than draw it near (Bates, O'Connell, & Shone, 1987, p. 161), although data supporting their argument had been meager.

Evidence presented in this chapter is consistent with the latter account, more specifically with the proposition that referential index-finger pointing emerges from index-finger extension, which is related to orienting the infant's own attention to an interesting object. Index-finger pointing does not emerge from actions that are related to gaining contact with objects through reaching and grasping or to pleading with adults for help.

Index-finger extension is traced back to 3 months of age, and its production seems to be correlated to the production of speechlike vocalizations. Until 8 months of age, infants produce index-finger extension as if to direct their own attention when they are exploring an object that interests them. This behavior, in combination with speechlike vocalization, induces adults' preferable impression of the infant in such cultures where index-finger pointing is regarded as a prevalent referential gesture. Finally, index-finger extension becomes index-finger pointing when it is augmented by an intentional arm extension toward an object or location that is capturing the infant's attention, presumably in order to share the attention with others. In summary, there is developmental continuity from index-finger extension to index-finger pointing.

ACKNOWLEDGMENTS

This research was partly supported by Grant-in-Aid 09207106 from the Japan Ministry of Education, Science, Culture, and Sports. I am grateful to Sotaro Kita and Alissa Melinger for reading the earlier version of the chapter and making a number of invaluable comments.

REFERENCES

Bates, E., Benigni, B., Bretherton, I., Camaioni, L., & Voltera, V. (1979). Cognition and communication from nine to thirteen months: Correlational findings. In E. Bates (Ed.), *The emergence of symbols: Cognition and communication in infancy* (pp. 69–140). New York: Academic Press.

Bates, E., O'Connell, B., & Shone, C. (1987). Language and communication in infancy. In J. D. Osofsky (Ed.), *Handbook of infant development* (2nd ed., pp. 149–203). New York: Wiley.

Bloom, K. (1988). Quality of adult vocalizations affects the quality of infant vocalizations. *Journal of Child Language, 15,* 469–480.

Bloom, K., D'Odorico, L., & Beaumont, S. (1993). Adult preferences for syllabic vocalizations: Generalizations to parity and native language. *Infant Behavior and Development, 16,* 109–120.

Bloom, K., & Lo, E. (1990). Adult perception of vocalizing infants. *Infant Behavior and Development, 13,* 209–219.

Bloom, K., Russell, A., & Wassenberg, K. (1987). Turn-taking affects the quality of infant vocalizations. *Journal of Child Language, 14,* 211–227.

Bruner, J. S. (1983). *Child's talk: Learning to use language.* Cambridge: Cambridge University Press.

Fogel, A., & Hannan, T. E. (1985). Manual actions of nine- to fifteen-week-old human infants during face-to-face interaction with their mothers. *Child Development, 56,* 1271–1279.

Leavens, D. A., & Hopkins, W. D. (1998). Communication by chimpanzees: A cross-sectional study of the use of referential gestures. *Developmental Psychology, 34,* 813–822.

Leung, E., & Rheingold, H. L. (1981). Development of pointing as a social gesture. *Developmental Psychology, 17,* 215–220.

Masataka, N. (1993). Effects of contingent and noncontingent maternal stimulation on the vocal behaviour of three- to four-month-old Japanese infants. *Journal of Child Language, 20,* 303–312.

Masataka, N. (1995). The relation between index-finger extension and the acoustic quality of cooing in three-month-old infants. *Journal of Child Language, 22,* 247–257.

Masataka, N. (1996, April). *Significance of synchronization between vocalizations and motor action for spoken language acquisition.* Paper presented at the 2nd European Research Conference on the Development of Sensory, Motor and Cognitive Abilities in Early Infancy: Antecedents of Language and the Symbolic Function, San Feliu de Guixols.

McArthur, L. Z., & Baron, R. M. (1983). Toward an ecological theory of social perception. *Psychological Review, 90,* 215–238.

McNeill, D. (1985). "So you think gestures are nonverbal?" *Psychological Review, 92,* 350–371.

Murphy, C. M., & Messer, D. J. (1977). Mothers, infants and pointing: A study of a gesture. In H. R. Shaffer (Ed.), *Studies of mother–infant interaction* (pp. 325–354). London: Academic Press.

Netsell, R. (1981). The acquisition of speech motor control: A perspective with directions for speech. In R. E. Stark (Ed.), *Language behavior in infancy and childhood* (pp. 117–156). Amsterdam: Elsevier.

Oller, D. K. (1980). The emergence of the sounds of speech in early infancy. In G. H. Yeni-Komshian, J. F. Kavanagh, & C. A. Ferguson (Eds.), *Child phonology* (Vol. 1, pp. 93–112). New York: Academic Press.

Oller, D. K. (1981). Infant vocalization: Exploration and reflexibility. In R. E. Stark (Ed.), *Language behavior in infancy and childhood* (pp. 156–218). Amsterdam: Elsevier.

Stark, R. E. (1978). Features of infant sounds: The emergence of cooing. *Journal of Child Language, 5,* 379–390.

Stark, R. E. (1981). Infant vocalization: A comprehensive view. *Infant Mental Health Journal, 2,* 118–128.

Vygotsky, L. S. (1961). *Thought and language.* Boston: MIT Press.

Werner, H., & Kaplan, B. (1963). *Symbol formation.* New York: Wiley.

Zebrowitz, L. A. (1990). *Social perception.* Buckingham: Open University Press.

Chapter 5

Pointing Toward Two-Word Speech in Young Children

Susan Goldin-Meadow
Cynthia Butcher
University of Chicago

The first two-word combinations that a child produces are significant for two reasons. First, they reflect the child's developing ability to express propositional information within a single communicative act. Rather than produce *baby* and *drink* in separate utterances, the child can now conjoin them within a single sentence, *baby drink*, thus explicitly signaling that there is a relationship between the two elements. Second, two-word combinations are the child's first step into syntax. Independent of the language they are learning, children across the globe tend to produce the words that comprise their sentences in a consistent order. The particular orders they use mirror the orders provided by the language models they experience—*baby drink* rather than *drink baby* for an English-learning child. Even when the language a child is learning has relatively free word order, the child tends to adhere to a consistent pattern based on a frequently occurring adult pattern.

These two features of early two-word combinations are robust. They are found in the first two-sign combinations produced by deaf children acquiring a conventional sign language from their deaf parents (Newport & Meier, 1985), and even in the first two-gesture combinations invented by deaf children not yet exposed to conventional sign language by their hearing parents (Goldin-Meadow, 1997, 2002a).

Children begin to produce two-word sentences at approximately 18 months of age. They have, however, been able to produce isolated words since 12 months. Why is there a delay between the onset of words and the onset of word combinations? Combining two words into a single communicative act requires a number of skills. Children not only need to be able to intend to convey a proposition; they must also be able to segment that proposition into elements, label those elements with words, and combine the words into a single string.

Until children actually produce two words in a single combination, there is no explicit evidence in their talk that they intend to convey a proposition. There is, however, evidence that children in the one-word period can produce two elements of a proposition in one communicative act—but only if one looks across modalities. One-word children can utter a word—*drink*—and indicate the object of that action through their gestures—a point at a bottle. Assuming that gesture and speech are functioning as a unit, the two modalities together convey, to the observant listener, two elements of a single proposition.

In this chapter, we explore whether combinations in which gesture and speech convey different but complementary information are a transitional bridge between one- and two-word speech. We require two lines of evidence to support this hypothesis. First, in order for this type of combination to be a stepping-stone, gesture and speech must be functioning as a unified system. We therefore begin by exploring the onset of this type of combination in relation to the moment when gesture and speech come together into a well-integrated system—an event that takes place sometime during the one-word period (Butcher & Goldin-Meadow, 2000).

Next, we ask if integrated gesture-speech combinations are a harbinger of two-word combinations. Specifically, we explore the onset of combinations in which gesture and speech convey different information in relation to the onset of two-word speech. Whether these gesture–speech combinations precede or co-occur with two-word speech can provide insight into the conditions needed to combine words within a single sentence. If all that is needed for two-word combinations is the cognitive ability to convey two elements within a single communicative act, then gesture–speech combinations of this sort ought to co-occur with, and not precede with any regularity, the onset of two-word speech. Alternatively, if additional language-specific skills are required for the onset of two-word combinations, then gesture–speech combinations in which the two modalities convey different information might be expected to reliably precede the onset of two-word speech.

Our goal here is to situate the onset of combinations in which gesture and speech convey different information relative to two events: (a) the onset of gesture–speech integration during the one-word period, and (b) the onset of two-word combinations.

THE CHILDREN AND THE CODING CATEGORIES

The subjects for this study were six children, three boys and three girls, also described in Butcher and Goldin-Meadow (2000). The children were video-taped in their homes over a period of months, beginning when each child was in the one-word period of language development and continuing until the child began producing two-word combinations. All of the data were collected in spontaneous and unstructured play situations during which children interacted with their primary caregivers and/or the experimenter around a standard set of toys and books. Four of the six children were seen approximately every 2 weeks; the remaining two subjects were seen approximately every 6 to 8 weeks. Table 5.1 reports the age range during which each child was observed and the number of videotaped sessions conducted during this period.

Table 5.1 also presents the age at which each child first produced a meaningful word (with or without a gesture) on our videotapes, and the age at which the child first produced a two-word combination on the videotapes. Because the videotaped sessions necessarily represent a small sample of each child's communications, the onset ages listed in Table 5.1 may inflate the actual onset ages for these children. Four of the children (Beth, Emily, Nicholas, and Joseph) were already producing meaningful words during their first observation sessions; the remaining two (Ann and Christopher) were not and produced their first meaningful words on the videotapes at ages 16.5 and 13 months, respectively. The ages at which the children began producing two-word combinations on our videotapes ranged from 18 to 26.5 months, an age span that falls within the range typically reported for the onset of two-word speech (cf. Bloom & Capatides, 1987; Bowerman, 1973; Braine, 1976).

TABLE 5.1
Subject Information

Subject Name	Sex	Ages Observed	Number of Sessions Observed	Age of First Meaningful Word	Age of First Two-Word Combination
Christopher	M	12 to 23.5 months	11	13.0	21.0
Emily	F	13.5 to 19 months	9	13.5[a]	18.0
Nicholas	M	15.5 to 21 months	11	15.5[a]	18.5
Beth	F	15.5 to 21 months	5	15.5[a]	18.0
Ann	F	15.5 to 25 months	6	16.5	22.5
Joseph	M	21 to 27.5 months	10	21.0[a]	26.5

[a]These four children produced meaningful words during their first observation sessions.

We focused in this study on gesture and speech that were used communicatively. All of the communicative gestures and words produced by each child during a half hour of videotape were transcribed and coded. If that half hour did not yield 100 communicative behaviors, additional tape was coded until 100 behaviors were transcribed. A *communicative behavior* was defined as either speech on its own, gesture on its own, or gesture and speech produced together. Children were given credit for having produced a spoken word if the vocalization sounded like an actual English word (e.g., *dog, cat, duck, hot, walking*) or if a sound was used consistently to refer to a specific object or action (e.g., *bah* used consistently to refer to a bottle).

Children were given credit for having produced a gesture if their hand movements were directed toward another person whose attention they had (i.e., if the hand movements were communicative) and if those movements were not themselves a direct manipulation of some relevant person or object (i.e., if the movements were symbolic). All acts that were done on objects were excluded, with one exception—if a child held up an object to bring it to another's attention, an act that serves the same function as the pointing gesture, it was counted as a gesture. The form of each gesture was described in terms of the shape of the hand, type of movement, and place of articulation. The vast majority of gestures that the children produced were deictics, either pointing at an object with the index finger or loose palm or holding up an object to call attention to it. The children also produced a few iconic gestures, in addition to nods, side-to-side shakes, and hand flips.

Gestures produced without speech and speech produced without gesture were identified and categorized but coded no further. Two additional coding decisions were made for gestures produced in combination with speech.

1. The timing of a gesture with respect to the speech it accompanied was coded to the nearest frame (1/30 sec) for the gesture–speech combinations produced by each child. Following McNeill (1992) and Kendon (1972, 1980), gesture–speech combinations were considered synchronous if the vocalization occurred on the stroke of the gesture or at the peak of the gesture (the farthest extension before the hand began to retract).

2. The relationship between the information conveyed in speech and the information conveyed in gesture in each gesture–speech combination was coded. Gesture–speech combinations were divided into two types: (a) combinations in which gesture conveyed the same referent as did speech— for example, a point at a dog accompanied by the word *dog*; and (b) combinations in which gesture conveyed a different referent from the referent conveyed in speech—for example, a point at a pair of glasses accompanied by the word *mommy*. Note that the child's intent may be to make a statement

with a gesture–speech combination (e.g., "those are mommy's glasses"), to make a request ("give me mommy's glasses"), or to ask a question ("are those mommy's glasses?"). For our purposes here, we focus only on the fact that *mommy* and *glasses*, the objects indicated in gesture and speech, are part of the utterance, whatever its function.

It is important to stress that gesture never conveys information that is completely redundant with the information conveyed in speech (McNeill & Duncan, 2000). For example, a point at a dog serves to draw an observer's attention to the object; it does not identify the object as a member of a category, as labeling the object with the word *dog* would. Nevertheless, pointing gestures do single out objects for attention, and it is in this loose sense that we say they "convey information" about those objects. If the object indicated by a point is also referred to in speech, we consider the point to convey the same information as the speech it accompanies; if not, we consider it to convey different information.

Reliability between two independent coders was assessed on a subset of the videotaped sessions and ranged between 84% and 100% agreement between the two coders, depending on the coding category (see Butcher & Goldin-Meadow, 2000, for further details on coding procedures and reliability).

GESTURE–SPEECH COMBINATIONS AND THE ONSET OF INTEGRATION ACROSS THE MODALITIES

The spontaneous gestures that adults produce as they speak can convey substantive information and, as a result, provide insight into a speaker's mental representations. Thus, gesture conveys meaning, although it does so differently from speech. Speech conveys meaning by rule-governed combinations of discrete units, codified according to the norms of that language. In contrast, gesture conveys meaning mimetically and idiosyncratically through continuously varying forms (Goldin-Meadow, 2002b; McNeill, 1992).[1]

Despite the fact that gesture and speech represent meaning in different ways, the two modalities form a single, integrated system in adults. Gesture and speech are integrated both semantically and temporally. For example, a speaker produced the following iconic gesture when describing a scene

---

[1]In this chapter, we consider gestures situated at one end of the continuum described by Kendon (1980)—spontaneous hand movements produced while talking (*gesticulation* in Kendon's terms). Thus, we leave aside more codified gestures such as emblems (e.g., OK, thumbs-up) that can be produced without speech.

from a comic book in which a character bends a tree back to the ground (McNeill, 1992): The speaker grasped his hand as if gripping something and pulled the hand back. He produced this gesture as he uttered the words *and he bends it way back*. The gesture was an iconic representation of the event described in speech, and thus contributed to a semantically coherent picture of a single scene. In addition, the speaker produced the "stroke" of the pulling-back gesture just as he said "bends it way back," synchronizing the gesture with speech (see also Kendon, 1980).

The Onset of Gesture–Speech Integration

When do young children's gestures become integrated with the speech they accompany? At a time when children are limited in what they can say, they gesture (Bates, 1976; Bates, Benigni, Bretherton, Camaioni, & Volterra, 1979; Petitto, 1988). The earliest gestures children use, typically beginning around 10 months, are deictics, gestures whose referential meaning is given entirely by the context and not by their form (McNeill, 1992). For example, a child may hold up an object to draw an adult's attention to that object or, later in development, point at the object. Children also occasionally use iconic gestures (McNeill, 1992). Unlike deictics, the form of an iconic gesture captures aspects of its intended referent. For example, a child might open and close her mouth to represent a fish or flap her hands to represent a bird (Iverson, Capirci, & Caselli, 1994; see also Acredolo & Goodwyn, 1985, 1988; Goodwyn & Acredolo, 1998).

Most of the gesture–speech combinations that children in the one-word period produce contain gestures that convey information redundant with the information conveyed in speech—for example, pointing at an object while naming it (de Laguna, 1927; Greenfield & Smith, 1976; Guillaume, 1927; Leopold, 1949). However, as described earlier, one-word speakers also produce gesture–speech combinations in which gesture conveys information that is different from the information conveyed in speech—for example, gesturing at an object while describing the action to be done on the object in speech (pointing to an apple and saying "give") or gesturing at an object and describing the owner of that object in speech (pointing at a toy and saying "mine"; Goldin-Meadow & Morford, 1985; Greenfield & Smith, 1976; Masur, 1982, 1983; Morford & Goldin-Meadow, 1992; Zinober & Martlew, 1985).

This second type of gesture–speech combination allows a child to express two elements of a sentence, one in gesture and one in speech. A child who produces such gesture–speech combinations can therefore be considered to have explicitly conveyed a proposition within a single communicative act—assuming, of course, that gesture and speech are working together as a unified system at this point in the child's development. We explore this assumption here and ask when children begin to produce combinations in which gesture and speech convey different information relative to when they have integrated gesture and speech into a unified system.

Butcher and Goldin-Meadow (2000) investigated the onset of gesture–speech integration during the transition from one- to two-word speech in the six children who participated in this study. They noted first that the proportion of each child's communications containing gesture remained relatively constant over the observation period (there were individual differences in the proportion of communications containing gesture, ranging from 20% to 40%, but each child's proportion remained constant within him or herself). What changed over the observation sessions was the relationship gesture held to speech. In the earliest sessions, gesture did not appear to be well integrated with speech in three senses:

1. Gesture tended to appear without speech. In five of the six children, over 60% of the child's communications containing gesture were produced without any accompanying sounds at all.

2. Gesture and speech did not form a temporally unified system. Only a small proportion of the few gesture–speech combinations that the five children produced at this early period were synchronous—that is, in most of their combinations, speech did not occur on the stroke or the peak of the gesture (cf. McNeill, 1992).

3. Gesture and speech did not form a semantically unified system. All of the few gestures that these five children produced with speech at this point in time were combined with meaningless sounds, despite the fact that all but one of these children were able to produce meaningful words. In other words, the children's gestures were either produced alone or, less often, with meaningless sounds. The meaningful words they produced were uttered without gesture.

The relationship between gesture and speech changed when the five children began to produce gesture in combination with a meaningful word that conveyed the same information as the gesture (e.g., point at bottle + "bottle"). Figure 5.1 presents three pieces of data for these six children superimposed on a single graph: (a) the proportion of gesture-alone communications, which declined over time; (b) the proportion of synchronized gesture–speech combinations, which increased over time; and (c) the onset of combinations containing gesture plus words conveying the same information, shown as a vertical line on each graph. Note that for each of the five children who began to produce gesture + word combinations conveying the same information during our observation sessions, the three events converge: Gesture-alone combinations began to decline and synchronous gesture–speech combinations began to increase at just the moment when ges-

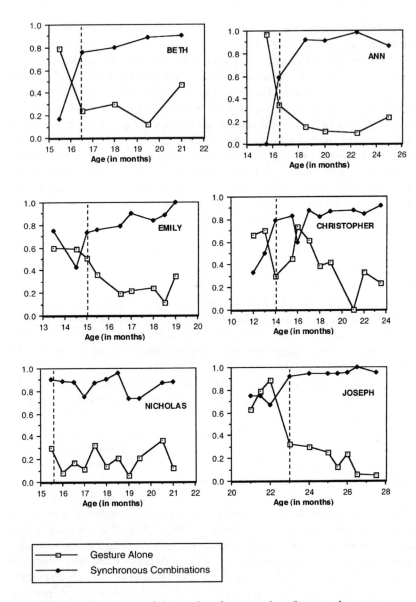

Gesture Alone

Synchronous Combinations

FIG. 5.1.   Gesture–speech integration: the proportion of gesture-alone combinations (black diamonds) and the proportion of synchronous gesture–speech combinations (white squares) for each child. The vertical line
demarcates the age at which each child first produced gestures in combination with words conveying the same information. The convergence point of
the three marks the integration of gesture and speech in terms of temporal
synchrony and semantic coherence. Adapted from Butcher and Goldin-
Meadow (2000), with permission.

ture was first combined in the same utterance with a word conveying the same meaning (the sixth child, Nicholas, had presumably gone through this convergence point prior to our observations).[2]

Thus, the age at which each of the children began to produce communicative gestures in combination with words conveying the same information was precisely the age when timing began to improve dramatically in each child's gesture–speech combinations. Butcher and Goldin-Meadow (2000) took this point to be the onset of gesture–speech integration in these children, the moment when gesture and speech become unified into a system characterized by both semantic and temporal coherence.

The Onset of Combinations in Which Gesture and Speech Convey Different Information

If combinations in which gesture and speech convey different information are a product of two modalities operating independently, we would expect these combinations to occur prior to the session at which gesture and speech begin to merge into a single system—that is, prior to the onset of combinations in which gesture and speech convey the same information. Alternatively, if such combinations are the product of a single system, we would expect them to follow, or at the least co-occur with, the onset of combinations in which gesture and speech convey the same information. The left-hand and middle columns of Table 5.2 present the ages at which each of the six children first produced gesture–speech combinations in which the two modalities conveyed the same information (left) versus different information (middle).[3] None of the six children produced combinations in which the modalities conveyed different information before they produced combinations in which the modalities conveyed the same information.

These onset data suggest that combinations in which gesture and speech convey different information are a product of a unified system in which the two modalities work together. Further evidence for this hypothesis comes from the fact that this type of gesture–speech combination displays the two properties that are the hallmark of gesture–speech integration: semantic coherence and temporal synchrony.

---

[2]The high proportion of synchronous combinations found in each child's communications after gesture–speech integration (i.e., to the right of the vertical line in Fig. 5.1) was not unique to gesture + word combinations, but was also characteristic of the gesture + meaningless sound combinations that the child produced at this time.

[3]Once a child began to produce combinations in which the two modalities conveyed different information, the child tended to continue to do so. In the 26 sessions that followed the onset of combinations in which gesture and speech conveyed different information, there were only three sessions across the six children in which a child failed to produce such a combination (two in Joseph and one in Emily).

TABLE 5.2
Age (in Months) of the First Appearance
of Three Types of Combinations

	Combinations in Which Gesture and Speech Convey the Same Information (one semantic element)	Combinations in Which Gesture and Speech Convey Different Information (two semantic elements)	Combinations in Which Two Words Convey Different Information (two semantic elements)
Christopher	14.0	18.0	21.0
Emily	15.0	15.0	18.0
Nicholas	15.5[a]	15.5[a]	18.5
Beth	16.5	16.5	18.0
Ann	16.5	20.0	22.5
Joseph	23.0	25.5	26.5

[a]This child produced these two types of combinations during his first observation session. Note that each of the children who began producing combinations in which gesture and speech conveyed different information during the study first produced them (a) at the same time as, or after, they began producing combinations in which gesture and speech conveyed the same information, and (b) before they began producing combinations in which two words conveyed different information.

Semantic Coherence in Combinations in Which Gesture and Speech Convey Different Information

In adult speakers, gesture and speech form an integrated system in the sense that the two modalities convey related, if not identical, information within an utterance. Thus, we asked whether the combinations that the children produced in which gesture conveyed different information from speech were semantically coherent.

In general, the gesture in combinations of this sort tended to indicate an object playing a semantic role in a proposition while the speech referred to another element of that same proposition. Table 5.3 presents examples of the types of these combinations that the six children produced. The most common gesture–speech combination of this type, the only one found in all six children, contained a word representing an action paired with a gesture, either a pointing gesture or a hold-up gesture, indicating the object involved in the action. Examples 1 through 6 in Table 5.3 are of this variety. The children also produced several other types of words combined with pointing or hold-up gestures: words representing the sound made by the object indicated in gesture (Examples 7–9), words representing an attribute of the object indicated in gesture (Examples 10–11), words representing other objects that were either the location (Example 12) or the owner (Example 13) of the object indicated in gesture, and negative words either rejecting the object indicated in gesture (Example 14) or noting its inappropriateness or lack of fit (Example 15).

TABLE 5.3
Examples of Combinations in Which Gesture
and Speech Convey Different Information

Speech		Gesture
1. "open"	+	point at drawer (Beth)
2. "out"	+	hold-up toy bag (Ann)
3. "go"	+	point at turtle (Christopher)
4. "do-it"	+	hold-up ball (Joseph)
5. "swing"	+	hold-up frog (Emily)
6. "blow-it"	+	hold-up frog (Nicholas)
7. "moo"	+	point at cow (Joseph)
8. "quack"	+	point at duck (Emily)
9. "boom-boom"	+	point at drum (Nicholas)
10. "hot"	+	point at furnace (Nicholas)
11. "pretty"	+	point at crab (Nicholas)
12. "key"	+	point at door (Nicholas)
13. "mama"	+	hold-up mother's glasses (Nicholas)
14. "no"	+	point at box (Christopher)
15. "no"	+	hold-up key at door with no keyhole (Emily)
16. "seal"	+	side-to-side headshake (Emily)
17. "ball"	+	two-hand flip [= where?] (Nicholas)
18. "monster"	+	two vertical palms spread wide [= BIG] (Christopher)
19. "bear"	+	palm scratches in air [= CLAW] (Nicholas)

In addition to pointing and hold-up gestures, the children also produced a few instances of other types of gestures combined with words that
conveyed different information: side-to-side head shakes (Example 16),
hand flips (Example 17), and iconic gestures (Examples 18–19).

Thus, the combinations that the children produced in which gesture
and speech conveyed different information tended to express two elements that held some semantic relationship with respect to one another.
Indeed, the number of combinations in which gesture and speech did not
convey elements of a single underlying proposition was quite small (e.g.,
Nicholas pointed at the moon while saying "mama," two referents for
which we could determine no propositional relationship[4]). Nicholas pro-

---

[4]We observed a few instances where the child pointed at an object (e.g., a pig) and labeled
it with the wrong word (e.g., *cow*). Gershkoff-Stowe and Smith (1997) also observed combinations in which gesture indicates one object and speech another, apparently unrelated object in
young one-word speakers naming pictures in a book. However, this type of combination might
not actually be an instance of gesture conveying different information from speech if, in fact,
the child really thinks that *cow* is the name for a pig. In their sample, Gershkoff-Stowe and
Smith were able to tell that a given child had the word *pig* in his or her vocabulary, suggesting
that these combinations were indeed an instance of gesture and speech conveying different information. We did not have enough data on each child's vocabulary to make comparable
claims for the children in our study. As a result, we did not count combinations of this type as
instances where gesture and speech convey different information.

duced five, Emily two, Joseph one, and Ann, Beth, and Christopher produced no such combinations at all. As a result, in most of the children's combinations in which gesture conveyed different information from speech, gesture and speech each conveyed an element of the same proposition, suggesting that these combinations were the product of a unified gesture–speech system.

Temporal Synchrony in Combinations in Which Gesture and Speech Convey Different Information

In adult speakers, when gesture conveys information that is different from the information conveyed in speech, that gesture nevertheless has a systematic temporal relation with the speech it accompanies (McNeill & Duncan, 2000). For example, one adult produced a downward gesture while saying "goes through the drainpipe" (thus conveying the direction of motion in gesture and the location where that motion took place in speech). Despite the fact that the information conveyed in the two modalities was not identical, the word "drainpipe" was produced in synchrony with the stroke of the gesture. As other examples, Kita (1993) described subtle cases in which speech and gesture adjust to each other in timing in adults; Morrel-Samuels and Krauss (1992) provided evidence that the timing of gesture and speech is related to the rated familiarity of the spoken word; and Mayberry, Jaques, and DeDe (1998) provided evidence that gesture and speech are synchronized even when, as in stuttering, the speech production process goes awry.

To explore whether combinations in which gesture and speech conveyed different information were synchronous, we examined the timing in these combinations and compared it to the timing in combinations in which gesture and speech conveyed the same information. Because the children were all one-word speakers, we defined a synchronous combination as one in which the vocalization occurred on the stroke or peak (the farthest extension) of the gesture. Figure 5.2 presents the proportion of each type of gesture–speech combination that was synchronous for each of the six children. There were no significant differences in timing between the two types of gesture–speech combinations [Ann $\chi^2(1)$ = .20, n.s.; Beth $\chi^2(1)$ = 0, n.s.; Emily $\chi^2(1)$ = .23, n.s.; Christopher $\chi^2(1)$ = .12, n.s.; Nicholas $\chi^2(1)$ = 1.34, n.s.; Joseph produced too few combinations in which gesture and speech conveyed different information to conduct a statistical analysis]. Thus, once gesture and speech become integrated, gesture–speech combinations tend to be synchronous, whether or not the information conveyed across the two modalities was the same.

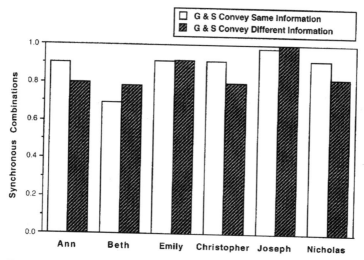

FIG. 5.2.   Temporal synchrony in gesture–speech combinations: proportion of synchronous combinations in two types of gesture–speech combinations: combinations in which gesture and speech conveyed the same information (white bars), and combinations in which gesture and speech conveyed different information (black bars). The proportion of synchronous combinations was the same, and high, in both types of combinations.

GESTURE–SPEECH COMBINATIONS AND THE ONSET OF TWO-WORD SPEECH

We have shown that combinations in which gesture and speech convey different information are not produced until gesture and speech are well integrated into a unified system, suggesting that the two pieces of information reflect two elements of a single proposition rather than two unrelated elements. Children who can produce this type of gesture–speech combination clearly have the ability to convey two elements of a proposition within a single communicative act and should be well on the way toward being able to produce two-word utterances. Indeed, if the lack of this skill is the only ability preventing children from producing two-word combinations, they should begin to put two words together in a single string as soon as they begin to produce combinations in which gesture and speech convey different information. If, however, this skill is only one among many necessary for children to produce two-word combinations, they might be expected to produce two words together some time after they begin to produce combinations in which gesture and speech convey different information.

The middle and right-hand columns of Table 5.2 present the ages at which each of the six children in our study began producing gesture–

speech combinations in which each modality conveys a different semantic element (middle) versus two-word combinations in which each word conveys a different semantic element (right). All six of the children began producing combinations in which gesture and speech conveyed different information prior to first producing two-word combinations. More impressive is the fact that, across the six children, the correlation between the age of onset of this type of gesture–speech combination and the age of onset of two-word combinations was quite high and reliable ($rs = .90$, $p < .05$, Spearman rank correlation coefficient, correcting for ties). The top graph in Fig. 5.3 displays the age at which each child began producing two-word combinations (y axis) as a function of the age at which that child began to produce combinations in which gesture and speech conveyed different information (x axis). Note that Joseph, who was substantially older than the other child and at the top of the scale in both measures, is an outlier inflating the correlation. However, even without Joseph, the correlation was .82 (correcting for ties). In other words, the children who were first to produce combinations in which gesture and speech conveyed different information were also first to produce two-word combinations.

It is important to note that the correlation between gesture–speech combinations and two-word speech is specific to combinations in which gesture and speech conveyed different information. The bottom graph in Fig. 5.3 displays the age at which each child began producing two-word combinations (y axis) as a function of the age at which that child began to produce combinations in which gesture and speech conveyed the same (single) semantic element (x axis). Although all six children began producing combinations in which gesture and speech conveyed the same information prior to first producing two-word combinations, the correlation between the age of onset of this type of gesture–speech combination and the age of onset of two-word combinations was relatively low ($rs = .46$, n.s., Spearman rank correlation coefficient, correcting for ties) and without Joseph, the outlier, dropped to .03 (correcting for ties).

Thus, the onset of combinations in which gesture and speech convey different information not only precedes the onset of two-word speech, it does so in a predictable fashion. The skills involved in producing this type of gesture–speech combination thus appear to be necessary for two-word speech but not sufficient to guarantee its onset.

DISCUSSION

This study explored the relationship between communicative symbolic gesture and speech in young children at the beginning stages of language development. It has two main findings. First, we found that combinations in

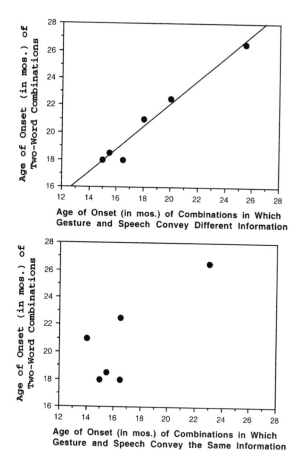

FIG. 5.3.   Onset of two-word combinations: age at which each child first produced two-word combinations as a function of the age at which that child began producing combinations in which gesture and speech conveyed different information (top graph), and age at which that child began producing combinations in which gesture and speech conveyed the same information (bottom graph). The onset of two-word combinations is reliably related to the onset of the first type of gesture–speech combination but not the second.

which gesture and speech convey different information, despite the fact that they might intuitively be thought to reflect two separate systems operating independently, begin to be produced after gesture and speech become integrated into a single system and thus appear to be a product of this unified system integrated across the modalities. Second, we found that the onset of combinations in which gesture and speech convey different information predicts the onset of two-word speech. We consider each of these findings in turn.

**Combinations in Which Gesture and Speech Convey
Different Information Reflect a System Integrated
Across Modalities**

All of the children in our study produced combinations in which gesture
conveyed information that was different from the information conveyed in
speech. At first glance, combinations of this sort might be thought to be a
product of the two modalities operating independently and in parallel.
However, the timing of these combinations suggests that they are indeed a
product of a single system integrated across the two modalities. Combinations in which gesture and speech conveyed different information were first
produced at the same age as, or after (but never before), combinations in
which gesture and speech conveyed the same information (Table 5.2)—the
point in development that can be taken to be the first sign of gesture–
speech integration in the child's communications (Butcher & Goldin-
Meadow, 2000; see Fig. 5.1). Combinations in which gesture and speech
conveyed different information would have been expected to occur throughout development—in particular, before the onset of gesture–speech integration as well as after it—if they had, in fact, been a product of the two modalities operating independently of one another.

Moreover, combinations in which gesture and speech convey different
information are characterized by the two properties that signal gesture-
speech integration:

1. *Semantic coherence.* Despite the fact that gesture conveyed different information from speech, the information conveyed in the two modalities almost always was related and reflected a single idea unit (Table
   5.3).
2. *Temporal synchrony.* Gestures that conveyed different information
   from the information conveyed in speech were nevertheless synchronously timed with respect to that speech (Fig. 5.2).

What happens over time to combinations in which gesture and speech
convey different information? Do they disappear as the child begins combining words into longer strings and developing further cognitive skills? Although the particular type of gesture–speech combination that we have described here is likely to drop out as the child becomes more and more
comfortable with two-word combinations, utterances in which gesture conveys information that is different from the information conveyed in speech
continue to be found throughout development. For example, a child asked
to solve a liquid quantity conservation task *says* that the transformed object
is different from the original because "this one is taller than this one" but,
in the same response, produces a *gesture* reflecting an awareness of the

widths of the objects; specifically, she indicates with her hands the skinny diameter of the original object and the wider diameter of the transformed object, thus revealing knowledge of the widths of the task objects that was not evident in her speech (Church & Goldin-Meadow, 1986).

Instances in which gesture and speech convey different information in a problem-solving situation have been called "mismatches" (Church & Goldin-Meadow, 1986) and have been observed when individuals, both adults and children, are asked to describe their reasoning about a task—in toddlers going through a vocabulary spurt (Gershkoff-Stowe & Smith, 1997; in preschool and elementary school children reasoning about a board game (Evans & Rubin, 1979), Piagetian conservation tasks (Church & Goldin-Meadow, 1986), mathematical equivalence problems (Alibali & Goldin-Meadow, 1993; Perry, Church, & Goldin-Meadow, 1988), and seasonal change problems (Crowder & Newman, 1993); in adolescents reasoning about Piagetian bending rods tasks (Stone, Webb, & Mahootian, 1991); in adults reasoning about problems involving gears (Perry & Elder, 1996) and problems involving constant change (Alibali, Bassok, Solomon, Syc, & Goldin-Meadow, 1999); and in individuals of many ages reasoning about moral dilemmas (Church, Schonert-Reichl, Goodman, Kelly, & Ayman-Nolley, 1995) and Tower of Hanoi puzzles (Garber & Goldin-Meadow, 2002). Thus, the behavior that we have observed in our study of the one-word period in language development—combinations in which gesture conveys different information from speech—is one that continues throughout the developmental life span.

Combinations in Which Gesture and Speech Convey Different Information Predict the Onset of Two-Word Speech

We found, in six English-learning children, that the onset of combinations in which gesture and speech convey different information predicts the onset of two-word speech (Fig. 5.3). Similar findings have been reported in a group of Italian-learning children observed during the transition from one-to two-word speech (Volterra & Iverson, 1995). Thus, at the earliest stages of language learning, the relationship between gesture and speech within a single utterance appears to herald change in the child's linguistic system.

There are, in fact, other areas in which the relationship between gesture and speech heralds change. For example, children who produce a relatively large number of gesture-speech mismatches in their explanations of a particular task (e.g., a conservation task or a mathematical equivalence task) are more likely to benefit from instruction in that task than children who produce few mismatches (Alibali & Goldin-Meadow, 1993; Church & Goldin-Meadow, 1986; Goldin-Meadow, Alibali, & Church, 1993; Perry et al.,

1988, 1992). Thus, gesture–speech mismatch signals that the child is in a transitional state with respect to a task, and is therefore ready to make progress on that task if given appropriate input.

Are the situations in which gesture–speech mismatch signals the child's readiness to learn a given task comparable to the situation we have described, in which one-word speakers made the transition to two-word speech? In both instances, it is the relationship between gesture and speech that predicts the likelihood of cognitive change. The question is whether the relationship between gesture and speech is comparable in the two situations. We argue that it is—precisely because, in both situations, gesture and speech convey pieces of information that would, if considered together, form a single notion. The one-word speaker produces one semantic element in speech (e.g., the action "go") and a second element within the same proposition in gesture (e.g., the actor, point at a turtle). If considered together, these two pieces of information convey a single proposition (i.e., actor–action, turtle go). Similarly, the nonconserver describes one dimension of the conservation task in speech (e.g., the height of the containers) and another dimension also relevant to the task in gesture (e.g., the width of the containers). If considered together, these two pieces of information convey a single conservation rationale (i.e., compensation, the fact that even though the glass is taller than the dish, it is also skinnier than the dish).[5]

At some level, the child knows all of the information needed to express a proposition (in the case of the one-word speaker) or a compensation rationale (in the case of the nonconserver), and can even express that information within the bounds of a single communicative act. However, the child does not yet appear to be able to express the information within a single modality in that communicative act. A new level of understanding is apparently reached when the child combines the two pieces of the problem within a single modality, that is, when the one-word speaker expresses both elements of the proposition in a two-word utterance, or when the nonconserver expresses both dimensions of the compensation rationale in speech. Thus, in both situations, knowledge that is not yet sufficiently developed to be expressed within a single (spoken) modality may be expressed across two modalities.

---

[5]In some cases of gesture–speech mismatch in older speakers, it is difficult to integrate the information conveyed across the two modalities into a single idea; for example, a child produces a *pour* gesture on the conservation task while talking about the container's width. Although these two pieces of information do not form a single conservation rationale, the child must have both in perspective in order to conserve—the child must understand that merely pouring the water is as irrelevant to its amount as the diameter of its new container. The pieces of information conveyed across the two modalities are very rarely in conflict even in older speakers; rather, they tend to reflect complementary aspects of the situation. Indeed, we suggest that mismatches reflect just those pieces of the situation that the speaker is currently working on integrating (Goldin-Meadow, 2002b).

Our data suggest that a one-word speaker who produces combinations in which gesture and speech together convey a single proposition fails to produce two-word combinations *not* because of a cognitive inability to grasp a proposition. Rather, the limitation appears to involve the ability to explicitly express a proposition entirely within the spoken modality. Although it may be the articulatory difficulty involved in producing two words in succession that prevents the child from expressing a two-element proposition in speech,[6] we suspect that the difficulty is deeper: that a child whose understanding of a proposition is tied in part to the manual modality cannot manipulate that proposition as well as one who can express the proposition entirely within the linguistic modality—in other words, that the child's understanding of the proposition is tied to a restricted range of uses and thus remains at an implicit level (cf. Goldin-Meadow & Alibali, 1994; Karmiloff-Smith, 1992). If so, making the transition to two-word speech would involve transforming this implicitly represented knowledge into an explicit form. By transposing information completely to the linguistic modality, the child generates a new level of representation, one that is a problem space in its own right and that can be worked on and improved as a modality of understanding (Karmiloff-Smith, 1979).

In summary, in both the young one-word speaker and the older child, a difference—or mismatch—between the information conveyed in gesture and the information conveyed in speech appears to signal readiness for cognitive growth. It is an open question as to whether the actual production of gesture–speech mismatch contributes to cognitive growth—that is, does the act of producing two different pieces of information across modalities but within a single communicative act improve the child's ability to transpose that knowledge to a new level and thus produce those pieces of information within a single modality? Our future work will investigate whether the act of producing gesture–speech mismatches itself facilitates transition (see Goldin-Meadow, Nusbaum, Kelly, & Wagner, 2001).

Even if it turns out that the production of gesture–speech mismatches has little role to play in facilitating cognitive change, mismatch remains a reliable marker of the speaker's potential for cognitive growth. As such, the

---

[6]One argument against articulatory difficulties being responsible for the relatively late onset of two-word speech is that two-sign combinations are developed at the same, relatively late age in deaf children learning American Sign Language from their deaf parents (Newport & Meier, 1985; Volterra & Caselli, 1985). If articulation were playing a major role, one would expect some differences in the onset of two-unit combinations across the two modalities. Moreover, within this particular sample, all of the children except Beth produced a small number of meaningful words in combination with meaningless vocalizations several sessions before they produced two-word combinations (Beth produced both types of combinations for the first time during the same session.) Thus, the ability to produce two vocalizations in succession was not what prevented most of the children in this sample from combining two meaningful words into a single utterance.

relationship between gesture and speech may prove to be useful in clinical populations. For example, there is some evidence that children who are delayed in the onset of two-word speech fall naturally into two groups: children who eventually achieve two-word speech, albeit later in development than the norm (i.e., late bloomers), and children who continue to have serious difficulties with spoken language and may never be able to combine words into a single string (Feldman, Holland, Kemp, & Janosky, 1992; Thal, Tobias, & Morrison, 1991). Indeed, in preliminary analyses of children with unilateral brain damage, we have found that some children display gesture-speech patterns comparable to those in Fig. 5.1 and Table 5.2 during their one-word period, whereas others display atypical gesture–speech patterns (e.g., gesture alone communications stay the same or even increase during this period, or gesture–speech synchrony decreases; Stare, 1996). Additional work is needed to determine whether atypical gesture–speech patterns early in development predict later language learning. If so, the relationship between spontaneous gestures and the speech they accompany may prove to be a useful clinical tool for distinguishing, at a relatively young age, children who will be late bloomers from those who will have difficulty mastering spoken language without intervention.

We have explored gesture's role in the transition from one- to two-word speech. The convergence of the semantic union and the temporal union of gesture and speech marks the beginning of gesture–speech integration in the one-word speaker. This integration sets the stage for the onset of gesture–speech combinations in which gesture conveys different (but related) information from the information that is conveyed in speech. These combinations, in turn, herald the onset of two-word speech. Thus, gesture provides the child with an important vehicle for information that is not yet expressed in speech, and, as such, it provides the listener (as well as the experimenter) with a unique window into the child's mind.

ACKNOWLEDGMENTS

This work was supported by grants from the March of Dimes Foundation and the National Institute on Deafness and other Communication Disorders (RO1 DC00491) to Goldin-Meadow, and by funding from the Home Health Care Foundation of Chicago through the section of Neonatology, Department of Pediatrics at the University of Chicago. We thank Samar Ali, Vera Joanna Burton, and Beth Stare for their help in coding the videotapes and establishing reliability; and Janellen Huttenlocher, Susan Levine, David McNeill, and William Meadow for their intellectual contributions throughout the project.

REFERENCES

Acredolo, L. P., & Goodwyn, S. W. (1985). Symbolic gesture in language development: A case study. *Human Development, 28,* 40–49.

Acredolo, L. P., & Goodwyn, S. W. (1988). Symbolic gesturing in normal infants. *Child Development, 59,* 450–466.

Alibali, M. W., Bassok, M., Solomon, K. O., Syc, S. E., & Goldin-Meadow, S. (1999). Illuminating mental representations through speech and gesture. *Psychological Science, 10,* 327–333.

Alibali, M. W., & Goldin-Meadow, S. (1993). Gesture-speech mismatch and mechanisms of learning: What the hands reveal about a child's state of mind. *Cognitive Psychology, 25,* 468–523.

Bates, E. (1976). *Language and context.* New York: Academic Press.

Bates, E., Benigni, L., Bretherton, I., Camaioni, L., & Volterra, V. (1979). *The emergence of symbols: Cognition and communication in infancy.* New York: Academic Press.

Bloom, L., & Capatides, J. B. (1987). Expression of affect and the emergence of language. *Child Development, 58,* 1513–1522.

Bowerman, M. (1973). *Early syntactic development: A cross-linguistic study with special reference to Finnish.* New York: Cambridge University Press.

Braine, M. D. S. (1976). Children's first word combinations. *Monographs of the Society for Research in Child Development, 41,* 164.

Butcher, C., & Goldin-Meadow, S. (2000). Gesture and the transition from one- to two-word speech: When hand and mouth come together. In D. McNeill (Ed.), *Language and gesture* (pp. 235–257). New York: Cambridge University Press.

Church, R. B., & Goldin-Meadow, S. (1986). The mismatch between gesture and speech as an index of transitional knowledge. *Cognition, 23,* 43–71.

Church, R. B., Schonert-Reichl, K., Goodman, N., Kelly, S. D., & Ayman-Nolley, S. (1995). The role of gesture and speech communication as reflections of cognitive understanding. *Journal of Contemporary Legal Issues, 6,* 123–154.

Crowder, E. M., & Newman, D. (1993). Telling what they know: The role of gesture and language in children's science explanations. *Pragmatics and Cognition, 1,* 341–376.

de Laguna, G. (1927). *Speech: Its function and development.* Bloomington: Indiana University Press.

Evans, M. A., & Rubin, K. H. (1979). Hand gestures as a communicative mode in school-aged children. *Journal of Genetic Psychology, 135,* 189–196.

Feldman, H. M., Holland, A. L., Kemp, S. S., & Janosky, J. E. (1992). Language development after unilateral brain injury. *Brain and Language, 42,* 89–102.

Garber, P., & Goldin-Meadow, S. (2002). Gesture offers insight into problem-solving in children and adults. *Cognitive Science.*

Gershkoff-Stowe, L., & Smith, L. B. (1997). A curvilinear trend in naming errors as a function of early vocabulary growth. *Cognitive Psychology, 34,* 37–71.

Goldin-Meadow, S. (1997). The resilience of language in humans. In C. T. Snowdon & M. Hausberger (Eds.), *Social influences on vocal development* (pp. 293–311). New York: Cambridge University Press.

Goldin-Meadow, S. (2002a). *The resilience of language: What gesture creation in deaf children can tell us about how all children learn language.* New York: Psychology Press.

Goldin-Meadow, S. (2002b). *Hearing gestures: How our hands help us think.* Cambridge, MA: Harvard University Press.

Goldin-Meadow, S., & Alibali, M. W. (1994). Do you have to be right to redescribe? *Behavioral and Brain Sciences, 17,* 718–719.

Goldin-Meadow, S., Alibali, M. W., & Church, R. B. (1993). Transitions in concept acquisition: Using the hand to read the mind. *Psychological Review, 100,* 279–297.

Goldin-Meadow, S., & Morford, M. (1985). Gesture in early child language: Studies of deaf and hearing children. *Merrill-Palmer Quarterly, 31,* 145–176.

Goldin-Meadow, S., Nusbaum, H., Kelly, S. D., & Wagner, S. (2001). Explaining math: Gesturing lightens the load. *Psychological Sciences, 12,* 516–522.

Goodwyn, S. W., & Acredolo, L. P. (2000). Encouraging symbolic gestures: A new perspective on the relationship between gesture and speech. In J. M. Iverson & S. Goldin-Meadow (Eds.), *The nature and functions of gesture in children's communications* (pp. 61–73). San Francisco: Jossey-Bass.

Greenfield, P., & Smith, J. (1976). *The structure of communication in early language development.* New York: Academic Press.

Guillaume, P. (1927). Les debuts de la phrase dans le langage de l'enfant. *Journal de Psychologie, 24,* 1–25.

Iverson, J. M., Capirci, O., & Caselli, M. C. (1994). From communication to language in two modalities. *Cognitive Development, 9,* 23–43.

Karmiloff-Smith, A. (1979). *A functional approach to child language: A study of determiners and reference.* Cambridge: Cambridge University Press.

Karmiloff-Smith, A. (1992). *Beyond modularity: A developmental perspective on cognitive science.* Cambridge, MA: MIT Press.

Kendon, A. (1972). Some relationships between body motion and speech. In A. Siegman & B. Pope (Eds.), *Studies in dyadic communication* (pp. 177–210). New York: Pergamon.

Kendon, A. (1980). Gesticulation and speech: Two aspects of the process of utterance. In M. R. Key (Ed.), *Relationship of verbal and nonverbal communication* (pp. 207–228). The Hague: Mouton.

Kita, S. (1993). *Language and thought interface: A study of spontaneous gestures and Japanese mimetics.* Unpublished doctoral dissertation, University of Chicago.

Leopold, W. (1949). *Speech development of a bilingual child: A linguist's record, Volume 3.* Evanston, IL: Northwestern University Press.

Masur, E. F. (1982). Mothers' responses to infants' object-related gestures: Influences on lexical development. *Journal of Child Language, 9,* 23–30.

Masur, E. F. (1983). Gestural development, dual-directional signaling, and the transition to words. *Journal of Psycholinguistic Research, 12,* 93–109.

Mayberry, R. I., Jaques, J., & DeDe, G. (2000). What stuttering reveals about the development of the gesture-speech relationship. In J. M. Iverson & S. Goldin-Meadow (Eds.), *The nature and functions of gesture in children's communication* (pp. 77–87). San Francisco: Jossey-Bass.

McNeill, D. (1992). *Hand and mind.* University of Chicago Press.

McNeill, D., & Duncan, S. (2000). Growth points in thinking-for-speaking. In D. McNeill (Ed.), *Language and gesture* (pp. 141–161). New York: Cambridge University Press.

Morford, M., & Goldin-Meadow, S. (1992). Comprehension and production of gesture in combination with speech in one-word speakers. *Journal of Child Language, 9,* 559–580.

Morrel-Samuels, P., & Krauss, R. M. (1992). Word familiarity predicts temporal asynchrony of hand gestures and speech. *Journal of Experimental Psychology: Learning, Memory, and Cognition, 18,* 615–622.

Newport, E. L., & Meier, R. P. (1985). The acquisition of American Sign Language. In D. I. Slobin (Ed.), *The cross-linguistic study of language acquisition: Volume 1. The data* (pp. 881–938). Hillsdale, NJ: Lawrence Erlbaum Associates.

Perry, M., Church, R. B., & Goldin-Meadow, S. (1988). Transitional knowledge in the acquisition of concepts. *Cognitive Development, 3,* 359–400.

Perry, M., Church, R. B., & Goldin-Meadow, S. (1992). Is gesture–speech mismatch a general index of transitional knowledge? *Cognitive Development, 7*(1), 109–122.

Perry, M., & Elder, A. D. (1996). Knowledge in transition: Adults' developing understanding of a principle of physical causality. *Cognitive Development, 12,* 131–157.

Petitto, L. A. (1988). "Language" in the pre-linguistic child. In F. Kessel (Ed.), *The development of language and language researchers: Essays in honor of Roger Brown* (pp. 187–221). Hillsdale, NJ: Lawrence Erlbaum Associates.

Stare, E. M. (1996). *Congenital unilateral brain injury, gesture, and the transition to two-words.* Unpublished master's thesis, University of Chicago.

Stone, A., Webb, R., & Mahootian, S. (1991). The generality of gesture-speech mismatch as an index of transitional knowledge: Evidence from a control-of-variables task. *Cognitive Development, 6,* 301–313.

Thal, D., Tobias, S., & Morrison, D. (1991). Language and gesture in late talkers: A one year followup. *Journal of Speech and Hearing Research, 34,* 604–612.

Volterra, V., & Caselli, C. (1985). From gestures and vocalizations to signs and words. In W. Stokoe & V. Volterra (Eds.), *SLR '83, Proceedings of the Third International Symposium on Sign Language Research* (pp. 1–9). Silver Spring, MD: Linstok.

Volterra, V., & Iverson, J. M. (1995). When do modality factors affect the course of language acquisition? In K. Emmorey & J. S. Reilly (Eds.), *Language, gesture, and space* (pp. 371–390). Hillsdale, NJ: Lawrence Erlbaum Associates.

Zinober, B., & Martlew, M. (1985). Developmental changes in four types of gesture in relation to acts and vocalizations from 10 to 21 months. *British Journal of Developmental Psychology, 3,* 293–306.

Chapter 6

Pointing by Hand
in "Neapolitan"[1]

Adam Kendon
Laura Versante
Istituto Universitario Orientale, Naples[2]

In this chapter, we examine *pointing*, here understood as gestures that are specialized for indicating an object (or a location) of some kind. Such gestures are commonly done with the hands, but they may also be done with the head, by certain movements of the eyes, by protruding the lips (cf. Sherzer, 1972), by a movement of the elbow, and in some circumstances even with the foot. In this chapter, however, we deal only with pointing as it is accomplished by the hands. We describe six different kinds of manual pointing, distinguished in terms of the shape of the hand and the rotation position of the forearm. From a consideration of the discourse contexts in which we have observed them in use, we conclude that the form of pointing adopted by a speaker is systematically related to the way the object being referred to is presented in the speaker's discourse. For example, if a speaker points to an object because it is to be an example of something, or because it illustrates a concept, then the form of pointing adopted will be different from the form adopted when the speaker points to an object when it is to be identified as something distinct from other objects. It as if the form of pointing adopted provides information about how the speaker wishes the object being indicated to be regarded.

---

[1]A fuller version of this report is found in Versante (1998), in which observations on pointing gestures as used by speakers in central England are also included. These observations are described and compared to our Neapolitan observations in another publication.

[2]This was the institutional affiliation of both authors when this chapter was written.

Few previous studies of pointing have been published in which the form of the pointing gesture itself has been taken into consideration. Many of the classifications of gestures that have been proposed, such as those by Wundt (1973), Efron (1972), Ekman and Friesen (1969), or McNeill (1992), have recognized, in one way or another, "pointing" or "deictic gestures" as a separate class, but in these discussions we find little in the way of a detailed description of what is done when someone "points." It is usually assumed that this is done by directing the hand toward the object to be indicated with the hand shaped so that only the index finger is extended. However, Calbris (1990) drew attention to the possibility that using a head movement instead of a hand movement in pointing, or using the thumb instead of an index finger, may make a difference for the meaning of the pointing action. Thus, she suggested (p. 128) that one designates another person with the forefinger "in order to command or accuse" but "[t]he hand, which constitutes a surface rather than a line, presents or offers. Its concrete designations are polite and not imperative . . ." The use of the head to designate something may appear "impolite" according to Calbris, and likewise the thumb, "probably because of the symbolic signification of rejection or offhandedness attached to thumb, its use [in designating] is cavalier and offhanded, even rude and authoritative . . ." Much earlier, de Jorio, writing in 1832 (de Jorio, 2000), noted that indicating something with the eyes, often combined with an almost imperceptible movement of the head, was done when it was wished to keep the act of indication inconspicuous. He also noted, as had Quintilian as long ago as 100 A.D. (Quintilian, 1922), that to point to someone or something to one's side or behind one with the thumb was also to express one's disparagement of what was being pointed to.

Observations of this sort encourage a study of pointing in which the different forms of the gestures used in pointing are compared in terms of the discourse contexts in which they appear. Are there consistencies in their use that would suggest that the pointing gesture does more than merely indicate, that it can also express certain kinds of differences in the acts of indication?

THE RECORDINGS

The examples discussed here are drawn from video recordings made in natural situations in April 1991 and March and April 1996 within an area in the south of Italy that, rather loosely, may be referred to as "Neapolitan." The recordings from 1991, referred to as Bocce I and Bocce II, were made in a village in the vicinity of Salerno. Here a small group of middle-aged men, all members of a bocce club (a club for a type of indoor bowls), were recorded in conversation, first as they were waiting to begin a meeting of the council of the club and then as the council meeting itself was held. The recordings from 1996 were made in a town on the Bay of Naples, situated at the foot of Vesuvius. These include recordings of buying and selling at various stalls in the open-air market in the *piazzetta* of the town (referred to as "Fruttivendolo"), a long recording of a stall owner and a few friends playing cards together while the stall owner waits for clients (referred to as "Commerciante"), and conversations with old sailors and fishermen who were asked questions by a university student who explained that she was interested in learning something about the lives of sailors and fishermen ("Marinai" and "Cappello Verde").[3]

The method followed in the study presented here has been to review these recordings and to identify all instances of manual pointing, differentiated according to the hand shape employed. These instances have been compared in terms of the discourse contexts in which they occur. We have tried to identify what appear to be the common features of these contexts, so that we can arrive at a formulation of the different ways in which the several forms of pointing we have distinguished appear to be used. In the exposition to follow we present a series of examples that illustrate the different usages we have observed.

WHAT IS "POINTING"?

Gestures recognized as "pointing" seem to have in common a certain characteristic movement pattern in which the body part carrying out the gesture is moved in a well-defined path, and the dynamics of the movement are such that at least the final path of the movement is linear. Commonly, but not always, once the body part doing the pointing reaches its furthest extent, it is then held in position briefly. In pointing, except when a moving object is being followed, the movement by which the gesture is accomplished is thus a movement that appears to be aimed in a clearly defined direction as if toward some specific target. Eco (1976, p. 119) referred to this feature of the act of pointing as "movement toward," and we use this term here also.[4]

---

[3]Bocce I and Bocce II were made by Adam Kendon. Thanks are due to Professor Pina Boggi Cavallo of the University of Salerno for her help. The talk was transcribed by Maria De Simone of Salerno and revised by Laura Versante. The 1996 recordings were made by Laura Versante, Mario Cimmino and Rosaria D'Alisa and the talk was transcribed by Laura Versante. Permission for the recordings was granted by the participants in advance. Financial assistance from the Wenner-Gren Foundation of New York and technical assistance from the Istituto Universitario Orientale of Naples are gratefully acknowledged.

[4]In describing the features of the act of pointing, Eco said that "//movement toward//" is a feature that must "always exist, even if imperceptible. In some other kinesic expressions it is absolutely indispensable, as occurs when somebody turns his head or glances toward something."

Gestures understood as pointing gestures are regarded as indicating an object or a location that is discovered by projecting a straight line from the furthest point of the body part that has been extended outward into the environment.[5] We shall not here enter into a discussion of this process of interpretation, how it arises, or how individuals come to adopt it. To do so would take us too far from our present aims. We would like to point out, however, that how the object or location that intersects with this straight line is identified as being the object or location referred to by the gesture is not well understood. It clearly depends on what else is being said or done as part of the utterance of which the gesture is a part, and also on the presuppositions shared by the interactants, in terms of which what is relevant and what is not relevant for the discourse are understood.

A good example of a pointing gesture is provided by a woman at a fruit stall (in Fruttivendolo 00.01.37) who extends her arm forward, holding it straight, with her hand held palm downward with only her index finger extended, just as she says to the fruit seller that she wants a kilo of apples (see Fig. 6.3A). Here we have a simple movement in which the arm is raised, directed forward, held still briefly, and then lowered. All the gesture seems to do is to indicate to the fruit seller which kind of apples the woman desires to buy.

However, it is important to remember that gestures can also occur in which that feature of it that is seen as "pointing" is combined with other features, whether of hand shape or of movement, so that the gesture not only indicates but at the same time accomplishes something else, such as depicting a characteristic of the object indicated. For example, a woman at Vincenzo's Fruit Stall is buying bananas (Example 1, Fruttivendolo 00.05.11, Fig. 6.1) and objects when the fruit seller removes the bananas she has asked for from the scales before the needle of the scales has stabilized. She calls out "Huà scennënë nu' scennënë! Monello!—Hey! They [the scales] go down they're not going down! Cheat!"[6] and as she does so she lifts up her arm, also straight, and directs it toward the scales with her index finger extended. Instead of simply holding her arm extended, however, she rotates her forearm back and forth three times at the same time.

---

[5]In most of the examples discussed in this chapter, pointing refers to real objects or locations present in the physical environment that speaker and addressees share. Pointing may also be done so that it indicates objects or locations that are not immediately visible or that are in a "narrative" or "metaphorical" space (Haviland, 1993; McNeill, Cassell, & Levy, 1993).

[6] The speakers in our material use both various forms of Neapolitan and a regionalized form of Italian. In transcribing Neapolitan we have followed the conventions of D'Ascoli (1993) except that we have used "k" where he would use "ch" and we have used "ë" to indicate where the vowel is atonal or indistinct, as commonly happens in final position (see De Blasi & Imperatore, 1998). Apostrophes are used to indicate environments where certain word segments are dropped.

FIG. 6.1. Example 1: Pointing combined with description: Customer at a fruit stall indicates the scales at the same time as she characterizes the movement of the needle by rotating her index finger back and forth.

Here, in directing her arm and extended index finger toward the scales she indicates them (and thus disambiguates what she refers to), but with the movements performed with her arm in this position she shows in gesture what she sees the needle of the scales to be doing. The extended index finger in this case thus appears to be not only an indicating finger, but it is also a "body model" for the needle of the scales, with the movement of the hand displaying the type of movement the woman sees. Here the gesture both indicates an object (the needle of the scales) and provides a description of the activity of something (the movement of the needle).

Such a combination of deictic with other functions can also occur with gestures that serve as discourse structure markers. For example, Giovanni, in the recording Bocce I (7.48.02), is characterizing the breaking down of a door in the office of the club as a type of vandalism (Fig. 6.2). As he speaks he twice uses the gesture sequence "finger-bunch-open-hand" in this utterance, a gesture sequence that is commonly used to mark "topic/comment" components in a discourse (see Kendon, 1995, for a description). Thus, he uses the "finger bunch" as he says "one must say that" and "open hand" as he says "a type of vandalism," then "finger bunch" again as he says "uh vandalism" and "open hand" as he says "over here." However, as he does so, his arm is extended well to his left, in the direction of the office where the "vandalism" he is talking about had occurred. Thus, at the same time as he uses a discourse structure marker gesture, he also adds, in his arm movement, a "movement toward" that serves to make reference to the location mentioned by the locative expression "over here."

In these examples, these descriptive or discourse structure marking gestures are combined with an inflection for direction, which carries with it a deictic reference. The gesture both describes and indicates, both marks dis-

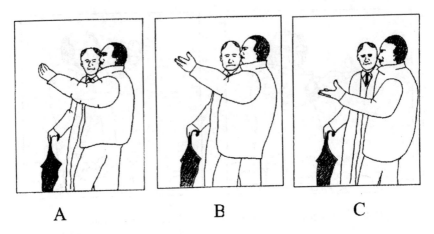

A   B   C

FIG. 6.2.   Example 2 (Bocce I 07.48.02): Discourse structure marker gesture
directionally inflected toward the location of the object the speaker is commenting on:

e allorë (.) s'adda ricërë ka e 'a tipë vandaliscëmë
|~~~~~~~~~~~~~~~~~~~~~~~/***************/*****/
                    [A]   [B]   [C]
e allora   si deve dire   che è un tipo di vandalismo
and well   one must say   that it is a type of vandalism

(A) Finger bunch hand lifted, directed left, as speaker states "topic." Note
speaker looks in the same direction as gesture, which is an additional clue to
the deictic component this gesture has. (B) Hand opens as speaker gives his
"comment." (C) Opened hand lowered and speaker turns to look at interlocutor as he completes his spoken phrase.

course structure and indicates. In our terminology, these are not gestures
of *pointing,* however, although they combine with a "pointing function."
These gestures may be said to have a "deictic component." Combined gestures of this sort will not be dealt with further here, although in a full treatment of deixis in gesture they merit much further analysis. For us, gestures
of *pointing* are those gestures in which the inflection for direction—"movement toward"—constitutes its only action.[7] That is, we deal only with gestures that seem *specialized* as gestures of pointing.

---

[7]It is often not easy to decide what the "action" of a gesture is. For example, a speaker may
engage in what is clearly a "pointing" gesture, but then sustains it for an extended stretch of
discourse during which the hand and arm engage in movements that are coordinated with the
rhythm of speech. These movements are not repetitions of the pointing action, nor are they
movements that convey substantive information about the object being pointed to. They have,
rather, "discourse marking" or "punctuating" functions, and to this extent they are not considered as "inflections" relevant to the meaning of the pointing gesture.

FORMS OF POINTING BY HAND

Six different forms of manual pointing are discussed here. These include two forms in which only the index finger is extended, one in which only the thumb is extended, and three in which the hand has all digits extended ("open hand"). For index finger pointing, there is one type where the hand is held so the palm faces downward (forearm is rotated to the supine position) and another where the hand is held with the forearm in "neutral" rotation, so that the palm of the hand faces sideways. The first will be referred to here as *index palm down*, while the second will be called *index palm vertical*. Pointing done either with the middle finger or the little finger has also been noted in our material, but it is not common and we shall not describe examples here. In *thumb pointing* the thumb is fully extended and adducted while the other digits are flexed.

In pointing with all fingers fully extended and held together—*open hand* pointing—the fingers are held straight and, typically, the thumb is held away from the fingers, rather than lying along the side of the hand. The three forms differ in the orientation of the palm. These are: *open hand palm up*, *open hand palm vertical*, and *open hand obliqua* (the palm is oriented obliquely upward). In open hand obliqua the fingers are typically extended to their fullest extent. In the other two forms there may be some relaxation in the extended fingers.

Index-Finger Pointing

As noted earlier, we distinguish two kinds of index-finger pointing, according to the way the forearm is oriented. These are used differently according to the kind of indication being undertaken in the speaker's discourse. In *index palm down* pointing (the forearm in prone position, palm facing downward), the speaker is typically engaged in what might be called *object individuation*. That is, it is the object itself, as distinct from other possible objects, that is the primary focus of the discourse; when an object is indicated as something to be attended to for itself, or when it is nominated separately as the topic of some discourse that is to follow, index palm down pointing is likely to be used. In *index palm vertical* pointing (forearm in "neutral" position, the palm of hand vertical), on the other hand, the object being indicated has relevance in the discourse but may not itself be the primary topical focus. Rather, the focus may be on the way in which the object indicated is being contrasted with other objects, or on some process or activity to which the object is related in some way, such as origin or cause, or as a concrete representation of something more abstract.

Examples of *index palm down* pointing, as used in object individuation, may be readily observed in shops or markets when customers point to spe-

FIG. 6.3.   Example 3 (Fruttivendolo 00.01.37): A woman uses index palm
down to point to the fruit she wants to buy. Example 4 (Marinai 00.58.38):
Luigi uses index palm down at he points out a "nostromo" (experienced seaman) to his interviewer.

cific objects to indicate to the vendor what they are interested in (Fig. 6.3).
Thus, a lady buying fruit at Vincenzo's fruit stall (Example 3, Fruttivendolo
Vincenzo 00.01.37, Fig. 6.3A) uses index palm down each time she indicates the fruit she wants—oranges, bananas, broccoli, tomatoes. Again,
when Luigi (Example 4, Fig. 6.3B, Marinai 00.58.38) points to a person
some distance off as he explains to the interviewer that this person is a

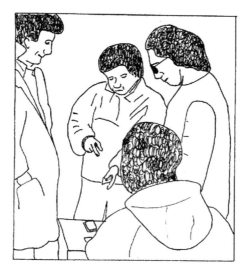

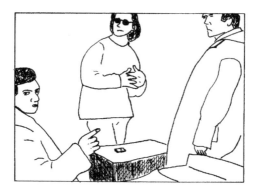

FIG. 6.4. (A) Example 6 (Commerciante 00.02.40): Peppe points with index palm vertical to cards just played as he asks, "Well what have we made?" (B) Example 7 (Commerciante 00.08.22): Peppe directs index palm vertical toward the camera as he says, "Mondo di Quark" suggesting, jokingly, that he and his friends are being video-taped for the television programme of that nature.

"nostromo" (i.e., an especially experienced seaman) who it would be worth her while to talk to, he uses index palm down.

Examples of this sort may be compared with the following, in which we see *index palm vertical* being used. In these cases, the object indicated is not the focus of the discourse, although it always has a connection of some sort to the focus.

A woman at a fruit stall wants to buy some lemons (Example 5, Fruttivendolo Via Falanga). The stall owner is talking to someone else, so she picks up some lemons and places them in the scales. Then she touches the stall owner to gain his attention and says "e guardë, mezzo kilo—look! Half a kilo," pointing at the scales with index finger palm vertical as she does so. Here the woman is not indicating a specific object; she is not saying "look at the lemons," for example. Rather, she is indicating the consequences of her action, in this case the weight of the lemons she has put in the balance. It is clear from what she says that the focus of her discourse is not the lemons themselves, but their weight.

A similar example may be drawn from Commericante (Example 6, 00.02.40). Peppe, holding cards in his left hand, touches with his right-hand index finger the cards he is holding and then directs the extended index fingers of both hands, both in the palm vertical position, toward the cards that are on the table that Aniello has won (Fig. 6.4A). As he does this he asks: "Allorë imma fattë? Well we have made [i.e., what points have we won]?" Here Peppe points to the cards not to single them out as objects in their own right, but because, interpreted in this particular context, the cards can provide the answer to his question.

Index palm vertical rather than index palm down is also used when a speaker indicates an object that provides the conditions or circumstances for what he is saying. For example, in Example 7 (Commerciante 00.08.22), Peppe is in conversation with Rosaria, as well as with his card-playing friends, about the topic of the film that Laura and Rosaria might be making. Salvatore asks, "Che titolo avrà 'stu film?—What will be the title of this film?" Peppe has an idea. He suggests that the film is being made for a well-known popular science television program *Il Mondo di Quark* on the theme of animals that are on their way to extinction. Earlier in the recording the idea that small street vendors such as himself are dying out had already been suggested. Peppe says "Ma è ooo (. . .) va al Mondo di Quark. Gli animali in via di estinzione—But it is, ooh, its for *Mondo di Quark*. Animals on the way to extinction." As he says "mondo di quark" he moves his right hand, index palm vertical, toward the television camera (Fig. 6.4B). By pointing at the camera here, however, he indicates the activity of the recording for the film that he suggests is being made. He is not singling out the video camera as an object to be specifically and directly attended to for its own sake.

Index Palm Down and Index Palm Vertical in Contrast

In some cases, we can observe how, within the same stretch of discourse, both forms of index finger pointing are used. For example, in Example 8 (Commerciante 00.09.33), Peppe has just had a brief conversation with a city official who passed by. As the official goes away he says to Rosaria, "That fellow is a city councilman, it doesn't seem so, but he's a city councilman."

With this utterance Peppe identifies a specific individual. As he says this, he points in the direction of the councilman, who is now crossing the piazza using index finger palm down. After a brief pause, Peppe then follows up with a comment. He says, "Maybe he is one of the few city councilmen honest and serious." He again points in the direction of the councilman, but this time he uses index finger palm vertical (Fig. 6.5). In this follow-up remark, although the councilman is indicated, it is not his individual identity that is the focus of the discourse but some quality that he has.

As a second example (Example 9, Marinai 01.04.00), we cite the following from an extract from the interview with Saverio (Fig. 6.6). This is particularly striking for the way in which we can see Saverio change from index palm down to index palm vertical pointing, and back again, all within the same gesture unit.

Saverio is talking about fishermen's cooperatives in Torre del Greco. His interviewer has just asked him if the name of a certain cooperative he has

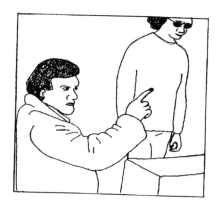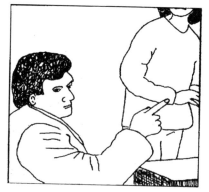

FIG. 6.5. Example 8 (Commerciante 00.09.33): Index palm down and index palm vertical in contrast. Peppe uses index palm down to identify the city councilman he refers to (A) and index palm vertical when he again points in his direction as he makes a comment about him. (B).

P: quello è 'n' assessore, non ci sembra, è 'n' assessore (.)
|~~~**-----|
      [A]
That fellow is a city councilman, it doesn't seem so, [but] he's a city councilman.

può darsi uno dei pochi assessori se - eee onesti e seri (.)
|~~~***************************~~~|
      [B]
maybe [he is] one of the few city councilmen ser- uh honest and serious

pëkkè n' a' mai approfittato, però purtroppo è sulë issë
because he has never profited, but unfortunately he is the only one

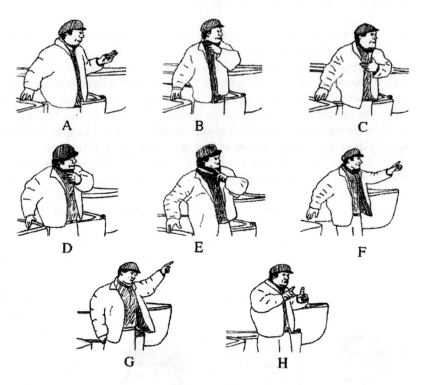

A   B   C

D   E   F

G   H

FIG. 6.6. Example 9 (Marinai 01.04.00): Contrast between use of index palm vertical (B, D, G), used when Saverio discusses the name of the two cooperatives he refers to, and index palm down (E, F), used when he re-refers to these coooperatives as a new topic.

S: Nooo eee (.) kellë so' dojë kooperativë
       /*************/
          [A]
No   those are two cooperatives
Sto purë 'n' atë sottë 'a Ripë (.) 'u Ko- 'u Ko- 'u Komitatë 'u Ko-
/***/ ------
                     [B]
There is another in the Riva too   the Co- the Co- the Committe the Co-
        'u Quartierë Komitatë   **ëëëëë**
            ****
            [C]
      the District Committee
I: = Comitato di quartiere   **S: Di quartierë së kjammë sta kooperativë**
                         /*************/
                          [D]
    Committee of the District   Of the District it's called, this cooperative
Però kestë e ku kellë (.) ko so' una kosë
/********/********/~~~***/**********/
  [E]   **[F]**   **[G]**   **[H]**
  but this   and with that   here they are just one thing

been a member of for many years is the correct one. He replies by saying it is not and then proceeds to explain that there are two cooperatives and he tries to give the name of one of them. As he is doing so, he points in its direction, using index palm vertical. When he gives its name, he changes to open hand palm up pointing (see below for further discussion) and then, as he confirms this name in a brief exchange with the interviewer, he again points with index palm vertical. Immediately thereafter, however, he refers to both cooperatives afresh, now newly identifying them as the topic of the next part of his discourse, and here, as he does so, he points first at one, then at the other, using index palm down. Here, as long as the name of the cooperatives was the focus of the discourse, index palm vertical was used in pointing. When the cooperative was rementioned as topic, it was pointed at with index palm down.

How can we account for this difference in usage between index palm down and index palm vertical? Perhaps the index palm down position is used in object individuation because, to achieve this position, an additional action of the arm (forearm pronation) is often required. This may make it "marked" or "distinct" relative to the palm vertical position. The gesture used for pointing at an object when it is to be attended to for its own sake, as happens in object individuation, is thus more fully differentiated as an act of indication.

Pointing with the Thumb

When the thumb is used in pointing, all the fingers are flexed to the palm of the hand and the thumb is fully extended. With this hand shape it is easy to direct the thumb upward, backward over the shoulder, or to the left or to the right. Perhaps for this reason it is often used to point to things that are either behind or the side of the speaker. However, hand shapes such as the index finger or open hand are also observed in use by people in pointing in these directions. Hence whether the thumb is used or not appears also to depend on other factors besides the convenience it might offer as a means for referring to something behind or to the side.

One general circumstance in which the thumb is used to point with appears to be when it is not important to establish the precise location or identity of what is pointed at. This may be because, among the participants, there is such shared knowledge of the environment that it is not necessary to indicate location or identity precisely. It may also be because the location or identity of the object referred to has been previously established. It is also clear from our examples that when the thumb is used in pointing in these circumstances the identity or location of the object pointed at is not the focus of the discourse.

The first example we cite comes from Bocce I, 7.54.47 (Example 10, Fig. 6.7) and is part of the burglary discussion. Here we see a contrast between the use of the index finger and the use of the thumb within the same interactional moment, which suggests how the thumb is used when the location of what is pointed at is known and where its location is no longer an issue in the discourse. Two speakers make reference to the same object—a door—and both, as they do so, point in its direction. In the first reference, however, the first speaker, Enzo, states specifically which door is being discussed, and here he points in the direction of the door using index finger palm vertical (A). His interlocutor, Giovanni, responds with a comment about the door—a comment about the way the door had been broken down—and here, as he refers to the door, he directs his thumb toward it (B). The example begins when Enzo enters the room with new information about a particular door. He says, "The lock was open, that door that leads on to the terrace." As he specifies which door he is talking about, he points

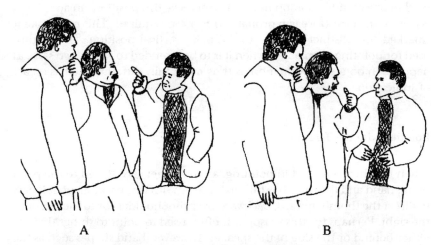

A   B

FIG. 6.7. Example 10 (Bocce I. 7.54.47): Contrast in use of thumb and index finger in pointing. Enzo points with index finger as he specifies a particular door (A). Giovanni makes a comment about this same door, points to it using his thumb (B).

E **'a mascëkature stevë apertë** (.) **quella porta che porta sul terrazzo**
/*****/
[A]
the lock was open   that door that leads on to the terrace
G **e allorë prufëssò e allorë è kummë**   **e allorë** (.)
and therefore, professor, and therefore it's like   and therefore
statëmë a sentì kella porta là è statë scekassatë sicurë a 'intë
/************/
[B]
listen to me,   that door there has surely been broken from inside

with his index finger. Giovanni then responds by saying that the door in question had been broken down from the inside (this is the mystery of the robbery: Why was an unlocked door broken down by the robbers?). Here the issue of which door it is becomes secondary. Enzo has already settled the matter. Now when Giovanni points in the direction of the door he does so with his thumb. When the discourse is focused on the question of which door it is, in pointing to it an index finger is used. When the discourse is focused on the state of the door and its identity is no longer in doubt, in pointing to it the thumb is used.

This example is similar to others that we have collected in which a speaker refers twice to the same location. When the location is first referred to the speaker may use his index finger, and commonly he glances in the direction of his pointing. For the second reference, if he points, the thumb tends to be used, and he does not glance in the direction of his point. In these cases it is as if the thumb point is an anaphora of the index-finger point.

As an illustration, we cite two passages from Marinai: 00.45.22 and 00.46.13. In these passages we find Luigi explaining to the interviewer how he worked for years in an abattoir (Example 11). He describes how he used to work as a sailor, and then he explains that he subsequently worked at the abattoir in Torre del Greco. As he explains this, he points behind him, in the direction of the abattoir, using his index finger to do so. Somewhat later in the same discussion the topic shifts to the pension he now receives. He says that nowadays he has enough money because he also has contributed to a pension scheme at the abattoir for 30 years. As he mentions the abattoir he again points to it, but this time he uses his thumb. Thus, when the focus of his discourse is the abattoir as a new location for his work he uses his index finger to locate it in pointing. When the abattoir is mentioned incidentally because it is the source of his pension, he points to it using his thumb.

To conclude this section, we cite an example that illustrates how the thumb is used when the location of what is being referred to is not important, in contrast to the use of the index finger, as soon as the location of the object does become important. As will be clear, it is not the relative location of the object pointed to—in this case behind the speaker—that determines whether the thumb is used or not. It is rather whether or not it is the location of the object that is the focus of the discourse. This example is also particularly interesting because in it we see how a speaker corrects his gesture so that it is more appropriate for the type of verbal expression he is using.

The speaker, Saverio (Example 12, Marinai 00.50.29, Fig. 6.8), is talking about the work his sons do. He explains that one of them is a fisherman who works in a certain fish shop. He singles out this fish shop, which is some distance away but actually visible in the setting, specifying it as "that" fish shop, pointing to it as he says this. He points to it twice, however. He first

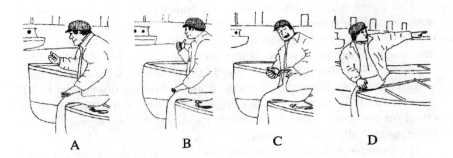

A   B   C   D

FIG. 6.8.   Example 12 (Marinai 00.50.29): Contrast in use of thumb and index
finger in pointing. Saverio raises thumb in an enumeration gesture as he mentions his first son (A); directs thumb backward as he begins to point toward the
fish shop where his second son works (B); in a pause in speech immediately after
"kella—that" he reorganizes his posture (C); points with index finger palm down
as he refers again to the fish shop where his second son works (D).

I: **Ma the lavoro Canno ? Voi avete detto il marittimo che avete detto ?**
      But what work do they do? You spoke of the sailor, what did you say?

S: **= eh unë fo 'u militarë (. . . .) 'n'atë fo 'u piscëkatorë (.) rinë'a kella . . .**
   /***************/~~~~~~~~~~***************************|
   [A]   [B]
   one is in the military   another is a fisherman   in that. . . .

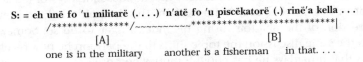

                kella piscëkaria a lo 'i ? (.) sto lo mo 'i?   Sto 'nu figljë ru mijë
   [-------Saverio changes posture-------]/~~~/************************/
                [C]   [D]
   that fish shop there, d'you see? He's there now, d'you see? One son of mine's there

   'n'atëvo vënnennë 'i fazzulëttinë
                /***********/
                [points behind with thumb]
   another goes around selling tissues

points to the fish shop with his thumb. He probably does this because, immediately before, he has used his thumb as an enumerator gesture to refer
to the first of his three sons (Fig. 6.8A). Since he proceeds at once to refer
to the next son, he simply continues with the same hand shape, now making use of it as a pointing gesture (Fig. 6.8B). However, as soon as he
reaches the demonstrative pronoun "kella—that," he breaks off his utterance, reorganizes his posture (Fig. 6.8C), and looks around and points at
the fish shop, extending his arm toward it with index finger palm down
(Fig. 6.8D). He then restarts his utterance and completes it. It is as if the
speaker caught himself using a mode of pointing that was inappropriate for
the kind of focus he was giving to what he was referring to. In consequence,

he reorganized his pointing to a more appropriate form and only then completed what he had to say. Finally, at the end of this passage, Saverio refers to his last son, who works as an ambulant salesman in the city. Here he resumes using his right hand to point with, again pointing with his thumb, directing it toward the city that is behind him to his right. In this case, since the son he is referring to moves around in an area of the city and there is no specific visible location where he can be found, the use of the thumb point seems entirely appropriate.

We have also collected observations that suggest that another circumstance in which the thumb is used in pointing is when what is pointed at is being placed in some kind of contrast or opposition with something else. In these cases, when the thumb is directed to the side or behind, it seems to be used to indicate what is "not here," "outside," "elsewhere," "not us," and the like. Space does not permit a detailed account of these examples, but we may mention two briefly. Thus, Saverio in Maranai (Example 13), comparing the behavior of non-Italian and Italian crew members, and saying that the non-Italians work much harder and for less money than the Italians, directs his index finger forward to the space in front of him as he talks of the Italians but directs his thumb sideways, to his left, as he refers to the non-Italians. Or again (Example 14), when Saverio speaks of how today parents must give money to their children and cannot expect their children to give parents money (as it used to be), as he refers to giving money to the children (referred to as "them") he directs his thumb backwards, behind him. A third example (Example 15) comes from the Commerciante recording. In this instance Vincenzo is complaining to Peppe's partner, Salvatore, that Peppe is always trying to claim more points than he is due. He suggests to Peppe that it is just as well he is not arguing directly with him. He says: "Meno malë ka mo sto parlannë ku killë!—it's better that now I am speaking with that fellow!" and as he does so, he points with his thumb to Salvatore. In this case it would seem that by pointing with his thumb in this fashion at Salvatore, who is sitting to his right, while at the same time he is oriented to Peppe, to whom he directs his remark and who sits to his left, he effectively indicates Salvatore as someone separate and in contrast with Peppe and in this case (as his words allow us to conclude), from Vincenzo's point of view, of greater value than Peppe.

OPEN-HAND POINTING

The term *open hand* is used here to refer to a hand shape in which all of the digits are extended and the fingers are more or less adducted. The thumb may either be extended or adducted, although it is usually extended. There can be some variation in the degree of 'tension' with which this hand shape is maintained, although, in general, in the 'open hand' pointing observed in the material examined here, the fingers show a good deal of tension in their extension.

As explained above, we observe three distinct 'open hand' orientations, which differ according to the contexts in which they are used. These orientations are: *palm vertical*, in which the hand is held so the palm is vertical and forearm rotation is 'neutral'; *palm up*, with the forearm supinated; and *obliqua*, with the palm held so it faces upward, but at an oblique angle.

In general, it may be said that when an 'open hand' is used to indicate something, this is not because the indicated object is simply to be distinguished from others, nor because it is to be put in some kind of contrastive relationship with another object or location. Rather, it is because of the implications that the object or location has for the current theme of the speaker's discourse. Thus, it may be that the object is being referred to because it serves as an example of something, because it stands for a concept, because it is the source of some information or activity that is being discussed, or because it is something that must be examined or taken into consideration as an exhibit.

When the open hand is in the palm vertical orientation in pointing, something is being attributed to the object indicated or the object indicated is being referred to as the source or cause of something. It is also used when the speaker makes comments on the qualities of the object indicated. With the open hand palm vertical it is as if the speaker indicates the object for the idea that it is taken to refer to, rather than for its material identity. Open hand palm vertical is also used when the object indicated is an exemplar of a class or when it serves as a symbol for a concept. The open hand palm up tends to be used when the object pointed at is referred to as something to be scrutinized as an example of something—in such pointings, often it seems that the speaker, metaphorically, is "offering" the object to his interlocutor. Finally, the open hand obliqua is used to point at something when a comment is being made about the object, or when a comment is being made about a relationship between the object and the speaker's interlocutor. In most cases the object pointed at in this way is another person and the comment is negative, sometimes strongly so. This use of open hand obliqua, in fact, appears to be rather well ritualized in the Neapolitan area and may possibly be regarded as having the status of a quotable gesture.[8]

---

[8]A quotable gesture is a conventionalized gestural expression that members of the community where it is used can cite or quote out of its context of use. Gestures that have this property may often be glossed with a verbal expression, often a conventional one. Gestures that have been referred to as *emblems* since the publication of Ekman and Friesen (1969) usually have this quotable property (see Kendon, 1992).

OPEN HAND PALM VERTICAL IN CONTRAST WITH INDEX-FINGER POINTING

First, we give examples in which, within the same stretch of discourse, a speaker is observed to use in pointing both a single extended finger (index finger) and then an open hand palm vertical. As we shall see, the form of the speaker's pointing gesture changes in relation to the way in which the object indicated is being made use of in the speaker's discourse.

Our first example comes from Marinai 00.43.54, where Luigi is responding to his interviewer's inquiry as to where she might find experienced sailors to talk to (Example 16, Fig. 6.9). He says: "Of sailors up here there's a whole bunch of sailors. You go close to there, they are all sailors." As he begins speaking he waves his arm in broad circular movements, extended in the direction of a location at some distance away, the hand formed as open hand palm vertical. When he says "You go close to there," however, he changes to point with index finger palm down. After two brief interventions

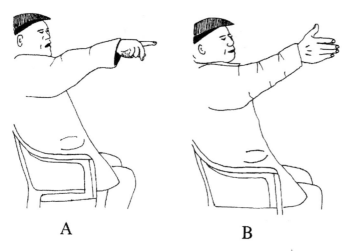

A   B

FIG. 6.9. Example 16 (Marinai 00.43.54): Contrast between index finger and open hand palm vertical. (A) Speaker points with index finger palm down as he says:

vujë 'jatë la vicinë la niente so' tuttë
/~~~~~~~************************/
you go there close to there they all are [sailors]

(B) Speaker points with open hand palm down as he says:

nientedimenë so' tuttë marittëmë la
/~~~~~~~*********************/
they actually are all sailors there

by another sailor and by the interviewer, Luigi returns to making reference
to the location he indicated before as he says, "Actually they are all sailors
there"—but this time he points with open hand palm vertical. Notice that
when, in his discourse, a precise location is foregrounded, when it is nominated as the location to which the interviewer should proceed, he uses index finger palm down, but when he then characterizes what is to be found
in that location his hand becomes open hand palm vertical.

In the next example (Example 17, Bocce I, 7.42.42), Sandro is talking to
Giovanni about Ninuccio, who went to Enzo (one of the club officials) to
obtain a certain telephone number, a telephone number that Enzo had got
from a poster on the wall in the bocce court. Giovanni opens the exchange
by asking why someone had come to tell Ninuccio about a new telephone
number he had gone away to call. Sandro replies by explaining that it was
not known that the new number was written underneath a certain poster.
Sandro directs an index finger palm vertical in the direction of the of the
bocce court (which is where Enzo had found the number on a poster) as he

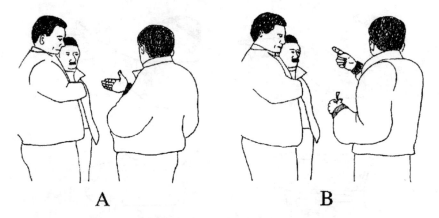

A   B

FIG. 6.10.   Example 18 (Bocce I 7.56.32): Contrast between pointing with
open hand palm up and index finger. (A) Enzo extends open hand palm up
toward Giovanni as he repeats Giovanni's completion of Enzo's phrase. (B)
Enzo directs index finger forward as he specifies a paritcular key as topic.

E   quando vennero a rubare la volta scorsa. . .
       when they came to steal   the last time . . .

G   =s'arrubbaj^{e}n^e pur^e 'a kjav^e
       =they stole   also the key

E   =s'arrubbajën purë 'a kjavë   kella kjavë la
       /*********************/   /**********/
                [A]   [B]
       they stole   also the key that key there

speaks about where Ninuccio went, but when he refers to the poster because the poster is the place where the telephone number could be found, he points in the direction of it, using an open hand palm vertical.

Another example (Bocce I 07.56.32, Example 18, Fig. 6.10) also illustrates the contrast between index finger and open hand in pointing, but it also illustrates another sort of use of the open hand. Here the participants are discussing a robbery that had taken place at the premises of the club a day or so before. Part of what was at issue was a key that was missing to a door that had been locked after the robbery, suggesting that the robbers themselves possessed the key. Enzo says, "When they came to rob the last time," and Giovanni immediately chimes in, completing his turn with "they stole the key." Enzo immediately resumes speaking. He repeats what Giovanni just said, "they stole the key," and immediately continues with "that key there." When he repeats Giovanni's words he directs an open hand palm up toward Giovanni. This is a common use of such a pointing gesture—here it serves to indicate the source of something that the speaker is now saying. When he continues with "that key there," however—an utterance that specifies a particular object with a particular location—Enzo points with an extended index finger.

The direction of this point does not seem to be in the direction of where, relative to Enzo, the door they are talking about is to be found (from a consideration of other examples, it seems the door is actually far to Enzo's left), and therefore where the key is to be found. However, precise specification of the location in this case is not important, since it is well known to everyone present. In this case, at this moment in Enzo's discourse, the individuality of the key becomes focal. In his linguistic expression Enzo uses both the demonstrative "kella" and the locative pronoun "la," and thus for Enzo the "focus" at this moment is the individuation in his discourse of the specific key. This is what his gesture also does. It points to something specific to individuate it, but in this case the gesture does not actually locate the object indicated. In this case it seems that we have a pointing gesture that gives expression to the idea of individuation without indicating a location for what is individuated.

In the three examples described, we have observed a contrast between the use in pointing of an extended index finger and an open hand palm vertical. In each case, as we have seen, the index-finger point is associated with an expression in which a demonstrative or locative pronoun is used and in which the focus of the discourse at that moment is that of distinguishing or individuating an object. In each case, the open hand palm vertical is used in pointing as soon as there is a shift in the focus of the discourse, when the object that is being referred to has some characteristic attributed to it, when the object is referred to in virtue of some property that it has, or when it is referred to because it is the source of something.

OPEN HAND PALM UP

As mentioned earlier, when the open hand palm up is used commonly in association with utterances in which something is being "presented" or "shown"—as if the speaker wishes to say that the object indicated be taken as an exhibit. When used in a pointing gesture, the object indicated is being indicated not just because it is an object referred to as a topic of discourse, but because it is an example to be scrutinized. By using the open hand palm up the speaker invites the recipient to look at the object indicated.

Thus, in Commerciante 00.08.14 (Example 19, Fig. 6.11), the card players have noticed that the two quite attractive young women who are filming them have been doing this for longer than might be expected. They wonder why. Vincenzo playfully suggests that it is because Aniello is such a handsome fellow. He says: "No pëkkè anna vistë Aniello 'nu bellu 'uaglionë—No because they have seen Aniello, a handsome fellow!" As he says this he extends his open hand palm up forward toward Aniello. As he begins the gesture, he looks round at the filmmakers and then he looks back at Aniello as he pronounces his name. In effect, thus, with this gesture Vincenzo invites one to look at Aniello, to appreciate him as a specimen of handsome manhood.

In Commerciante 00.19.55 (Example 20), Vincenzo tells Peppe it is his turn to play his cards. Peppe declares he has played and directs an open hand palm up toward the cards on the table he has just put down. Here the hand indicates the cards, but it indicates them as objects to be seen for the

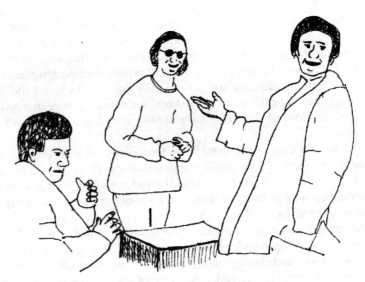

FIG. 6.11.   Example 19 (Commerciante 00.08.14): Vincenzo directs palm up open hand toward Aniello. For explanation see text.

evidence they provide of Peppe's action, not just as objects to be individuated. In Capello Verde 00.03.10 (Example 21) an old fisherman discussing
his work complains about the many persons who fish without a license.
This, he says, makes it hard for legitimate fishermen to make money. He refers to a colleague who is sitting close by, and says " 'stu povërë 'uagljonë e
me akkusì imma fattë 'i përukkjë tantë—This poor boy and I, thus, we have
made beans because of that." As he says "This poor boy" he directs his open
hand, palm up, toward his colleague. Later, in the same discussion, he
again refers to his colleague, saying that he hardly brings any food home,
and again, as he says this, he directs his open hand palm up toward his colleague. Here it seems that the speaker's colleague is being presented to the
interlocutor as a case to consider, and the use of the open hand palm up directed toward the object of reference in both cases indicates who is being
referred to and, by virtue of the hand configuration employed, how this object is to be treated in the context of the speaker's discourse—he is being
presented as an example—is suggested.

OPEN HAND OBLIQUA

As stated earlier, the open hand obliqua, when used as a form of pointing,
indicates an object when a comment is being made either about the object
itself or, in some cases it seems, about the relationship between the interloc-

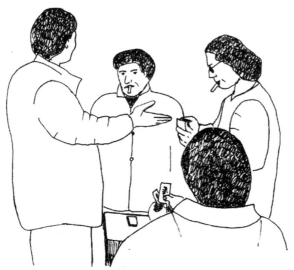

FIG. 6.12.   Example 22 (Commerciante 00.04.25): Vincenzo directs an open
hand obliqua toward Aniello at the same time as he addresses Peppe.

utor and the object. Commonly, the object indicated is a person, and the comment being made is negative. Thus, in Commerciante 00.04.25 (Example 22, Fig. 6.12), Vincenzo directs an open hand obliqua toward Aniello while he first criticizes Peppe for looking at Aniello's cards and then criticizes Aniello for holding his cards so that another can see them.

Immediately prior to Vincenzo's intervention the four players have been occupied by looking at the cards they have just been dealt. Suddenly Vincenzo looks at Peppe and tells him not to "look at the cards of this fellow" and as he does so he extends his right hand, open hand obliqua, toward Aniello who stands opposite him. The open hand obliqua here serves as pointing, and disambiguates the pronoun "kistë—this." At the same time, directing the open hand obliqua to Aniello already conveys a critical attitude toward Aniello on the part of Vincenzo. This becomes clear when Vincenzo addresses Aniello directly, declaring that he has allowed others to see his cards.

In Commerciante 00:05:38 (Example 23), Salvatore, Peppe's partner in the game, asks the score of Vincenzo, who is of the opposite team. Vincenzo reproves him and tells him he should ask his "compagno." He says: "stattë zittë 'ddumantë 'u kumpagnë tuojë—Be quiet, ask your partner!" As he says "Be quiet" Vincenzo rapidly lifts an open hand upwards toward himself in what may be a gesture of throwing something over the shoulder, which, in this context, when addressed to another, as here, can mean "throw away what you are doing."[9] As he says "ask your partner" he directs open hand obliqua toward Peppe while looking toward Salvatore as he speaks. In this context, Vincenzo's expression " 'u kumpagnë tuojë—your partner" conveys a scornful attitude to Salvatore, for it refers to Peppe only in his capacity as Salvatore's coplayer in the opposing team. The open hand obliqua here indicates Peppe for Salvatore's benefit, the form here conveying a negative attitude toward him on the part of Vincenzo.

A third example comes from Marinai 00.41.39 (Example 24). This is at the beginning of the recording where two old sailors have been approached by the interviewer to see if they would be willing to talk about their life as mariners. They call to another to call him over. They say he has much experience. However, he is a bit shy about talking about his life and Saverio makes fun of him and says Aniello will speak only if the interviewer pays him. Aniello says: "vo 'i sordë vo truannë 'i sordë—He wants money, he wants to find money." This means, "you are the one who need money while I have enough." In saying this, he addresses the interviewer and as he does so he directs his right hand, formed as open hand obliqua, toward Saverio.

In each of these examples, we see how the open hand obliqua is used as a way of indicating an object, in all cases another person, who is in some way

---

[9]Compare de Jorio (1832/2000, p. 312).

the butt of a critical remark or a critical attitude. In each case, however, it is to be noted that there is always a third participant in the interchange. That is to say, the critical remark or attitude is not only directed to the person being criticized, but it is made in the hearing of others and, most commonly, the addressee of the utterance is another and not directly the object of the criticism. Thus, in the first example, although Vincenzo criticizes Aniello for letting his cards be visible, he does this indirectly by a remark directed to Peppe. Although in the second example Vincenzo addresses Salvatore, he simultaneously directs his gesture to Peppe, thus drawing Peppe in as a second addressee in the interchange. In the third example, the disparaging comment about Saverio is directed to the interviewer. Thus, in these examples, the open hand obliqua seems to be a gesture that directs a third person to attend to the target of the criticism and thus plays a role in making that criticism public.

DISCUSSION

Deixis refers to those linguistic features or expressions that relate utterances to the circumstances of space and time in which they occur. When the conditions that allow these expressions to function are discussed, there is usually some reference to 'pointing', for it is recognized that, in a fundamental sense, it is only through some nonlinguistic action or nonlinguistic aspect of the situation that the tie between an utterance and its spatial or temporal circumstance can ultimately be established (Bühler, 1990, pp. 126–128), and the gesture of pointing is one of the most obvious ways in which this is done. In many circumstances, indeed, it cannot be done without.

Despite this, it is commonly assumed that the gesture of pointing does no more than establish this necessary tie between word and circumstance. It serves to indicate what the referent of a deictic word might be, but it does not make any of the distinctions that deictic words can make, such as between gender and participation status (as in personal pronouns), singularity and plurality (*this* vs. *these*), closeness and far-offness (*this* vs. *that* vs. *that yonder*), and so on. The idea that distinctions of this sort might also be made gesturally has hardly been explored.

Birdwhistell (1966), in his discussion of certain so-called *kinesic markers*, observed that directionally distinctive movements of the head or other body parts associated with stressed pronominals varied according to closeness and singularity and plurality; Eco (1976, p. 119) suggested that variations in what he called "dynamic stress" in finger-pointing gestures conveyed the semantic markers of "closeness" and "distance." Apart from these two discussions, and those of Calbris (1990) and de Jorio (2000) already noted, it seems that the idea that the character of the pointing gesture itself might vary systematically in relation to semantic distinctions of various sorts has never been seriously examined. The investigation reported here takes a step in this direction. We have concentrated on the configuration of hand-with-forearm rotation in manual pointing gestures. We have described six different configurations, and, through the examples we have presented, we have suggested that these are used in a consistent manner as if to make certain distinctions with regard to the way the objects referred to are presented in the discourse. Another way to put this might be to say that the various forms of hand pointing we have described relate to the way the speaker regards the object being referred to.

Thus when the object referred to is to be considered directly as a material object, individuated with respect to other material objects, it is pointed to with extended index finger palm down (Examples 3 and 4). When the individual object pointed to is to be considered in terms of certain attributes it has, is placed in some kind of relationship with other objects in respect to certain attributes, or if it is to be considered for its causal role in a situation, or for its symbolic significance, then extended index finger palm vertical is likely to be used (Examples 5, 6, and 7). This distinction between the use of these two kinds of index finger pointing was illustrated in Examples 8 and 9 where, within the same unit of discourse, as the way in which the objects referred to changed, so also did the form of the index finger pointing gesture change.

These usages appear to contrast with instances where some form of open hand is used in pointing. When the open hand is used in pointing with a palm vertical orientation (palm oriented vertically), the object indicated is referred to because of certain characteristics associated with it; the object stands for a concept, or is the source of information or activity that is the topic of discussion, or is linked to such a source or it is an example of a class (Examples 16, 17, and 18). Open hand palm up appears to be used in contexts where the object being referred to either is presented as an example to be inspected or is being presented because of certain characteristics it has that are in discussion (Examples 19, 20, and 21). There is also a more specialized use of the open hand when it has an obliqua orientation, when the object being indicated, which is usually a person, is the butt of a criticism that is being addressed to a third party (Examples 22, 23, and 24).

Turning now to the thumb, the examples we presented show how it is used in pointing when the location or the identity of the object indicated is not in the foreground of discussion; the thumb point thus is used as a means of parenthetical reference to the object (Example 10). This may be linked to what could be called its "anaphoric" use, where something referred to a second time is indicated by the thumb, where it had been indicated by an index finger the first time (Example 11). Of particular interest here is Example 12, in which the speaker, embarking upon a particular linguistic expression that foregrounds the location and identity of something, is yet using a thumb point to indicate it. He interrupts his own speech, changes his bodily orientation, and then rebegins, with the same linguistic expression, but this time using an index-finger point. The same speaker in the same passage then again uses a thumb point, but here he makes a reference to an area behind him that is not precisely specified. This example shows well how pointing with the thumb carries implications for what is being referred to that are different from index finger pointing, and that a speaker can make a choice accordingly.

As we noted at the beginning of this chapter, more than one writer has suggested that using the thumb to point with implies that the speaker has disdain for the object indicated in this way (Calbris, 1990; de Jorio, 2000; Quintilian, 1922). However, this may be but a particular elaboration from the use of the thumb to point to something that is "not present" or "beyond" rather than "present" or "here." To point to someone who is, in fact, copresent, using the thumb, might be a mode of referring to them as if they are "not present" or "beyond," and this could certainly imply disdain for them. We mentioned (but did not describe) examples that suggest that thumb pointing is used when the speaker is placing objects or locations in some kind of symbolic opposition to one another, but we need more instances before the network of implications carried by thumb pointing can be articulated more clearly and completely.

To understand the relationship between the forms of pointing distinguished and the different semantic implications they appear to have, it may be useful to compare the forms in these gestures with those found in other nonpointing gestures. For example, a general contrast seems to be marked by whether the index finger is used in pointing or the open hand is, such that in index-finger pointing there is always present the idea of the singularity of the object being referred to, whereas when the open hand is used the object pointed to is being referred to not in its singularity but in its status as a symbolic, conceptual, or exemplary object.

If we look beyond pointing gestures and consider differences between other gestures that use the extended index finger and those that use an open hand, there seem to be certain parallels. Thus, there is a gesture of negation in which the hand, with the index finger only extended, held vertical with the palm of the hand facing outward, is moved in a well-defined manner, laterally away from the speaker's midline. This is used when something specific is being denied. Another gesture of negation, which has the same lateral movement, uses the open hand with the palm facing away. This is used as an expression of refusal or as an expression that can be glossed with an expression such as "basta—it is enough," thereby indicating that whatever has been in progress (e.g., the filling of a grocery order, food being served or consumed, or the like) one now wishes to stop. It seems, in short, that the index-finger negation negates something specific within a transaction, but does not negate the entire transaction, whereas the open-hand negation negates an entire transaction—something much more general (de Jorio, 2000; Kendon, 2001).

In the same way, we can compare the contrasts between the three different orientations of the open hand that we have described for pointing gestures with like contrasts found in nonpointing gestures. For example, the open hand palm up is used not only in pointing but also in gestures in which one offers something or requests something or in which one expects to receive something (Mueller, 2002). It seems to us that the use of the palm up open hand in pointing, when it serves as a way of showing that the object indicated is being treated as an "exhibit" by the speaker, is semantically linked to these other uses of the palm up open hand, and this stands in contrast with the gestures in which one sees, for example, open hand palm vertical. In nonpointing gestures, this is commonly seen in gestures that serve as dividers of space or, in another usage, in gestures that indicate movement along a route.

More generally, we suggest that it will be useful to pursue an analysis of gesture in which different features of form are compared across different contexts of use (cf. the approach initiated by Calbris, 1990, and followed also by Webb, 1996, 1998). That is, we suggest, that an analysis of gestures in terms of their various components of form (hand shape, hand orientation, relative spatial location and movement) will show corresponding semantic components. Just how these semantic components are to be referred to still remains a problem to be solved, but contrasts such as those between "singularity" and "concreteness" on the one hand and "generality and "abstractness" on the other are among those referred to here that appear to "map onto" contrasts in gestural form.

This approach can also be applied with respect to the movement component of gesture. In the discussion in which we sought to define just which kinds of gestures were to be examined in this chapter, we made reference to the movement component of pointing gestures—Eco's "movement toward"—and pointed out how gestures that were not pointing gestures could, nevertheless, be combined with a "movement toward" and could thus acquire a deictic significance. For present purposes we defined pointing gestures as those in which the "movement toward" was the only dynamic component. Yet as we saw in our discussion of "What is pointing?," gestures can vary in terms of the "balance" between these components. Perhaps gestures could be arranged on a scale in which the "movement toward" feature ranges continuously from zero through various degrees of subordination or dominance in respect to other movement components, until it is so dominant that no other movement component can be observed. From this point of view, the gestures we have defined as "pointing" are those that are at the extreme end of this range, where "movement toward" dominates over everything else.

REFERENCES

Birdwhistell, R. L. (1966). Some relationships between American kinesics and spoken American English. In A. G. Smith (Ed.), *Communication and culture* (pp. 182–189). New York: Holt, Rinehart & Winston.

Bühler, K. (1990). *Theory of language* (D. F. Goodwin, Trans.). Philadelphia: John Benjamins. (Original title *Sprachtheorie*, Jena and Stuttgart, 1934)

Calbris, G. (1990). *Semiotics of French gesture*. Bloomington: Indiana University Press.

D'Ascoli, F. (1993). *Nuovo Vocabolario Dialettale Napoletano*. Naples: Adriano Gallina.

De Blasi, N., & Imperatore, L. (1998). *Il Napoletano parlato e scritto*. Naples: Fausto Fiorentino.

de Jorio, A. (2000). *Gesture in Naples and gesture in classical antiquity*. (A translation of *La mimica degli antichi investigata nel gestire napoletano* [1832], and with an Introduction and Notes by A. Kendon.) Bloomington: Indiana University Press.

Eco, U. (1976). *A theory of semiotics*. Bloomington: Indiana University Press.

Efron, D. (1972). *Gesture, race and culture*. The Hague: Mouton.

Ekman, P., & Friesen, W. (1969). The repertoire of non-verbal behavior: Categories, origins, usage and coding. *Semiotica*, *1*(1), 49–98.

Haviland, J. B. (1993). Anchoring, iconicity and orientation in Guugu Yimithirr pointing gestures. *Journal of Linguistic Anthropology*, *3*(1), 3–45.

Kendon, A. (1992). Some recent work from Italy on quotable gestures ("emblems"). *Journal of Linguistic Anthropology*, *2*(1), 77–93.

Kendon, A. (1995). Gestures as illocutionary and discourse structure markers in Southern Italian conversation. *Journal of Pragmatics*, *23*, 247–279.

Kendon, A. (2001). *Context of use studies of the "headshake" and some manual "negation" gestures among Neapolitans and among speakers of English in Northamptonshire and elsewhere*. Report to CILA, Istituto Universitario Orientale, Naples.

McNeill, D. (1992). *Hand and mind*. Chicago: Chicago University Press.

McNeill, D., Cassell, J., & Levy, E. (1993). Abstract deixis. *Semiotica*, *95*, 5–19.

Mueller, C. (2002). Forms and uses of the palm up open hand. A case of a gesture family? In C. Mueller & R. Posner (Eds.), *Semantics and pragmatics of everyday gesture*. The Berlin conference. Berlin: Weidler Verlag.

Quintilian, M. F. (1922). *Institutio oratoria* (H. E. Butler, Trans.). London: William Heinemann.

Sherzer, J. (1972). Verbal and nonverbal deixis: The pointed lip gesture among the San Blas Cuna. *Language in Society*, *2*(1), 117–131.

Versante, L. (1998). *Osservazioni comparative sulla deissi verbale e gestuale in alcune zone della Campania e dell'Inghilterra centrale*. Tesi di Laurea, Anno Accademico 1996–1997. Facoltà di Lingue e Letterature Straniere, Istituto Universitario Orientale, Naples.

Webb, R. (1996). *Linguistic features of metaphoric gestures*. Doctoral dissertation, University of Rochester.

Webb, R. (1998). The lexicon and componentiality of American metaphoric gestures. In S. Santi, I. Guaïtella, C. Cavé, & G. Konopczynski (Eds.), *Oralité et getualité: Communication multimodale, interaction* (pp. 387–391). Paris: L'Harmattan.

Wundt, W. (1973). *The language of gestures* (J. S. Thayer, C. M. Greenleaf, & M. D. Silberman, Trans.). The Hague: Mouton.

Chapter 7

How to Point in Zinacantán

John B. Haviland
Reed College/CIESAS-Sureste, Chiapas, Mexico

This chapter takes as its raw material pointing in the speech of two different individuals from Zinacantán, a Tzotzil (Mayan)-speaking peasant community in Chiapas, Mexico: a 3-year-old girl named Mal immersed in learning how to interact with other people, and her grandfather Petul, a partially blind octogenarian. Field material from Zinacantán suggests the possibility of a "natural history of pointing" that encompasses a range of narrative and nonnarrative discourses, different sorts of speakers and interactive contexts, and both the emerging skills of language-learning infants and the full-blown competence of adult speakers. As a preliminary to such a study, in this chapter I present several examples of apparent pointing, first to argue against the oft-assumed simplicity of "pointing gestures." Second, I suggest the essentially linguistic nature of pointing, as part of the system of determiners and pronouns, using as evidence links between pointing and spoken language, the form of pointing, and its use by young Tzotzil children.

Consider first the alleged conceptual and functional simplicity of pointing gestures, evidenced by the status of pointing in proposed typologies of gesture. For example, in his influential classification, McNeill (1992) posited a class of deictic gestures taken as definitionally unproblematic; "the familiar pointing" (p. 18) gestures are described with unabashed circularity as "pointing movements, which are prototypically performed with the pointing finger, although any extensible object or body part can be used" (p. 80). Indeed, McNeill found what he called "concrete pointing," which "has the obvious function of indicating objects and events in the concrete world" (p. 18), relatively straightforward in contrast with "abstract pointing," where "there is nothing objectively present to point at" (p. 18).

Hand in hand with the evident formal and functional simplicity of pointing goes a purported conceptual and developmental link between pointing gestures and referential devices in language generally. Again, McNeill (1992) encapsulated the standard view: "Pointing . . . has been regarded as a precursor of speech developments" (p. 300). In his discussion of "protogestures" (as opposed to "true gestures") he summarized literature on early acquisition as follows: "By 12 months of age, or so, gesture movements with definite referential significance have emerged in the form of concrete pointing. . . . A convincing demonstration of the referential significance of this early pointing is when a child reaches out in the direction of a desired object, and *looks away from the object and to the adult* who is in a different direction" (McNeill, 1992, p. 300, citing Bates, Bretherton, Shore, & McNew [1983] and Lock [1978]). Researchers seem to have little difficulty identifying a child's movements as instances of pointing, nor do they hesitate to ascribe referential intent by linking the gestures to apparent concrete referents. The later development of more complex referential devices in language is assumed to build on these early pointing gestures.

When researchers on child language (or the caregivers on whom they rely as interpreters and with whom they usually share a language) operate with their own native category of pointing they are free to apply it as they like. Matters are more complex in a different communicative tradition. David Wilkins (chap. 8, this volume) insists on the use of native categories of action in launching our descriptions. Accordingly, he bases his categorization of certain Arrernte gestures on Arrernte descriptive terms and an accompanying native theory. Applying this perspective to speakers of Zinacantec Tzotzil, however, yields unsatisfying results. It is not clear that Zinacantec communicative metatheory will yield *any* category of "pointing," or for that matter of "gesture," as a distinct and recognizable class of actions.

In English, to describe a pointing gesture we might use the verbs *point at* (or *to*) or *indicate* with a specific direct object denoting the presumed referent. *"She pointed at her mother." "He indicated where the ball fell."* In some contexts, we might prefer the verb *show* with appropriate complements. *"He showed me his toy."* The syntax of these expressions seems to presume that the corresponding actions are *referential*—that is, that they have *referents* denoted by their direct objects.

In Zinacantec Tzotzil, I know of no equivalent expressions. The only verbs we might translate as *point* have specific anatomical connotations. For example, the verb stem *bech* is "stick out (e.g., a limb, a finger, the end of a hose), hand over, deliver." Thus, *isbech sk'ob* means "she stuck out her hand," with no necessary implication of pointing *at* something. There are many expressions that we might gloss as "show"—mostly causative constructions like *ak' iluk*, lit., "make (another person) see (something)"—but none is specific to gesturing, nor is a presumed "pointing" movement a particularly appropriate action to be so described.[1]

Furthermore, Zinacantec Tzotzil seems to provide neither a description of the common "pointing hand," nor even a distinctive name for the index finger.[2] In local terminology, pointing gestures seem to be accorded no special recognition or status.[3] Instead, in Zinacantán, gestures that appear to an outside observer to be instances of pointing are characterized like *spoken linguistic communicative acts*. That is, they are glossed with the same sort of metapragmatic frame used to gloss speech, typically with the form *xi*, "he/she says."[4] We show examples in the spontaneous glosses offered for little Mal's gestures, to which I now turn.

---

[1]Although the expression is much more general, Laughlin (1975) does gloss *ak' iluk* by offering a series of exemplary gestures whose specific hand-shape morphology is culturally and communicationally salient: to "show /by pointing, by holding palm down to show height of object, cornfield, or animal, with forefinger raised to show height of child/." Zinacantecs thus observe a widely cited conventional use of different handshapes to signal size. Compare the classic description of such conventions in Foster (1948, p. 237), whose original citation was brought to my attention by David Wilkins.

[2]There are a few descriptive expressions for other hand shapes, for example, *much' k'ob* or *mich' k'ob*, "make a fist (lit., squeeze one's hand)," *ch'ivet k'ob*, "with fingers widespread." A number of verbs in Laughlin's (1975) dictionary of Zinacantec Tzotzil suggest conventional gestures or uses of the hands: *velu*, "motion (to someone) with circular motion of the hand"; *yom*, "hold in both hands"; *vutz' ba*, "push down on shoulders with hands"; *ixin*, "shell corn with the hand"; *ak' k'ob*, "shake hands"; *nup k'ob*, "bow (to meet with one's forehead the extended hand of an older person in greeting)"; *tom*, "hold (in hand)"; *t'ax k'ob*, "clap"; *p'is krus*, "hold hand in sign of cross"; *mich'*, "squeeze in fist or hands"; *net'*, "press (with side of hand)"; *nup' k'ob*, "fold hands (in prayer)"; *k'et*, "hold or scoop in hand"; *jop*, "cup in both hands"; *tz'it*, "clean with second joint of forefinger /inside of gourd or bowl/"; *xek*, "pick up or carry by holding between thumb and forefinger"; and so on. Similarly, a number of conventional measures involve specific hand configurations: for example, *ch'ix*, "handspan"; *kejlej*, "span between thumb and knuckle of forefinger."

[3]This situation contrasts with what we can infer for other native American languages. For example, Rigsby (1965) wrote about the Nez Perce numeral *túska:s*, "seven." "*Seven* is a descriptive formation which may be segmented into /túsk-/ *point (with a finger)* and /-a:s/, a common suffix for body parts which might be considered a 'fossilized' allomorph of the first person singular pronominal clitic. *Seven*, then, may be translated literally as *pointer-my*. Starting with either hand, the seventh finger is always the first finger of the opposite hand. Unlike some American Indians of the Plains who 'point' at objects by protruding the lips, the Sahaptins pointed with their first or index fingers, as do Euroamericans. In fact, the index finger is called /tuskáwas/ *point for the purpose of* in the Northwest and Colombia River dialects" (Rigsby, 1965, p. 117). I am indebted to Courtney Handman for bringing this passage to my attention.

[4]The word is derived from the defective intransitive stem *-chi*, "say"; see Haviland (1998a). Lucy (1993) gives an extended treatment of the cognate expression in Yucatec Mayan. In other contexts, the same word functions as a demonstrative meaning "thus" and also in a construction where it suggests "all of a sudden, just."

MAL AT 18 MONTHS

Consider the following examples of what a barely verbal Zinacantec child can communicate using word and gesture. Mal (shown as M on the transcripts) is a Zinacantec infant who in this sequence is 18 months old, barely into the "one-word" stage in her spoken Tzotzil.[5] She is strapped to the back of her 18-year-old cousin (shown as L on the transcripts), one of her principal caregivers. The cousin and T, an aunt who is an occasional visitor in the household, are engaged in conversation about where Mal's mother has gone. There follows a complex interaction, from which I have extracted several evident pointing gestures.

(1) **V9607:44:27** *me' "mother"*

   5 T; much'u tzna ibat taj sme'e?
              Whose house did her mother go to?

   6 L; an, tzna me'el Alyax
              Why, to the house of old lady Arias.

   7 T; aaa?
              Oh?

   8 L; jmm.
              Mm hmm.

As the women talk, Mal has been feeding chicks, and L is cleaning corn dough off her hand. Mal has also evidently been following the conversation, and she now stares intently at T. After a short pause, she simultaneously reaches out in a "pointing" gesture and intones a word (see Fig. 7.1).[6]

       ((Mal gazes at T as tortilla dough is being brushed off her right hand)
       ((Mal extends her left hand with index finger extended, out to her left side))
       [

   9 M; me'
              Mother

---

[5]Lourdes de León studied Mal from birth; I am indebted to her for sharing her videotapes, which have allowed us to trace the genesis of Mal's gestures (see de León, 1998). Support for our research was provided by National Science Foundation grant SBR-9222394.

[6]In the transcripts, descriptions of gestures, sometimes individually labeled with letters or attributed to particular interactants for clarity, appear above and linked with an open square bracket [to the corresponding transcribed simultaneous speech.

FIG. 7.1. Mal points, "Mother."

Both women understand the combination of Mal's word and gesture to be a contribution to the conversation about the child's absent mother, as evidenced by their spontaneous "glosses" of what she has said.

10 L; bat lame'?
    Did your mother go?
11 T; bat lame'?
    Did your mother go?

Mal apparently replies to T's question, although T misunderstands her. Mal's word at line 19 sounds like the adult *ja'* "yes," which is how T interprets it. L, a frequent interpreter of Mal's utterances, corrects this reading, glossing Mal's word instead as *sa'*, a bare verb stem[7] meaning "look for." At line 17, T now understands Mal's childish pronunciation *xi'* as *si'* "firewood," as evidenced by the comments that follow.

---

[7]See de León (1999) on the remarkable ability of Zinacantec children to isolate roots from the adult stream of speech, which ordinarily clothes them in inflectional and derivational morphology.

12 M; ja'
    Yes (But: sa' = [went to] look)

13 T; ja'?
    Yes?

14 L; ba sa' xi
    *"She went to **look**," she says.*

15 M; xi'
    Firewood

16 L; si'
    "Firewood"
    [

17 T; ba sa' si' ((laughs)),
    "She went to look for firewood."

18   lek xa ka' xlok' yu'un.
    I see that she pronounces well now.

19 L; ba sa' si' xi.
    "She went to look for firewood," she says.

This little interaction illustrates several complexities that belie the presumed simplicity of pointing. First, it is unclear toward what Mal is pointing. Mal's mother—one possible "referent" of her gesture—is absent, although she has left the house compound by the path that lies in the direction Mal indicates. This direction itself illustrates the limited spatial knowledge Mal possesses; she herself rarely leaves the house compound, but she knows that it is by this path that people depart. Finally, Mal's interlocutors apparently have glossed the pointing gesture as a proto-predicate: "go that way."

Mal wants to try to feed the baby chicks, to which she refers repeatedly as *nene'* "baby." Her aunt, T, engages the little girl in "conversation," noting that the chicks have moved to another part of the yard.

(2) V9607:45:27 *taj* "over there"

42 T; bu lanene'e
    Where is your baby?

43   buy
    Where?

L, who frequently prompts Mal with suggestions about what to say, tells her to look for the chicks, guiding her with a gaze. Mal looks around, raises her arm in another clear pointing gesture in the direction of the chicks (see Fig. 7.2), and repeats L's deictic *taj* "there [distal]"—the only deictic in Mal's verbal repertoire at this point.

FIG. 7.2. *taj* "Over there."

44 L; taje vi
Over there, look.
((Mal looks, points with her left hand to her left))
((holding the pointing gesture as she speaks))
[

45 M; ta:j
Over there

46 T; a: ja' le',
Oh, there?

47   ja' anene' le'e.
That's your baby there?

48 M; *((nods))*

T continues the virtual dialogue at lines 46–47, interpreting Mal's utterance for her and eliciting a nodding assent in line 48.

In Sequence 3, Mal and her interlocutors engage in a little routinized game. The child is now clearly the center of interactional attention, and she is aping for her aunt, closing her eyes as if asleep, and pounding on her own head. Suddenly she pretends to pluck a louse from her head and pop it into her mouth (to bite it—the normal way to kill lice).

(3) V9607:46:39 *oy nan uk* "(I) have (lice), too"

76 L; oy la yuch'.
She says she has lice.

FIG. 7.3.   *tzakbo* "Grab her (louse)!"

L glosses the routine *just as she would gloss speech*: She uses the "quotative" particle *la*, which marks reported speech[8]: "*she says* she has lice." Mal now takes another "louse" from L's head and "eats" it (see Fig. 7.3). T takes up the commentary.

> M;   *((reaches for L's head and "picks a louse"))*
> 77   T;   oy la yuch' noxtok
> > *She(L) has lice, too, she (Mal) says.*
> 78   an tzakbo che'e
> > *Why, go ahead and grab them.*

Now Mal reaches out in T's direction, extending a pointing hand (see Fig. 7.4), in an obvious request to continues the game. T's reaction (spoken at line 80) makes it clear that she interprets the gesture as having both referential and imperative significance: She offers her own head for Mal to examine.

> M;   *((points at T))*
> 79   T;   aaii
> 80   oy nan uk a'a
> > *Why, perhaps (I) have (lice), too.*

---

[8]See Haviland (1987, 1989).

FIG. 7.4. *oy nan uk* "I have (lice), too."

Immediately afterward, Mal informed me that she wished to pick "lice" from my head, too, using a point aimed at my head, and repeated insistently with a grabbing hand (see Fig. 7.5).

The last of Mal's apparent pointing gestures comes as L carries the child toward the house to put her down for a nap. The sound of a baby crying in a neighboring courtyard elicits an utterance from Mal, which her aunt interprets (at line 148). Mal then amplifies her "commentary" at line 149, supplementing it with a further pointing gesture in the direction of the sound.

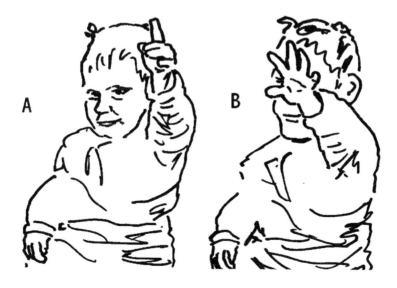

FIG. 7.5. Reaching insistently for lice.

(4) V9607:49:44

147 M; nene‘
         Baby
148 T; yu‘un la chve‘ nene‘
         (She says that) the baby wants to eat.
149 M; titi‘
         Meat
     M; ((*points out to left with hand held low.*))
     L; ((*L repeats Mal's point as she amplifies her meaning*))
         [
     M; ((*Mal raises her pointing hand*))
         [
150 L; sk'an la titi‘ taj nene‘ ch'ok'e
         (She says that) that baby wants meat, (that's why) it's crying.

At line 150, L integrates into a single complex gloss the three parts of Mal's communication (the two spoken words and the gesture), simultaneously echoing Mal's point with her own, perhaps to accompany the spoken deictic *taj* "that one." Mal's "pointing gesture" has a trajectory: It moves from low to high, suggesting to observers a relatively distant "referent" (see Fig. 7.6).

MAL'S GRANDFATHER PETUL

To get an idea of the adult pointing that provides Mal with her targets, let us turn briefly to Petul, Mal's grandfather now in his late eighties. Petul's pointing gestures are notable for their formal and conceptual complexity, and for their interactive delicacy.

FIG. 7.6. *titi‘* "(It wants) meat."

In Example (5), Petul is talking with another man who is stacking boards
he has just carried up to the path from his woodlands. Petul has adjacent
property, and he is asking about other large trees in the area that might also
be used for timber. He accompanies his questions with changes of gaze and
hand gestures that both "point to" the areas he is asking about and illustrate
iconically aspects of the terrain and the configuration of the objects there.

(5) v9611:1:7

> A: ((*left hand out South, back*))
>
> 82   p;   much'u ma yu'un ali xi ta olon
>
> *Whose is that down below . . . ?*
>
> B: ((*fingers pointing and wiggling*))____ . . .
>
> 83   olon sba li tulantik
>
> *down, above the oak trees.*
>
> 84   mol tulantik
>
> *big oak trees . . .*
>
> 85   ali tojtik oy to
>
> *There's still pine there.*
>
> 86   bu alok'es o ate'
>
> *where you got your wood from*
>
> C: ((*outstretched fingers curl inward, hand dips down, held*))____
>
> [
>
> 87   amol toj vo'ne
>
> *that big old pine tree of yours long ago?*
>
> 88   m;   . ja' yu'un i kitz'intake
>
> *That belongs to my younger brothers.*

Petul first extends his arm (A) in the direction of the particular stand of
pine trees he has in mind. He then shows by the trajectory of his backhand
sweep (B) that the pines lie in a specific direction "above" a different group
of oak trees. Finally, he identifies a specific "large pine" by showing with his
hand where it stands in relation to the reference point just established (C)
(see Fig. 7.7). Petul's pointing hand thus indicates both location via a series
of directional vectors, and also relative position (and perhaps contour of
the terrain), by changes in shape and finger motion. His gestures add considerable locational specificity to the very general spatial terms he speaks:
olon "below" and *sba* "on top of."[9]

---

[9]See de León (1995) and Brown and Levinson (1993) on the use of words denoting *up* and
down for geocentric location.

FIG. 7.7.   The pine trees below, above the oaks.

Later in the same conversation, the two men discuss several small pine trees wantonly chopped down by thieves. M, the owner, complains angrily of the destruction, directing an extended index finger in the direction (south-southeast from where the men stand) of the affected tract of land (see the left side of Fig. 7.8). Petul shortly thereafter offers a possible explanation: that the gate in the fence around that tract had been left wide open.

(6) V9611: 1:54

                          ((points and sights along index finger, South-southeast))
126   M; animal **ep** laj yixtalan ya'ele
          They just messed with LOTS(of tree)s.

     . . .

                        ((arm sweeps out right, points North-northeast)
131   P; ja' nan i level to'ox . li ti' be
          Perhaps because before the gate was gaping open

Petul points north-northeast as he speaks of the gate (see the right side of Fig. 7.8). Because the gate in question actually lies to the southeast of where the men are standing, it appears that Petul has *transposed* his perspective to the field where the baby trees were destroyed. Calculating from that position, the gate lies in the direction Petul indicates.[10] For such transposed directional gestures to work, the interlocutors must share knowledge of both the geography referred to and the principles of direction as applied to gestures.

---

[10]Systematic uses of such directional transpositions in gesture are described in Haviland (1993, 1996b).

M points SSE   P points NNE

FIG. 7.8. The gate was open before.

One can also use precisely oriented referential gestures in a hypothetical or imagined space, incorporating as appropriate props from the local surround (Haviland, 1998a, 2000). Petul, for example, once described to me how to make a cane press, known in Tzotzil as *k'av-te'* "split wood." The contraption uses two logs mounted on supporting posts; twisting the logs squeezed the juice out of cane stalks inserted between them. To illustrate one of the supporting posts, Petul used a real house post conveniently located to the right of where he was sitting. The other supporting post he created with gestures in an imaginary space to his left. To show how the cross bars were inserted into the posts he pointed to his right with his index fingers, using the real house post as a prop, first with a single index finger to show where holes were drilled (see Fig. 7.9A), and then with two fingers (Fig. 7.9B) to represent the bars themselves. The transition between A and B was rapid: first pointing to the house post (standing for imagined canepress post) with an outstretched index finger, then actually touching the post as he said *xi* "thus," then swiftly extending the second finger as he said *xchibal* "both (bars)."

(7) K'av-te'

A: ((*index finger extended out, touching house post*))
3 p; xch'ojojbe sat xi to vi
    they put holes in it this way, see?

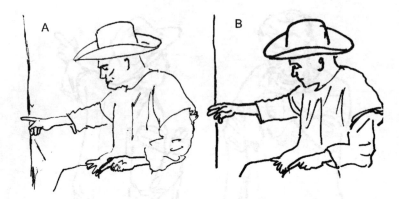

FIG. 7.9. *kav-te'* "Cane press"—"hole(s), two sticks."

> *B: ((two fingers extended, still touching post))*
> 6 p;   te matz'al xchibal li te' xi to vi
> *Both of them stuck in this way, see?*
>
>   . . .

To refer later to the two bars, Petul again used his index fingers, first illustrating how the crossbars connected to an imagined post to his left (C, in Fig. 7.10), then extending both index fingers in parallel back to his right (D) to show how the bars were supported between the two posts.

> *C: ((index fingers of both hands crossing to left)).*
> 12   ochem xchibal xi ta jote
> *And the two entered thus, on the side.*

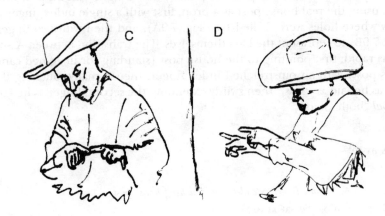

FIG. 7.10. *k'av-te'* "Cane press"—"two bars."

D: ((*both index fingers extended pointing to right*))

13 ochem xchibal xi to ta jote

The two entered thus, on the side.

Petul ends his illustration of the machine by bringing both index fingers together in the gesture space in front of his body (Fig. 7.11) to illustrate how the two bars worked together to crush the sugarcane.

As a final example, consider how Petul uses what I call *sociocentric* pointing as part of a complex genealogical discussion. Petul is telling me about the relatives of a recently deceased man, José. To locate José's father, whom I call Mol Sebastian, in genealogical space for me he glances up to the east and raises a pointing hand (see Fig. 7.12). This gesture (also shown as A in Fig. 7.13) points toward where one of José's surviving relatives, Maria, now lives. Maria is my *comadre* or "co-mother," a fictive kinswoman related to me through shared ritual obligations, and Petul thus uses *my* kinship relations to anchor his descriptions of the referents. The woman Maria and the recently deceased José were both children of the same father, Mol Sebastian. Next, to be sure I know about whom he's talking, Petul further identifies Mol Sebastian as the grandfather of my *compadre* or "co-father," Juan, and Maria as his mother. Petul now points back over his right shoulder (at Fig. 7.13B) toward where Juan lives with his father-in-law, Domingo.

FIG. 7.11. "Together."

FIG. 7.12. Sociocentric pointing: "your compadre."

FIG. 7.13. "Your compadre."

(8) Chon

               A ((left hand points up east))
13 P; ja' stot ti yajnil ti akumpa Manvele

        That was the father of the wife of your compadre Manuel.
14   smuk'totik i xun

        the grandfather of Juan

        B: ((left hand points back northwest, behind))
15   akumpa xun te sni' li romine

        your compadre Juan, the son-in-law of Domingo

        . . .

Another son of Mol Sebastian Petul identifies as the "brother-in-law of Domingo," but this man had a different mother, Mol Sebastian's first wife. In speaking about this other woman he points (at Fig. 7.14C) somewhat vaguely to his right, south, perhaps toward the house of her son, "Domingo's brother-in-law," whom Petul has just mentioned. However, the original deceased man José and my previously mentioned comadre Maria shared the same mother, as he tells me (at Fig. 7.14D), once again pointing in the direction of Maria's house.

36   sbol li romine

      The brother-in-law of Domingo

FIG. 7.14. "His mother."

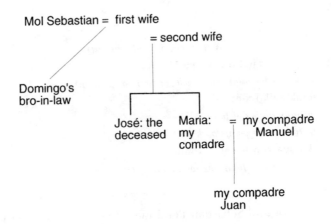

FIG. 7.15.   The deceased José's (partial) genealogical tree.

      C: ((index finger extended right, level, palm up))

37   pero . jun o sme'

     had a different mother

     . . .

     D: ((index finger up, pointing east))

45   Ja' xa sme'ik taje

     But that was their mother

The genealogical relations mentioned are diagrammed in Fig. 7.15, where the equals sign (=) symbolizes a marriage.

    Petul constructed a genealogical chain built around people he knew me to be able to identify, indeed, using my own fictive kinship links with them as a basis for his characterizations. His gestures in turn indexed the social geography of the village where we sat (see Fig. 7.16), and they functioned much like spoken anaphors to refer to, distinguish, and locate individuals. However, the precise directions of his pointing gestures, as well as his combinations of locational index with characterizing words, required indirect "sociocentric" inferences to establish links to specific individuals, a matter to which I return later.

COMPLEXITY IN POINTING

Mal's gestures and those of her grandfather illustrate the complexity of pointing and its close integration with spoken language. Although pointing may seem a primeval referential device, it is far from simple: It is complex

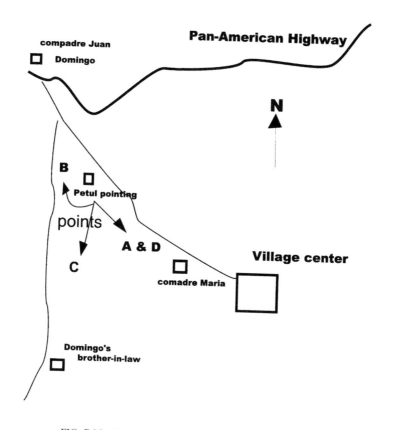

FIG. 7.16. Map of the village, showing Petul's gestures.

(a) conceptually, (b) morphologically, (c) linguistically, and (d) socio-culturally as a device for communication.

Pointing Is Conceptually Complex

Elucidating a central Peircean trichotomy of signs that distinguishes icons, indexes, and symbols, Silverstein (1976) in a classic paper underscored the dual nature of all indexical signs, including pointing gestures: They can have both a creative (or "entailing") relationship and a dependent (or pre-supposing) relationship with the "context" they index. When Petul points in the direction of my compadre's house in order to help me identify the particular woman—this compadre's wife—to whom he refers, he exploits a particular preexisting geographic and social space in the village, and our shared knowledge of who lives where within it. To be successful as a refer-ring device—to allow me to identify the woman he has in mind—his gesture *presupposes* a set of spatial relationships and my knowledge of them. The spatial context thus comes first, and the pointing gesture both depends upon and exploits it. Contrast Petul's *creative* use of the house post and the space in front of him to describe the cane press; his gestures do not rely on a previously existing space of potential referents but instead *populate* the space, establishing their referents by placing them into the interactive arena. The house post becomes a support, and Petul's pointing fingers create the "holes" into which imagined cross bars "fit." Indexical signs, in Silverstein's parlance, "project" their contexts (Silverstein, 1993): They both draw on presupposable aspects of, and help to create and structure, the contextual surround.

The dichotomy between relatively presupposing indexical signs and relatively entailing or creative ones is actually a continuum, and like other such signs pointing gestures typically have both creative and presupposing aspects. Even little Mal, pointing in roughly the same direction in three separate utterances, indexes presumed referents of quite different characters: once the chickens that are within her view (Fig. 7.2), once a neighbor child out of sight but whose cries can be heard (Fig. 7.6), and once her mother, nowhere to be seen but departed in the indicated direction (Fig. 7.1).

That interactants rely on mutual knowledge or common ground (which is precisely what is presupposed or creatively altered by indexical signs) is nowhere more apparent than in the "meaning" of *direction* in pointing gestures. In other work (especially Haviland, 1993, 1996a) I have argued that pointing makes crucial use of highly structured conceptual spaces that include points, vectors, and areas, all of which may be variously presupposed or created by the corresponding gestures. When Petul remarks to me, "That was the father of the wife of your compadre" (see again Fig. 7.13A) by the time he says the Tzotzil word for *his wife* his pointing finger has already located my compadre geographically from where we sit. The direction of his gesture (roughly toward the house of the compadre in question) helps fix his referent for both of us, although in slightly different ways. His gesture is not toward a named individual but rather (as I must infer) to a house compound. He knows to which person he is referring, and he reckons that person's place of residence to be a salient identifying feature for me. I must narrow down the *comadre* in question—one of many—taking a hint from where Petul has placed her husband (my *compadre*) on the landscape.

Moreover, pointing transposes and laminates these conceptual spaces in characteristically complicated ways. In the second frame of Fig. 7.8, Petul points to the north while referring to a "gate." The gate in question actually lies south of where he stands, but the two interlocutors have relocated themselves discursively in a field still farther to the south. Petul can point north and be understood thus to index the perspective of a man in the field

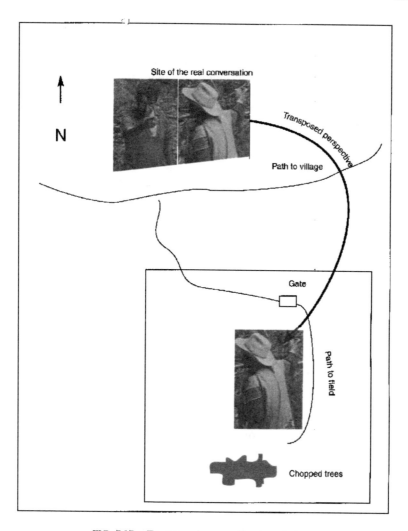

FIG. 7.17. Transposed perspective in pointing.

where the destroyed trees lay, looking north *from there* to the gate both men can identify (see Fig. 7.17). That is, Petul and his interlocutor must imagine themselves to be standing not on the path to the village where they actually are, but rather in the field where the fallen trees are. At the same time, they must hold constant the directional orientation of Petul's gesture, transposing only its origo, to locate the gate conceptually. Such transpositions, signaled and at once exploited by pointing, are perhaps the clearest expression of the conceptual complexity underlying such indexical reference.

Pointing Is Morphologically Complex

In the exhibits, Mal and Petul point with outstretched index fingers using a familiar "pointing hand." Nonetheless, in Zinacantán in addition to the "index" finger various body parts (as well as other objects—hoe handles and machetes, for example) are used to "point out" things, and there are multiple accompanying bodily attitudes. Gaze alone can do the dual job of calling one's interlocutors' attention to something and indicating a direction, and one can use not only the eyes but also the chin, the shoulders, or even the lips.[11] Before his first pointing gesture in Fig. 7.14, Petul first looked up with a brief eyebrow flash in the direction he was about to indicate, anticipating his reference to my compadre who lived over that way. Moreover, although Mal points with a loose fist and outstretched index finger (a hand shape she began to master at about 11 months of age), her grandfather's gestures show at least one further standardized Zinacantec handshape for "pointing": the flat hand illustrated in Fig. 7.6.

Petul uses the flat hand (with the palm held vertically, thumb side up, fingers grouped and extended outwards) to indicate vectors or directions, in contrast with the extended index finger, which seems to denote individual referents located in particular directions. A distinction akin to that between linguistically marked genders or noun classes appears to be conventionalized here in *symbolic* hand shapes[12] that distinguish reference to individuals from reference to pure direction.[13] The flat hand apparently indicates "that away" as opposed to the index finger's "that one."

As we have seen, Tzotzil speakers can also indicate direction by gaze alone (sighting a "point" above the horizon, for example, to indicate a time of day), or by a combination of components: Petul sights along his outstretched hand in Fig. 7.7A, and his interlocutor does something similar in Fig. 7.8. Both actions suggest that there is, indeed, something to "see" in the direction of their gaze. All in all, the morphological complexity of "indicating direction" reminds us of further conceptual indeterminacies with the notion of "direction" itself. In which space are the directions to be calculated? Are they attached to individual loci, to pure vectors, to orientations (e.g., "running north-south," specifying, as it were, the shaft of an arrow but omitting the arrowhead), or to areas? At what level of resolution are entities specified? What sorts of perceptual access are available (if any, since one can point to imaginary entities in virtual spaces)? And so forth.

---

[11]See Sherzer (1972).

[12]See footnote 1 for another example of such gestural gender marking, symbolized in handshape combined with orientation.

[13]A similar distinction can be observed in the gestural accompaniments to the ubiquitous Guugu Yimithirr directional terms described in Haviland (1993), especially in gestures that accompany or appear to replace the "side terms" that denote such notions as "on the eastern side." See also Haviland (1979, 1998b).

Although a pointing gesture *indexes*, in the Peircean sense, the direction it is meant to signify—the direction "meant" is recovered from directional aspects of the physical production of the gesture itself, although perhaps in complex or transposed ways—other aspects of the significance of the gesture may be *iconically* encoded. A clear example is Mal's "grabbing" gesture in Fig. 7.5, where the form of her open, grasping hand iconically "projects" its "referent"—presumably an imagined louse—as being something graspable. (Contrast, for example, an outstretched open hand with palm face up—a familiar begging gesture that combines a conventional, symbolic action with an iconically suggestive handshape—"projecting" a desired object that can be laid in such an open hand.)

Moreover, in addition to the familiar sweeping rise of the hand or punctual extension of an outstretched limb, other sorts of formatives, including motion, accompany apparent pointing gestures. In example 5 Petul moves his outstretched flat hand evidently to indicate both the direction of the place he has in mind, the lay of the land there, and the location of one large pine in relation to a stand of oak trees. He traces details of a trajectory that corresponds to the path leading to the place he speaks about, mapping in the air relative locations and directions. Using a different convention,[14] he appears to indicate the relative distance of referents by altering the height of his index-finger point. For example in Fig. 7.14 (A and D), he suggests that the compadre he refers to with a raised pointing gesture is relatively distant, by comparison with the other compadre he mentions, toward whose house he gestures with a relatively lower backward point (Fig. 7.14B).

Different aspects of the form of pointing gestures thus relate to different "semantic domains": not just direction, but also aspects of shape (or manipulability), and proximity. The list does not stop here, however, as pointing gestures also seem to encode information about individuation or quantity. Petul's description of the cane press provides a clear example. In Fig. 7.10, he uses one outstretched finger to illustrate the hole drilled in the support posts for the cane press. He adds a second pointing digit when he mentions the second crossbar, and he continues to model the double bars with two fingers (from one hand or both) as he "points" to show where the bars are attached. In each case, his double fingers move into action just as he pronounces the corresponding word *xchibal* "both."

In talking about his interlocutor's pine tree, in example 5, Petul also appears to use gesture to individuate. He has located a stand of trees with a sweeping pointing gesture; when he mentions a specific tree—*amol toj* "your big pine tree"—his hand, still extended in the appropriate direction, appears to dip, suggesting that he now refers to a single known tree.

---

[14]The association of height of pointing gesture with distance of referent may be a widely shared convention; see Calbris (1990).

Slightly different is Petul's gesture in Fig. 7.14C. He has been enumerating different relatives of the deceased man, relating them to fictive kin of mine. Two of the individuals he has located clearly in social space, pointing with an outstretched finger in the direction of their houses at A and B. As he mentions a third relative, who had a different mother from his previous referent, he says *jun o sme'*, literally "one other [his] mother," simultaneously turning the hand palm upward and extending another outstretched index finger. The change in palm orientation seems to correspond to Petul's contrast between the two groups of people, corresponding to the two wives and families of Mol Sebastian. The extended finger appears precisely as Petul, in word and gesture, individuates his new referent—the old man's long deceased first wife—placing her in a spot in the interactional space in front of him. He thus gesturally distinguishes her from the second wife, to whom he returns at D, and who has a specific if indirect locus in space defined by the house compound of her living daughter.

The complex morphology of pointing gestures means that they are typically not "simple referring devices" but rather complex semantic portmanteaux. Indeed, pointing gestures seem much like spoken deictics, linking in a single morphological guise many of the same semantic domains—quantity, shape (or "gender"), and proximity—that characterize spoken demonstratives.

Moreover, the link between a "natural" gestural expression of a notion like *one* (a single raised digit, for example) and referential pointing suggests the possibility for gesture of a process akin to "grammaticalization." In particular, it recalls two paradigm cases of historical developments in spoken languages: the movement from demonstrative to definite article (Greenberg, 1978a), and from the numeral "one" to an indefinite marker (Givón, 1981; Hopper & Closs Traugott, 1993).[15] Some of Petul's pointing suggests that his "pointing hand" is at once a conventionalized individuating gestured numeral "one" merged with a pure directional vector "there/that." The directional significance of the deictic element (the fact that the finger points a certain way) may be bleached away, leaving only the gestural equivalent of "definiteness" ("this" as opposed to "another'), and the icon-

---

[15]The well-known use of pointing gestures as full pronouns in ASL (Bellugi & Klima, 1982) suggests a similar conclusion. Consider the following just-so story, adduced to explain the development of Germanic articles from cognate demonstratives: "The natural way of giving linguistic expression to the desire to draw attention to the definite or familiar is to qualify the noun in question with a demonstrative pronoun, i.e. with a word meaning 'this' or 'that' or both. But in this new function, the demonstrative force of the word automatically diminishes, eventually disappearing altogether; when this happens the article is born" (Lockwood, 1968, p. 86), quoted in Heine, Claudi, & Hünnemeyer, 1991). Suggestive, too, is the link between demonstratives and relative clause markers (see Heine et al., 1991, p. 183ff) in light of McNeill's suggestions about the metanarrative functions of deictics and the gestures he calls "beats" (1992, p. 188ff).

ically signaled "oneness" may be conventionally reduced to the assertion of individuation and existence ("[He had] *another* wife").

Pointing gestures serve clear anaphoric ends, even in the short exemplary fragments of Mal and Petul's discourse. For Mal, pointing gestures substitute for arguments, and for Petul they act as virtual resumptive pronouns. Moreover, they are integrated into discourse in an especially languagelike way, a topic to which I now turn.

Pointing Is Linguistically Complex

Standard wisdom links pointing to speech directly. Here is a particularly clear account that divides a pointing event into subcomponents:

> Suppose George points at a book for Helen and says "That is mine." His act of pointing is the index (*index* is Latin for "forefinger") and the book is the object. His intention is to get Helen to recognize that he is using the index to locate the book for her. To that end, he must point while she is attending. He must locate the book for her by the direction of his forefinger—a physical connection. And he must get her to see that he is pointing at the object *qua* "book" and not *qua* "example of blue," "piece of junk," or whatever. (Clark, 1996, p. 165)

On Clark's account, George wants to refer to the book, and he must locate his referent in space and time for his interlocutor. He accomplishes this dually, in this example, by pointing and simultaneously talking. Moreover, in this hypothetical case the pointing gesture is evidently linked to a specific spoken element, the demonstrative *that*. Clark argued that "[i]n language use, indicating is usually combined with describing or demonstrating" (1996, p. 168), citing as the paradigm example the use of demonstrative pronouns, linguistic elements sometimes analyzed as virtually requiring gestural specification (Levelt, Richardson, & La Heij, 1985). Of course, there is no necessity that the locating be done both by gesture and the accompanying "characterizing" speech,[16] although this is perhaps a typical case.

In the naturally occurring examples from Zinacantán one can thus ask how pointing gestures are synchronized with the accompanying talk. In Petul's conversation in the forest, some of his directional pointing follows Clark's general description of "composite signals" (1996, p. 176). In Example 5 at line 82, just as he says the demonstrative *xi* "this way," his hand sweeps out in the direction of the field he is speaking about. He further

---

[16]Indeed, the division of labor between pointing gesture and accompanying talk may be quite different, as when Petul characterizes the two hypothetical crossbars of the cane press both in words and with double extended fingers.

specifies the direction in words: *ta olon* "below," referring to the lay of the land. Here demonstrative, descriptor, and pointing gesture all coincide temporally and complement one another referentially.

However, when the two men talk about the destruction of small trees, the pointing gestures bear a more problematic relation to the talk. In example 6, both men point, but neither issues an explicit spoken demonstrative. When Petul refers in speech to the "open gate," one might associate his gesture with the (transposed) location of his referent. In the same exchange, Petul's interlocutor's sights along his pointing finger exactly when he says *ep* "lots," referring to the baby trees felled by the thieves. Both gestures are simultaneous with descriptive predicates, and in neither case is there a clear spoken referent—demonstrative or otherwise—to associate with the gesture. Petul's description of the cane press at example 7 uses spoken demonstratives (*xi* to "this way"), but now his pointing gestures are produced well before the demonstratives are pronounced. Similarly, in example 8, Petul makes a pointing gesture precisely when he begins to utter the noun phrase associated with each new referent (relatives of the dead man), but the "locating" relation that may typically obtain between referent and index is nowhere expressed in words. (Only in line 45 is there a verbal demonstrative, *taj* "that one yonder," but the gesture has been in place since the beginning of the breath group.)

One may conclude that although pointing gestures may frequently, perhaps even canonically, be associated both referentially and synchronously with spoken demonstratives, such a link is not always present. Spoken demonstratives, of course, occur in nondemonstrative uses (e.g., as relative pronouns), which expect no gestural complements. And pointing gestures can occur emancipated from any specifically indexical expressions, perhaps even with no associated verbalized referents.

This functional complementarity (or autonomy) between gesture and speech is even clearer in the utterances of young children. Mal's pointing gesture in the opening example (Fig. 7.1) appears together with or just after her spoken *me'* "mother." Later in the sequence, having been instructed to look at some baby chicks *taj* "over there," Mal first looks, then points, and while holding the point repeats *taj* (Fig. 7.2). In the lice-picking game, Mal makes her pointing and reaching gestures without words (although she utters a little demanding syllable, *aa'*, when she insists on picking *my* lice at Fig. 7.5). In each of these cases, there is no clear synchronization between word and point: If there is a "lexical affiliate" in any of these cases, it is *taj* "over there"—a deictic that, as we have seen, frequently receives gestural supplementation in adult speech. Here the gesture comes well before the echoed verbalization.

In the other cases, either the gesture is independent of speech, or it seems to act as a kind of proto-syntactic frame for which the single word utterance is more like an argument. Indeed, in example 1 the adult gloss for Mal's little performance is exactly "Mother went." The caregivers appear to treat the *combination* of word and gesture as a virtual (proto-syntactic) construction, with the spoken *me'* "mother" providing the "subject" and the pointing gesture supplying the predicate (something like "[go] thataway").

In Fragment 4, the relative timing between Mal's words and her gesture is more complex. A baby is heard crying in a neighboring yard. Mal begins the sequence with a spoken word, *nene'* "baby." Her caregiver provides a fuller gloss—"(She says that) the baby wants to eat"—after which once again Mal speaks a word, *titi'*, a baby-talk word for "meat." Only now does her gesture appear: She points in the direction of the baby's cry. Once again, the caregiver offers a "gloss" that encompasses the whole sequence, Mal's two words and her pointing gesture: "(She says that) that baby wants meat, (that's why) it's crying." This holophrastic gloss also appears to treat gesture as a proto-predicate (or at least some kind of virtual frame) to which the spoken arguments are attached.[17]

Although Tzotzil provides no satisfying metalinguistic label for "pointing gesture," the fact that caregivers gloss children's discrete gestures as virtual equivalents to speech suggests that the movements are both segmentable and recognizable in the stream of communicative behavior. They are treated much the way spoken deictics are treated, integrated into metalinguistic glosses just as spoken counterparts might be. In the examples, we see two strategies for glossing the child's intended communications. One uses the explicit verb of speaking *xi* "[she] says," as illustrated in Example 1. The other attaches the "hearsay" particle *la* to a putative interpretation, marking it as illocutionarily attributable to the gesturer. Yet although they are treated metalinguistically as "utterances," the gestures are synchronically autonomous, or at least are potentially decoupled from any explicit verbalizations.

The influential typology of gestures known as "Kendon's continuum" (McNeill, 1992, p. 37; Kendon, 1988) orders different sorts of gestural phenomena according to their "languagelike properties" and their relationship to speech. It puts "gesticulation"—which McNeill characterizes as "id-

---

[17]Longitudinal Zinacantec data, in the research of Lourdes de León, suggest the early integration of pointing and verbalization during acquisition, and likely links to a kind of proto-syntax—including such hallmark characteristics as compositionality, sequencing, and argument structure—that precede verbalization. The anecdotal examples shown provide only a glimpse of the combinatorial possibilities, whose full exposition is impossible here. Space limitations also prevent me from describing the genesis of pointing in Mal's emerging linguistic abilities—part of the original conference presentation on which this chapter is based. Pointing appears in Mal's repertoire by about 8 months of age, although it develops adultlike morphology only at 11 months. It is integrated with her first verbalizations, and it continues to play a central role in her communications, with or without accompanying talk, well into her third year. See Haviland (1998a).

iosyncratic spontaneous movements of the hands and arms accompanying speech" (1992, p. 37) and which he takes to include deictic gestures such as pointing—at the least languagelike end of the spectrum. Such gestures are opposed, for example, to conventionalized "emblems," which must meet languagelike standards of well-formedness and which, unlike gesticulation, "have as their characteristic use production in the absence of speech" (McNeill, 1992, p. 38). There is thus an apparent paradox. Deictic gestures are included among the least languagelike gesticulations in terms of their formation and their characteristic appearance *together with* verbalization—on some accounts, necessary accompaniments to such words as demonstratives. Yet in terms of their segmentability, glossability, and potential temporal autonomy from speech (not to mention the apparent conventions of well-formedness that may sometimes apply to them), pointing gestures are much more emblematic in character than, for example, iconic gestures.[18] Indeed, the considerations in this section suggest that pointing is simply *part of language*, albeit an unspoken part: like emblems, autonomous from speech while serving speechlike ends, and also unlike emblems tightly linked pragmatically to such parts of spoken language as deictic shifters.[19]

Pointing Is Socioculturally Complex

Let me conclude my excursion into the wilds of pointing[20] by returning to the ethnographic interests that prompted it in the first place. Spoken language involves elaborate descriptors, lexical hypertrophy, and a variety of devices to emancipate interlocutors from the confines of the immediate here and now. In some cases—the "essential indexicals" (Perry, 1979)—links to this I-here-now are necessarily built into language. However, in many other cases—the shifty inspecificity of demonstratives, for example—explicit definite descriptions might do the job better, on at least some philosophers' semantico-referential accounts of language. Why say *that* when one could avoid confusion by intoning *the blue book balanced on the corner of*

---

[18]As we have seen, pointing disobeys the apparent tight synchrony between iconic gestures and their "lexical affiliates" (Kendon, 1980a; Schegloff, 1984), in which iconic gestures just precede or coincide with the associated words.

[19]Little wonder, if this is true, that in signed languages deictic shifters *are* pointing gestures.

[20]In the conference to which the original presentation of this chapter was a contribution, one section was devoted to the study of "pointing in the wild." As a specimen collector, I recognize that my reflections on the particular items pinned by their wings to my ethnographic wall have been collectively informed by the comments and criticisms of other participants in the conference. I wish particularly to thank Laura Petitto, Susan Goldin-Meadow, Adam Kendon, Herb Clark, and especially Chuck Goodwin and Danny Povinelli for their insights on this material, insights that I have not always managed to assimilate into my own understanding.

the desk in Room 114? And why, of all things, point, when the resulting referential indeterminacy is potentially even worse?[21]

Common arguments about the efficiency of linguistic expressions (Barwise & Perry, 1983) go a long way toward answering such deliberately naive questions. Petul's conversation with his interlocutor in the forest illustrates how pointing and the judicious use of spoken demonstratives can
replace whole reams of difficult explanation. Indeed, the two men largely
work out in the process of description just what it is they are describing—
among other things, *which* stand of trees in *which* field. However, other
communicative virtues of pointing—some linked firmly to interactive
sociocultural practice—emerge from exhibits like those I have adduced
from Zinacantán.

For one thing, pointing can accomplish otherwise impossible reference.
Mal at the "one-word stage" has a highly limited repertoire of referring expressions, the majority of which are verbs.[22] When she points to indicate a
referent, no words are spoken, largely because she has no words to speak.
When there are no obvious available descriptors (e.g., when one can't think
of the appropriate words) adults have recourse to the same device.

More interesting is the expressiveness of the unspoken. The well-known
Australian prohibition on speaking the names of the dead is a single example of more general culturally driven reluctance to speak certain words or
names, prohibitions that can be neatly observed and circumvented by
pointing. A large part of Petul's gesturally rich genealogical discourse in example 8 is motivated by strained relations with some of the individuals he
must mention, whose usual names and exact kin relations he is unwilling to
state explicitly. At the time he was in an active feud with both my compadres
Domingo and Juan (Domingo's son-in-law), and thus he chose both an
alterocentric descriptive phrase—based on my relationship with them
rather than his own much closer genealogical tie—and a distancing gesture
to insert them into the conversation. That is, although there were many
referentially clearer alternative ways for Petul to identify the people in question, the indirection of his chosen means of referring—pointing (sometimes fleetingly and almost covertly, as in Fig. 7.13B) in the general direction of houses of relatives of the referents—invited me to infer about whom
he was talking without having simply to come out and say their names
plainly. The Cuna "pointed lip gesture" (Sherzer, 1972) sometimes associates derogatory, if not downright vulgar, connotations with its referent, and
thus has the virtue of silence. Signaling a pick in basketball or a desired set
in volleyball, with a pointing finger discretely hidden from certain others'
eyes, is a related phenomenon.

---

[21]See Wittgenstein (1958, section 85) and Quine (1960).
[22]See de León (1999).

The interactive potency of pointing can go further still. Zinacantec children are notoriously shy around non-family members, and in some circumstances they simply will not talk to strangers. When she will sometimes not *say* what she wants, Mal is nonetheless often willing to *point*, as if the words are more difficult (or more dangerous) than the gesture, or as if the gesture is less compromising than the words.

Most striking to the anthropologist, perhaps, is the inferential and interactive potency of pointing. Indexicals are, in general, potentially *creative*; they effect changes on the "spaces" they implicate, populating them, transforming them, and rendering these changes exploitable in subsequent interaction. To have such an effect, however, they draw interlocutors into active participation. Petul, when a younger man not yet deaf and blind, was renowned in Zinacantán as a master speaker. His graphic description of the cane press, in which he virtually reconstructs the contraption before my very eyes, is a mild example of the techniques he employs to involve his interlocutors in his narratives. A central device for invoking the visible and the invisible, the present and the absent, in Petul's discourse is pointing.

REFERENCES

Barwise, J., & Perry, J. (1983). *Situations and attitudes.* Cambridge, MA: MIT Press.

Bates, E., Bretherton, I., Shore, C., & McNew, S. (1983). Names, gestures, and objects: Symbolization in infancy and aphasia. In K. E. Nelson (Ed.), *Children's language* (Vol. 4, pp. 59–123). Hillsdale, NJ: Lawrence Erlbaum Associates.

Bellugi, U., & Klima, E. (1982). From gesture to sign: Deixis in a visual-gestural language. In R. J. Jarvella & W. Klein (Eds.), *Speech, place, and action. Studies in deixis and related topics* (pp. 297–314). Chichester: Wiley.

Brown, P., & Levinson, S. C. (1993). "Uphill" and "downhill" in Tzeltal. *Journal of Linguistic Anthropology, 3*(1), 46–74.

Calbris, G. (1990). *The semiotics of French gesture.* Bloomington: University of Indiana Press.

Clark, H. H. (1996). *Using language.* New York: Cambridge University Press.

de León, L. (1995). *The acquisition of geocentric location by Guugu Yimithirr (Australia) children.* Working Paper 31. Cognitive Anthropology Research Group at the Max Planck Institute for Psycholinguistics, Nijmegen, the Netherlands.

de León, L. (1998). The emergent participant: Interactive patterns in the socialization of Tzotzil (Mayan) infants. *Journal of Linguistic Anthropology, 8*(2), 131–161.

de León, L. (1999). Verb roots and caregiver speech in early Tzotzil (Mayan) acquisition. In B. A. Fox, D. Jurafsky, & L. A. Michaels (Eds.), *Cognition and function in language* (pp. 99–119). Stanford, CA: CSLI.

Foster, G. M. (1948). *Empire's children, The people of Tzinzuntzan* (Publ. No. 6). Washington, DC: Smithsonian Institute of Social Anthropology.

Givón, T. (1981). On the development of the numeral "one" as an indefinite marker. *Folia Linguistica Historica, 2*(1), 31–53.

Greenberg, J. H. (1978). How does a language acquire gender markers? In J. H. Greenberg (Ed.), *Universals of human language* (Vol. 3, pp. 47–82). Stanford, CA: Stanford University Press.

Haviland, J. B. (1979). Guugu Yimidhirr. In R. M. W. Dixon & B. Blake (Eds.), *Handbook of Australian languages, 1* (pp. 27–182). Canberra: Australian National University Press.

Haviland, J. B. (1987). Fighting words: Evidential particles, affect and argument. *Proceedings of the Berkeley Linguistics Society, 13.*

Haviland, J. B. (1989). Sure, sure: Evidence and affect. *Text, 9*(1), 27–68.

Haviland, J. B. (1993). Anchoring, iconicity, and orientation in Guugu Yimithirr pointing gestures. *Journal of Linguistic Anthropology, 3*(1), 3–45.

Haviland, J. B. (1996a). *Pointing, gesture spaces, and mental maps.* Electronically published multimedia discussion paper, Language-Culture List, http://www.cs.uchicago.edu/l-c/archives/subs/haviland-john/, April 22.

Haviland, J. B. (1996b). Projections, transpositions, and relativity. In J. J. Gumperz & S. C. Levinson (Eds.), *Rethinking linguistic relativity* (pp. 271–323). Cambridge: Cambridge University Press.

Haviland, J. B. (1998a). Early pointing gestures in Zinacantán. *Journal of Linguistic Anthropology, 8*(2), 162–196.

Haviland, J. B. (1998b). Guugu Yimithirr cardinal directions. *Ethos, 26*(1), 25–47.

Haviland, J. B. (2000). Pointing, gesture spaces, and mental maps. In D. McNeill (Ed.), *Language and gesture* (pp. 13–46). Cambridge: Cambridge University Press.

Heine, B., Claudi, U., & Hünnemeyer, F. (1991). *Grammaticalization, a conceptual framework.* Chicago: University of Chicago Press.

Hopper, P. J., & Closs Traugott, E. (1993). *Grammatizalization.* Cambridge: Cambridge University Press.

Kendon, A. (1980). Gesticulation and speech: Two aspects of the process of utterance. In M. R. Key (Ed.), *Relationship between verbal and nonverbal communication* (pp. 207–227). The Hague: Mouton.

Kendon, A. (1988). How gestures can become like words. In F. Poyatos (Ed.), *Cross-cultural perspectives in nonverbal communication* (pp. 131–141). Toronto: Hogrefe.

Laughlin, R. M. (1975). *The Great Tzotzil dictionary of San Lorenzo Zinacantan.* Washington, DC: Smithsonian Institution.

Levelt, W. J. M., Richardson, G., & La Heij, W. (1985). Pointing and voicing in deictic expressions. *Journal of Memory and Language, 24*(2), 133–164.

Lock, A. (1978). *Action, gesture and symbol: The emergence of language.* London: Academic Press.

Lockwood, W. B. (1968). *Historical German syntax.* Oxford: Clarendon.

Lucy, J. A. (1993). Metapragmatic presentationals: Reporting speech with quotatives in Yucatec Maya. In J. A. Lucy (Ed.), *Reflexive language* (pp. 91–125). Cambridge: Cambridge University Press.

McNeill, D. (1992). *Hand and mind: What gestures reveal about thought.* Chicago: University of Chicago Press.

Perry, J. (1979). The problem of the essential indexical. *Nous, 13,* 3–21.

Quine, W. V. O. (1960). *Word and object.* Cambridge, MA: MIT Press.

Schegloff, E. (1984). On some gestures' relation to talk. In J. M. Atkinson & J. Heritage (Eds.), *Structures of social action: Studies in conversation analysis* (pp. 266–296). Cambridge: Cambridge University Press.

Sherzer, J. (1972). Verbal and nonverbal deixis: The pointed lip gesture among the San Blas Cuna. *Language and Society, 2*(1), 117–131.

Silverstein, M. (1976). Shifters, linguistic categories, and cultural description. In K. Basso & H. Selby (Eds.), *Meaning in anthropology* (pp. 11–56). Albuquerque: University of New Mexico Press.

Silverstein, M. (1993). Metapragmatic discourse and metapragmatic function. In J. A. Lucy (Ed.), *Reflexive language* (pp. 33–58). Cambridge: Cambridge University Press.

Wittgenstein, L. (1958). *Philosophical investigations.* Oxford: Blackwell.

Chapter 8

Why Pointing With the Index
Finger Is Not a Universal
(in Sociocultural and Semiotic Terms)

David Wilkins
Center for Aphasia and Related Disorders,
VA Northern California Health Care System

This chapter examines cultural variation in pointing gestures and discusses what this reveals about cross-cultural differences in the semiotics of pointing. In particular, I use data from speakers of Arrernte, a central Australian (Pama-Nyungan) language, to challenge and clarify two widely held views: (a) that pointing with the index finger is a universal human behavior, and (b) that pointing with the index finger is not socially transmitted but is a basic (natural) form of reference. Although some Arrernte pointing forms, including an "index-finger point," may look familiar to "Standard Average Europeans," a close examination of the form and function of such pointing gestures reveals that they are, in fact, quite culture specific in the range and nature of allomorphic variants of the points, the range of possible interpretations given to the points, the body space they are deployed in, and typical contexts of use. In short, I utilize data from an Australian cultural group that appears to manifest index-finger pointing to argue that pointing with the index finger is *not* a universal in sociocultural and semiotic terms. Pivotal in this argument is the fact that the Arrernte have both a fixed metalanguage for talking about pointing, and they have their own native theory concerning how pointing is a structured semiotic that plays a critical role in interactive communication.

In a number of recent papers, Haviland (1993, 1996a, 1996b) used data from speakers of another Australian language, Guugu Yimithirr (Pama-Nyungan), to make several important observations concerning pointing as a culturally and semiotically complex phenomenon. His work concentrated primarily on broader pragmatic and discourse-functional issues concerning pointing in relation to both speech and cognition, but has not looked in detail at the formal properties of pointing gestures, nor has it explored the degree to which Guugu Yimithirr speakers are conscious, or meta-aware, of their pointing behaviors. I am interested in meta-awareness and available standard terminology for methodological reasons: Such evidence allows us to more readily explore the boundary between those aspects of a system that are above the level of conscious awareness and those that are below it, and thereby allows one to investigate the nature of conventionalization and sign structure more clearly. So, in what follows, I extend and complement Haviland's research by discussing the role of pointing as it is understood and described by a different Australian group. In particular, I hope to demonstrate that the Arrernte native classification and theory of pointing add another dimension to the discussion of pointing that allows us to step back and take a fresh view of what may be culture specific and what may be universal. As far as the index finger is concerned, we see that, cross-culturally, the index-finger pointing form varies in the functions it is used for, and that the functions "Standard Average Europeans" attribute to the index-finger point are regularly, and conventionally, carried out by other morphological forms of pointing, including other body parts beyond the hand (e.g., lip pointing and eye pointing). Thus, there is no absolute universal alignment of form and function.

This chapter is organized as follows. After describing and assessing previous claims concerning index-finger pointing, I describe the Arrernte folk classification of pointing. Then, I briefly discuss the teaching and transmission of pointing behavior. Finally, I discuss the bearing that the Arrernte facts have on the two main claims that I am challenging in this chapter, and I conclude.

WHAT IS MEANT BY THE PROPOSITION THAT "POINTING WITH THE INDEX FINGER IS A HUMAN UNIVERSAL"?

Despite that researchers generally lament that there has been little cross-cultural research on gestural behavior, it has still been common to regard deictic pointing with the index finger as a human universal. Moreover, it is no trivial universal; the "index-finger point" has been taken as a critical stepping-stone in the evolution of language (Hewes, 1981, 1996; Rolfe, 1996), a key distinguishing feature between humans and other primates (Povinelli & Davis, 1994), an innate component of the human language acquisition device (Bates, Oconnell, & Shore, 1987), a form of reference basic to human nonverbal communication (Butterworth, 1995), and "the royal road to language for babies" (Butterworth, chap. 2, this volume). The following are typical of the statements made:

Pointing with the index finger is a universal human (*Homo sapiens*) behavior found in cultures around the world. (Povinelli & Davis, 1994, p. 134)

The use of an outstretched arm and index finger to denote an object in visual space may reflect hominid evolutionary adaptations of the index finger and thumb and be species-specific to man. . . . *The most plausible interpretation of our data, when it is taken in this wider context, is that pointing is not socially transmitted, nor is it derived from prehension. Our findings support the view that pointing is a species specific form of reference that is basic to human nonverbal communication.* (emphasis added; Butterworth, 1995, pp. 334– 335, based on laboratory child acquisition studies of children to 2 years, in a Western context)

The most popular form of deliberate guide-signing in our species is undoubtedly the Forefinger Point. (Morris, 1978, p. 64)

Two contributions to this volume that argue carefully, and quite persuasively, for the privileged nature of the index finger in pointing are those of Butterworth and Povinelli et al. However, when, for instance, Povinelli and colleagues (chap. 3, this volume) say of the index-finger point that "to our knowledge, the pointing gesture has been found in every human culture examined thus far," how are we best to interpret the claim? What is the pointing gesture such that it can be claimed to have been found in each culture examined? Because at this point in their discussion they are only discussing the structural form of the point—taking Franco and Butterworth's (1996) definition of the canonical pointing gesture as "the simultaneous extension of the arm and index finger towards a target"—one might assume they are merely talking about a universal ability to extend one's index finger and move it into (or toward) a position (as in picking one's nose; or poking someone in the ribs; or reaching to touch something with the tip of the index finger). If this is the extent of the universality claim, then there are no objections. Certainly a prerequisite to being able to point with the index finger is the ability to physically isolate the index finger, and Povinelli and Davis' (1994, p. 137) findings that there is "a topological difference between chimpanzees and humans in the resting state of the index finger" and that "[h]umans appear to possess a natural inclination for the index finger to protrude above the level of the other fingers, whereas chimpanzees do not" are instructive regarding species-specific morphological differences that could, down the line, influence the manifestation of the structural aspects of pointing as a semiotic act. But those same morphological differences would presumably influence countless different potential uses of the extended index finger (either for instrumental use or for other gestures beyond pointing, like baton beats or gesturing the number "one"). It seems clear, however, that Povinelli and his colleagues have a stake in more than just the universality of the structural form of pointing because they are interested in the "psychological operations that attend (and perhaps cause)" pointing as a communicative referential behavior. Moreover, I suspect the definition of the structural form they have chosen is not as free of such psychological interests as they might like us to believe because, in its usual application by developmental psychologists, the actual interpretation of the definitional element *towards a target* already precludes a number of behavioral acts (ones not considered to be referential pointing).

As an initial challenge to the focus that has been placed on the index finger in pointing, I take a brief look at what we know about the distribution of index-finger pointing cross-culturally. For current purposes, I presume that researchers at the very least identified the three criteria offered by Rolfe (1996, p. 776) for identifying a behavioral act as an act of ostension. He wrote: "Ostension has three important facets: it is for another (and is hence situated in the earlier dialogic frame); it implies the addressee understands what is being pointed at; and it is oriented on the speaker—that is, it is 'deictic.' " To pursue issues of occurrence and distribution, I also set up a contrast of index-finger pointing and lip pointing cross-culturally. Unfortunately, in a number of instances, because of the paucity of available descriptions, I have had to rely on personal communications from trusted researchers.

"Index-Finger Pointing" Versus "Lip Pointing" in Seven Cultures

One culturally widespread deliberate pointing behavior that can often be found as the preferred referential pointing strategy, supplanting index-finger pointing for that honor, is lip pointing. The relation between lip pointing and index-finger pointing is little studied, and claims about the former in relation to the latter are often premised more on conjecture than actual research. Although Butterworth (chap. 2, this volume) boldly claims that "[w]e may describe pointing as a universal gesture in babies, given the geographical dispersion of the longitudinal studies," he cites neither the geographical spread nor any supporting studies, and it is quite clear that no one has studied the child development of pointing in a culture where lip pointing is the dominant referential strategy. Two unsupported assertions in the literature concerning lip pointing in comparison to index finger pointing are:

1. That deliberate lip pointing arises as a cultural preference to index finger pointing, only where finger pointing is considered taboo or impolite

(Hewes, 1996; Morris, 1978). This is a line of argument that follows Wundt (1921/1973), who spoke of the suppression of pointing in certain cultures on the assumption that pointing developed independently and spontaneously in children.

2. That lip pointing is less precise than index-finger pointing (e.g., Hewes, 1981).

Lip pointing is far more common than researchers (e.g., Hewes, 1981) suggest. It can be found in indigenous communities on all inhabited continents, which strongly indicates independent development. Sherzer (1973, 1983, 1993), whose description of the lip point of the Kuna Indians of the Comarca de San Blas (Panama), is the best information we have on lip pointing for any group, noted:

> This Kuna gesture shares features of both form and meaning with similar pointing facial gestures that have been reported throughout the Americas, including the North American Southwest, Guatemala, and parts of South America. Questions of typological areal comparison, including the possibility of diffusion, remain to be explored. (Sherzer, 1983, p. 246)

A lip point is also common in much of central and northern Australia, where it occurs alongside index-finger and other kinds of body points, and it appears to be common and often predominant in areas of Papua New Guinea. Although apparently of more restricted distribution, instances of lip pointing also occur in Europe and Africa.

In many communities where lip pointing is predominant, hand and finger points are not ruled out. Thus, writing about the Kuna, Sherzer placed lip pointing in relation to other gestures as follows:

> Some Kuna call the [lip point] gesture *kaya sui sai* (to make a long or pointed face). . . . While the Kuna use hand gestures as batons, to accent the rhythm of their speech, there is relatively little gesturing of other kinds. Mediterranean-like gestures, which replace specific words, are unknown. *Hand and finger pointing occurs infrequently and has a set of usages essentially identical to that of the deictic pointed lip gesture; however, the latter is more common by far.* . . . all uses of the gesture are related precisely because pointing is involved in all of them. Differences in meaning result from the various communicative contexts in which the gesture occurs. (Sherzer, 1983, p. 169, italics added)

Similarly, we find the following statement by Feldman concerning the Awtuw-speaking people who inhabit the southern foothills of the Torricelli Range in northwestern Papua New Guinea:

Awtuw speakers typically point with pouted lips, sometimes accompanied by a
fortis bilabial trill with egressive velar air. One occasionally points with the index finger. (Feldman, 1986, p. 196)

Mike Olson (personal communication) contended that there is no conventional index-finger pointing among the Barai of Papua New Guinea. Lip
pointing, in contrast, is the ubiquitous deictic behavior and is highly conventionalized. Certainly the Barai were confounded when Olson used index-finger points with respect to objects as a means for getting names for
them. It was not apparently a question of reading the behavior as impolite,
but merely not understanding the referential intent. Lip pointing is the primary means of drawing a person's attention to something for naming, and
his attempts at index-finger pointing could not engage the same dialogic interaction. When I sent these observations on Barai to Bill Foley, asking for
his response to Olson's statements and any published articles that might
clarify the situation, he kindly replied as follows: "As to pointing, both
Yimas and Watam [both groups of Papua New Guinea] are as Olson describes it, pointing with the extended lower lips. I don't recall ever seeing
them point with their fingers, but I can't rule out that they don't. . . . As far
as I know, there are no published sources on this topic" (Foley, e-mail, 12
March 1996].

With respect to the Arrernte, we show that both lip pointing and index-
finger pointing coexist. In this case, lip pointing is considered more informal than index-finger pointing, which can be used in much more formal
discursive contexts. Moreover, the lip point can be used in circumstances
where someone is being secretive about reference, whereas manual points
are considered fully public acts. Among Ewe speakers of Ghana (Essegbey,
personal communication; Ameka, personal communication), there is a
similar differential distribution of index-finger pointing and lip pointing
according to circumstance. First, it should be said that for the Ewe, index-
finger pointing with the right hand is ubiquitous, but any form of gesturing
with the left hand is considered taboo. Lip points can serve most of the
same referential functions as index-finger pointing for the Ewe, but are typically used when the hands (particularly the right hand) are "out of action"
for either physical or social reasons (e.g., one has one's hands full or one is
in a context where it would be impolite to use the hands to gesture). Like
Arrernte speakers, Ewe speakers may also choose to use lip pointing when
they want to make the pointing less obvious to potential onlookers, and
thereby invoke a sort of conspiratorial relation with their interlocutor(s).[1]

---

[1]Saitz and Cervenka (1972, p. 33) provided an illustration of Colombian "lip pointing."
They presented this gesture under the heading "Directions" and described it as follows: "Lips
are pursed and then moved in the direction the performer wishes to indicate. Used for nearby
people and objects."

TABLE 8.1
Index-Finger Pointing Versus Lip Pointing in Seven Cultural Groups

	Index-Finger Pointing	*Lip Pointing*
English Speakers (U.S.)	Ubiquitous	No
Ewe speakers (Ghana)	Ubiquitous (right hand only)	Common
Arrernte speakers (Australia)	Common	Common
Kuna (Panama)	Infrequent	Ubiquitous
Awtuw (Papua New Guinea)	Infrequent	Ubiquitous
Barai (Papua New Guinea)	No	Ubiquitous

A rough overview of the kind of differential distribution of index-finger pointing and lip pointing that can be found cross-culturally is given in Table 8.1. Hewes (1981), in questioning the precision of lip pointing, has probably premised his position on a false presumption of what constitutes the totality of the deliberate behavior. It is rarely simply pointing of the lips. This discussion is particularly relevant given Butterworth's (chap. 2, this volume) suggestion that "the arm and pointing hand may have become specialized for referential communication because it is particularly useful in taking attention further to the extreme periphery," because "[f]or any given spatial separation between a pair of targets, the angular excursion of a long lever like the arm, will be greater than that of a shorter lever, like the head and nose or a pair of very short levers, like the eyes." In Sherzer's (1973, 1983, 1993) description of the Kuna lip point, he was clear that this referential action does not only involve the lips. He wrote:

> The gesture consists of looking in a particular direction and raising the head; during the raising of the head, the mouth is first opened and then closed with the lower lip thrust outward from the face. The gesture is completed by a lowering of the head to its original position. It is this constellation of raising the head and opening and closing the lips which gives the impression of pointing lips. (Sherzer, 1983, p. 169)

Although any one short lever might afford less accuracy, the coordination of eyes, head, and lips can afford detailed and precise localization and appears to be typical of lip pointing behaviors around the world. Among the Arrernte, one can easily indicate which of two similar objects next to one another in space is intended, by pointing with the lips to the relevant space and shifting the eyes towards the side of the intended entity. Moreover, sighting behavior that looks as though one is trying to see something in the distance, rather than up close, can help determine whether the extreme periphery is intended or not.

With respect to the issue of whether index-finger pointing is being culturally suppressed, due to politeness factors and/or taboos, thus leading to the predominance of an alternate deictic mechanism like lip pointing, all one can say is that the research has not been done.[2] Certainly, it is the case that in the few accounts we have of lip-pointing predominance, there is no suggestion that index pointing is being suppressed by other cultural factors. Sherzer, for instance, simply refers to index-finger points among the Kuna as a less preferred alternate that can be used in the same way as lip pointing. Furthermore, as we have seen, in some groups both types of pointing serve different functions, and either politeness is not the distinguishing factor or, in cases where features related to politeness like formality and secrecy are involved, as in the Arrernte case, the assignment of pointing behaviors does not go in the predicted direction. All we can say is that both types of pointing seem to be widespread and are able to perform very similar functions.

So, on the basis of the preceding excursion, I would say that one should rightly be cautious about statements concerning the universality of the index-finger point. Certainly groups like the Barai, Yimas, and Watam of Papua New Guinea need to be investigated more closely. Even if it were the case that we found something looking like index-finger pointing behavior among individuals, one would need to assess group understanding and group use. This brings us to the question of convention: Olson's story for the Barai given earlier is salutary because, if accurate, it suggests that index finger pointing is not "universally understandable within our species," as proclaimed by Hewes (1996, p. 588), but requires an understanding of the conventions of use. If it turns out that these groups, like the Awtuw and Kuna, do show infrequent index-finger pointing behavior alongside ubiquitous lip pointing, then we are left to ponder what conditions could possibly lead lip pointing to being favored over index-finger pointing if it is supposed to be an innate or, at the very least, a much better solution to the problem of gestural reference. The fact that so many unrelated cultures

---

[2]Hewes (1996), for instance, wrote: "The few cultural groups in which finger-pointing is tabooed, for example the Navajo of North America, do not appear to me to constitute genuine exceptions to the universality of deixis, but only specialized rules of etiquette which would be unnecessary if the gesture were in fact totally unknown (p. 588)." However, it is surely more important to stress that they *do* point with other parts of their body. Navajo is another lip-pointing dominant culture, and it is also possible to point with one's arm and hand as long as all fingers are extended. For an interesting description of this and other aspects of Navajo Culture, see the FAQs list (especially 132 and 133) at http://ourworld.compuserve.com/homepages/larry_dilucchio/faq02b.htm As is discussed later, although tabooing of index-finger pointing might be an explanation for a group like the Navajo, there is no reason to believe that this is true for all groups in which lip pointing (or some other body-based alternate to index-finger pointing) is dominant. For an interesting and critical discussion of the relation of pointing to impoliteness, which explores the complex factors involved, see Müller (1996).

have hit on lip pointing as a reasonable solution to giving gestural deictic indications must surely lead us to find more general principles underlying the development of pointing behavior than have been advanced on the basis of the presumption that index-finger pointing is king of the hill. It remains an empirical question whether, in cultures where lip pointing is dominant, babies and young toddlers actually go through a phase where they use the index finger for making reference. I have no doubt that they show index-finger extension and may do index-finger exploration of objects and may even reach for things with the index finger extended, but as Povinelli et al. (chap. 3, this volume) rightly elucidated, the "pulling out" of the pointing gesture in young infants will depend on cultural and attributional influences in interaction, which may channel them into other, culturally dominant forms. At any rate, one can now propose a comparative investigation of "pointing" acquisition among index-finger dominant pointing cultures, lip-pointing dominant cultures, and cultures where both forms of pointing are copresent and common.

In the preceding discussion, I relied on a big simplification that I am not at all content with: namely, that index-finger pointing is really the same, or sufficiently comparable, in each of the cultures that manifest it. In other words, even this presumption fails to stand up to cross-cultural scrutiny. We cannot, as outsiders, confidently identify all acts of index-finger pointing—either etically or emically—that occur in interaction in another culture. I am particularly aware of this because during my long period of interaction with the Arrernte I have had to be retrained in how to point "properly." My own use of pointing led to confusions and misunderstandings, and I have often inaccurately interpreted the content of other people's pointing. Although I am willing to concede that both Butterworth (chap. 2, this volume) and Povinelli et al. (chap. 3, this volume) have hit on factors that help to explain why the use of the index finger for pointing is so widespread and natural (even if it may not be the only candidate body part), and they have some convincing explanations for aspects of child development, I cannot possibly concede that the adult use of index-finger pointing in any one culture is identical to that in another. Certainly, as the data to be discussed next reveal, index-finger pointing among English speakers and Dutch speakers is semiotically very distinct from that of Arrernte speakers. There is a level of generational transmission, perhaps overlaid on universal underpinnings, that creates pointing anew for each generation and each culture. In the next section I go on to back up my claims by demonstrating that the index-finger point:

1. Is embedded in differently structured sign systems with different functional–pragmatic considerations (sections "Three Categories of Orienting Behavior" and "True Pointing From the Arrernte Perspective").

2. Is characterized by distinct combinatorial properties (with both linguistic and nonlinguistic signs) (sections "True Pointing From the Arrernte
Perspective" and "The Three Recognized Types of Manual Pointing").

3. Possesses a different semantic range cross-culturally (section "The
Three Recognized Types of Manual Pointing").

4. Has different physical forms cross-culturally (section "The 'One-
Finger Point' ").

5. Has a deployment in gesture space that varies cross-culturally (section
"Manual Points, Gesture Space, and System").

6. Invokes, and is only interpretable against, the unique culture-specific
(communal) common grounds of each community (section "Manual
Points, Gesture Space, and System").

One outcome of these observations is the realization that the index-
finger point is, to use Peirce's term, a mixed sign having not only indexical
properties, but also iconic and symbolic properties. In Clark's (1996)
terms, to deploy a simple index-finger point, each of three basic methods of
signaling are appealed to—indicating, demonstrating, and describing-as.
The logical conclusion is that even index-finger pointing is subject to some
degree of social and semiotic shaping that must be socially transmitted.

THE ARRERNTE VIEW OF POINTING

Background

This study is based on work with speakers of Eastern Arrernte and
Mparntwe Arrernte who are residents of Alice Springs, in the Northern Territory of Australia. Gesture behavior is ubiquitous in interaction, but is especially prevalent when speakers are describing their traditional country and
discussing events and happenings (both traditional and nontraditional) in
their home territory. As well as high rates of cospeech gesture, Arrernte
speakers also use an auxiliary (manual) sign language that is a simplified
auxiliary communication code (with its own grammar), is used on an everyday basis by all members of the speech community, and is *not* the fully elaborated sign language that Kendon (1988) describes for older Warlpiri and
Warumungu women under a speech taboo. *Quotable gestures*[3] from this auxiliary sign language may accompany speech or can be used independently
from it (see Wilkins, 1997a).

---

[3] This term is used in the sense of Kendon (1992, 1994).

For the Arrernte, pointing seems to fall somewhere between spontaneous cospeech gesture and the highly conventional signs of the sign language. I say this for two reasons. First, although there are conventional pointing handshapes (see "The Three Recognized Types of Manual Pointing"), they appear to allow greater allomorphic variation than the hand signs. Second, when Arrernte speakers signal in speech that the addressee should attend to a nonconventionalized cospeech gesture, they tend to use the demonstrating form *alakenhe* "like this; like so" in their utterance, and when they are drawing attention to a cospeech (conventional) hand sign they tend to use *nhenge-ulkere* "this sign; you know the one of this kind," but when speakers are referring to a cospeech point, there are some occasions when they use *alakenhe* "like this; like so" and some occasions when they use *nhenge-ulkere* "this sign; you know the one of this kind" to draw attention to the gesture space. These facts in themselves, I would submit, constitute the sort of evidence that is needed to establish that the group maintains some level of categorical distinction between "spontaneous gestures," "points," and "hand signs," but more direct and substantive evidence is presented later.

In the rest of the chapter, I presume as background to the Arrernte situation much of what Haviland has already established for the Guugu Yimithirr speakers living at the Hopevale Aboriginal community in northeast Queensland. Through examination of videotaped episodes of Guugu Yimithirr story telling and conversation, Haviland (1993, 1996a, 1996b) demonstrated that:

1. In talk about location and motion, both language and pointing gestures tend to be directionally anchored "in terms of what we can calculate to be the 'correct' directions, which in the G[uugu] Y[imithirr] context means correct *compass* directions." That is to say, language and gesture are both absolutely oriented in such contexts (see also Levinson, 1997, on this point).

2. Guugu Yimithirr speakers are highly gesture conscious, in the sense that gestures, especially orientational gestures, will be attended to by interlocutors and taken to be part of the asserted propositional meaning. This holds not only for obligatory cospeech gestures (like points that would accompany a phrase like "the camp that is over there"), but any oriented gesture that may occur with speech. Levinson (in press), in referring to this aspect of Haviland's work, wrote: "Haviland has put it another way: Guugu Yimithirr speakers can lie with their gestures, while we—except in limited demonstrative contexts—can hardly be said to do so."

3. One has to take account of a number of distinct deictic spaces to correctly interpret a pointing gesture—the *locally anchored space* (immediate environs of the speech event), the *interactional space* (the interpersonal space

of the interlocutors), and the *narrative space* (the space that the narrative refers to as laminated on to the immediate spaces). Shifts between spaces
have pragmatic consequences that correlate with distinct linguistic and gestural behaviors and interpretations.

4. The Guugu Yimithirr deployment of pointing gestures in narratives
demonstrates a constant awareness of social factors, such as kinship relations, language etiquette, and the geographical and directional knowledge
that others possess.

5. Knowledge of traditional country involves orientational precision,
and the use of space in communicative interaction "suggests the mnemonic
function of gesture in reconstructing knowledge about land."

Apart from the fact that the use of cardinal-point terms in Arrernte speech
is far less prevalent than in Guugu Yimithirr speech, the preceding five
points also hold for the Arrernte, who live 1,500 km to the southwest. Of
particular relevance to remember is that we are talking about a highly ges-
ture-conscious culture with predominant absolute orientational behavior
(see Pederson et al., 1998).[4]

EXPLORING THE ARRERNTE FOLK CLASSIFICATION
OF "ORIENTING BEHAVIORS"

To explore the Arrernte folk categorization of Arrernte "pointing" behaviors, videotapes made during previous field trips were shown, during two
field trips in 1995, to three adult women, and these tapes were used as the
basis of free elicitation centering on what the women could tell me about
the cospeech movements of the participants. Each consultant was interviewed separately, and the selected video clips contained episodes that were
rich with discussions of location and movement, and that contained (what
to me were) obvious examples of bodily orienting behavior. Among the
video clips were clips of natural interactive conversation, narratives about
country, elicitation games focusing on spatial issues, and direction giving.
Each woman was a participant in at least one of the video clips. The results
from these individual elicitations were then discussed with other adult
members of the Arrernte community to further confirm the degree of
agreement and meta-awareness concerning the behaviors observed. In fact,
there was a high degree of agreement as to what constituted meaningful
communicative orienting behavior, and what was not to be considered such
behavior (e.g., gaze turns that were part of the narrative, vs. gaze turns that

---

[4]Discussion of Arrernte spatial language can also be found in Wilkins (1991, 1993, 1997c)
and Wilkins and Hill (1995). Discussion of the spatial properties of another semiotic system
used by the Arrernte can be found in Wilkins (1997b).

were just responses to "eye-catching" things happening in the local space). There was also a high degree of agreement as to how these behaviors are to be named and talked about. This is significant because, as Haviland (chap. 7, this volume) notes in his discussion of pointing in Zinacantec Tzotzil, there are cultures that do not possess descriptive terms for pointing, and for whom it is not clear that "communicative metatheory will yield any category of 'pointing,' or for that matter of 'gesture,' as a distinct and recognizable class of actions." So when a cultural group, like that of the Arrernte, does provide us with a clear guide to native categories of "pointing" and "gesture," we should pay close attention to it in our descriptions and see whether it reveals any new understanding of this class of communicative actions. This section, therefore, contains an overview of the system of semantically differentiated "orienting behaviors" identified by Arrernte speakers in the task just described.

To establish the embeddedness of the Arrernte "index-finger point" within a complex, culturally determined semiotic system, the discussion that follows moves from recognized categories of orienting behavior (see "Three Categories of Orienting Behavior"), to "pointing" generally (see "True Pointing From the Arrernte Perspective"), and finally to manual pointing and its distinct subtypes (see "The Three Recognized Types of Manual Pointing"). In other words, the investigation proceeds down through a hierarchy of recognized classes of communicative action, and it is not until discussion in "The 'One-Finger Point' " that we finally encounter a canonical index-finger pointing form as one of a set of conditioned alternant morphologies of a particular Arrernte pointing gesture.

Three Categories of Orienting Behavior

The observed orienting behaviors—that is, communicative behaviors that identify a particular direction [vector] that the interlocutor is to attend to— were regularly classified by consultants into three distinct categories: *thileme* "is pointing"; *iltyeme-iltyeme* "a hand sign"; *aremele ileme* "tell by gazing."

The term *thileme* is a transitive verb that refers to intentional uses of various body parts to indicate to an interlocutor that he or she is supposed to attend to, recognize, or identify some region of space that is in the direction which the body part is oriented toward. As such, acts that are classified as being *thileme* are deictically anchored at the speaker[5] or at another discourse center as represented by the speaker. With the verb *thileme*, a noun phrase marked with accusative case (i.e., the object of the transitive verb) will refer to the thing or place that is being pointed at, whereas a noun phrase (NP) marked with the allative case -*werne*, or the spatial suffix -*theke* "-wards," indi-

---

[5] The use of *speaker* here is problematic because speech may not always be involved. Thus *pointer*, *gesturer*, and *communicator* are all also appropriate.

cates the general direction toward which the point is aimed, without necessarily entailing that the referent of the NP that is so marked is the referent of the point. In this way the difference between "pointing at camp" and "pointing camp-wards (at the dog)" is established. A common phrase used by consultants was *thilemele ileme* "to indicate by pointing (or, more literally, 'pointingly tell')". Anything that is considered an act of *thileme* is here treated as a "true" point from the Arrernte perspective, and the bulk of the rest of this chapter can be considered to be about *thileme*, rather than "pointing."

The Arrernte term *iltyeme-iltyeme* "hand signs; the act of using hand signs to communicate" actually covers a set of several hundred hand signs (see Strehlow, 1978; Wilkins, 1997a), most of which do not have an orienting function. When referring to actual uses of the auxiliary hand-sign language, consultants talk of *iltye-le ile-me* (hand-INST tell-present) "telling something with the hands" (i.e., using sign language) or *iltye-le angke-rre-me* (hand-INST speak-RECIP-pres) "speaking to each other with the hands." The term for conventionalized hand signs is a reduplicated form that is also based on the word *iltye* "hand; finger," *iltye-me-iltye-me*. A small subset of conventional (quotable) hand signs are deictic and communicate vector in an analog fashion. Most notably, the "going off toward a place" hand sign is especially common. This hand sign, illustrated in Fig. 8.1, may be called the *horned*

Form:

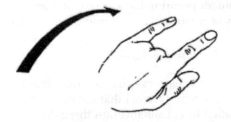

Examples:

a) "The Dreaming travels through   b) "We're going off to that   c) "They two left and walked off
to Ilewerre there, according   old camping spot."   to where there's lots of witchetty
to Aboriginal law."   grubs there in the west."

FIG. 8.1.   The horned hand sign: form and examples.

sign and is made with the little finger and index finger out, and middle and ring finger contracted. This sign is used to indicate the "global orientation of a place that is being moved to," independent of the orientation of the subpaths used to get there, with these subpaths being signaled by the "flat hand point" as described later. The *horned* sign is moved toward the target and then rapidly retracted, and is never held for any length of time at its apex. The fact that one cannot hold this sign in place relates iconically to the fact that the sign encodes motion rather than static location—it shows us where the goal of motion is oriented, not the location of the place. Although oriented and clearly deictic, such signs are never considered points. Even when used on their own as cospeech gestures, which is extremely common, consultants refused to use the verb *thileme* "is pointing" to describe the act. This was a revelation to me because I had previously observed that the use of the horned hand patterned in almost all ways like the other behaviors I had taken to be pointing behaviors and so I had assumed it was one of the ways people *thileme.*

Finally, in the context of examining meaningful orienting behavior, consultants used the phrase *aremele ileme* (seeingly tell) "tell by gazing" to refer to significant shifts of the head position and/or eye movement that they considered meaningful in the context of use. A typical phrase that was used to describe this kind of behavior was *alknge-le aremele il-irtnaneme* (eye-with gazing tell-always) "always sort of telling it by gazing with your eyes," where the thing being "told" was the location of a thing or place. This corresponds essentially to what has been called *deictic gaze* in the literature. Interestingly, in the few cases where people in the video excerpts I showed looked as if they were surveying their surroundings in order to more accurately calibrate their bearings, my consultant viewers did not consider this meaningful "gaze" behavior: Although they were "looking" they weren't "telling by looking." It is common for gaze with accompanying head turn to be moved toward places and things that cannot actually be seen by the speaker, but that are "seen in the head" (M.H.) "because of having the actual memories of the place" (V.D.).[6] Such deictic gazes may or may not co-occur with other

---

[6]In speaking about how people can "look" accurately at places that they cannot see, one consultant said *Re itelaremele ahirre areme pmere renhe.* (she/he knowingly imagining see place the) "She/he through knowing (the country) can have a vision of the place (in their mind)." Levinson (1997), in discussing absolutely oriented behavior in language and gesture among the Guugu Yimithirr, noted that, to explain the type of absolutely oriented behavior that the Guugu Yimithirr demonstrate, "a mental map of one's world with accurate absolute angles must be accessible" (p. 105), and this mental map will have the location of the place of speaking within it. I believe that quotes from my Arrernte consultants, like the one just mentioned and those represented by their English versions in the body of the article, suggest there is also a folk view of mental maps involving people's memory of places, their ability to willingly call those places up and accurately envision where the places are oriented relative to the deictic center.

body points. In fact, independent deployment of "gaze" and manual gesture is very common. Consultants were most in agreement that such "deictic gaze" was necessary for the interpretation of what was going on, and was regarded as intentional, when the shifting gaze occurred without any further body point and when it referred to something that could not possibly have been seen from the speaker's current location. Previously, in a brief report on one Arrernte man's pointing behavior, I noted (in Hendriks & McQueen, 1996) that:

> Gaze and pointing function independently of one another, although they could align. Most of the "oriented" gesturing was done *without* accompanying gaze. A consistent use of gaze without accompanying deictic point was used to identify the direction of the region that formed the deictic center for his narrative (which was distinct from his interpersonal deictic center). Gaze and pointing did align when significant new places were being introduced for the first time in narrative. (p. 123)

Before leaving the topic of deictic gaze, I should point out that this is the category of behaviors that was least certainly identified and classified by consultants.

In summary, orienting behaviors were classified into three broad classes of meaningful interactive behavior: *thileme* "pointing"; *iltyeme-iltyeme* "hand signs"; and *aremele ileme* "meaningful gaze (deictic gaze)." Some behaviors that might have been taken by a non-Arrernte analyst as "meaningful orienting behavior" were not regarded by Arrernte consultants as being "meaningful" (e.g., there were gaze behaviors that did not "tell" anything). Furthermore, a manual gesture that I, as an outside analyst, would have regarded as a deictic "pointing" gesture and so would have expected to be describable by the verb *thileme* "pointing" was instead classed by Arrernte consultants as a hand sign. Finally, manual pointing and deictic gaze are able to function as disengaged and independently meaningful systems, and this is in distinct contrast to the English and Dutch speakers we have observed (see also Levinson, in press). Having thus embedded "pointing" within the context of other recognized meaningful orienting behaviors, we can now turn to an examination of the subclassification of "true pointing," or to be more accurate, *thileme*.

True Pointing From the Arrernte Perspective

From the Arrernte perspective, there are three different body parts that can conventionally be used to *thileme* "point": the hand, mouth, and eyes. Speakers' own metacommentaries on how, why, and when these different body points are deployed, coupled with observations of actual use in day-to-day interaction, reveal that Arrernte pointing is a structured semiotic field. The relevant parameters in this field involve the visible availability of the referent, the formality of the context, and whether one is attempting to create or maintain an air of secrecy.

When you "tell by pointing with the eye"—*alknge-le thilemele ileme* (lit. eye-with pointingly tell)—you first catch your interlocutor's eye and then shift your eye noticeably within the socket toward a particular referent. There is typically no accompanying head movement. This is considered a "secret" point, and is used with close familiars in an informal interactive context, and reflects a conspiratorial mood. It is used when one does not want other potential onlookers to see what is being referred to, and is often accompanied by hushed speech or restricted (hidden) signing. The eye point is always directed toward a visibly available object in local space, but this object may only serve to refer indirectly to the actual intended conceptual referent. Thus, when two Arrernte women were speaking conspiratorially about a colleague who works in the same office, they made reference to the colleague through an eye-point to her empty chair.

Earlier, I noted that Arrernte people also use lip pointing. In fact, their term for this form of pointing is *arrakerte-le thilemele ileme* (mouth-with pointingly tell) "telling by pointing with the mouth." The mouth point is made by orienting one's head face-on toward a referent while protruding both lips (sometimes just the bottom lip). When several like objects are in close proximity to one another, the eyes shift toward the intended referent. In cases where the referent is not visible or not readily accessible, the degree of head tilt helps indicate distance. An exaggerated squinting of the eyes may accompany the mouth point when large relative distance is being indicated, and when an object is particularly close and available. Thus, the mouth point may saliently involve the lips, but also involves the coordinated action of the head (in both rotation and tilt) and eyes (both the eyeballs and eyelids). This point is only used with close familiars, although one also sees it used in extreme cases when both hands are occupied. It can be used for both secret and openly public pointing, and it can refer either to visibly available local objects or objects that are not visible and are beyond the local space. In this latter case, pointing is absolutely oriented, and the mouth point gives the bearings of the intended referent.

Such mouth pointing is so widespread among Central Australian groups that manuals for language learners often include tips or warnings about this phenomenon. For instance, in the section on demonstratives in *Wangka Wiṟu: A Handbook for the Pitjantjatjara Language Learner* (Eckert & Hudson, 1988), the authors provided a special note that stated, "[a] common way of pointing to something in Pitjantjatjara culture is to extend the bottom lip and raise the chin at the same time" (p. 87). As in Arrernte, this form of pointing also tends to have a conventionalized term or phrase that is used to refer to it. Thus, the Kukatja Dictionary (Valiquette, 1993) records both the verb form *tjaa yurrila* (lit. move the mouth) "show direction

with one's lips" and the nominal form *tjaa yurri* "indicating by mouth movement" (p. 283). A note appended to this last entry states with respect to
Kukatja mouth pointing that, "[w]hen asked about a direction or the time
of the day in words or in sign language, people will frequently answer by
raising the head and turning it in the compass direction being indicated or
towards the sun and its height in the sky." Mouth pointing is encountered
so frequently that non-Aboriginal people who have come to work with Aboriginal people in Central Australia readily pick up the convention and often tend to overuse it or use it inappropriately.

Finally, we come to manual points. The phrase for this form of pointing
in Arrernte is *iltye-le thilemele ileme* (lit. hand/finger pointingly tells) "tell by
pointing with the hand/finger." Like many Australian languages, Arrernte
does not distinguish lexically between "hand" and "finger," and the same
term *iltye* refers to both. There are three distinct forms of manual pointing
that are recognized by the Arrernte, and each of these is dealt with in the
following subsection. However, there are several attributes that are associated with manual pointing generally. First, manual points are considered
fully public gestures. This does not mean there are not more discrete and/
or indirect uses of manual pointing, but such uses appear to have more to
do with the speaker's relation to the referent or are a metacomment on the
content rather than reflecting the degree of public accessibility to what is
being said. Second, although manual pointing can be used in informal
everyday interaction, it is also regularly used in the most formal of situations, for example, in ceremony and public oration. In certain highly restricted and formal contexts, as when undertaking minimal interaction with
"respected" kin-relations that are to be "avoided," the only form of pointing
that is permitted is manual pointing. Among other things, unlike "eye
pointing" and "mouth pointing," manual pointing does not require the interlocutors to be facing one another for effective execution and, given the
regular prohibition on any form of direct face-to-face contact with certain
"respected" kin relations, this makes it the only plausible method of pointing when interaction is required. Finally, like "mouth-pointing," manual
pointing is used for indicating both visibly available referents as well as nonvisible referents. In the case of nonvisible referents, once again pointing is
absolutely oriented, and the angle at which the arm is held will show relative distance (in a range of between 30° and 140° from rest at the side of the
body). Figure 8.2 provides a rough indication of how arm angling in manual pointing corresponds to the use of the three Arrernte demonstrative
terms—*nhenhe* "this; here," *yanhe* "that (mid); there (mid)," *nhakwe* "that
over there; there yonder"—when referring to nonvisible referents (typically
places and landmarks).

To conclude this subsection, we can see that acts labeled as conventional
instances of *thileme*—that is, true instances of pointing from the Arrernte

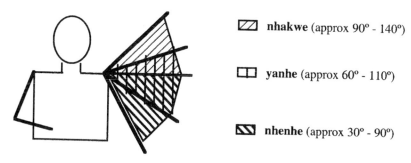

nhakwe (approx 90° - 140°)

yanhe (approx 60° - 110°)

nhenhe (approx 30° - 90°)

FIG. 8.2.   Relation of degree of upward/downward arm angling to use of demonstratives. *Note.* This is relevant only to relative indications of objects/ places that are not visible, and inhabiting a horizontal space whose areal scale is in the order of hundreds to thousands of square kilometers.

perspective—are enacted by three different parts of the body. Choice of body part for pointing is culturally determined and semiotically governed. Table 8.2 summarizes the distinctions among the three general forms of pointing in terms of *referent visibility, formality of context* (i.e. relation to inter-locutor), and *degree of secrecy* intended.

The Three Recognized Types of Manual Pointing

As noted earlier, there are three distinct forms of manual pointing that are identified and named by Arrernte speakers. Each of these is next de-scribed in turn, and it is at this point we first encounter the index-finger form in pointing.

The "One-Finger Point": Home of the Index Finger.   Acts of pointing that most English speakers would identify as the common-and-garden index-finger points are described by Arrernte consultants with the phrase *iltye anyente-le thilemele ileme* (hand/finger one with pointingly tell) "telling by pointing with one hand/finger." Although the most common hand shape of this point is pretty much the same as the index-finger point used by Eng-lish speakers, it has some common allomorphic variants that are probably

TABLE 8.2
Differences in Arrernte Use of Pointing With Hand, Mouth, or Eye

	Referent Visibility	Formality of Context	Degree of Secrecy
Manual point	+/− Visible	+/− Formal	− Secret
Mouth point	+/− Visible	− Formal	+/− Secret
Eye point	+ Visible	− Formal	+ Secret

not as familiar to English speakers. The "one-finger point" can be made with palm down or palm to the side (*di taglio* in Kendon and Versante's terms). In the palm down condition, there are roughly four shape variants (see Fig. 8.3): one with the index finger extended and all other fingers tightly retracted and thumb resting on the retracted middle finger (i.e., the canonical pointing form described by authors such as Butterworth in this volume), one with the index finger extended and the other fingers only loosely retracted and essentially pointing down, one where the fingers are basically not retracted at all but the index finger is raised up from what is essentially a flat palm down hand, and finally, one where it is the middle finger, not the index finger, that is pointed toward a target.

It is these last two variants of the pointing form that we have not encountered in comparative English and Dutch data. First, in the English and Dutch data I have been able to observe, speakers always make index-finger points with fairly substantial contraction of the other fingers, although it may be tighter or looser, but always within the range provided by (a) and (b) in Fig. 8.3. Indeed, with my own English-colored spectacles, in doing transcriptions of video data, I had trouble identifying anything with a looser (and flatter) hand configuration as a one-finger point and regularly coded it as another form of manual pointing. The Arrernte consultants I worked with had no trouble identifying such points (with or without further supporting context). Second, pointing with the middle finger occurred with a number of Arrernte speakers, but I have not picked it up in any of the English or Dutch data. I have, however, noted English speakers using a middle-finger variant "in the wild" under two conditions, one where they are pointing at something they are also touching (like a paper, or a map, or an overhead sheet) and one where they are holding something and their index finger is otherwise occupied.[7] Arrernte speakers, in contrast, can use the middle finger variant much the same way as the index-finger variant. For instance, it is used with full arm extension to point to places and objects in the distance. Of course, the relative paucity of the middle-finger variant for English speakers may not be independent of the fact that it is formally associated with a rude and derogatory "middle finger" emblematic sign. Certainly, when English-speaking audiences see examples of the Arrernte middle-finger variant, they can't help but make the association with the emblematic form that is so much a part of their own culture.

It is worth stressing that these variant forms of the "one-finger point" are all regarded as being "the same" by Arrernte speakers. They do, of course, see the differences once they are pointed out, and then it is possible to elicit

---

[7]Kendon and Versante (chap. 6, this volume) note that they have observed middle-finger and little-finger pointing in their Neapolitan data, but state that such points were not common, and they give them no further consideration in their chapter. They do, however, recognize that these two forms of pointing must be taken into account in future investigations.

Variant forms:

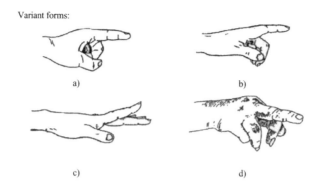

a)   b)

c)   d)

Examples:

a) "That place there has a lot of native honey."   b) "That (mid-distant) is the main site of Ilewerre."

c) "One more egg is still hidden."   d) "We found another grind stone just a little bit up on the other side of the creek."

FIG. 8.3. The one-finger point: variant forms and examples.

a more specific description of the form. For instance, under elicitation, some speakers describe the index-finger variants by the phrase *iltye anyente-le thilemele ileme iltye arratye-le* (hand/finger one with pointingly tell hand/finger true) "make a one-finger point using the index finger," but this is not a fixed phrase and only serves to highlight that this category of point is not thought to uniquely cover just the use of the index finger. In other words, the canonical index-finger point is merely one of a number of etic variants of a more general emic category. It is an "allo-gesture" (i.e., one of several allomorphic variants) of a basic "gesture-eme." The factors that determine which variant is selected are discussed momentarily, but first we examine the function and meaning attributed to the "one-finger point" as an emic gesture.

All variants of the "one-finger point" encode the same functional and semantic content. It is used to identify a single object or place by showing its location in space or its bearing from the deictic center. As a related function, it is used to indicate the direction toward which a featured object is statically facing. In its function of picking out a single referent, it shares the object individuation function that Kendon and Versante (chap. 6, this volume) observe for the index palm down pointing of Neapolitan speakers. However, remember, this function is not restricted to a single variant form in Arrernte, and palm orientation is not relevant at this level. Moreover, we need to be clear about what is meant by the object individuation function. The Arrernte one-finger point fairly strictly applies to picking out just a single referent; if more than one referent is to be identified then another pointing form is used. English speakers have, for instance, been observed using an index-finger point when saying things like "give me those two cups"—the point may either be a single direct gesture to the area of the cups or may move in an alternating fashion between cups. This is the sort of function the one-finger point does not perform, and speakers reject its co-occurrence with the Arrernte equivalent of "give me those two cups" and require the use of a wide hand point (to be discussed in a later section).[8] Another function that is *not* accomplished by the one-finger point in Arrernte, but is accomplished by the index-finger point used by English speakers, is the indication of paths of motion to be traveled or turns to be negotiated in moving.[9] In giving directions, for instance, Arrernte speakers quite systematically use the horned hand hand sign (discussed in "Three Categories of

---

[8]An alternate phrasing like "give me the two cups sitting *there*" does allow the one-finger point, but the referent of the point in such a case is the single location, not the two cups.

[9]One sometimes sees an Arrernte one-finger point apparently tracing a motion path, but all the cases I have observed fall into two categories: (a) pointing at an individual referent that happens to be in motion, and (b) tracing the extension of linearly extended single referent (like a creek bed) that is statically located in space.

Orienting Behavior" and illustrated in Fig. 8.1) to give the overall goal of
motion, whereas the flat hand (discussed in a later section) is used to give
path segments and turns and compass point bearings, and the one-finger
point is used to localize individual sites and landmarks. In giving directions,
English speakers regularly employ the index-finger point to encode meanings and perform functions that are restricted to the horned hand hand
sign and the flat hand point for Arrernte speakers. In short, although the
Arrernte one-finger point and the English index-finger point have overlapping uses, they are semantically and functionally quite distinct.

So does this mean that the variant forms of the Arrernte one-finger point
are just randomly generated alternant morphologies? No. Although the intuitions of Arrernte speakers break down at this point, and they are unable
to identify functional or semantic differences among the variants, close observation of usage does suggest some pattern as to when particular variants
are deployed. For instance, the degree of finger closure or openness among
the three index-finger variants of the one-finger point appears to correlate
with certain discourse factors. Emphatic mentions, or first mentions of entities that continue to be important, are regularly accompanied by the canonical (tightly bunched) index-finger point (which is often held in place). In
follow-up anaphoric mentions, or the mentioning of nonimportant participants, a looser hand is used (and the action is executed more quickly). In
the case of the two more closed variants, the utterance is often constructed
so as to require an accompanying point. In contrast, the most open variant
of the index-finger point, the one that is hardest to identify for an outsider,
tends not to be used in the context of obligatory pointing, but is used instead to quickly point out something that has already been identified and
mentioned explicitly in speech. Not surprisingly, this point tends to be performed rapidly and tends not to be held. Put crudely, the more semantically important the gesture is to the ongoing discourse; the more it takes
the shape of canonical index-finger pointing, the less semantically important it is, the looser and more open it is, and the quicker is its performance.
In this sense, then, the occurrence of alternant forms is environmentally
determined, and the variants are in complementary, rather than contrastive, distribution.

Although less well understood, due to fewer attestations, the middle-finger variant of the one-finger point also seems to have a fairly predictable
distribution. It appears to arise when individuating among potential alternates, all of which are also relevant to the discourse. Two such contexts
have been observed. First, the middle-finger variant follows the use of an index-finger variant to pick out a different single referent. In the few cases
available, the referents lay in the same areal quadrant. Second, this variant
has been observed when picking out a middle referent of a series of referents that have previously been established. Especially this latter use may be

associated iconically with the selection of the middle finger and may explain why this variant is only observed in palm down uses (i.e., all attestations are with localization of objects on the horizontal, and the middle finger leaves alternates on either side). However, more examples are required to see whether this pattern holds. As I have said, such apparent differences in the morphological shapes of these related variants are not at the level of consciousness, and the differences may in fact reflect natural responses to discourse context and/or other environmental conditions that determine the shape. That is to say, the variants of the one-finger point appear not to be determined by convention in the sense of Lewis (1969) or Clark (1996) and so are not each individual signs conveying different meanings from one another.[10]

In summary, the Arrernte recognize a gesture that they call a one-finger point. This gesture has a clear function and semantics. Although there are a number of variant forms of this gesture, Arrernte speakers do not seem to be overtly conscious of this fact. The variant forms of the gesture are not randomly distributed but seem to arise predictably in different discourse contexts—that is to say, they appear to be in complementary rather than contrastive distribution. One of these variant forms happens to be a canonical index-finger point, and although there is evidence to suggest this is a privileged variant of sorts, its actual distribution, use, and meaning differ significantly from those of its English counterpart. In particular, the one-finger point cannot be used in a number of contexts where the English index-finger point is regularly used. Although there are semantic similarities, the Arrernte one-finger point clearly conveys, for instance, a different notion of individuation.

The Wide Hand Point. The second of the three recognized Arrernte manual points is referred to by the standard phrase *iltye anteke-le thilemele ileme* (hand wide-with pointingly tell) "telling by pointing with the wide (spread) hand." For convenience, I refer to this as the wide hand point. It is made with digits extended and spread out (see Fig. 8.4). In contrast to the one-finger point, the wide hand point regularly carries with it the notion of non-singularity or nonindividuation. It can be used to identify regions or expanses of country (i.e., areas which contain multiple individual places), and is also used to refer to the multiple objects in an area. In this last use it can even be performed when standing next to an object, like a bush laden with fruit, and indicating the fruit on the tree. The orientation of the palm

---

[10]In other words, to borrow terms from Clark (1996), each variant form realizes the same *coordination device* and solves the same *recurrent coordination problem* in the community. They may be slightly different behaviors but they realize just one meaning and function that is "common ground in the community," and although the differences are regular they do not, through convention, convey any distinct content.

Form:

Examples:

a) "... the snakes spread out all over (this area) here." [note: both hands used]

b) "They used to live all over the area on that side."

c) The (group of) saltpans on the mid-distant side there is Anmatyerre (country).

FIG. 8.4.   The wide hand point: form and examples.

tells the relative orientation of the surface upon which things are extended or spread. For example, when the palm is down and horizontal, it may indicate salt pans spread out over flat ground. If the palm were facing out and vertical, it could indicate, for instance, paintings spread out over a cliff face. When identifying large regions, or indicating the degree of *spreadness* of a mass object (like water), this point often co-occurs with a sweeping, rotating motion. Moreover, this is the only manual point that can be performed two-handed as well as one-handed. When performed with both hands, one is emphasizing either the extent of a region, the degree of spread, or the large number of objects referred to.

In Arrernte grammar, there is no obligatory marking in noun phrases to indicate singular or plural (i.e., number is not marked in NPs). So, for instance, a phrase like *arne nhenhe* (tree this) can mean either "this tree" or "these trees." However, the singular/nonsingular distinction is frequently made gesturally: When the one-finger point accompanies the phrase, the interpretation is "this tree," whereas when the wide hand point accompanies the phrase the interpretation is "these trees."[11] I have been pulled up in

---

[11]As Haviland (chap. 7, this volume) observes, "[t]he complex morphology of pointing gestures means that they are typically not 'simple referring devices' but rather complex semantic portmanteaux . . . linking in a single morphological guise many of the same semantic domains—quantity, shape (or 'gender'), and proximity—that characterize spoken demonstratives."

the past by Arrernte consultants frustrated with the fact that I used an index-finger point when I intended reference to multiple objects. It is in this
sense that the wide finger point and the one finger point are in contrastive
distribution. They can occur with the same phrase or utterance and totally
change the basic (propositional) interpretation of the communicative act.

The "Flat Hand Point." The final manual point is referred to by the
phrase *iltye ilperrele thilemele ileme* (hand-flat pointingly tell) "telling by pointing with the flat hand." In the flat hand point, all the fingers are extended
and drawn together (abducted). The form of the point is usually with the
palm to the side (i.e., it conforms closely in its morphology to the Neapolitan point described by Kendon and Versante as "open hand di taglio").
However, especially when it is used to point to something behind the
speaker and is launched over the shoulder, it can take on an orientation
where the palm either faces up or down. Further, this gesture regularly
identifies the line along which extended objects (like mountain ranges) lie,
and can sometimes be used to partially model the referent, in the sense that
the angle of the palm may convey information such as the nature and absolute direction of side slope (cf. Levinson, in press). Finally, it needs to be
mentioned that there is a two-fingered variant of the flat hand point in
which only the index finger and middle finger are extended (with the
thumb aligning with them) and the ring and little finger are drawn in. Although radically different in formal appearance, once again Arrernte
speakers do not regard it as anything but an instantiation of the flat hand
point (see Fig. 8.5).

To be more explicit about the meaning and function of the flat hand
point, it is used to project lines and paths. For instance, it is used to identify
the linear orientation of extended objects such as a creek, road, or range of
hills that lie in a particular direction. It is also typically used to indicate the
orientation of subpaths traveled or to be traveled in getting toward an overall goal and so is commonly found in direction giving. This is the form of
point that is used to identify the cardinal directions, and here again we find
a contrast with the typical behavior of English speakers. Of 20 Australian
English speakers, interviewed individually, whom I asked to show me where
north is, 14 used an index-finger point to indicate direction. Of 16 Arrernte
speakers who were asked the same thing, all 16 used the flat hand point. So
once again, we get a clear sense that an English speaker's deployment of an
index-finger point diverges significantly from that of an Arrernte speaker's.

As well as projecting lines and paths, the flat hand point can sweep out
laterally to indicate a sector or quadrant. This use contrasts with the use of
the wide hand point to indicate regions in that the wide hand point is used
to pick out identifiable or known regions, whereas the lateral sweep of the

Variant forms:

Examples:

a) "That range lies like this."   b) "South."
   [from east to west]

c) 'Prepare to curve around to the   d) 'Make a sharp turn here to the
   north'   northeast'

FIG. 8.5. The flat hand point: variant forms and examples.

flat hand creates a region of interest. For instance, it can be used to delimit an area in which a search for bush food should take place.

With respect to the two-fingered variant of the flat hand point, once again we come to a point where Arrernte speakers are unable to call on conscious reflection to elucidate their understanding of the form. However, as in the case of variant forms of the one-finger point, the deployment of the two-fingered variant of the flat hand point appears to be governed by contextual factors. Although I do not have many examples, the examples I have suggest the following generalizations. First, the two-fingered variant is made much more rapidly than the full-hand variant. Second, this component of speed seems to be related to the content of the co-occurring speech. Third, the two-fingered variant is more likely when (a) an individual is being told to move rapidly along the indicated subpath, or (b) the driver of a vehicle is being warned by a navigator that upcoming turn to the direction indicated is particularly close and/or tight (i.e., one will have to act quickly to take the turn appropriately).

Manual Points, Gesture Space, and System: Where's the Thumb Point?

Having briefly described the three recognized manual points individually, we return for a moment to issues concerning manual points as a system. In particular, I wish to touch on some aspects of how manual points are deployed within the gesture space of Arrernte speakers. This issue is related, in part, to a feature of the English (and Dutch and Neapolitan) pointing system that is absent from the Arrernte system, namely, the use of thumb pointing. That is, Arrernte speakers do not use thumb points as part of their system, whereas English speakers use a thumb point in opposition to an index-finger point in a manner at least partially determined by different body-based divisions of space, as described next.

In a paper subtitled "Cultural Differences in the Use of Body-Schema for Spatial Thinking and Gesture," Levinson (in press) presented data that argue strongly for the view that speakers of languages (like Arrernte) that rely heavily on the absolute frame of reference for spatial localization (even on a small scale) use spatial gestures in a way that varies systematically from those of speakers of languages (like English) that rely heavily on a (body-based) relative frame of reference. Based on the analysis of videotaped data of Tzeltal speakers and Guugu Yimithirr speakers, supplemented by my observations of video data of Arrernte speakers, Levinson identified a number of features that seem to characterize "gesture morphology" in communities using an absolute (cardinal or geo-based) system. A few of these features include: (a) Absolute gestures tend be large and expansive; (b) gesturing tends to be more evenly distributed across the dominant and nondominant hands; and (c) the "gesture space consists of a two-metre sphere with the front 180 degrees more heavily used but the full 360 degrees being available," in contrast to McNeill's characterization of the American English speaker's gesture space as a "shallow disk in front of the speaker." In a more systematic comparison of 180 Arrernte and Dutch spatially oriented gestures (de Ruiter & Wilkins, 1998; Wilkins & de Ruiter, 2001), we have further confirmed and expanded on Levinson's findings: Arrernte speakers use a significantly larger gesture space than the Dutch, one that more frequently uses full arm extension, and frequent (and deep) breaking of the back plane. Moreover, although Dutch speakers regularly used one hand dominantly for talking about the space around them, and consistently made contralaterally oriented gestures, the Arrernte speakers in the sample deployed gesture in a systematic manner such that they used the left hand to gesture to places located in the region on the left side of their body, and the right hand to point to places on the right side (i.e., all gestures were ipsilateral, and there were no contralateral points).

One of the common differences we've found is the manner in which Dutch and Arrernte speakers refer to locations that are behind them. The Dutch speakers would either rotate their bodies, as if sighting their location (although it was rarely a place that was visible from their perspective), and then launch an index-finger point, or more commonly they would use a thumb point without rotation or sighting. As Kendon and Versante (chap. 6, this volume) write with respect to thumb pointing among the Neapolitans:

> When the thumb is used in pointing, all the fingers are flexed to the palm of the hand and the thumb is fully extended. With this hand shape it is easy to direct the thumb upward, backward over the shoulder, or to the left or to the right. Perhaps for this reason it is often used to point to things that are either behind or to the side of the speaker. However, hand shapes such as the index finger or open hand are also observed in use by people pointing in these directions. Hence whether the thumb is used or not appears also to depend on other factors besides the convenience it might offer as a means for referring to something behind or to the side.

For current purposes, all we need to recognize is that thumb pointing is a common Anglo and European gesture behavior, strongly associated with the back plane, and it may bring with it further connotations that put it in contrast with index-finger pointing.[12]

This contrasts with Arrernte pointing behavior. When referring to the back plane, the most common means of gesturing was to launch one of the

---

[12]Saitz and Cervenka (1972) observed that thumb pointing is common in both Colombia and the United States, but noted that the uses differ in their connotations. They wrote: "Thumb protruding from fist indicates the direction. Whereas in the U.S. this gestures is strong and often rude, in Colombia it is a more acceptable way of indicating direction" (p. 34).

three Arrernte manual points over the shoulder, pressing it deep into the back plane in a manner that looks "awkward" or "unnatural" to English speakers (see Fig. 8.6). Such gestures would often also rise above head level, in keeping with a more extensive gesture space. On a few occasions, references to the back plane were made using points in which the arm was at full stretch and swung out laterally to the side of the body and again "strained" deeply into the region behind the body axis. Also attested to were cases in which the pointing looked like it was targeting a front part of the body (e.g., it looked like the speaker was pointing to their chest or the shoulder), but what was intended was a reference to a location with the indicated bearing at a position behind the speaker. As Levinson (in press) noted, on the basis of similar occurrences in his own work, "[t]his observation perhaps has some bearing on the 'disembodied' kind of spatial reckoning involved: the self becomes as it were wholly transparent." In all of these different cases of Arrernte pointing to the back plane, I have attested to the same three distinct manual point types that have just been described (and only these).

On the basis of the preceding observations, it should be obvious that the index-finger point of an English or Dutch (or Neapolitan) speaker is made under different understandings of gesture space and system when compared to that of an Arrernte (or Tzeltal or Guugu Yimithirr) speaker. Children growing up in the Netherlands, for instance, and learning to speak Dutch have to learn to constrain their gestures to a smaller space than Arrernte children, and they have to learn the contrast between the index-finger point and the thumb point—a contrast that belongs to a set with different oppositional dimensions than that which the Arrernte child

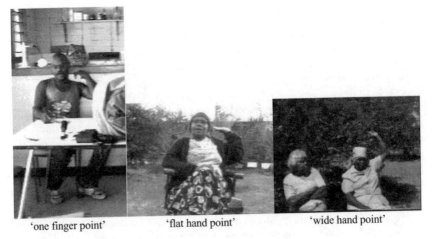

'one finger point'   'flat hand point'   'wide hand point'

FIG. 8.6.   Examples of unsighted pointing (over the shoulder) to the backward plane.

must master. In the end, Arrernte children will have acquired a system that allows them to freely launch an index-finger point over their shoulder without body rotation and in an unsighted and seemingly awkward fashion, whereas this will not be part of the Dutch children's repertoire because they have simply acquired a different system, which cannot be said to have the same index-finger point. The comparative work of Levinson suggests that these differences are not independent of differences that also manifest themselves in differences in language use and that rest on deeper distinctions in the specific cognitive strategies that are culturally selected for employing coordinate systems in spatial reckoning (e.g., absolute vs. relative).

OBSERVATIONS ON ARRERNTE TRANSMISSION
AND ACQUISITION OF POINTING

In preceding sections, some presumed consequences of system differences for the acquisition of pointing have been mentioned in passing, but what do we know about the actual transmission and acquisition of Arrernte pointing? In this section, I touch on this question briefly by presenting three forms of available evidence: (a) native speakers' own comments on teaching practice, (b) observed instances where children's pointing behavior has been corrected, and (c) actual observations of change in pointing behavior in the acquisition process. These three lines of evidence converge and lead to the conclusion that pointing behaviors, including pointing forms, are subject to social transmission.

Arrernte speakers readily talk about how they learned to point and the right way to go about teaching pointing. Such discussions are usually in the context of learning about country and learning about directions. That is to say, there seems to be a strong association between teaching about sociogeographical surroundings (i.e., place names, Dreaming stories, paths of travel), way-finding, and practices associated with the traditional hunter-gatherer lifestyle, on the one hand, and teaching pointing as one of the appropriate means for communicating and discussing such knowledge, on the other hand. I next present a free English translation of one such discussion at length. It comes from a videotaped session with two Arrernte women whom I interviewed about directions and route-finding knowledge in February 1995. The main speaker in the discussion given next is V.D., one of the most knowledgeable, skilled, and important of Arrernte teachers and language experts, and a strong voice for the preservation and continuation of Arrernte cultural and linguistic practices. She is supported in this discussion by her colleague S.T. Sections that especially address teaching of pointing are in bold type.

V.D.:   *It used to be that really young kids knew about that before* [i.e., directions and how to point], *but not anymore. They're slower now, 'cause they're not taught properly—not like the old people taught us. The old people, they'd test young kids. "Where's East?" you'd ask a young kid, especially kids from the bush—not town kids—and they'd point to the directions, y'know.* **They mightn't know which direction the exact place is but they normally can point, and point the proper way, holding the hand the right way.** *That's how it was before. "Which way is west?" they might ask, and the kid would point straight away. They used to learn a lot from the old people in the early days. Yeah, y'know,* **if they asked a little kid, the kid'll point direct to where they've been asked. "Where's North?" "There" the kid would say** [demonstrates pointing to the north with the flat hand point]. **And if he points wrong, they say "No, not there, it's there!"** [again demonstrating the correct bearing with the flat hand point]. **And if he didn't use his hand right, you know, to point, they'd say "Don't point like that!"** [demonstrates a "wide hand point"] **"Point like this!** [demonstrates a "flat hand point"] **Do it this way so you can be understood properly."** *And they used to really force that onto you to make sure that you learned it. But nowadays it's not like that. . . .*

And they used to always do that [i.e., test the kids], *even if you were traveling too. You know, if you were traveling from one place to another, they'd tell you which direction you had come from and which direction you're going to.* **And they'd ask, "So, where are we going to today?"** *And the young kids would just have to point, and maybe they'd know the direction but they wouldn't show it the right way* [demonstrates an index-finger point, which is wrong in conjunction with motion]. **So, the old people would say, "Do it like this, with this sign"** [demonstrates the "horned hand" sign for global direction of motion]. **Older kids would also have to say the right thing as well** (as pointing properly). *They had to know those words "East," "South," "West," "upstream."—"Towards that way is called what?"* [making a flat hand point to the east], *and they'd have to answer "East." The same with "North," "South," things like that.*

S.T.   *We were taught a lot of good things by the old people, a lot of strict rules we had to obey at the time.*

This passage is a further demonstration of how conscious Arrernte speakers are of pointing as a significant communicative act. Moreover, as well as indicating that there was overt teaching, testing, correction, and demonstration of pointing behavior, at least in relation to direction and travel, it also suggests a natural staging to the transmission process: Arrernte children would be expected to learn how to point properly before they were expected to know the appropriate terms, or ways of speaking, that would accompany pointing.

Also embedded in this passage are two examples that V.D. made up on the spot to demonstrate the types of corrections older people would make in relation to children's pointing forms. First, she shows the correction from a wide hand point to a flat hand point in the context of teaching how best to indicate which way the cardinal point directions lie. Second, she shows the correction from a one-finger point (index-finger variant) to the use of the horned hand sign in the context of teaching how best to show the endpoint goal of motion. In this first instance, she explicitly notes that the reason for choosing the right form of pointing is "*so you can be understood properly.*" One cannot underestimate how important accurate guide signing is in harsh desert conditions, especially in more traditional times when people had to travel great distances on foot. Because pointing, as an analogue mode, is more accurate than language, it is not surprising that adults would want children to learn to point according to the recognized conventions "so they could be understood properly."

Quite fortuitously, I have two videotaped instances of children being corrected in their pointing behavior, one child by his mother and the other child by her 9-year-old sister. Both children are 4 years of age and were taking part in a pilot project designed to elicit pointing behavior and demonstrative terms from both adults and children. The design is a variant on the "walnut game." This involves a ball and three (opaque) cups, and the ball is rapidly moved back and forth from under different cups in full view of the person playing the game. Once the investigator has finished shuffling the ball and the cups around, the respondent has to point and say which cup he or she thinks the ball is hidden under (Pederson & Wilkins, 1996, p. 14). In this game, Arrernte adults always produced a one-finger point, typically the index-finger variant, because only one cup is being selected out of the three. In both cases of correction, the child was failing to use a one-finger point, and the child was forcefully shown how to make a good index-finger variant. In the first instance, the young boy had used a wide hand point (which is used for multiple, not singular objects), and although the intended target was clear, the mother grabbed his hand and with her own hand wrapped all fingers except his index finger tightly closed such that his index finger was pointing in the manner of a canonical index-finger point. The older sister performed the identical operation on her younger sister, but in this case it was to prevent the younger sister from actually reaching down to pick up the chosen cup. Thus, in both cases, caregivers are physically shaping children's points when they perceive that their indicating behaviors are inappropriate for the context. That they shape the children's hands into a tight index-finger point suggests that this form is indeed the canonical form of one-finger pointing for the Arrernte. However, it also shows that children might not select it as the natural option in a given context, and when that happens, caregivers quickly recognize the fact and are willing to intervene to physically "teach" the appropriate form for the context.[13]

---

[13]I believe that these facts further support Haviland's contention (chap. 8, this volume) that pointing gestures can be far more conventionalized and emblematic in character than the literature on gesture has heretofore allowed. He observes that "in terms of their segmentability,

As a brief digression, I would like to insert quite a different sort of example that further demonstrates the perceived need to monitor and train accurate orientation behavior. One Arrernte consultant told me of an old blind man who would train younger men in traditional knowledge about country. When testing the young men to determine whether they had accurately remembered what they needed to learn, he would sit next to the individual to be examined with his hand lightly on the young man's forearm and in that way feel whether the gestures the young man made were oriented in the appropriate direction.[14] Indeed, absolutely oriented gestures are so much a part of traditional narrative performance that it is often very difficult to reconstruct the actual content and force of a text from an audio recording alone. As Levinson (in press) wrote, "in Absolute gesture systems truth-conditional information is happily conveyed in the gesture channel, and may then be picked up by an interlocutor in speech." A further consequence of this "is the care and consistency with which gestures are made and monitored—they must add up to a consistent picture, and apparent inconsistencies will lead to interactional repair sequences just as verbal inconsistencies may do."

Although the factors just described speak to the issue of conscious teaching and transmission, they do not really say anything about the actual acquisition of pointing. Here I lay out some cursory details of a study that I intend to report on in greater detail later. In early 1995, I undertook a short trip out bush with an extended family of 14 people wishing to return to the heart of their traditional country. During the trip, I was able to make sys-

---

glossability, and potential temporal autonomy from speech (not to mention the apparent conventions of well-formedness that may sometimes apply to them), pointing gestures are much more emblematic in character than, for example, iconic gestures." I would, however, caution against his suggestion that this means "pointing is simply part of language." It may be that pointing is differently systematized in different cultures—in some it may be integrated as part of language, and in others it may be separated into an independently structured semiotic system that is used in parallel with language, and in still others pointing may have fewer emblematic qualities than Haviland suggests. In other words, pointing in different cultures may vary along a number of different continua, including a continuum of conventionalization and a continuum of systematicity.

[14]In reference to the orienting abilities of blind people in Kukatja communities, Peile (1997) wrote that, when directed,

a blind person will unerringly go north, south, east or west as he is told to do so (these compass directions are also given to a blind person to find a chair to sit down in a room, etc.). The blind person is not directed to go to the right or left, backwards or forwards, as the case may be. (pp. 46–47)

This is yet another demonstration of the prevalence of absolute over relative spatial orienting behavior in Desert Aboriginal communities. It also shows that ability to keep track of one's absolute orientation can be independent of vision and visual cues.

tematic observations of the spatial deictic gesture behavior of the members of this family (between ages 20 months and 59 years). On the trip there were five children under the age of 5. The exact ages were: 1;8, 2;2, 3, 4;6, and 4;9 (years;months). A surprising finding was that the three youngest children all used a pointing form that has not been observed with adults, and they used this form for all instances of pointing. The pointing form was like a cross between the adult wide hand point and the middle-finger variant of the one finger point: a loosely spread hand with the middle finger raised and directed (see Fig. 8.7). Of more than 40 observations of pointing for these children, with at least 10 instances for each of the three children, there was never a deviation from this pointing form. Even when children were mimicking the pointing behavior of an adult, which happened in two observed cases, they used this form of the pointing hand rather than the form the adult had chosen. Obviously, what was striking was the complete absence of any index-finger point even in typical contexts where one would have expected it. The two 4-year-old children, in contrast, had acquired more than one pointing form and both showed usage of a canonical index-finger point alongside a wide hand point.

Although the literature on the development of pointing does not report any occurrences of middle-finger pointing, when George Butterworth saw these Arrernte examples he noted that he had observed some of the English children in his laboratory also making middle-finger points, although he did not say how systematic this was. In discussing my chapter, Butterworth (chap. 2, this volume), writes that "such middle-finger pointing is occasionally observed in Western infants too," and he acknowledges that there seems to be "a permissible (but narrow) envelope of variation in the form of the gesture that, during development, converges on the canonical indexical form." What I find significant about the Arrernte case, though, is that it was all three of the

(pointing to bird in hollow of tree)

(pointing to father on hill top)

FIG. 8.7.   Two examples of the unique pointing form used by a cohort of three young Arrernte children (the form involves the middle finger extended from a spread hand).

youngest children together, and that, given the timeline for the development of pointing suggested by Butterworth, one would have expected the emergence of the privileged form by age 3. I was able to do follow-up observations of two of these three children about 7 months later (when they were 2;9 and 3;7), and both showed no evidence of their earlier "unique" pointing form, but instead manifested a canonical one-finger point as well as at least one of the other conventional adult pointing forms.

So why, in a culture that supports the public use of the "index finger" for pointing, would these three young children not have this form (a supposedly universal basic form of human nonverbal communication) until so late in their communicative development? First, I suggest that the fact that all three used the same unique form is not independent of the fact that they formed a cohort of close playmates—a peer group. This is a social factor.[15] Second, it seems significant that once there is another conventional manual pointing form in the child's system (wide hand point or flat hand point), then the index-finger variant of the one-finger point becomes available. This suggests a systemic influence on these three young children's choice of point. In particular, I propose that the "unique" form of pointing this cohort of three children converged on may be an intermediate mixed ("compromise") form between the one-finger point and the wide hand point—the two most common points for picking out visually available objects. The form may in fact represent the first recognition of the adult system, and later, once the children gain further understanding of the system, the form then "unpacks" into the more conventional forms. In a sense, this is like Petitto's (1987, 1997) argumentation concerning the transition in the acquisition of ASL from pointing as a gesture to pointing as a pronominal sign in the language system; it is only when pointing becomes a sign in the structured system that there is "confusion" as to how to correctly target the form. If the Arrernte data were analogous, then I would not be surprised if, at some stage prior to my first observations of these children, one or more of them did manifest index-finger pointing behavior of the type described by Butterworth for children earlier on in infancy. However, the combination of social factors (the power of the peer cohort) and the first recognition of the existence of a structured system of adult Arrernte nonverbal behavior could eradicate the index-finger point in favor of the compromise point, only to see it reemerge again once the system starts developing oppositions.[16]

---

[15]So I am in no way suggesting that all Arrernte children go through a stage of using this unique form, and in fact I have observed other young Arrernte infants who seem to start out with something like an index-finger point.

[16]As Melissa Bowerman pointed out to me, this scenario of appearance followed by disappearance and then subsequent reappearance conforms to the U-shaped behavioral growth curve that is found in many other areas of cognitive development (see, e.g., Strauss, 1982).

I admit that much of this is speculative. However, the facts driving the speculation should themselves be sufficient to bring into question claims concerning the privileged nature of index-finger pointing and the lack of social transmission in pointing. The position that adults only "provide models of the frames within which pointing may be used, not models of the action itself" (Lock et al., 1990, p. 55) is not consistent with the Arrernte data presented in this section.

DISCUSSION

The stated aim of this chapter was to challenge and clarify the following common views: (a) that pointing with the index finger is a universal human behavior, and (b) that pointing with the index finger is not socially transmitted but is a basic (natural) form of reference. I undertook this crusade against the notion that the index finger is universally privileged in pointing primarily as a means to help clarify the extent to which pointing is shaped by cultural and semiotic factors. More particularly, I have used the opportunity to describe what is known about the Arrernte use and understanding of pointing in daily interactive communication. I believe this Arrernte window on pointing is fairly unique because Arrernte speakers can guide us through much of the complex structure of their system of pointing due to the fact that they are highly conscious about much of their nonverbal communicative behavior, and, as a consequence, they have a structured and conventionalized way of talking about these behaviors.

It has not been my intention to pursue a radically relativist position. There do appear to be some important universals. All cultures do, for instance, appear to make systematic use of some part of the body for deictic reference to places and inanimate objects. As shown in "What Is Meant by the Proposition That 'Pointing With the Index Finger Is a Human Universal'?" however, there appear to be cultures in which the canonical form of pointing is a lip point and there is no, or little, evidence of systematic pointing with the index finger (nor is there evidence that index-finger pointing is being suppressed or tabooed).

Of course, before making claims about the universality (or non-universality) of index-finger pointing, or any form of pointing for that matter, the notion of what one takes pointing to be must be clarified. Do we merely mean the etic behavior or the emic structure? As an analogy, consider the question "Do all languages have a 'b'?" It is a different question depending on whether we mean [b] as a phonetic unit or /b/ as a phoneme. Of course, more languages are likely to have [b] than /b/, but the answer to both questions would be interesting and revealing, although for different reasons. One tells us about physical gestures regularly realized in the flow of speech, and the other is suggestive of how those gestures are structured at a more abstract level to form meaningfully contrastive oppositions in a system. It does appear that the index-finger point is such a natural etic behavior that it has an extremely widespread occurrence across cultures, but I have been interested in it as an emic phenomenon.

So like Haviland (chap. 7, this volume) and Kendon and Versante (chap. 6, this volume), I have chosen to further clarify the notion of what pointing is and can be by exploring nonverbal deictic behaviors in another culture (i.e., a non-Anglo culture). All three studies converge on the conclusion that pointing is socioculturally complex, the forms are shaped by social convention, and there tends to be a system of pointing signs in oppositional contrast. However, I believe that the results of the Arrernte study suggest that we should be somewhat cautious in how we interpret the findings from both Haviland's Tzotzil study and Kendon and Versante's Neapolitan study. What the Arrernte study suggests (see especially "The Three Recognized Types of Manual Pointing") is that we need to be careful to distinguish between the etic variant forms of a pointing sign, and the emic units that are in contrastive opposition. I could be guided to this distinction in Arrernte because there was a clear point at which Arrernte speakers were no longer conscious of observed differences and could no longer employ conventional labels. Although the form and distribution of etic variants of a given emic pointing type were systematically governed by factors of discourse context, one would not want to say that they conventionally conveyed any other informational content beyond that which can be attributed to the emic pointing type. If I had relied solely on the same observational methodology as Kendon and Versante or Haviland, I would have been tempted to treat the middle-finger pointing variant of the one-finger point as a sign different from the canonical index-finger pointing variant, and similarly would have treated the two-fingered variant of the wide hand point as being a sign contentfully different from the standard fully spread hand variant. In other words, I would have missed the structure in the system and have paired every form difference with a content difference without realizing that some formal variants are in truly contrastive distribution, whereas others are in complementary distribution, and in this latter case one should not confuse the environmental features that condition etic occurrence with semantic features of content conveyed. This is not to say, for instance, that the Tzotzil or Neapolitan systems are anything but what the authors very insightfully describe them as; it is simply to say that it is not clear whether the methodology they have have employed successfully distinguishes etics from emics (i.e., contextual determination of meaning from conventional semantic encoding). Moreover, I do not claim that it is only in cultures where we have access to native metadescriptions and clear intuitions where we can discover and explore the distinction between etics and emics in gesture, only that the Arrernte case helps us see that gesture studies must identify methods, techniques, and discovery procedures which clearly recognize this distinction. Only in this way will we fully appreciate the complexity of the phenomena we are studying and come to understand the way in which pointing gestures actually communicate information.

As demonstrated in "The Arrernte View of Pointing," the Arrernte system of orienting behaviors is hierarchically structured and the canonical index-finger point is merely an etic variant at the fourth level in the system. This hierarchy is given in Fig. 8.8. Note that in this figure I have not shown all possible branchings, only those branchings that I discussed specifically in this chapter.

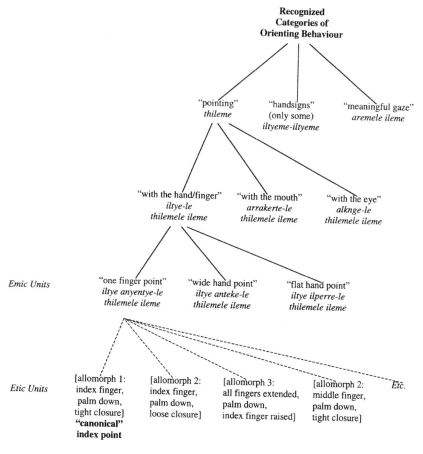

FIG. 8.8.   The hierarchical structure of Arrernte orienting behaviors, showing the embeddedness of the canonical index-finger point as an etic form variant of the one-finger point.

As far as index-finger pointing is concerned, the discussion of the Arrernte system warrants the following conclusions.

1. *Index-finger points in different cultures are embedded in differently structured sign systems with different functional–pragmatic considerations.* That is to say, to understand precisely what an index-finger point means, and when and how it should be used, we must understand the broader system of deictic gestures and their function. The broader Arrernte system was represented in Fig. 8.8. It is clear that the English system does not have the same structured system. For instance, there is no recognized mouth pointing that English speakers deploy in informal situations with familiars (see "True Pointing From the Arrernte Perspective"), and there is no recognized "thumb point" that Arrernte speakers deploy to refer to the back plane (with perhaps a hint of informality or rudeness).

2. *Index-finger points are cross-culturally divergent in their combinatorial properties, with both linguistic and other nonlinguistic signs.* As noted in "The One-Finger Point," the English sentence "give me those two cups" can be accompanied by an index-finger point, but its propositional equivalent in Arrernte cannot. This is because of stricter understanding of "individuation." In relation to its combination with other nonlinguistic conventions, I observed at the end of "True Pointing From the Arrernte Perspective" that all forms of manual pointing can systematically occur with a nonlinguistic convention in which angle of the arm shows relative distance in horizontal space, as long as the objects and places referred to are nonvisible. A similar convention is not present for English speakers, so the index-finger point does not have this combinatorial possibility (cf. Haviland, 1996b).

3. *Index-finger points possess a different semantic and functional range cross-culturally.* In the case of Arrernte, a one-finger point is used neither to refer to paths of motion, nor to point out compass point directions. Both of these functions are, however, common for the English index-finger point, and are conveyed in Arrernte through other manual gestures. Thus, we see a different form-to-function mapping and a different function-to-form mapping. Further, as noted in 2, the Arrernte one-finger point was shown to be used under a different (and stricter) understanding of individuation than the corresponding English pointing form.

4. *Index-finger points have different physical forms cross-culturally.* That is to say, the forefinger point does not have the same shape or range of alternate forms in different cultures. We have seen that Arrernte speakers, for instance, use a very open-handed index-finger pointing variant that is not attested to among English speakers. Moreover, we have seen that the middle finger variant is classed together with all of the index-finger variants as being manifestations of the one sign—the one-finger point (see "The One-Finger Point").

5. *Index-finger points have a deployment in gesture space that varies cross-culturally.* In "Manual Points, Gesture Space, and System," I observed that all Arrernte manual points, including index-finger variants, were deployed in a gesture space that is significantly larger than that used by Dutch speakers. Moreover, when making references to entities in the back plane, Arrernte speakers regularly launched one of the manual points over their shoulder in a fashion unattested to in the English and Dutch data examined. In similar circumstances, English and Dutch speakers use a thumb point or turn to sight their point. The Arrernte do not, themselves, recognize a "thumb point."

6. *Index-finger points invoke, and are only interpretable against, the unique culture-specific (communal) common grounds of each community.* Throughout the chapter, the absolute orienting behavior of Arrernte speakers has been mentioned in contrast to the relative (body-based) orienting behavior of English and Dutch speakers. Because of this difference in the primary coordinate system used for spatial reckoning and the communication of spatial information, an Arrernte speaker will regularly expect manual points to be absolutely oriented, and so interpret them as conveying correct information about actual bearings. English speakers do not make the same presumption, and this can lead to cross-cultural misunderstanding in which an Arrernte speaker presumes that an English speaker is saying something in gesture that the English speaker did not in fact intend (see "Manual Points, Gesture Space, and System").

In short, on all semiotic parameters, the Arrernte one-finger point diverges from the English index-finger point. As such, it can hardly be surprising that all the evidence mustered together in "Observations on Arrernte Transmission and Acquisition of Pointing" strongly suggests that Arrernte children do, in a very real sense, learn how to point through social transmission, and this includes learning the appropriate way to make and use the index-finger variants of the one-finger point. Three forms of evidence were brought to bear on this issue: a native speaker's own commentary on how pointing was (and should be) taught, observations concerning how adults correct the pointing behavior of children, and the unique case of a cohort of three young Arrernte children whose only form of pointing was not attested to in adult pointing and involved the extension of the middle finger rather than the index finger. An examination of this third line of evidence strongly indicated the role of both social factors and systemic factors in determining the shape of the pointing form. According to Povinelli, Bering, and Giambrone (chap. 3, this volume), the morphological constraints model proposed by Povinelli and Davis (1994) to account for the universality of the pointing gesture in humans can account for the Arrernte data. I leave readers to judge for themselves whether they think that is the case.

To conclude, pointing (i.e., the use of some part of the body to make deictic gestural reference) appears to be universal. However, the use of the index finger for pointing does not appear to be universal. Where it does occur, it is subject to cross-cultural variation along a number of semiotic parameters. Although it is easy to find the etic behavior of a canonical index-finger point in many different cultures all across the world, without detailed research it is impossible to be sure about either the exact content of such a behavior or the patterns of complementary and contrastive distribution this behavior has in relation to other etic behaviors. In fact, simply observing the behavior cannot tell us whether the behavior was purely ad hoc, like an English speaker's occasional use of the foot, knee, or elbow to point, or whether it was a conventional sign in a structured system of signs. Further, although it may be true that the cross-cultural range of associated forms and types of content conveyed may fall within a motivated and predictable range of possibilities, the exact determination of the sign form, the sign content, and the sign system will all be subject to cultural shaping and social transmission. Butterworth (chap. 2, this volume) gives some convincing arguments as to what makes the index finger a natural candidate for pointing, but it is important to realize that these do not make it so privileged that it is to be considered an absolute universal. The meta-understandings of other cultural groups concerning pointing can provide a useful alternative perspective on this topic and lead us to reconsider such long-held, pretheoretical presumptions. Finally, I believe that a better understanding of what the Arrernte mean by the term *thileme* helps us to better refine what we want to mean in using the term *pointing*.

ACKNOWLEDGMENTS

I would like to acknowledge the important contribution made to this chapter by those members of the Arrernte community living in Alice Springs who have patiently worked with me over several years. In particular, Margaret Heffernan and Veronica Dobson helped facilitate my research on pointing. This chapter has changed significantly due to the discussion generated at the Workshop on Pointing Gestures at Oud-Turnhout, Belgium, 1997, and I would like to thank all the participants for their contributions. I have been fortunate to be able to discuss the Arrernte data separately with several scholars who have provided useful advice and input. These include Felix Ameka, Melissa Bowerman, Herb Clark, Eve Danziger, John Haviland, Adam Kendon, Sotaro Kita, Steve Levinson, David Nash, Eric Pederson, and Jan-Peter de Ruiter. For comments on an earlier draft of this chapter, I thank Bill McGregor, Mandana Seyfeddinipur, and Barbara Villanova. My general research program on pointing by Arrernte speakers has been nurtured within the Gesture Project of the Max Planck Institute, and I would like to thank the MPG for funding regular fieldtrips to Central Australia between 1993 and 1997.

REFERENCES

Bates, E., Oconnell, B., & Shore, C. (1987). Language and communication in infancy. In J. D. Osofsky (Ed.), *Handbook of infant competence* (2nd ed., pp. 149–203). New York: Wiley.

Butterworth, G. E. (1995). Factors in visual attention eliciting manual pointing in human infancy. In H. L. Roitblat & J.-A. Meyer (Eds.), *Comparative approaches to cognitive science* (pp. 329–338). Cambridge, MA: MIT Press.

Clark, H. (1996). *Using language*. Cambridge: Cambridge University Press.

Eckert, P., & Hudson, J. (1988). *Wangka Wiru: A handbook for the Pitjantjatjara language learner*. Adelaide: University of South Australia [ARI & SLI].

Feldman, H. (1986). *A grammar of Awtuw*. Pacific Linguistics (Series B, No. 94). Canberra: Australian National University.

Franco, F., & Butterworth, G. E. (1996). Pointing and social awareness: Declaring and requesting in the second year of life. *Journal of Child Language, 23*, 307–336.

Haviland, J. B. (1993). Anchoring, iconicity, and orientation in Guugu Yimithirr pointing gestures. *Journal of Linguistic Anthropology, 3*(1), 3–45.

Haviland, J. B. (1996a). Projections, transpositions, and relativity. In J. J. Gumperz & S. C. Levinson (Eds.), *Rethinking linguistic relativity* (pp. 269–323). Cambridge: Cambridge University Press.

Haviland, J. B. (1996b, April). *Pointing, gesture spaces, and mental maps* [Electronically published multimedia discussion paper]. Language-Culture List. Available: http:/www.cs.uchicago.edu/l-c/archives/subs/haviland-john/

Hendriks, H., & McQueen, J. (Eds.). (1996). *Max Planck Institute for Psycholinguistics annual report 1995*. Nijmegen: MPI.

Hewes, G. W. (1981). Pointing and language. In T. Myers, J. Laver, & J. Anderson (Eds.), *The cognitive representation of speech* (pp. 263–269). Amsterdam: North-Holland.

Hewes, G. W. (1996). A history of the study of language origins and the gestural primacy hypothesis. In A. Lock & C. R. Peters (Eds.), *Handbook of human symbolic evolution* (pp. 571–595). Oxford: Clarendon.

Kendon, A. (1988). *Sign languages of Aboriginal Australia: Cultural, semiotic and communicative perspectives*. Cambridge: Cambridge University Press.

Kendon, A. (1992). Some recent work from Italy on quotable gestures ("emblems"). *Journal of Linguistic Anthropology, 2*(1), 72–93.

Kendon, A. (1994). Do gestures communicate? A review. *Research on Language and Social Interaction, 27*(3), 175–200.

Levinson, S. C. (1997). Language and cognition: The cognitive consequences of spatial description in Guugu Yimithirr. *Journal of Linguistic Anthropology, 7*(1), 98–131.

Levinson, S. C. (in press). *The body in space: Cultural differences in the use of body-schema for spatial thinking and gesture*. Paper circulated for the Fyssen Colloquium: Culture and the Uses of the Body, December 1995.

Lewis, D. K. (1969). *Convention: A philosophical study*. Cambridge, MA: Harvard University Press.

Lock, A., Young, A., Service, V., & Chandler, P. (1990). Some observations on the origins of the pointing gesture. In V. Volterra & C. J. Erting (Eds.), *From gesture to language in hearing and deaf children* (pp. 42–55). Berlin: Springer-Verlag.

Morris, D. (1978). *Manwatching: A field guide to human behavior*. St. Albans, England: Triad Panther.

Müller, C. (1996). Zur Unhöflichkeit von Zeigegesten. *Osnabrücker Beiträge zur Sprachtheorie, 52*, 196–222.

Pederson, E., Danziger, E., Wilkins, D. P., Levinson, S., Senft, G., & Kita, S. (1998). Semantic typology and spatial conceptualization. *Language, 74*, 557–589.

Pederson, E., & Wilkins, D. P. (1996). A cross-linguistic questionnaire on "demonstratives." In CARG (Ed.), *"Manual" for the 1996 field season* (pp. 1–14). Nijmegen: Cognitive Anthropology Research Group, Max Planck Institute for Psycholinguistics.

Peile, A. R. (1997). *Body and soul: An Aboriginal view.* Carlisle, West Australia: Hesperian.

Petitto, L. A. (1987). On the autonomy of language and gesture: Evidence form the acquisition of personal pronouns in American Sign Language. *Cognition, 27*, 1–52.

Petitto, L. A. (1997, June). *Ontogenesis of early pointing and language: Evidence from languages where gestures are linguistic.* Paper presented at the Max Planck Institute Workshop on Pointing Gestures, Oud-Turnhout.

Povinelli, D. J., & Davis, D. R. (1994). Differences between chimpanzees (*Pan troglodytes*) and humans (*Homo sapiens*) in the resting state of the index finger: Implications for pointing. *Journal of Comparative Psychology, 108*, 134–139.

Rolfe, L. (1996). Theoretical stages in the prehistory of grammar. In A. Lock & C. R. Peters (Eds.), *Handbook of human symbolic evolution* (pp. 776–792). Oxford: Clarendon.

Ruiter, J. P. A. de, & Wilkins, D. P. (1998). The synchronization of gesture and speech in Dutch and Arrernte. In S. Santi, I. Guaïtella, C. Cavé, & G. Konopczynski (Eds.), *Oralité et gestualité: Communication multimodale, interaction* (pp. 603–607). Paris: L'Harmattan.

Saitz, R. L., & Cervenka, E. J. (1972). *Handbook of gestures: Colombia and the United States* (M. Pekarsky, Illus.). The Hague: Mouton.

Sherzer, J. (1973). Verbal and non-verbal deixis: The pointed lip gesture among the San Blas Cuna. *Language in Society, 2*(1), 117–131.

Sherzer, J. (1983). *Kuna ways of speaking: An ethnographic perspective.* Austin: University of Texas Press.

Sherzer, J. (1993). Pointed lips, thumbs up, and cheek puffs: Some emblematic gestures in social interactional and ethnographic context. SALSA I, 197–212.

Strauss, S. (Ed.). (1982). *U-Shaped behavioral growth.* New York: Academic Press.

Strehlow, C. (1978). The sign language of the Aranda. In D. J. Umiker-Sebeok & T. A. Sebeok (Eds.), *Aboriginal sign languages of the Americas and Australia* (Vol. 2, pp. 349–370). New York: Plenum. (Translation by C. Chewings of Chapter 12 of Strehlow, originally published 1915)

Valiquette, H. (1993). *A basic Kukatja to English dictionary.* Balgo, West Australia: Luurnpa Catholic School.

Wilkins, D. P. (1991). The semantics, pragmatics and diachronic development of "associated motion" in Mparntwe Arrernte. *Buffalo Papers in Linguistics, 1*, 207–257.

Wilkins, D. P. (1993). Linguistic evidence in support of a holistic approach to traditional ecological knowledge. In N. Williams & G. Baines (Eds.), *Traditional ecological knowledge: Wisdom for sustainable development* (pp. 71–93). Canberra: CRES.

Wilkins, D. P. (1995). More than just wishful thinking: The survival of Arrernte worldview is historical fact, not romantic fiction. *Oceania Newsletter, 15*, 8–12.

Wilkins, D. P. (1997a). Handsigns and hyperpolysemy: Exploring the cultural foundations of semantic association. *Pacific Linguistics, C-136*, 413–444.

Wilkins, D. P. (1997b). Alternative representations of space: Arrernte narratives in sand. *Proceedings of the CLS Opening Academic Year '97/'98*, pp. 133–164.

Wilkins, D. P. (1997c). The verbalization of motion events in Arrernte (Central Australia). In E. Clark (Ed.), *The proceedings of the twenty-eighth annual child language research forum* (pp. 295–308). Stanford, CA: CSLI.

Wilkins, D. (to appear). Learning to point the Arrernte way. *Proceedings of 2002 Child Language Research Forum.*

Wilkins, D. P., & de Ruiter, J. P. A. (2001). *A cross-cultural investigation of the relations between speech, gesture and brain lateralisation: Is everybody right?* Invited keynote speech at 2001 Australian Linguistic Society Conference.

Wilkins, D. P., & Hill, D. (1995). When GO means COME: Questioning the basicness of basic motion verbs. *Cognitive Linguistics, 6,* 209–259.

Wundt, W. (1973). *The language of gestures.* The Hague: Mouton. (Original work published 1921)

Chapter 9

Pointing as Situated Practice

Charles Goodwin
UCLA Applied Linguistics

One of the legendary moments in American baseball occurred during the third game of the 1932 World Series when Babe Ruth, with two strikes against him and the game tied, pointed to center field and then hit the next pitch to where he had pointed for a home run. The classic version of this story has, however, been challenged on numerous occasions. For example, Woody English, the captain of the team opposing Ruth, claims that Ruth never pointed:

> Babe Ruth did *not* call his H.R. I was playing third base that game and he held two fingers up indicating two strike[s]—The press indicated he pointed, which he did *not*—He never said he called it. When asked, he replied "the papers *said I did.*" (Martin, 1996, p. E7; italics original)

Both the reporters and Woody English saw exactly the same posture assumed by Babe Ruth's body at a crucial moment: In the midst of his turn at bat, after having swung twice at the ball and missed, Ruth raises his arm into the air in front of him, and extends a finger or two. In the legend the arm with its extended fingers performs the action of pointing toward a particular place; for Woody English, Ruth's hand was displaying the number *two*, the current strike count.

The action that Ruth performed cannot be defined within a framework that focuses on his body in isolation, for example, disambiguating a point-

ing from a counting hand through ever finer analysis of postural configuration and hand shape. Instead, each version of the event is built by juxtapos-
ing to the visible configuration of Ruth's body a different set of phenomena
selected from the scene in progress. The legend, by depicting Ruth pointing, links his arm to a specific place in the surrounding scene. That place is
not a mere, undifferentiated space, but a highly structured cultural entity, a
playing field. The legend would be impossible if Ruth were described pointing to a part of the field where a hit ball would be classified as foul. This
configuration of an actor's body displaying intentional orientation to a culturally formulated space is then tied to a second event that occurred a short
time later: hitting the ball to the place pointed at for a home run. Note that
in making this link, a host of other events that also occurred within the park
during this time (e.g., the actions of other team members, fans eating
hotdogs, etc.) are treated as irrelevant. By way of contrast, Woody English's
version links the upraised hand not to a space in the surround or a future
action, but instead to prior events in the unfolding course of a turn at bat.
Here something that was invisible in the legendary account, the number of
fingers being raised, emerges as crucial for the visible production of a particular kind of action, for example, using the hand to display a number.
The encompassing game and the events that had just occurred provide
grounds for seeing the fingers as referring to the strike count, rather than
something else. In short, the particular action being seen selectively parses
the scene within which it is embedded, including a gesturing hand, by
bringing a particular subset of culturally formulated phenomena into juxtaposition with each other while ignoring others. Pointing is not a simple act,
a way of picking out things in the world that avoids the complexities of formulating a scene through language or other semiotic systems,[1] but is instead an action that can only be successfully performed by tying the act of
pointing to the construals of entities and events provided by other meaning
making resources as participants work to carry out courses of collaborative
action with each other.

---

[1]Pointing has frequently been treated as a simple, indeed primitive technique for doing
reference, a way of directly indicating entities in the immediate environment that avoids the
complexity of formulating what is being indicated through semiotic systems such as language.
From such a perspective, pointing tied to practices such as naming can act as the crucial bridge
between the categories provided by an abstract mental calculus such as language and the objects in the world around us. Thus, in a passage that constituted the point for departure for
Wittgenstein's (1958) critique of the unproblematic use of ostensive definition to link language to objects in the world (see also Quine, 1971), Saint Augustine (1996, I.8) stated that
"When they (my elders) named some object, and accordingly moved toward something, I saw
this and I grasped that the thing was called by the sound they uttered when they meant to
point it out."

POINTING AS A SITUATED INTERACTIVE ACTIVITY

A central locus for the act of pointing is a situation that contains at least two participants, one of whom is attempting to establish a particular space as a shared focus for the organization of cognition and action. Within such a field, pointing is constituted as a meaningful act through the mutual contextualization of a range of semiotic resources including at least (a) a body visibly performing an act of pointing; (b) talk that both elaborates and is elaborated by the act of pointing; (c) the properties of the space that is the target of the point; (d) the orientation of relevant participants toward both each other and the space that is the locus of the point; and (e) the larger activity within which the act of pointing is embedded.[2] In the remainder of this chapter this process is investigated by looking in detail at the organization of pointing in videotapes of multiparty talk-in-interaction recorded in two settings: (a) an archaeological field excavation, and (b) conversations in the home of man almost completely unable to produce spoken language because of a stroke. The catastrophically limited speech production of the man with aphasia (he can speak only three words) vividly demonstrates how the ability of both participants and analysts to easily, indeed almost transparently, find meaning in gesture is very much a situated accomplishment. Without the semiotic shaping of both space and the act of pointing provided by a rich language system, this man and his interlocutors must go to considerable work to establish where he is pointing (e.g., the location and conceptual structure of the space that is the target of his point) and what he is trying to say with an act of pointing. However, precisely because he has such limited ability to produce speech (although he has excellent ability to understand the talk of others), this man makes extensive use of points toward spaces already sedimented with meaning in his lifeworld as a way of trying to say something to others, the catch of course being that all of these spaces can be seen and understood in multiple ways. What is required to understand this process is study of how a complex visual field that must be parsed and understood in a congruent fashion by multiple participants is structured and elaborated through language, pointing, and mutual action. The work of the archaeologists as they articulate for each other the visibility and structure of relevant phenomena in the dirt they are excavating provides one site for such investigation.

---

[2]See Agha (1996), Hutchins and Palen (1997), and Ochs, Gonzales, and Jacoby (1996) for other most relevant analysis of how gestural meaning is accomplished through the mutual elaboration of multiple semiotic fields. Haviland (1993a, 1993b, 1996) provided extensive analysis of how pointing is organized with reference to both narrated spaces and directional coordinates.

DEFINING FEATURES AS ARCHAEOLOGICAL PRACTICE

A perspicuous site for the study of pointing can be found in work environments where participants must establish for each other how a relevant space should be construed in order to perform the tasks that make up the work of their setting. This chapter focuses on a group of archaeologists excavating an ancient native American village. Pointing is pervasive in their work, in large part, because archaeologists in the field are repetitively faced with the task of locating with precision relevant entities in the complex visual field provided by the dirt they are excavating, and of agreeing how to classify what they see. Issues posed for the analysis of pointing within such an environment can best be demonstrated through a specific example. Some brief background on the work of the archaeologists is necessary.

Many phenomena of interest to archaeologists, what they call *features* (Fig. 9.1), are visible only as color changes in the dirt they are excavating. For example, the cinders produced by an ancient hearth will leave a black stain, and the decaying material in an old posthole will produce a tube of dirt with color systematically different from the soil around the post. The activity of excavating features systematically destroys them. As dirt is removed to dig deeper, the patterns of visible color difference are destroyed. In part because of this, careful records, including maps, photographs, and coding forms of various types, have to be kept of each stage in the excavation. The data we examine were collected during one of the first working days of an archaeological field school. Personnel at the school included

FIG. 9.1. Archaeological features.

Ann, the senior archaeologist, graduate students with different levels of experience, undergraduates, and volunteers. For some of the newcomers, this is their first experience performing actual excavation. At the end of the last digging season, the current structure of the site was protected from weather and vandalism by covering exposed surfaces, including the features then visible, with dirt. The archaeologists are now removing this layer of dirt and comparing the surfaces they uncover with the maps made during the previous season.

JUXTAPOSING MULTIPLE SEMIOTIC FIELDS
TO ACCOMPLISH POINTING

Example 1 (Fig. 9.2) provides an opportunity to examine some of the different kinds of phenomena implicated in a single act of pointing. Ray Jones, a graduate student, calls the senior archaeologist, Ann Wesley, and shows her a feature he has found (Ann's laughter, dimmed in the transcript, is not relevant to the present analysis). In line 10, Ray shows Ann a feature. One of the places where that feature can be found in the current scene is on a map that Ray is holding on a clipboard. Over the word *found* in line 10 he uses his trowel to point to the image of that feature on the map. A number of different kinds of sign systems, instantiated in different semiotic media, are relevant to the organization of this point. First, there is the *pointing gesture*, here the hand using the trowel. That gesture points toward a particular place in the surround, a *domain of scrutiny*, where the addressee should look to find the *target* of the point, the particular entity being pointed at. Here the particular domain of scrutiny being pointed at is a map, a *graphic field* within which signs of a particular type can occur, in this case graphic representations of phenomena to be found in another territory.

The system that provides organization for the entities that can function as targets of a point is called the *activity framework*. An activity framework can encompass a number of different kinds of phenomena. Thus, on a baseball diamond the physical object that marks a base is not simply a bag, but a game-relevant semiotic object of a particular type. Similarly, by virtue of their placement on the graphic field constituted by a map, irregular squiggles are situated within a complex relationship both toward each other and to the territory that they describe. A second component of the activity framework is the encompassing activity that endows phenomena such as a graphic field and the semiotic objects situated within it with particular kinds of relevance; for example, the maps being used here constitute specific kinds of tools within the larger process of archaeological excavation that defines the work of this setting. A single domain of scrutiny can con-

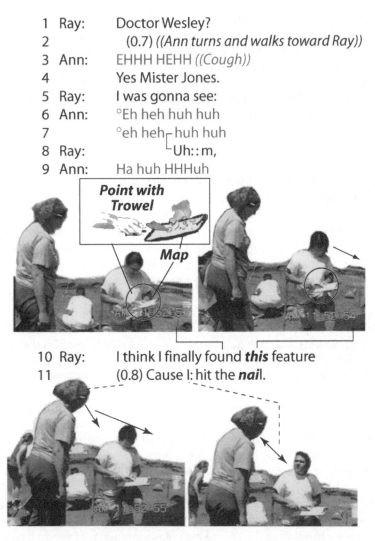

1 Ray: Doctor Wesley?
2   (0.7) ((Ann turns and walks toward Ray))
3 Ann: EHHH HEHH ((Cough))
4   Yes Mister Jones.
5 Ray: I was gonna see:
6 Ann: °Eh heh huh huh
7   °eh heh⌐huh huh
8 Ray: └Uh::m,
9 Ann: Ha huh HHHuh

Point with Trowel

Map

10 Ray: I think I finally found *this* feature
11   (0.8) Cause I: hit the *nail*.

FIG. 9.2.   Example 1: Multiple targets.

tain multiple targets linked in complex ways to a variety of different activity frameworks. An example is provided later when interaction with the man with aphasia is examined.

As an embodied action, a pointing gesture is lodged within a larger *hierarchy of displays being performed by the body* of the party doing the point. Just before he performs the trowel point, Ray picks up the map and gazes toward it, and thus displays to others that the map is the explicit focus of his current attention. The trowel point thus occurs within a larger framework of *postural orientation* by the pointer, which also displays focus toward the domain of scrutiny relevant to the action of the moment. Insofar as the point is being performed precisely to show someone else where the feature is to be found, *addressee orientation* is as relevant as the postural orientation of the pointer. Indeed, here Ray goes to considerable work to secure the orientation of his addressee, summoning her by name in line 1, and delaying the performance of his action until she is positioned to perceive it (note, for example, the "Uh::m" in line 8 and the silence that follows it). The separate, interlocking displays of pointer and addressee form a whole that is greater than the sum of its parts, a particular kind of *participation framework*.

Note that the participation framework relevant to the act of pointing includes not only orientation toward other participants (e.g., the situation described by Goodwin, 1981, in which speakers work to secure the orientation of a hearer before producing a complete utterance), but also orientation toward specific phenomena located beyond the participants in the surround. How these different possible foci of orientation (e.g., other participants versus targets in the surround) may be organized relative to each other within the activity of pointing is investigated shortly.

Crucial semiotic resources for shaping what is pointed at, and what is being done through a point, are provided by the talk that typically co-occurs with the point. In the present data, two different kinds of signs within Ray's utterance are briefly noted. First, the deictic term *this* not only instructs the hearer to attend to something beyond the talk itself, that is, the point, to locate what is being indicated, but also specifies that what is being pointed at is a single, countable entity (e.g., *this* not *these*), that is being formulated in terms of its thinglike attributes, as opposed to, say, the locative formulation that would result from use of a alternative deictic such as *here* or *there*. Second, the *semantic structure* of the term *feature* construes what is being pointed at as a particular kind of entity, for example, a cultural structure of interest to the archaeologists (as opposed to, say, a rock).

However, although located on the map, "*this* feature" has a second instantiation in a quite different spatial framework: the dirt being excavated. Moreover, both of these spatial frameworks are implicated in what is being said in Ray's utterance: Ray is reporting that he has found in the dirt a feature specified on the map. Over the word "*this*" in line 10 Ray moves his head away from the map and visibly gazes toward the place in the dirt that he is talking about. As a deictic term, *this* points toward a referent that exists in two separate, mutually relevant spaces in the current scene, the map and the dirt (which provide two quite distinct graphic fields for their separate targets). As Ray speaks the word "*this*" his body makes visible a complex pointing gesture, with the hand and trowel indicating one of the places where the entity identified through the semantic structure of his talk is to be found, while his gaze locates the second. Although the trowel point is no longer framed by his gaze toward the map, the postural configuration of his lower body and the sustained orientation of both of his hands toward the map continue to mark that field as the primary locus of his ongoing orientation (for detailed analysis of how the lower body displays a primary orientation framework see Kendon, 1990, and Schegloff, 1989). Through the way in which he organizes his point, Ray visibly indicates that what is being pointed at exists simultaneously in two different spaces in the local surround.

What consequences does this *dual point* have for the coparticipation of his addressee in the activity of pointing? Does she attend to the multiplicity of spaces that he marks as relevant? As the utterance begins, Ann is just finishing walking toward Ray. As soon as she stops she looks briefly at the map, the place indicated by Ray's trowel, and then leans forward to look over the map toward the dirt that is the target of his gaze. Her actions thus visibly orient to both of the spaces indicated by his complex point. Finally, as further demonstration of how what is at issue here is shared seeing embedded within collaborative action, Ray then moves his gaze away from the dirt back to Ann. From this position he can both take into account her looking and possible responses, and locate her as the addressee of his continuing talk.

Rather than being a simple way of indicating some prelinguistic "thing" in the surround, the pointing that occurs here is a complex semiotic act accomplished through the juxtaposition of an array of quite different kinds of meaning-producing systems. Within the activity of pointing, participants are faced with the task of attending to multiple visual fields, including both the region being pointed at and each other's bodies. Indeed, as seen here, within pointing a progression of gaze shifts is frequently found; for example, the pointer may initially look toward the region being pointed at and then to the addressee in order to both judge the addressee's orientation (e.g., has he or she looked toward the appropriate region) and evaluate how he or she is responding to the action being performed through the point. Similarly, the addressee is typically faced with the task of using something in one spatial field—the pointer's body—to locate something else in a different spatial field. Rather than just looking somewhere, coparticipants engaged in pointing are faced with the task of coordinating multiple visual fields if they are to successfully accomplish the activities in progress.

Moreover, one of these fields, the human body, is quite unlike most other visual phenomena in the scene. Within interaction the body is a dynamic, temporally unfolding field that displays a reflexive stance toward other coparticipants, the current talk, and the actions in progress. As demonstrated through their responses to the displays made visible in each other's bodies (e.g., performing the point only after the addressee is positioned to see it, looking toward the various spaces indicated by the pointer's body, etc.), Ann and Ray treat each other's bodies as fields that provide a mutable locus for the ongoing production of intentional action. Moreover, the visible body is a complex entity that can construct multiple displays that mutually frame each other (e.g., points can be framed by larger postural configurations). The body is thus a very different kind of entity than, say, the *feature* that constitutes the target(s) of the points here. Thus, parties engaged in the activity of pointing must attend to not only multiple visual fields, but fields that differ significantly in their structure and properties.

Pointing is accomplished through the juxtaposition of very different kinds of semiotic phenomena (the body, talk, structures of different kinds in the surrounding scene, etc.). How is this heterogeneity within a common course of action to be analyzed? A framework is needed that can encompass both the differentiated actions of multiple participants (e.g., the party performing the point, and responsive actions of his or her addressee[s]) and a diverse collection of signs lodged within media with quite different properties (e.g., talk, gesture, visible structure in the field being pointed at, such as a map, etc.). Other work on the organization of talk-in-interaction has demonstrated the value of analyzing a course of recognizable action as a *situated activity system* (Goffman, 1961; C. Goodwin, 1996; M. H. Goodwin, 1990; Goodwin & Goodwin, 1987). For example, a concurrent assessment (e.g., two participants simultaneously evaluating something through both overlapping talk and visible embodied displays of affect and appreciation—see Goodwin, 1996, for an actual example) integrates into a common course of action syntactic and semantic structure, intonation, gesture, participation frameworks, and inferential processes projecting events that haven't actually occurred yet, into a common course of interactively sustained action. In this chapter, pointing is investigated as a situated activity system in which action is built by assembling diverse semiotic resources into locally relevant multimodal packages, which I have elsewhere analyzed as contextual configurations (Goodwin, 2000a).

APHASIA: POINTING WITHOUT A SEMANTIC CONSTRUAL

In the data just examined, many of the organizational frameworks being described converge at precisely the same place. Thus, when Ray's trowel touches his map, it locates with fine precision in a single space a target, a graphic field, and a domain of scrutiny, while his talk formulates that target as a particular kind of entity. Are these alternative frameworks simply distinctions being made by the analyst, or do participants orient to them differentially as they perform the tasks made relevant by the activity of pointing? To probe this issue, data of a quite different kind are briefly examined before returning to the archaeologists. Because of a massive stroke, Chil has been left with the ability to say only three words, *Yes, No,* and *And.* Elsewhere (Goodwin, 1995, 2000b) I described how Chil is nonetheless able to perform relevant conversational action, and say quite subtle things, by embedding his sparse vocabulary and gesture within larger sequences of talk produced by others. Frequently, as in the data examined here, what Chil wants to say is worked out through a sequence in which his interlocutors produce guesses that he accepts or rejects. Example 2 occurred after Chil and his son Chuck had finished breakfast and were making plans for what to do that day. The sequence begins when Peggy calls from another room and suggests a walk. After securing Chuck's gaze, Chil in line 7 points toward something on the table between them. For clarity, proposals Chuck makes about what Chil might be pointing at are highlighted with boxes (Fig. 9.3). Using Chil's outstretched finger as a guide, Chuck correctly treats the table between them as the domain of scrutiny where the target of the point is to be found. However, the kitchen table is the base of a complex space that contains many different kinds of objects, such as a plate with an assortment of pastries, a box of Kleenex, a plastic cup that held the morning's pills, newspapers, silverware, the table itself, and so on. Moreover, Chil is unable to produce co-occurring talk that would formulate the target as particular kind of entity and thus constrain the search. Locating the target of the point becomes a practical problem for Chuck, who produces a series of guesses—"Bagel." "Put this away?" "Chocolate." "Do you want something to eat?"—before at last establishing that what is being pointed at is his newspaper with its movie schedule. As Chuck guesses incorrectly, Chil responds by leaning forward in an attempt to move his pointing finger past the plate of pastries that Chuck repetitively returns to. However, in the absence of a semantic gloss this movement can also be read as an attempt to get the pastry plate itself, and Chuck responds to Chil's second point by moving the plate toward him. Only when Chil finally moves his finger entirely past the plate during the silence in line 18 does Chuck at last shift his attention to the movie schedule in the newspaper that now lies directly under Chil's pointing finger. In these data the way in which the *domain of scrutiny,* the *target, co-occurring talk,* and temporally unfolding changes in *the body of the party performing the point* constitute distinct phenomena differentially implicated in the activity of pointing is clear.

Note that in attempting to figure out where Chil is pointing, Chuck is not simply trying to locate the target of the point, that is, successfully accomplish reference, but is simultaneously attempting to locate the action Chil is performing—that is, does he want something to eat, or the table to be cleared, or movies to be checked. The way in which seeable targets are each embedded within webs of recognizable activities is central to this process. As noted earlier, the term *activity framework* is used to refer to a candi-

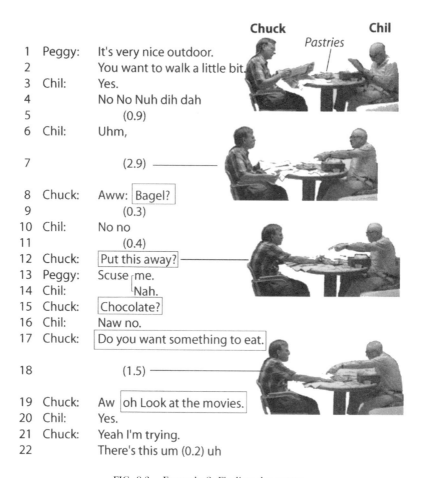

			Chuck	Chil
1	Peggy:	It's very nice outdoor.		
2		You want to walk a little bit.		
3	Chil:	Yes.		
4		No No Nuh dih dah		
5		(0.9)		
6	Chil:	Uhm,		
7		(2.9) ——————		
8	Chuck:	Aww: Bagel?		
9		(0.3)		
10	Chil:	No no		
11		(0.4)		
12	Chuck:	Put this away? ———		
13	Peggy:	Scuse ⌈me.		
14	Chil:	⌊Nah.		
15	Chuck:	Chocolate?		
16	Chil:	Naw no.		
17	Chuck:	Do you want something to eat.		
18		(1.5) ——————		
19	Chuck:	Aw oh Look at the movies.		
20	Chil:	Yes.		
21	Chuck:	Yeah I'm trying.		
22		There's this um (0.2) uh		

FIG. 9.3. Example 2: Finding the target.

date target, such as a bagel or a newspaper, and the webs of recognizable activities within which that target is embedded. Although different targets make relevant different activity systems—for example, bagels but not newspapers are eaten—each target is embedded within multiple activities that can overlap with activities appropriate to another target (e.g., both leftover bagels and newspapers are things to be put away when the table is cleared after breakfast). Moreover the entities that can serve as the targets of points can themselves be quite complex activity frameworks, such as the newspapers being read here, which contain within them news, comics, ads, pictures, movie and television schedules, and so on.

The way in which the objects that inhabit his lifeworld are already sedimented with visible, public meaning and tied to typical courses of action provides Chil with crucial semiotic resources for saying something meaningful to others despite his lack of speech. For example, by pointing toward a thermostat in his living room, he can be seen as requesting that the temperature in the house be changed. Indeed, it is the systematic availability of such differentiated but relevant structure in his environment that makes pointing such a crucial resource for Chil. However, as we see here, the multiplicity of phenomena within a single domain of scrutiny poses for addressees the task of locating which of the available candidates is the target of the point. Indeed, the practical problem faced by Chil's interlocutors of using his pointing finger to parse the current scene and its candidate actions in a relevant fashion by selecting an appropriate subset of phenomena from a host of competing possibilities provides a mundane, real-world example of the interpretative issues raised by Babe Ruth's legendary point to a future home run.

A final resource that is central to the organization of Chil's point in the data we have been examining is the *sequential framework* (Sacks, 1992/1995; Schegloff, 1968) provided by the talk from which Chil's initial point emerges. In line 2, Peggy suggests that Chil take a walk. Chil's point is being used to invoke an alternative to Peggy's suggestion for how to spend the afternoon. The activity of pointing is prefaced by a *No* tied to Peggy's proposal, and this formulates the point as offering something that stands in contrast to what was said there. The point emerges within a field already endowed with meaning. Going to the movies, but not having a bagel, constitutes an alternative to "walk a little bit" as a way to spend the time after breakfast. It appears that Chuck, who is intently looking at the paper until summoned by Chil, does not hear this, and thus produces guesses that are inconsistent with the framing provided by Chil's point as an alternative to something said in earlier talk. Chuck's failure to take this into account demonstrates how assembling the mix of multiple semiotic fields that is relevant to the appropriate construal of a particular act of pointing is not something automatic or specified in advance, but is instead a contingent accomplishment.

TRACING: SUPERIMPOSING ICONIC SHAPE ON A POINTING GESTURE

Returning to the archaeological data, Example 3 (Fig. 9.4) provides an example of a different kind of dual point. Once again the participants are trying to locate in the dirt a feature marked on the map that Ray is holding on a clipboard. As Ray's utterance begins, his index finger is tracing the shape of the feature being examined on the map. He has just solicited Jane's gaze, and the finger highlighting a particular spot on the map provides a way of showing her, and probably himself as well, the precise placement and shape

Ray: This is an **ex**tra thing here. (0.5) Little curve.

FIG. 9.4.   Example 3: Tracing.

of the feature on the map. Ray's index finger remains on the map until the beginning of the word *here*. While speaking *here*, he moves his pointing finger from the map to the instantiation of the feature in the dirt. Thus, while pronouncing this word he points at two quite distinct, although intimately linked, spaces. Here, rather than doing dual points with separate parts of his body (e.g., gaze and hand), a single moving gesture points toward two quite different spaces, both of which contain what is being pointed at. Note that his talk does not formulate what is happening as a moving series of discrete points that targets two contrasting semiotic entities (e.g., the sequence of separate points to different places over *this* and *that* in a phrase such as "It should be on this table, not that one"). Instead, what is being pointed at is formulated as singular: "an extra thing." However, that "thing" manifests itself in two separate spaces that are treated as equivalent loci for the co-occurring *here*, and that both constitute almost simultaneous (e.g., within the scope and duration of a single monosyllabic deictic term) targets of a single, albeit moving, point. Rather than performing primitive reference to a prelinguistic "thing" in the surround, Ray's pointing finger sits at the nexus of a complex process through which the semiotic construals provided by multiple meaning-producing systems (semantic structure, the map, seeable structure in the dirt being excavated, the framing of the action provided by Ray's body and Jane's visible orientation, the encompassing task, etc.) are juxtaposed to each other so as to permit their mutual elaboration in a way that is relevant to the work at hand (e.g., finding the phenomena on the map in the dirt in front of them).

In most typologies of gesture (see McNeill, 1992, p. 76, for a summary), *iconic* gestures and *deictic* (pointing) gestures are treated as separate kinds of gesture. This does not seem to be correct. Pointing gestures can trace the shape of what is being pointed at, and thus superimpose an iconic display on a deictic point within the performance of a single gesture. Instead of using this distinction to separate gestures into distinct classes, it seems more fruitful to focus analysis on an *indexical component* or an *iconic component* of a gesture, either or both of which may contribute to the organization of a particular gesture (see also Clark, 1996, p. 159).

The features that archaeologists focus on typically manifest themselves as irregularly shaped patches of color in the dirt being excavated. Quite frequently an archaeologist will not simply point toward a feature with his or her finger or a trowel, but will instead trace the shape of the feature with a moving point. Thus, just before Ray moved from the map to the dirt in the data just examined, he traced the shape of the "extra thing" on the map (i.e., moved his finger around the line defining its shape), and then when his pointing finger reached the dirt, again traced a shape while glossing it as "little curve." Through this *tracing* an *iconic representation* is superimposed on the indexical orientation of the point. Note that the *resemblance* between gesture and referent that constitutes iconicity can be specified in terms of the relationship between the gesture and two quite distinct semiotic fields: (a) the semantic structure of the talk, and (b) visible phenomena in the domain of scrutiny being pointed toward. Thus, here Ray's tracing movement has an iconic tie to both (a) *curve* in the stream of speech, and (b) the pattern in the dirt under his moving finger. Each of these construals of what is pointed at contextualizes the others. Most previous work on gesture has focused on ties between the gesture and only one of these fields, the talk. Thus for McNeill (1992, p. 78), "a gesture is *iconic* if it bears a close formal relationship to the semantic content of the speech." In the experimental situation used by McNeill, the entity being described through the gesture, a scene on a cartoon that the subject had just seen, was no longer present. McNeill recognized the crucial importance of looking not just at the speech, but also at the scene being described. However, because that scene was not actually present, phenomena such as tracing were inaccessible to analysis.

Tracing has a number of consequences. First, the moving finger and the target of the point are brought into a dynamic relationship in which each is used to understand the other. The activity of pointing continues after reference per se has been accomplished. Second, tracing provides a way of indicating precise information about what is pointed at, such as the exact shape of a color stain in the dirt, that would be difficult to specify through language alone. Third, typologies of gesture have almost completely ignored those that get their distinctive organization from the way in which the gesturing body interacts with other phenomena within a domain of scrutiny, such as tracing, touches, and so on (but see LeBaron, 1998; LeBaron & Streeck, 2000; and Streeck, 1996a, 1996b, for powerful demonstrations of how gesture is tied to its environment and analysis that is most relevant to the points being argued here). However, as anyone who has ever attended a scientific talk, a military briefing, a planning meeting, and so on, or even looked at a finger-smeared computer screen, can testify, such gestures are absolutely central to the way in which the work of the world gets done.

INSCRIPTION

When the act of tracing leaves a mark in the domain of scrutiny, it creates an *inscription*. There is an intimate, systematic progression within pointing from tracing to inscription. As he or she traces the outline of a proposed feature in the air above an a set of color patches, an archaeologist typically holds a trowel, the default tool used to excavate features. When defining a feature (outlining its shape in the dirt as a preliminary to mapping it), the point of the trowel is lowered just enough to cut into the dirt itself so that the tracing movement leaves a mark. The tracing point is thus transduced into a new medium, the dirt, where it leaves an enduring mark (Fig. 9.5). Leaving a visible trace of a pointing gesture within the field being pointed at has a range of consequences. A few are briefly noted. First, such inscription constitutes a form of *highlighting* (Goodwin, 1994), a way of reorganizing a domain of scrutiny in terms of the tasks of the moment. Indeed, through inscription the material structure of the domain of scrutiny is transformed through pointing. Second, this can act as a powerful rhetorical move. In the midst of an argument about whether or not a particular set of color patches does in fact provide evidence for a feature, or where the boundaries of a feature should be located, such inscription can lead others

FIG. 9.5.   Inscribing.

to see the shape it delineates as forming the pattern being argued for. Third, such inscription creates a special kind of liminal representation. Unlike what happens when the pattern is further transduced, say into a map, here the representation and the entity being represented coexist within the same perceptual field, and thus remain in a state where each can be used to judge the other. Fourth, by virtue of the way in which the original pointing action now has a new physical and temporal existence, new forms of mediated action become possible. In Example 4, a young student, Sue, is defining a feature under the watchful eye of her archaeology professor, Ann (i.e., to help the reader easily see who is who in the transcripts the name beginning with *S* is a student, and the name beginning with *A* is a senior archaeologist). Immediately after Sue finishes her inscription, Ann moves her own pointing finger just to the side of the student's line, and traces a slightly different path (Fig. 9.6). Here one person's pointing finger is carrying on a dialogue with the trace of another's gesture inscribed in the dirt. The inscription provides a precise record, enduring in time, that the professor can use to evaluate the work-relevant seeing of her student. In turn,

Ann:	En I- I would'a put it
	a *ti::ny* bit out there.
	(0.2)
Ann:	But *that*'s no big deal.
Sue:	°Okay.
	(0.5)
Ann:	But do you *see*: *hhh uhm
	(0.6)
Ann:	Right there.
	(1.5)
Ann:	⌈Okay.
Sue:	⌊I didn't see that one at all.

FIG. 9.6.   Example 4: Gesture dialogue.

within this public field of visible, meaningful action, the student can see how the professor would organize the very same materials that she has been working with. Inscription here provides an arena within which the judgments required to perform the practices used to constitute the phenomena that define the work of a community (e.g., the mapping of features within archaeology) can be publicly calibrated.

PROGRESSIVE REFORMULATION THROUGH CHANGING POINTS TO A COMMON TARGET

Inscription provides a particularly clear example of how pointing can transform features in the domain of scrutiny being pointed at, and of how this might be relevant to the social organization of the embodied practices that constitute the work of a profession. However, such transformations can be accomplished in other ways as well, for example, through the semantic construals that accompany a series of linked points. In Fig. 9.7 the same

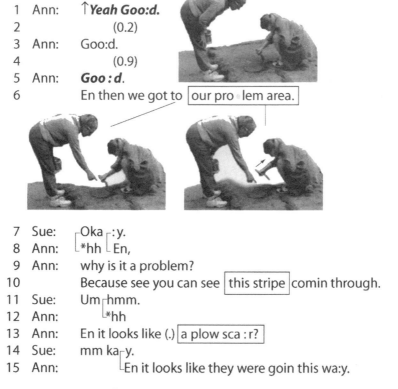

```
1   Ann:    ↑Yeah Goo:d.
2           (0.2)
3   Ann:    Goo:d.
4           (0.9)
5   Ann:    Goo:d.
6           En then we got to  our pro lem area.

7   Sue:    ⌈Oka⌈:y.
8   Ann:    ⌊*hh ⌊En,
9   Ann:    why is it a problem?
10          Because see you can see  this stripe comin through.
11  Sue:    Um⌈hmm.
12  Ann:      ⌊*hh
13  Ann:    En it looks like (.)  a plow sca:r?
14  Sue:    mm ka⌈y.
15  Ann:         ⌊En it looks like they were goin this wa:y.
```

FIG. 9.7.   Example 5: Progressive reformulation.

patch of color stains in the dirt is described in three different ways: (a) as a *problem area*, (b) as a *stripe*, and (c) as a *plow scar*. Each of these terms formulates what is being pointed at in a quite different way.

POINTING AS ACTION

The formulation of the space being pointed at as a *problem area* in line 6 of Fig. 9.7 is linked to a number of different action frameworks, and this is done not only through talk, but also through the precise way in which Ann's point here is done. As the sequence begins, Sue is tracing the outline of a feature, a postmold. In lines 1–5 Ann is intently scrutinizing Sue's moving trowel while praising her performance. Ann's point in line 6 and the statement about arrival at the problem area that accompanies it are not sequenced to actions in other talk, but instead occur precisely at the moment when Sue's trowel is about to extend the inscription into the space being formulated as a "problem area." The arm movement that brings Ann's point to the space being indicated almost touches Sue's moving trowel. When this happens, Sue quickly retracts the trowel and thus stops tracing. Indeed, if the sequence is viewed without sound, it looks like Ann's pointing movement has the effect of pushing Sue's hand away. The possibility that Ann might be attempting to stop Sue from continuing further is quite consistent with the formulation of the space being pointed at as a *problem area*; for example, because of the disturbance intruding into the postmold, its outline shouldn't be traced until it is examined more carefully. The past tense and distal temporal deictic used in line 6 also project that the ongoing action being observed in lines 1–5 has come to some type of completion (e.g., not "And *now* we *get* to our problem area" but "And *then* we *got* to our problem area"). In brief, in addition to indicating a relevant space, the embodied performance of Ann's point constrains Sue's ongoing action in a manner that attends to the temporally unfolding configuration of activity and task-relevant graphic field; it stops the tracing at the place where it enters the problem area. Note how this action depends on Ann's point being simultaneously contextualized by an array of different semiotic fields. Thus, in addition to indicating a target in a particular graphic field that is shaped as a domain of collaborative scrutiny through both the joint visual focus of multiple participants and the work being performed there, it also functions as a visible action within the current participation framework by intruding into the line of orientation being sustained through Sue's gaze and moving hand. Simultaneously, Ann's point constitutes a particular kind of move within the encompassing activity of outlining a feature. The force of that move as something designed to terminate an ongoing action is further specified by the grammatical organization (e.g., past tense) and semantic structure (problem area) of the talk that co-occurs with the point.

LEARNING TO SEE AS A PROFESSIONAL
THROUGH POINTING

The ensemble of action in line 6 not only orients to the course of action it emerges from, but also looks forward by the setting the agenda for a future course of action. The term *problem area* constitutes a *prospective indexical* (Goodwin, 1996, p. 384). Although the space being pointed at is characterized in a particular way, the nature of the problem with it is not specified. What precisely that consists of is something to be developed in subsequent interaction.

Ann immediately instructs Sue as to why this space should be seen as a problem through an ensemble of coordinated talk and pointing. As she asks rhetorically in line 9 "Why is it a problem?", her hand moves from right to left over the color patches that will be described in line 10 as a stripe. This gesture both anticipates and puts her body in position for the semantic and gestural exposition of this same line of patches that will occur in line 10. As her hand starts this gesture, it switches from a pointing index finger to an inverted *U* shape. The area within the *U* seems to mark the width of the color patches that will later be described as a "stripe." Although the talk in line 9 does not yet offer a solution to the question it poses, both the place where that solution will be found and some of the semantic features that will be used to characterize it (e.g., a long, straight extended space with seeable width, i.e., some of the defining features of a "stripe") are already being made visible with Ann's gesture.

Ann then sweeps her index finger in a long line over the dirt, tracing the shape of the color stain while characterizing the entity being pointed at as a stripe. This stripe is treated as something that can be readily seen and recognized: "you can see this stripe coming through." This unproblematic visibility of an entity of a particular type is made possible through a range of resources, including the shared public space that is being pointed at, the work that Ann performs to ensure that Sue is looking right where she is pointing, and the way in which the term *stripe* is lodged within a descriptive frame of reference that can be applied generically to particular types of patterns on diverse visible surfaces from paintings to jackets to landscapes. It offers a neutral characterization of structure being treated as clearly visible on the surface being examined. Note, however, that it is not at all clear that Sue would have seen, recognized, or focused on this pattern without Ann's exposition. The combined activity of description and pointing has made salient and relevant to the activities of the moment a particular kind of entity that is now clearly positioned in front of them.

After Sue acknowledges this in line 11, Ann, in line 13, describes this same pattern in a quite different way: "En it looks like (.) a plow sca:r?" Instead of offering a neutral description of phenomena being treated as clearly visible on the surface being examined, this new characterization of the color stain proposes a theory about no longer visible agents or processes that might have caused such a pattern—that is, the stripe was made by a plow moving through the dirt. The weakened epistemic status of this characterization is marked with the phrase "it looks like."

POINTING AS DEMONSTRATION

In line 15 (Fig. 9.8), the properties of the plow scar are further elaborated through a new, quite different, combination of talk and gesture. Ann holds her hand in a loose cup shape, with fingers facing to her left, that is, toward the line formed by the color stain, and moves the hand from right to left over the space she's just described as a plow scar. As she does this she says (line 15) "En it looks like they were goin this way." This gesture, which makes visible the direction and motion of the plow, is quite different from the earlier pointing gestures. In those, a pointing finger led the eye of the addressee to something beyond the finger: the dirt being pointed at. Here the moving hand is itself the focus of vision, and what is being referred to and characterized is not the dirt, but the motion of the invisible plow "going this way." This is indicated not only by the term *way* as the complement to the deictic term *this* indexing the gesture, but also by the new hand shape, which no longer points to the dirt below it, but instead focuses gaze on the hand and the direction in which it is moving. This gesture is still a form of pointing, only now what is being pointed at and demonstrated through the pointing motion is a direction rather than a specific place in the dirt. Although not being pointed at, the dirt being explicated remains a most relevant constituent of the field of action that provides the gesture with its visible intelligibility, as demonstrated through the way in which the hand moves right above the stripe. Like the liminal inscribed outline of a feature traced within an amorphous patch of color differences, the moving hand and the seeable structure in the dirt beneath it mutually elaborate each other while both are further construed by the talk that accompanies the gesture. Although what is being described occurred long ago, that past

13 Ann: En it looks like (.) a plow sca : r?
14 Sue: mm ka⌐y.

15 Ann: └En it looks like they were goin this wa:y.

FIG. 9.8. Example 6: Seeing the past in the present.

event is not a self-contained narrative bubble, but instead something that can only be perceived by attending to specific phenomena in the here and now. The current scene, and specifically the visible structure in the dirt under Ann's moving hand, interpenetrates the narrated past. Indeed, what Sue is being taught through the web of action invoked through this pointing is how to see the past in the present, by looking at its visible traces through the eyes of an archaeologist.

What has been seen in this sequence provides further support for the argument that what is being indicated with a pointing gesture is not a simple place or space, but a complex semiotic object constituted through the mutual conjunction of multiple meaning-producing systems. Here the same spot in the dirt is constituted as a series of quite different kinds of entities through changes in the semiotic fields within which the point is embedded. Although this is most clearly demonstrated through changes in semantic frameworks (*problem area* ⇒ *stripe* ⇒ *plow scar*), it is also constituted through relevant changes in the practices of pointing, such as the different hand shapes and movement patterns that distinguish a point toward the stripe from a demonstration of the plow moving through the dirt.

This act of locating something in a complex visual field, and thus dividing that field into a salient figure against a more amorphous ground, while using the semantic resources of language to construe what is to be seen there can have enormous rhetorical and political consequences. In the trial of the Los Angeles policemen who beat Rodney King, the pointing finger of a witness defending the policemen shaped what could be seen on the videotape of the beating in a way that led to the acquittal of the policemen. By pointing to Rodney King, indeed touching his image on the screen, the witness established Mr. King's actions as the focal event in the scene, while the policemen who were beating him faded into the background (see Goodwin, 1994, for more extended analysis of this process). Simultaneously, the witness used semantic categories such as *aggressive* to formulate Mr. King as the instigator rather than the recipient of the violence in progress. The power of pointing to structure what is to be seen in a domain of scrutiny transformed the tape that had led to the policemen being charged with a crime into the evidence that exonerated them.

In the plow scar data, through a sequence of pointing elaborated by other semiotic systems, Sue is being taught not only to see in a complex visual field the entities that constitute the working environment of her profession, postmolds for example, but also to see such entities as embedded within a complex layering of space and time. The native American postmold that is the focus of her current work is to be seen as something deformed by the work of later farmers. Moreover, by attending to the patterning of color in the dirt, Sue can even figure out in what direction that plow was moving. Such seeing is not available to just any speaker of English. I cannot do it.

However, being able to see the world in this way is central to what it means to be an archaeologist. Such seeing is a publicly organized constitutive feature of the profession of archaeology. Through the act of pointing, the senior archaeologist is able to juxtapose in a work-relevant fashion the visual field being scrutinized, the dirt that constitutes the primordial ground for all subsequent archaeological theory, semantic categories for describing and locating relevant entities within that field, and seeable evidence for the processes that shaped what can now be seen. Ann's moving finger weaves together into a single coherent package two semiotic modalities—visual fields populated by structured phenomenal entities, and language—in a way that is central to the cognitive organization of her profession.

CONCLUSION

This chapter has attempted to demonstrate that pointing is an inherently interstitial action, something that exists precisely at the place where a heterogeneous array of different kinds of sign vehicles instantiated in diverse semiotic media (the body, talk, phenomena in the surrounding scene, etc.) are being juxtaposed to each other to create a coherent package of meaning and action (see also Goodwin, 2000a). The heterogeneity of phenomena implicated in even a single act of pointing poses a range of methodological and theoretical problems, and indeed an enormously successful strategy for analysis has involved ignoring the structural diversity of multiple semiotic fields by isolating relatively independent, self-contained subsystems for study (e.g., language, space, gesture, etc.). Why then study pointing? A primordial site for the organization of human action, cognition, language, and social organization consists of a situation within which multiple participants are building in concert with each other the actions that define and shape their lifeworld (e.g., excavating an archaeological site, playing baseball, making plans for the day after breakfast, etc.). In this process, they make use of both language and semiotic materials provided by their setting (tools, objects sedimented with meaning and activity, culturally defined spaces such as playing fields, kitchen tables, maps, structure visible to an archaeologist as color differences within a patch of dirt, etc.). The issues posed for the analysis of action in such a setting involve not simply the resources provided by different semiotic systems as self-contained wholes, but also the interactive practices required to juxtapose them so that they mutually elaborate each other in a way relevant to the accomplishment of the actions that make up the setting. Pointing provides an opportunity to investigate within a single interactive practice the details of language use, the body as a socially organized field for temporally unfolding displays of meaning tied to relevant action, and material and semiotic phenomena in the surround. Looking at these issues in a different way, the semantic system of a language would be extraordinarily cumbersome if it had to provide separate terms for all the possible shapes that could be distinguished in even as simple a domain of scrutiny as a patch of dirt. However, the work of adequately locating and characterizing relevant phenomena in the surround can be readily accomplished within talk-in-interaction if sign systems containing different kinds of resources for construing phenomena, such as language and pointing, are used in conjunction with each other. For example, tracing provides resources for displaying an almost infinite variety of shapes but, as Chil's situation vividly demonstrates, frequently requires a simultaneous formulation of what is being pointed at through language. More generally, this suggests the importance of not focusing analysis exclusively on the properties of individual sign systems, but instead investigating the organization of the ecology of sign systems that have evolved in conjunction with each other within the primordial site for human action: multiple participants using talk to build action while attending to the distinctive properties of a relevant setting. From such a perspective, pointing cannot be explained by studying the body in isolation, but must be seen vis-à-vis shifting backgrounds of settings and situated language practices that are themselves structured by activities and semiotic resources. Pointing thus provides one perspicuous site for investigating the range of resources deployed by human beings to structure their cognition and build meaning and action within the endogenous settings that constitute the social world of a society.

ACKNOWLEDGMENTS

I am most indebted to Dr. Gail Wagner, and the students at her archaeological field school, and to Chil and his family, for allowing me access to relevant events in their lives, which made the analysis developed in this chapter possible. I thank Candy Goodwin, Makoto Hayashi, John Haviland, Adam Kendon, David Wilkinson, one anonymous reviewer, and the participants at the Max Planck Workshop on Pointing Gestures, organized by Sotaro Kita, for insightful and helpful comments on an earlier version of this chapter.

REFERENCES

Agha, A. (1996). Schema and superposition in spatial deixis. *Journal of Linguistic Anthropology*, *38*(4), 643–682.
Augustine, W. W., & Rouse, W. H. D. (1996). *Confessions*. Cambridge, MA: Harvard University Press.
Clark, H. (1996). *Using language*. Cambridge: Cambridge University Press.

Goffman, E. (1961). *Encounters: Two studies in the sociology of interaction.* Indianapolis: Bobbs-Merrill.

Goodwin, C. (1981). *Conversational organization: Interaction between speakers and hearers.* New York: Academic Press.

Goodwin, C. (1994). Professional vision. *American Anthropologist, 96*(3), 606–633.

Goodwin, C. (1995). Co-constructing meaning in conversations with an aphasic man. *Research on Language and Social Interaction, 28*(3), 233–260.

Goodwin, C. (1996). Transparent vision. In E. Ochs, E. A. Schegloff, & S. Thompson (Eds.), *Interaction and grammar* (pp. 370–404). Cambridge: Cambridge University Press.

Goodwin, C. (2000a). Action and embodiment within situated human interaction. *Journal of Pragmatics, 32*(1489–1522).

Goodwin, C. (2000b). Gesture, aphasia and interaction. In D. McNeill (Ed.), *Language and gesture* (pp. 84–98). Cambridge: Cambridge University Press.

Goodwin, C., & Goodwin, M. H. (1987). Concurrent operations on talk: Notes on the interactive organization of assessments. *IPrA Papers in Pragmatics, 1*(1), 1–52.

Goodwin, M. H. (1990). *He-said-she-said: Talk as social organization among Black children.* Bloomington: Indiana University Press.

Haviland, J. B. (1993a). Anchoring, iconicity, and orientation in Guugu Yimidhirr pointing gestures. *Journal of Linguistic Anthropology, 3*(1), 3–45.

Haviland, J. B. (1993b). *Pointing, gesture spaces, and mental maps.* Paper published online in the Third Language and Culture Symposium. http://www.language-culture.org//archives/subs/haviland-john/.

Haviland, J. B. (1996). Projections, transpositions, and relativity. In J. J. Gumperz & S. C. Levinson (Eds.), *Rethinking linguistic relativity* (pp. 271–323). Cambridge: Cambridge University Press.

Hutchins, E., & Palen, L. (1997). Constructing meaning from space, gesture, and speech. In L. Resnick, R. Säljö, C. Pontecorvo, & B. Burge (Eds.), *Discourse, tools and reasoning: Essays on situated cognition* (pp. 23–40). New York: Springer-Verlag.

Kendon, A. (1990). Spatial organization in social encounters: The F-formation system. In A. Kendon (Ed.), *Conducting interaction: Patterns of behavior in focused encounters* (pp. 209–238). Cambridge: Cambridge University Press.

LeBaron, C. (1998). *Building communication: Architectural gestures and the embodiment of ideas.* Dissertation submitted in partial fulfillment of the requirements for the degree of Doctor of Philosophy, The University of Texas at Austin.

LeBaron, C. D., & Streeck, J. (2000). Gestures, knowledge, and the world. In D. McNeill (Ed.), *Gestures in action, language, and culture.* Cambridge: Cambridge University Press.

Martin, D. (1996, September 29). "Word for Word/Baseball Letters" Excerpts from Seth Swirsky's "Baseball Letters: A Fan's Correspondence with His Heroes." *The New York Times,* p. E7.

McNeill, D. (1992). *Hand and mind: What gestures reveal about thought.* Chicago: University of Chicago Press.

Ochs, E., Gonzales, P., & Jacoby, S. (1996). When I come down, I'm in a domain state: Grammar and graphic representation in the interpretive activity of physicists. In E. Ochs, E. A. Schegloff, & S. Thompson (Eds.), *Interaction and grammar* (pp. 328–369). Cambridge: Cambridge University Press.

Quine, W. V. (1971). The inscrutability of reference. In D. D. Steinberg & L. A. Jacobovits (Eds.), *Semantics: An interdisciplinary reader in philosophy, linguistics and psychology* (pp. 142–154). Cambridge: Cambridge University Press.

Sacks, H. (1995 [1992]). *Lectures on conversation: Volumes I & II* (Edited by Gail Jefferson, with an Introduction by Emanuel A. Schegloff). Oxford: Basil Blackwell.

Schegloff, E. A. (1968). Sequencing in conversational openings. *American Anthropologist, 70,* 1075–1095.

Schegloff, E. A. (1990, November 30). *Body torque*. Presentation in the invited session on "Spacing, Orientation and the Environment in Co-Present Interaction" at the 89th annual meeting of the American Anthropological Association, New Orleans.

Streeck, J. (1996a). How to do things with things. *Human Studies, 19*, 365–384.

Streeck, J. (1996b, November 21). *Vis-à-vis an embodied mind*. Paper presented to the panel "Between Cognitive Science and Anthropology: A Re-Emerging Dialogue" at the annual meeting of the American Anthropological Association, San Francisco, CA.

Wittgenstein, L. (1958). *Philosophical investigations* (Edited by G. E. M. Anscombe and R. Rhees, Translated by G. E. M. Anscombe, 2nd ed.). Oxford: Blackwell.

Chapter 10

Pointing and Placing

Herbert H. Clark
Stanford University

Communication is ordinarily anchored to the material world—to actual people, artifacts, rooms, buildings, landscapes, events, processes. One way it gets anchored is through pointing. One day I went into a drugstore, picked out some soap and shampoo, and laid them on the counter for the clerk to ring up (see Clark, 1996). As it happened, the clerk had not seen me put them there, so when she looked for the items to be purchased, I pointed and said, "These two things over here." I used two expressions, "these two things" and "over here," that she could not understand without anchoring them to our material surroundings. I created the anchor by pointing at the soap and shampoo, and she acknowledged the action by picking them up.

Pointing is often thought to be the only, or prototypical, way to anchor communication, but it is neither. In the drugstore, the clerk and I created many other anchors by *placing* things in just the right manner. I identified myself as the next customer by placing myself in front of the counter, and she identified herself as a clerk by standing behind it. I tried—although I failed—to identify the soap and shampoo as items I wanted to buy by placing them on the counter. Later I identified a $20 bill as payment for the items by placing it on the counter, and she identified certain bills and coins as my change by placing them on the counter, and so on. Our transaction might have succeeded without pointing, but it could not have succeeded without placing.

At the heart of the issue is the notion of context. Every act of communication takes place in a material situation that plays an essential role in that communication. In the drugstore, it was essential that the clerk and I placed ourselves where we did, that I placed the soap and shampoo on the counter, that we were in a drugstore, and so much more. Most theories of language use are happy to acknowledge these actions, but as presuppositions of the communication. The actions are not considered part of the communication proper. Why not? If pointing is a communicative act, I argue, then so is placement. Yet if it is, we must revise our views of both communication and context. Much of what is now called *context* are really acts of communication.

Pointing and placing are indicative acts—forms of indicating—but they are only two of many possible forms. My goal here is to develop the notions of *directing-to* and *placing-for* as two basic techniques of indicating. The indicative acts that are prototypical of directing-to and placing-for are simple pointing and placing, but directing-to and placing-for are part of other communicative acts as well. I first consider the foundations of indicative acts and then show how these lead to directing-to and placing-for as two basic indicative techniques. At the end I return to the notion of context and how we must revise our understanding of what it is.

WHAT IS INDICATING?

Indicating has fundamentally to do with creating indexes for things. When I pointed at the soap and shampoo, I used my finger—*index* in Latin—as an index for them. To understand indicating, we must understand indexes, and for that I turn to Charles Sanders Peirce and his analysis of signs.

Indexes and Indicating

Signs, according to Peirce (Buchler, 1940), come in three basic types: icons, symbols, and indexes. Every sign "stands for something, its object" and "addresses somebody," creating in the mind of that person an idea that Peirce called the *interpretant* of the sign. Every sign is part of a three-place relation, sign, object, and interpretant, as illustrated in Table 10.1.

What distinguishes symbols, icons, and indexes is the relation between the sign and the object (Table 10.2). Symbols are *associated* with their objects *by rule*; in traffic signals, the red light is conventionally associated with the command to stop. Icons bear a *perceptual resemblance* to their objects; Picasso's sketch of Gertrude Stein is a selective depiction of Gertrude Stein.

Indexes are yet another case. An index, in Peirce's view, designates its object "because it is in dynamical (including spatial) connection both with

TABLE 10.1
Three Types of Signs

Type	Sign	Object	Interpretant
Symbol	Red light	Stop	Command to motorists
Icon	Sketch of Gertrude Stein	Gertrude Stein	The author Gertrude Stein
Index	Weathervane pointing north	North	The direction wind is blowing

TABLE 10.2
Relations of Signs to Objects

Sign	Relation of Sign s to Its Object o
Symbol	s is **associated by rule** with o
Icon	s **resembles** o **perceptually**
Index	s is **physically connected** with o

the individual object, on the one hand, and with the senses or memory of the person for whom it serves as a sign, on the other hand" (Buchler, 1940, p. 109). One such index is a weathervane. When it is pointing north, it is an index for north: It bears a "dynamical (including spatial) connection" with north and with you and me, the people "for whom it serves as a sign." The connection between index and object can occur naturally, or it can be arranged or engineered. The calluses on a shoemaker's thumb are a natural index to his occupation, but weathervanes are engineered to index the direction of the wind.

People communicate, I suggest, by creating signs by which they mean things for others (Clark, 1996). The act of creating such a sign I call a *signal*. Table 10.3 shows three *methods of signaling* that correspond to Peirce's three types of signs.

When I *describe* something *as* a dog, as in "I have a dog," I am producing *dog* as a symbol to signify a category of things. When I demonstrate a pear by drawing its shape in the air, I am producing an icon to signify a pear. And when I indicate my car by pointing at it, I am creating an index to that particular car.

Note that describing-as, demonstrating, and indicating are not *types* of signals, but *methods* of signaling. Most signals are *composites* of one or more

TABLE 10.3
Three Methods of Signaling

Signaling Method	Signaling Schema
Describing-as	Using **symbols** to signify categories of things
Demonstrating	Creating **icons**, or selective depictions of things
Indicating	Forming **indexes** to individual things

of these methods (Clark, 1996; Engle, 1998). Consider this utterance, recorded on videotape by Charles Goodwin, of a man named Gary telling his friends about a driver who had stopped just after a car race:

(1) Gary: and he takes his helmet off and "clunk" it goes on the top of the car.

As Gary says "clunk" he demonstrates the driver in the car swinging an imaginary helmet out of the car window onto the top of the car. So with "clunk" we have a composite of three things (see Clark & Gerrig, 1990): (a) a *description* of the sound *as* "a dull sound," (b) a demonstration of the sound by means of an exaggerated pronunciation of the word *clunk*, and (c) a demonstration of the driver's action of striking the helmet on the top of the car. These actions are all of a piece. They are three parts of the composite signal of saying how the driver slammed his helmet on the top of the car. So it is with many signals.

Prerequisites for Indicating

Every indication must establish an *intrinsic connection* between the signal and its object. When we think of signs, we tend to think of symbols such as *dog* and *run*, which are associated with their objects "canine animals" and "move swiftly on foot" by rule. These rules happen to be arbitrary conventions, and they could have been different (Lewis, 1969). Indexes, in contrast, are based on *intrinsic connections*. One day when a woman named Kay and I were in a parking lot, she asked, "Which car is yours?" and I responded by pointing to a nearby car. With that gesture, I expected her to work out a nonarbitrary link between my finger and that car. For an indication to work, addressees must be able to work out that connection with ease. Generally, the more transparent the connection, the easier it is to work it out.

Indicating an object in space must also lead the participants to *focus attention* on that object. As Peirce put it, "A rap at the door is an index. Anything which focuses the attention is an index" (Buchler, 1940, pp. 108–109). In pointing my finger at the car for Kay, I was trying to do more than designate it as the object. I was trying to draw her attention to it at its particular location.

Finally, every indication must establish a particular *interpretation* of its object. When people indicate an object, they do not designate it *simpliciter*. They designate it under a particular description or construal. When Kay asked, "Which car is yours?" and I pointed at a nearby car, I was indicating the thing I was pointing at *as* "a car," not *as* "a piece of junk" or *as* "a good example of modern technology." What I was bringing to her attention was not the thing as nothing in particular, but as "a car." This, it seems, is what Peirce meant by interpretant. The index is my pointing; the object is my car; and for Kay and me, the interpretant is "a car." Most accounts of indicating neglect interpretations, and they do so at their peril.

Taken together, these prerequisites give us a picture of what it takes to be an effective indicative act—at least for objects in space. Each indication must establish an intrinsic connection between the act and the object—for Peirce, a defining feature of indexes. That connection must focus the addressee's attention on the object, and on that object under a particular description. What is remarkable is the number of ways we have for doing that, and pointing is just one.

DIRECTING-TO VERSUS PLACING-FOR

Indicating is a matter of social engineering. Speakers arrange for their addressees to locate and focus attention on a particular object, relying on intrinsic spatial connections between the index and object. When I pointed at my car for Kay, she and I relied on a directional vector that ran from my finger to the car. What forms does this social engineering take?

Two Techniques for Indicating

Many forms of indicating exploit one of two basic techniques—directing-to and placing-for. To see how these differ, let us begin with two prototypical examples:

(2)   Clark to Kay: [Points at car]

(3)   Clark to clerk: [Places soap and shampoo on drugstore counter]

In 2 and 3, the index, object, description, and connection are as follows in Table 10.4. In both 2 and 3, my index consists of performing an action; in both, I signify an object under a particular description. The difference lies

TABLE 10.4
Four Properties of Pointing and Placing

	Pointing	*Placing*
Index	Pointing finger at car	Placing items on counter
Object	Car	Soap, shampoo
Description	"A car"	"Items to be purchased"
Connection	Vector from finger to car	Location of items on counter

in how I achieve this signification. In 2, Kay is to find a vector from my finger to the car. In 3, the clerk is to see the items as being on the counter.

What, then, is the essential difference between pointing and placing? In pointing, speakers try to *direct* their addressees' attention *to* the object they are indicating. In 2, I tried to direct Kay's attention to my car. In placing, speakers try to *place* the object they are indicating so that it falls within the addressees' focus of attention. In 3, I placed my soap and shampoo on the counter before the drugstore clerk. Briefly:

1. Directing-to: Speaker's signal directs addressee's attention to object *o*.
2. Placing-for: Speaker's signal places object *o* for addressee's attention.

In directing-to, speakers try to move the addressees' attention to the object. In placing-for, they try to move the object into the addressees' attention. Schematically:

1. Directing-to: A's attention → object *o*.
2. Placing-for: object *o* → A's attention.

The two techniques contrast on what speakers try to manipulate: the addressees' attention, or the object of the indication.

Directing-to and placing-for are designed to get addressees to focus on the *object of the indication*—on the car, soap, or shampoo. I call these *signaling techniques*. These are distinct from the techniques speakers have for getting addressees to focus on the *signal* itself—on the pointing finger, or on the act of placement. I call these *presentation techniques* (see Clark, 1996). Most signals require addressees to attend to the signals themselves. When Kay asks, "Which car is yours?" she must get me to attend to her vocalization so that I can identify the sentence she is presenting and understand the question she is asking. The same goes for indicating. When I pointed at my car, I had to get Kay to attend to my *finger* so that she could identify it as a communicative gesture and determine what I was pointing at. Likewise, when I laid the soap and shampoo on the drugstore counter for the clerk, I tried to get her to attend to that action in order to see the items as "items to be purchased." Presentation techniques are an important part of signaling, but my focus here is on the signaling techniques themselves.

What is the relation between directing-to and placing-for? One proposal is that they are strictly complementary. In most of the phenomena I survey here, speakers exploit directing-to, or placing-for, but not both in the same signal. Another proposal is that they are independent techniques, so they may both be used in the same signal. When I handed the drugstore clerk a $20 bill, I might be taken as simultaneously placing the bill for the clerk and directing her attention to it. At this point, I lean toward the second view.

If directing-to and placing-for are really different techniques, they should contrast in the way they satisfy the prerequisites for indicating—intrinsic connections, focus of attention, and interpretation. Let me consider the three prerequisites in turn.

Intrinsic Connections and Indexing Sites

In directing-to and placing-for, speakers try to establish a connection, often spatial, between the index they create and the object of that index. They do that in part to focus their addressees' attention on the object of that index. But what connections do they establish, and how? It is on these questions that the two techniques differ.

When Kay asked, "Which car is yours?" I could indicate the car in several ways. If I had been some distance from the car, I could have waved vaguely in its direction. I would have directed Kay's attention to a 50-square-meter area with the car at its center. If I had been standing next to my car, I could have tapped on its hood, directing Kay's attention to a 2-square-centimeter area on its surface. Let me call these areas *indexing sites*, or simply *sites.* With both gestures, I intend to bring Kay's attention to an indexing site and get her to identify the referred-to car by its intrinsic connection to that site. In one case, the car is at the site's center. In the other, it contains the site.[1] There was also an indexing site when I placed the soap and shampoo on the drugstore counter, and it was the one-meter-square countertop. Here, again, I intended the clerk to recognize the intrinsic connection between my referent and the site. In this case, the items are in the middle of the site. Both techniques, then, rely on an intrinsic relation between the indexing site and the object of the index.

The difference between directing-to and placing-for is this. With directing-to, speakers *create* the indexing site with respect to the referent. My tapping on the hood of my car created an indexing site where none existed before. With placing-for, speakers *presuppose* an existing indexing site and establish the referent with respect to it. In the drugstore, I took advantage of an indexing site, the countertop, that was already available, and established a connection from the soap and shampoo to the site by placing them on it.

1. Directing-to: Speaker's communicative act creates an indexing site that is connected with object *o.*

---

[1]I could have used the same two sites to answer "What color is your sister's car?" "What's the make of your car?" or "How are you getting home tonight?" I need only assume that Kay will recognize the different intrinsic connections between site and referent (Clark, Schreuder, & Buttrick, 1983; Nunberg, 1979).

2. Placing-for: Speaker's communicative act exploits a preexisting indexing site and connects object *o* with it.

As indicative acts, directing-to is *site-creating*, whereas placing-for is *site-exploiting*.

Interpretations

In directing-to and placing-for, speakers must get their addressees to view the object under a particular description. Kay was to view the object pointed at as "a car," and the clerk was to see the shampoo and soap as "items I wish to purchase now." How speakers and addressees establish these descriptions is different for the two techniques.

All indications require a description. Suppose Kay and I are walking in the woods when I suddenly and silently point in a particular direction. "What is it?" she asks. "A squirrel, that oak tree, the curious branch on that oak tree, a hidden nuthatch, or what?" Even if I point with care, she still needs to ask, "Do you mean the bark of the tree, its color, the mold, or what?" To complete my indication, she and I must arrive at a joint construal of the object, so I might I reply, "the oak tree," and she might nod in acknowledgment. Only then will I have completed my indication.

Directing-to ordinarily gets its description from outside, usually from the accompanying talk. Pointing, for example, is typically part of demonstrative references, as when I pointed at the shampoo and soap and said "those two things." The demonstrative reference provides the intended description of the object, "two things." At other times descriptions may come from other sources. When Kay asked "Which car is yours?" it was her question that provided the description "a car." These are just two of many ways of establishing a joint construal.

In placing-for, speakers and addressees usually establish joint construals by other means. In the drugstore, the checkout counter is a special place. It is conventional for customers and clerks to designate articles as part of their transaction by placing them on the counter. So, for example, I tried to designate the soap and shampoo as "items I wished to buy" by placing them on the counter at the start of our transaction. This way the clerk and I could be assured that we would mutually construe the purchasable items on the counter at that point in our transaction as "items I wished to buy." The description was derived from conventions about how things *at that site* are to be interpreted. Placing-for often doesn't rely on accompanying talk for its interpretation.

We are now in a position to examine directing-to and placing-for more closely. How do they work, and what are they good for?

DIRECTING-TO

Pointing is often assumed to be in a class by itself. It may vary conventionally with the body part used (forefinger, thumb, or lips), the distance of the objects, or the type of object indicated. Otherwise, it is a coherent category: If I want to indicate a thing, I can point at it. Let me call this the *standard view of pointing.*

The standard view has problems. For one thing, pointing is just one form of directing-to, and its use contrasts with other forms. For another, directing-to is often part of composite signals. These forms are easy to overlook or treat as distinct from pointing. We must look at directing-to in its many forms if we are to see the system behind indicating—even how it works in standard pointing. I next briefly survey many varieties of directing-to with two questions in mind: How do speakers direct their addressees' attention, and how do they use directing-to as a part of composite signals?

Devices for Directing-To

Speakers can direct their addressees' attention to objects via any number of devices. The most obvious of these, among North Americans at least, are the fingers and hand, but they are hardly the only ones. In principle, speakers can exploit any body part with which they can create a vector (Clark, 1996). Table 10.5 provides a few examples, each listed with an utterance to aid in imagining the gesture. Just how addressees are to direct their attention varies with the gesture. With the pointing finger, they are to treat the major axis as a vector that they are to follow from the body to a site at the object. But with a tapping finger, they are to ignore the major axis and attend to the site being tapped. With nodding, they are to compute the vector of the head's back and forth motion and follow that vector from the body. With the face and torso, they are to follow a vector that is not along but per-

TABLE 10.5
Methods of Directing-To

Instrument	Index i	Example
Finger	Pointing at *o*	"**That** is the book I want."
Arm	Sweeping *o*	"**All this** is yours."
Head	Nodding at *o*	"She was standing **there**."
Finger	Tapping on *o*	"**This** is the book I want."
Foot	Tapping on *o*	[of carpet samples] "I like **this** best."
Torso	Turning to *o*	"Let **us** talk."
Face	Directing at *o*	[looking up from papers on desk] "Can I help **you**?"
Eyes	Gazing at *o*	"I want **you** [person A] and **you** [person B] to come with me."

pendicular to the major axes of the body. Vector calculation isn't as trivial as it first appears. And it is not part of the repertoire of dogs or very young babies.

Eye gaze is special (Goodwin, 1981; Kendon, 1967). People use the direction of their gaze to designate the person or thing they are attending to and, thereby, to imply, among other things, that they are attending to that person or thing. Take an example simplified a bit from Goodwin (1981):

> (4) Elsie: See first we were gonna have
> [gazing at Ann] Teema, Carrie and Clara, (0.2) a::nd myself.
> [gazing at Bessie] The four of us.
> The four [gazing at Clara] children.
> But then—uh:: I said how is that gonna look.

Elsie directs her gaze in turn at Ann, Bessie, and Clara, designing her references to fit the person she is addressing. "Teema, Carrie, and Clara and myself" is for Ann, "the four of us" for Bessie, and "the four children" for Clara. Eye gaze isn't effective unless it is registered by the person being gazed at, so it is usually grounded by *mutual* gaze. This is one reason why not just gaze, but mutual gaze is so important in managing face-to-face conversation. Gaze is often used along with face and torso direction and even pointing.

Another attention-directing device is the voice. Speakers can use it to indicate themselves as *speakers*, their precise location as *here*, or the time of utterance as *now*. Table 10.6 offers some examples. Vector calculation seems simpler in these cases. Addressees are to locate the site from which the voice emanated. Sounds are ideal for this purpose because they are easy to localize at least to a certain degree of precision. The voice is often used along with directing the face and torso.

People also indicate with artificial devices. Lecturers can use wooden or laser pointers. They can use chalk or other markers to underline or circle things, leaving behind a semipermanent indication. At track meets, officials generally use starting guns to indicate the starting moment of races. Artificial pointers are common.

TABLE 10.6
Vocal Methods of Directing-To

Instrument	Index i	Example
Voice	Locating *o*	To roomful of people: "Whose keys are these?" "**Mine.**"
Voice	Locating *o*	In the dark: "Where are you, Helen?" "**Over here.**"
Voice	Identifying *o*	On telephone: "It's **me.**"
Voice	Timing *o*	At start of race: "Ready, set, **go.**"

Directing-To in Composite Signals

Directing-to is rarely used on its own. It ordinarily comes as part of composite signals as in "That car [pointing at a car] is mine." It is a genuine part of these signals because it is *essential* to their interpretation. I illustrate with five types of composite signals—demonstrative pronouns, demonstrative adjectives, summonses, emblems, and iconic gestures.

Take the English demonstrative pronouns *this, that, these,* and *those.* When speakers point at things in using these pronouns, their indications become an essential part of the composite signals. Two examples are:

(5) Duncan: [Pointing at a painting by Picasso] **That**'s beautiful.

(6) Helen: [Tapping on a box of cookies] **These** are delicious.

Without their directing-to, Duncan's and Helen's references to the painting and cookies would be incomplete. Directing-to can be used with other pronouns as well, as in these examples:

(7) Duncan: [Pointing at a painting of Henry VIII] **He** looks frightening.

(8) Helen: [Nodding at a diver] **She**'s doing a half gainer.

(9) Ken: Where are you, Margaret?
    Margaret: **I**'m upstairs.

(10) Ken: Where's our car?
    Margaret: [Pointing at a car] **There** it is.

Paradoxically, *I* and *we* appear to be the only pronouns that require directing-to as part of their composite signals, even though they are not normally considered demonstrative pronouns. All the rest can be used with or without directing-to as a composite part.

But what are the speakers pointing at—what are they indicating? Consider 11 and 12:

(11) Duncan: [Pointing at a man in a photo] **That**'s the guy who robbed me.

(12) Duncan: [Pointing at a man in a photo] **That** robbed me.

In 11, Duncan could not be indicating the actual man pictured in the photo. If he were, he would be able to say 12, which he cannot. What he is indicating is not a person or object, but a location, which he intends to be taken under the description of "a part of the picture before us." I call that location a *perceptually conspicuous site*, or *PCS*, a site that is perceptually conspicuous relative to the speaker and interlocutor's current common ground (Clark, Schreuder, & Buttrick, 1983).

That, however, isn't the end of the story, because the PCS is not the referent of the demonstrative pronoun in 5, 6, or 11. To get those referents, we must treat the PCS as a second index with its own object. References with demonstrative pronouns take two steps (Clark, 1996). Here are the two steps for 6:

Step 1: By tapping on a box of cookies, Helen is indicating a PCS, to be taken as "a box of cookies."

Step 2: By indicating the box of cookies, she is indicating the cookies in that box, to be taken as "cookies in this box."

We need these two steps if we are to make sense of examples like these:

(13)   Helen: [Pointing at a single cookie] **These** are delicious.

(14)   Helen: [Pointing at an ad for Mom's Cookies] **Those** are delicious.

In using demonstrative pronouns, people do not point at the referents of the pronouns. They point at locatable indexes to those referents.

Demonstrative reference is in general a two-step process. Suppose that Ken is tapping on a copy of Mark Twain's *Huckleberry Finn*. He could say:

(15)   **This book** is heavy.

(16)   **This novel** is great.

(17)   **This author** was born in Hannibal, Missouri.

(18)   **This character** is one of the most interesting in American literature.

By tapping on the book, Ken is indicating a PCS, but that is not what he is referring to with *this book, this novel, this author*, or *this character*. Indeed, he could not be pointing at the novel, author, or characters because the novel is an abstract object, Twain is dead and gone, and Huckleberry Finn is fictional. Rather, he is using the PCSs as indexes to other referents. In 15 through 18, these referents are to be taken as "the physical book at this PCS," "the novel represented in this PCS," "the author of the novel represented in this PCS," and "the main character of the novel represented in this PCS." Ken intends his addressees to come to these descriptions, largely from the head nouns *book, novel, author*, and *character*. Demonstrative references, then, are a composite of an indication to a PCS and a description of the referent in the demonstrative noun phrase.

Summonses are another composite signal that makes essential use of directing-to. Here are two characteristic examples (see Schegloff, 1968):

(19) Duncan: Helen [with raised voice].
     Helen: Yes?

(20) Alan: Hey, you!
     Barbara: What?

In 19, Duncan uses Helen's name and raises his voice to direct her attention to him. But why? To indicate himself as "a person who wishes to enter a conversation with her now." Once again, he does this via a two-step process. His voice directs her attention to a PCS at his body, and that indexes him in turn as "a person who wishes to enter a conversation with her now." Much the same analysis holds for 20. Summonses are composites of an indication to a PCS plus a description in a vocative or an interjection.

Emblems, too, rely on directing-to. An emblem is a conventional gesture that can stand on its own, like a good-bye wave, a thumbs-up, or a shoulder shrug (Ekman & Friesen, 1969; Kendon, 1981; McNeill, 1992). Suppose I wave good-bye to Barbara and Peter as they are about to board a train. I flap my hand first toward Barbara and then toward Peter as they both watch. In this way, I indicate Barbara as "the addressee of the first wave" and Peter as "the addressee of the second wave." With the timing of my waves, I indicate the moments at which I mean "farewell": I bid them good-bye at precisely the moment they are about to board the train, Barbara first and Peter second (cf. Wilkins, 1992). Many emblems are like good-bye waves and rely on directing-to for indicating a nearby person, object, or place. All emblems appear to rely on directing-to for indicating a moment in time.

Directing-to also turns up in iconic gestures. As illustration, consider a gesture made by a person explaining to another how a cylinder lock works (Engle, 1998). While the explainer held an actual lock in his left hand, he used his right index finger to trace the movement of the cotter pins within the tumbler, or stator, of that lock: "the pins are going down like that." During "going down like that," he traced his finger from the top of the keyface down to the keyhole. That is, he did not do the tracing just anywhere. He did it on the lock he was holding to indicate the actual location and direction of cotter pin's movement. The explainer's gesture was a composite of at least two methods: (a) *demonstrating* the motion of the cotter pins, and (b) *indicating* their location in the actual lock.

Directing-to, then, turns up in a number of composite signals, from demonstrative references to iconic gestures. In each case, speakers indicate by directing their addressees' attention to a mutually conspicuous site in their perceptual field, and they use that site as an index to other objects, real or fictional, material or immaterial.

PLACING-FOR

Placing-for is different from directing-to. For one thing, it works not by directing a person's attention to an object, but by placing an object for that person's attention. Also the objects of placement usually get their interpretations from the place where they are placed. The principles behind these interpretations are very different from those behind the interpretations of directing-to. And signals based on placing-for can endure, making their potential uses different from those of directing-to. In this section, I take up three dimensions of placing-for—what objects get placed, where they get placed, and by what actions they get placed. In each case, I begin with the drugstore transaction and move to other examples.

Objects of Placement-For

Placing-for is basically about manipulating material things. People place two basic types of things: (a) themselves, and (b) material things other than themselves. I call these *self-objects* and *other-objects*. In the drugstore, we find people placing a plethora of other-objects (Table 10.6). We also find people placing themselves (Table 10.7). These are only a few of the objects people place in the drugstore.

TABLE 10.6
Methods of Placement in Drugstore

Agent	Object	Placement	Description of Object
Manager	Shampoo	On store shelf	"Shampoo for sale"
Customer	Shampoo	On counter	"Shampoo to be purchased"
Customer	Money	In clerk's hand	"Payment for purchase"
Clerk	Money	In customer's hand	"Change for payment"
Clerk	Shampoo	In paper bag	"Shampoo already purchased"

TABLE 10.7
Methods of Self-Placement in Drugstore

Agent	Object	Placement	Description of Object
Clerk	Self	Behind counter	"Available clerk"
Customer 1	Self	In front of counter	"Current customer"
Customer 2	Self	Behind customer 1	"Next customer"

TABLE 10.8
Methods of Placement

Agent	Object	Placement	Description of Object
Waiter	Plate of spaghetti	In front of customer	"Food for customer"
Student	Exam	On teacher's desk	"Completed exam"
Secretary	Memo	In Ann's box	"Memo for Ann"
Card player	Card	Face-up in center of table	"Card in play"
Pedestrian	Candy wrapper	In litter basket	"Waste"

People place other-objects in many types of communication. Table 10.8 is a small sample. In a restaurant, a waiter might place a plate of spaghetti on the table in front of Ken and a bowl of soup in front of Margaret. In doing that, he would indicate the spaghetti as "food for Ken" and the soup as "food for Margaret." He could be mistaken, but he communicates his intent by his placement of the dishes. So it goes with the other examples.

People also place themselves across a variety of situations. Examples are everywhere (Table 10.9). When I place myself at the end of a queue in a bank, I indicate myself as "the next customer for service after the person in front of me." I indicate this not only to the bank teller and the customers in front of me, but to anyone who arrives after me; I expect them to indicate themselves as later customers by getting into the queue behind me. People communicate by placing themselves in a variety of circumstances.

The idea, in brief, is that people can place either themselves or other objects as a way of indicating these for their addressees.

Placement Sites

The sites where people place objects are the usual basis for the interpretations of those objects. Drugstores, for example, have a highly differentiated and conventional set of such sites. The store's shelves, for example, are sites where managers place merchandise to indicate them as "available for purchase." Some shelves are reserved for vitamins, others for hair care prod-

TABLE 10.9
Methods of Self-Placement

Agent	Object	Placement	Description of Object
Customer	Self	In queue at bank	"Nth customer for service"
Pedestrian	Self	In crosswalk	"Person with right-of-way"
Speaker	Self	At podium	"Person ready to speak"
Tennis player	Self	At service line	"Player ready to serve"
Secretary	Self	Behind desk	"Person at work"

ucts, and still others for headache remedies. Areas such as the back room and the space below the checkout counter are sites where managers place merchandise that is not available for purchase.

The placement sites around the checkout counter are worth a closer look. Some are pictured here:

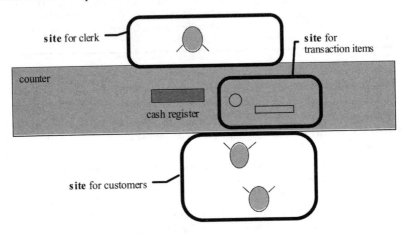

The counter has a front and a back. People place themselves in front of it to indicate themselves as "current customer" or "waiting customer," and other people place themselves behind it to indicate themselves as clerks.

The counter top is special. Parts of the clerk's and my transaction took place in a delimited space next to the cash register. That is the site where I placed the shampoo and soap, and where the clerk expected to find them. That is also the site where I placed my payment, where she placed my change, and where she placed the bag with the goods and receipt in it. If I had placed a bottle of vitamins next to the shampoo and soap, she would have had reason to believe that I was indicating them also as "items I wish to buy." The cash register is also special. Once the clerk places money in the cash drawer, it is designated the property of the drugstore. By convention, only the clerk has access to items at that site. There are still other sites on the clerk's and my persons. If I place a $20 bill in her hand, I am indicating that bill as "sufficient payment for my purchases," and if she places change in my hand, she is indicating that as "change for overpayment."

The drugstore shelves, checkout counter, and cash register are what I call *absolute* placement sites: They impose particular interpretations on objects more or less independently of where the participants are—within limits. Most of these sites get their interpretations from well-developed conventions about drugstores, checking out, cash registers, and monetary exchange. But absolute sites can also be ad hoc. A tour leader in Paris might say to her charges, "Those of you who want to visit the Louvre today stand here, and those who want to visit the Touilleries stand there." Once she has stipulated the two places, people signal which museum they want to visit by placing themselves in one place or the other. Finally, placement sites can be *relative* to the location of the speaker, addressee, or other landmarks. A person's place in a queue, for example, is relative: When I take my place behind Kay, I am indicating myself as the customer immediately after her.

Placing-for is closely related to orienting-for. Consider a study by Kendon (1990) on the way people stand in conversation. If we limit ourselves to two people, they typically assume one of three arrangements:

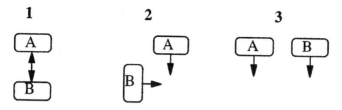

Kendon called these arrangements *vis-à-vis*, *L*, and *side-by-side*. In the conversations Kendon analyzed, people placed themselves in one or another of these arrangements based on a number of factors, one of which was topic. People signaled their orientation to the same topic by maintaining, say, a vis-à-vis arrangement, and they signaled the move to a new topic by rearranging themselves in an L. As Kendon demonstrated in detail, it takes the tight coordination of *both* parties to maintain such an arrangement, so in circumstances like these, placement and orientation are jointly achieved.

Phases of Placement

Most objects of placement persist in the same location and orientation until they are replaced or abandoned. Placing-for, therefore, divides into three phases:

1. *Initiation:* placing an object per se.
2. *Maintenance:* maintaining the object in place.
3. *Termination:* replacing, removing, or abandoning the object.

When a hostess asks, "Who'd like some coffee?" and I nudge my cup forward, it is the initiating phase, the nudge, that counts. She may not otherwise notice the cup's new location, which was relative to where it was before. In many venues, the initiating phase is essential in indicating who did the placing. A supermarket clerk who wants to know who to charge for a melon on the counter may need to see the act of placement itself. In contrast, when a drugstore manager places items on the shelves, we don't need to know when or how they got there. All we need to recognize is their presence on the shelves—the maintaining phase of the manager's placement.

The terminating phase is important for repairs. Suppose I had placed a bottle of vitamins on the drugstore counter along with my shampoo and soap. I could have revoked my indication by removing the bottle from the counter. That would terminate my placement and signal that I no longer intended the bottle to be taken as "an item I wished to purchase." My placement is in effect only as long as I am taken as maintaining it.

Speakers and addressees apply the same logic in grounding what speakers are doing. In the drugstore, the clerk moved my shampoo and soap to a new area on the counter as she rang them up. In doing that, she signaled that she had understood my placement of the shampoo and soap; by terminating the continuing phase of my signal, she was reaching closure on it. Her move also prevented me from revoking my indication—from backing out of buying the shampoo. Likewise, at the party, once I have nudged my coffee cup toward my hostess, she can signal that she has understood the act by filling the cup with coffee. By initiating the next relevant action, she terminates the continuing phase of my placement, preventing me from terminating the indication myself—say, to repair it or back out of it.

Preparatory Principle

Most acts of placing-for prepare for the next joint action. When I stepped up to the drugstore counter, I put myself in an optimal place for the next step in the clerk's and my joint activity—the beginning of our transaction. Then, when I placed the shampoo and soap on the counter, I put them in an optimal place for the next step after that—the clerk's ringing up of the two items, and so on. Each time I intended the clerk to interpret my placements by recognizing them as preparation for what she and I were to do next. The principle I wish to propose is this:

> *Preparatory principle.* The participants in a joint activity are to interpret acts of placement by considering them as direct preparation for the next steps in that activity.

The clerk should reason as if she had read Grice (1957, 1968, 1991): "That man has just placed himself in a location that is optimal, and conventional, for beginning a business transaction with me. Moreover, he seems to have done it with the intention that I recognize his very intention in doing that.

He must therefore mean that he wishes to begin a business transaction with me now."

The preparatory principle helps explain the evolution of conventional places. Why did the front, back, and top of checkout counters become conventional places for the placement of customers, clerks, and the items of transactions? Because these are the optimal sites for customers, clerks, and items in such transactions. Why did the queue become a conventional way of ordering people at bank windows, cinema windows, and airline counters? Because it satisfies these constraints, among others: (a) It delivers one person at a time to the server, (b) it delivers people in the order in which they chose to be served, and (c) the first person in the queue is optimal for engagement with server.

The preparatory principle also helps account for people's interpretation of relative placements. When the hostess asked, "Who'd like some coffee?" and I nudged my cup forward, I was making the cup more accessible for the next step in our joint activity—her pouring coffee into that cup. I could therefore be confident she would interpret my action as signaling, "Yes, I would like some coffee." I could have signaled, "No, I wouldn't like any coffee" by pulling my cup back, making it less accessible for the next step. This example illustrates an adjunct to the preparatory principle:

> *Accessibility principle:* All other things being equal, an object is in a better place for the next step in a joint activity when it is more accessible for the vision, audition, touch, or manipulation required in the next step.

Nudging my cup forward made it more accessible to the hostess for pouring; pulling it back would have made it less accessible. The same principle applies to customers in bank queues, customers stepping up to drugstore counters, waiters stepping up to restaurant tables, and two people in a vis-à-vis versus L arrangement.

For an action to be an indication, there must be an intrinsic connection between that action and its object, and it is the preparatory and accessibility principles that provide that connection. When I stepped up to the drugstore counter, my action was causally connected to beginning a transaction with the clerk. I could therefore intend my action to be an index to me as "a customer wishing to begin a transaction with the clerk." Likewise, when I nudged my cup forward, my action was causally connected to a place where the hostess would find it easier to pour coffee into it. That way I could intend my action to index the cup as "a cup in which I wanted more coffee." With placing-for, there is a direct spatial relation between the object and the site it is placed at, where that site has a natural interpretation in the current joint activity.

DIRECTING-TO VERSUS PLACING-FOR

Directing-to and placing-for are two techniques for indicating objects, but they differ in how they do that. The primary distinction between them is in whether they direct a person's attention to the object or place the object for a person's attention. Other differences go along with the primary distinction. Directing-to tends to be transitory, and placing-for, continuing. Also directing-to generally gets its interpretation from language associated with the indication, and placing-for, from its indexing site. The two techniques also differ in how they get extended to new domains. Let us look at these differences.

Time Course

Pointing tends to be a transitory signal and placing a continuing signal. Suppose I buy a cake in one of two settings. In Setting 1, it is in the display case of a bakery, so I must point at it while the clerk is looking. My signal is transitory. In Setting 2, the cake is on a shelf of a supermarket, so I pick it up and place it on the checkout counter. This time my signal is continuing. Technically, pointing and placing both have initiating, maintaining, and terminating phases, but with pointing, the maintaining phase tends to be brief.

The maintaining phase of placing-for gives it certain advantages over directing-to. The most obvious are these:

1. *Joint accessibility of signal.* The place of the object is accessible to everyone in a conversation for an extended period of time, and during that time, they can check on it as often as they wish. That makes the placement of the object ideal as a basis for their mutual belief that the speaker has performed precisely that signal.
2. *Clarity of signal.* The continuing presence of an object makes it easy to resolve disputes about what is being indicated. In Setting 1, the bakery clerk might ask "Did you want this cake or that one?" or "Do you want the cake or not?" In Setting 2, the clerk can resolve these questions by noting the continuing presence of the cake on the counter.
3. *Revocation of signal.* Placement is usually easier to revoke than pointing. To revoke my choice in Setting 1, I would have to tell the clerk, "Oh, forget the cake—I've changed my mind." To do so in Setting 2, I would simply remove the cake from the counter.
4. *Memory aid.* The continuing presence of the object is highly effective as a memory aid. In Setting 2, the cake on the counter is both a re-

minder to me that I am committed to buying it, and a reminder to the clerk that he or she has yet to ring it up.

5. *Preparation for next joint action.* Placement generally leaves the object in an optimal place for the next step in the joint activity. In Setting 2, I left the cake in a convenient place for the clerk to ring it up.

These five properties work together to establish, maintain, and make accessible crucial pieces of the participants' common ground in the current joint activity.

Directing-to, however, also has certain advantages. These include:

1. *Immovable objects.* It is easy to indicate objects that are difficult, impossible, or inappropriate to move or place—such as houses, cars, roads, trees, and other people.

2. *Dispersed objects.* It is easy to indicate objects one by one that are dispersed over a wide area.

3. *Directions.* With directing-to, speakers can indicate a direction—such as which way a car went. This is not easy to do with placing-for.

4. *Complex referents.* I can point at a bottle of shampoo and, by saying "that company," refer to Procter & Gamble, the company that made it. I cannot do anything comparable by placing the same bottle on the countertop in a drugstore. In placing-for, I am ordinarily limited to conventional interpretations associated with the indexing site.

5. *Precision timing.* Many indications depend on precise timing, and it takes the beat of a gesture or the timing of the voice to achieve that. If I tell the baker, "I want that, that, and that, but not that," I must time my pointing to coincide with the right *that*'s. That is harder to do with placement. Directing-to is usually quicker and more evanescent, and that has advantages in the right settings.

As a result of their comparative advantages, directing-to and placing-for tend to be used for different purposes.

Interpretations

Recall that directing-to and placing-for differ in how they establish the interpretation of the indicated object. In directing-to, the interpretation ordinarily comes from an external description, but in placing-for, it tends to come instead from the object's new site. Let me call these interpretations *adjunct-based* and *site-based.*

Site-based interpretations are advantageous in some settings, and adjunct-based in others. Site-based interpretations, for example, can be established without language. In the drugstore, the clerk and I could have carried out our entire transaction by means of placement. The drugstore could have been in Tokyo or Istanbul, and we still could have succeeded. Adjunct-based interpretations, in contrast, can be established with greater precision by the careful choice of the adjunct language. In a clothing store, I could point and say, "I'd like that tie with the floral pattern that is just next to the tie with black and yellow stripes." Or I could add an epithet, as I point at a car and say, "That idiot almost ran over me." Neither of these seems possible with placing-for without language.

Chains and Extensions

Directing-to and placing-for can both be used in chains of indications. First consider 21:

(21)   Clark: Did you know that *he* [tapping on a copy of *Angle of Repose*] won the Pulitzer Prize in 1972?

In 21, I used my finger as an index to the book. But by indicating the book, I used it as an index to the author of the book Wallace Stegner. Briefly:

(21′)   finger → copy of *Angle of Repose* → Wallace Stegner

Next consider 22:

(22)   Clark: [leaves his coat on seat D13 in movie theater to save the seat]

In 22, I used the chair as an index to my coat, which I used in turn as an index to myself, briefly as follows:

(22′)   seat D13 → Clark's coat → Clark

In other circumstances, I might have pointed at Wallace Stegner himself or sat in the seat myself, avoiding the chain of indications. Directing-to and placing-for are as useful as they are in part because they allow complex chaining.

Societies have evolved extended systems of chaining based both on directing-to and on placing-for. Those based on directing-to use *buttons*, broadly conceived. In 21, I tapped on a book as a way of indicating its author. Likewise, I can ring a doorbell or activate a telephone or beeper to indicate both the people I wish to summons and me as the person making the summons.

The extensions of placement are far more striking. These systems are built on *markers*. In 22, I used my coat as an artificial index, or marker, for me: Rather than placing myself in seat D13, I placed a marker for myself. Society has evolved a truly astonishing number of markers for such purposes, and they each belong to their own conventional system of indexing. Here is a small sample:

Commerce: coins and paper money; checks; credit cards; bills; receipts; tickets; coupons.

Government: drivers' licenses; car number plates; passports.

Armed forces: uniforms; insignias; flags.

Games: cards in card games; chips in gambling; chess pieces; balls in ball games; batons in relay races; markers in Monopoly.

In the drugstore, I laid down a $20 bill in payment for the shampoo and soap. I used that bill as a marker for the value of $20 within a monetary system; by moving the marker from me to the clerk, I changed the possessor of that value from me to the drugstore. Games such as poker and Monopoly would be impossible without markers.

Graphical user interfaces on computers rely on two basic operations, clicking and dragging. These are simply extended notions of directing-to and placing-for. The metaphor for these interfaces is a desktop on which icons correspond to files, folders, or applications. Users can select a file by pointing and clicking on its icon, and once they have selected the file, they can open it, print it, and do other things to it. They can initiate an application (such as a mail program) in much the same way. Clicking is a virtual form of pointing. Users can also drag a file's icon, say, from one folder to another, thereby changing its location in the virtual filing system. Dragging is a virtual form of placement. If directing-to and placing-for are the two basic techniques for indicating, it is no accident that they evolved into the two basic operations of clicking and dragging.

CONCLUSIONS

Whenever we communicate, we anchor what we do to the material world around us. Not only do we direct our partners' attention to things, as in pointing, but we place things for their attention, as in placement. Directing-to, or at least pointing, has long been accepted as a part of communication, but placing-for has been almost totally disregarded. And yet placing-for is just as valid a technique for indicating as directing-to, and it may even be more common.

Placing-for adds a great deal to the analysis of communication. Take my encounter with the clerk in the drugstore. In one tradition, our communicative acts consist entirely of the turns at talk, and the first three turns were these (in boldface):

(23) Clerk: **I'll be right there**
      Clark: **Okay.**
              (15 sec pause)
      Clerk: **These two things over there.**

The turns at talk might suffice in an analysis of gossip or telephone conversations, but they don't suffice here. Why did the clerk say that she would be right there, and why did I answer okay? Our utterances seem to have come out of the blue. They didn't, of course. The clerk and I were doing something else communicatively. But what?

Let us now add pointing—or, more generally, directing-to. Here are the same three turns expanded to include directing-to (in brackets and boldface):

(24) Clark: [**gazes at clerk**]
      Clerk: [**returns eye gaze**] I'll be right there.
      Clark: Okay.
              (15 sec pause)
      Clerk: [**manifestly looks for items to be rung up**]
      Clark: [**points at soap and shampoo**] These two things over here.

We now discover much more communication. I gazed at the clerk to indicate her as addressee and to imply that I was ready to be served. She gazed back at me to acknowledge me as a person requesting service, and she said "I'll be right there" in response to that request, and so it went with the pointing. But this analysis still has holes. How did the clerk know I wanted service? What was she looking for, and why?

Let us finally add placing-for. The problem is, placing-for has three phases—initiation, maintenance, and termination—and these are hard to represent in a transcript. The transcript here represents only the initiating and terminating phrases, so we must remind ourselves that the signal is in force in between. Here are the three turns with placing-for in brackets, italics, and boldface:

(25) Clerk: [*maintains standing far behind counter*, checking an inventory
              sheet]

Clark	[*initiates standing at counter*]
	[*initiates placement of soap and shampoo on counter*]
	[gazes at clerk]
Clerk	[returns eye gaze] I'll be right there.
Clark	Okay.
	(15 sec pause)
Clerk	[*initiates standing just behind counter, facing Clark*]
	[manifestly looks for items to be rung up]
Clark	[points at soap and shampoo] These two things over here.
Clerk	[*picks up soap and shampoo*, terminating Clark's placement]

The transcript reveals several new pieces of communication. First, the clerk had placed herself away from the counter, signaling that she was unavailable for service. Second, I tried to open the transaction by placing myself at the counter, by placing the soap and shampoo on the counter, and only then by catching the clerk's eye. Third, although she read my intentions, returned the gaze, and promised to "be right there," she maintained her distant placement throughout the 15-sec pause to signal that she was not yet ready to serve me. Fourth, when she was ready, she signaled that she was ready by replacing herself just behind the counter, and only then did I say "These two things over here." Fifth, she showed that she recognized my placement of the shampoo and soap by picking them up. In short, knowledge of what the clerk and I placed for each other is essential to a full understanding of what we did.

The lesson is clear. People have at least two basic techniques for indicating: directing-to and placing-for. We will never understand indicating and its role in communication without recognizing both.

ACKNOWLEDGMENTS

Work on this chapter was supported in part by grant N000140010660 from the Office of Naval Research. I thank Sotaro Kita for his constructive comments.

REFERENCES

Buchler, J. (Ed.). (1940). *Philosophical writings of Peirce*. London: Routledge & Kegan Paul.
Clark, H. H. (1996). *Using language*. Cambridge: Cambridge University Press.
Clark, H. H., & Gerrig, R. J. (1990). Quotations as demonstrations. *Language, 66*, 764–805.
Clark, H. H., Schreuder, R., & Buttrick, S. (1983). Common ground and the understanding of demonstrative reference. *Journal of Verbal Learning and Verbal Behavior, 22*, 1–39.

Ekman, P., & Friesen, W. (1969). The repertoire of nonverbal behavior: Categories, origins, usage and coding. *Semiotica, 1,* 49–98.

Engle, R. A. (1998). Not channels but composite signals: Speech, gesture, diagrams, and object demonstrations are integrated in multimodal explanations. In M. A. Gernsbacher & S. J. Derry (Eds.), *Proceedings of the Twentieth Annual Conference of the Cognitive Science Society* (pp. 321–326). Mahwah, NJ: Lawrence Erlbaum Associates.

Goodwin, C. (1981). *Conversational organization: Interaction between speakers and hearers.* New York: Academic Press.

Grice, H. P. (1957). Meaning. *Philosophical Review, 66,* 377–388.

Grice, H. P. (1968). Utterer's meaning, sentence-meaning, and word-meaning. *Foundations of Language, 4,* 225–242.

Grice, H. P. (1991). *In the way of words.* Cambridge, MA: Harvard University Press.

Kendon, A. (1967). Some functions of gaze-direction in social interaction. *Acta Psychologica, 26,* 22–63.

Kendon, A. (1981). Geography of gesture. *Semiotica, 37,* 129–163.

Kendon, A. (1990). *Conducting interaction: Patterns of behavior in focused encounters.* Cambridge: Cambridge University Press.

Lewis, D. K. (1969). *Convention: A philosophical study.* Cambridge, MA: Harvard University Press.

McNeill, D. (1992). *Hand and mind.* Chicago: University of Chicago Press.

Nunberg, G. (1979). The non-uniqueness of semantic solutions: Polysemy. *Linguistics and Philosophy, 3,* 143–184.

Schegloff, E. A. (1968). Sequencing in conversational openings. *American Anthropologist, 70*(4), 1075–1095.

Wilkins, D. P. (1992). Interjections as deictics. *Journal of Pragmatics, 17,* 119–158.

Chapter 11

From Pointing to Reference and Predication: Pointing Signs, Eyegaze, and Head and Body Orientation in Danish Sign Language

Elisabeth Engberg-Pedersen
University of Copenhagen

THE FUNCTIONS OF A POINTING GESTURE

Once a deaf mother signed CHARLOTTE WHERE ("Where is Charlotte?"), Charlotte being her daughter standing right next to her. Charlotte responded by pointing energetically to herself. She did not point to the ground where she was standing as a way of answering the request for a location. Neither did she point first to herself and then to the location to indicate who was where. A point to an entity X in a location Y as a response to the question *Where is X?* can be seen as a condensed way of saying *X is at Y*; the point has the same communicative function as a simple proposition used to refer to X and predicate of X its existence at Y. But while the pointing gesture simply links two entities, X and Y, Y is predicated of X in the linguistic expression *X is at Y*, and in this sense Y is subordinate to X (Greenberg, 1985, pp. 277–278; Lakoff, 1987, pp. 489–491; Lyons, 1977, pp. 646–657). When we point to entities in locations, we do exactly that: we point to the entity, not the location. We focus on entities, but use space to keep track of them. The indexical aspect of a pointing gesture is its use of a location in space, but in a pointing gesture the two functions, reference and predication, are expressed by one form.

In this chapter I demonstrate how the referring and predicating aspects of a holophrastic pointing gesture are differentiated in pointing signs in a language that is intimately connected with space—namely, Danish Sign

Language.[1] Pointing signs in a sign language take on specific grammatical roles and may lose their indexical aspect.

Not only pointing signs have an indexical aspect in signed discourse, however. Signers' eyegaze and head and body orientation may also be indexical, that is, make use of space to link what is said with a particular referent. Indexical eyegaze and head and body orientation contribute to reference tracking and accompany predicational signs in a manner reminiscent of mime. Their function can, however, only be interpreted from their interaction with manual signs; they are not formally differentiated as pointing signs are.

In the next section, I introduce the notion of locus, a direction from the signer that represents a referent in signed discourse. The third section looks at the differentiation of the pointing gesture into a pronoun, a determiner, and different types of verbs, and the fourth and fifth sections demonstrate the functions of eyegaze and head and body orientation, respectively.

LOCI IN SIGNED DISCOURSE

In sign languages, reference to present entities is usually made by points to the entities. When signers want to refer to nonpresent entities, they may represent the referents by means of directions in the signing space and refer anaphorically to these entities—for instance, by means of a point in the relevant direction. The term *locus* denotes a direction in the signing space or the situational context that represents a referent in signed discourse (Engberg-Pedersen, 1993). Referents represented by loci may be individuals, objects, locations, moments or periods in time, and abstract ideas. Not all referents are represented by a locus, however. More concrete referents such as geographical locations and individuals are more likely to be represented by a locus than more abstract referents such as plans, hopes, or decisions. Moreover, the higher an item's discourse relevance or general relevance to the participants in the discourse, the more likely it is to be represented by a locus. The signer's locus is the center of the signing space and represents either the signer or some other holder of the point of view.

Loci can be manifested in all signs that are not articulated on the body, in eyegaze and head and body orientation. Manual signs indicate loci by being articulated with the hand(s) oriented toward, moving out, or moved out in the direction of a locus. Moreover, signers may look in the direction

---

[1]Danish Sign Language is the primary language of 3,000 to 4,000 deaf Danes. A tradition has developed in sign language research of distinguishing between *Deaf* to describe a cultural-linguistic group and *deaf* to describe individuals with a hearing loss. Because I do not know whether individual deaf people see themselves as members of a cultural-linguistic group or not, I do not follow this practice.

of a locus, rotate their body or head so that they face the direction of the locus, or, more rarely, move their body in the direction of a locus.

At one point, it was suggested that sign languages distinguish two uses of space: topographical and grammatical (Poizner, Klima, & Bellugi, 1987). Spatial mapping was claimed to be a more or less iconic use of space to represent location, whereas space in spatialized syntax with arbitrarily chosen loci was said to serve syntactic purposes only. Liddell (1990, 1995, 1996) and Engberg-Pedersen (1993) argued against this view. All spatial representations in signing are part of a topographically organized or semantically motivated space. Loci for anaphoric purposes are chosen according to certain conventions (Engberg-Pedersen, 1993), for example, the convention of semantic affinity, which is the metonymic principle that unless two referents need to be distinguished for discourse reasons, the same locus is used to represent both referents if they belong together, such as a father and his child, a woman and the place where she works, or the time of one's vacation and the travel agency. The specific direction or locus from the signer in signed discourse is thus not irrelevant, but part of the message conveyed and should not be represented in transcriptions as indexes of (non-)coreferentiality as suggested, for instance, by Lillo-Martin and Klima (1990).

Especially Liddell (1996; Liddell & Metzger, 1998) argued that spatial representations are not linguistic. In a spatially modified sign, he distinguished the linguistic part expressed by the hand form, the type of movement, and certain aspects of the hand's orientation from the nonlinguistic—indexical—part that relates the sign to the locus, that is, other aspects of the hand's orientation, its location, and/or the direction in which it is moved.

The anaphoric use of space in sign languages is quite complex with subtle, meaningful shifts in the configuration of loci in signed discourse (e.g., Engberg-Pedersen, 1993; Liddell & Metzger, 1998). Yet the basic use of loci for anaphoric purposes has also been observed both accompanying speech (Gullberg, 1996, 1998) and in the self-invented signing of deaf children who have not been exposed to a sign language (Butcher, Mylander, & Goldin-Meadow, 1991).

POINTING SIGNS

Formal Differences

Signed discourse abounds with pointing signs.[2] On the average, almost every fourth sign[3] in signed discourse is a pointing sign, and many more

---

[2]The analysis of pointing signs presented here is largely identical with the analysis in Engberg-Pedersen (1993).

[3]Counting pointing signs (including the first-person pronoun) in 1 min of discourse from each of a dialogue and two monologues involving four different signers, I found the following

signs are indexical in the sense that they relate to loci. In Danish Sign Language, the functional difference between pointing signs in referential expressions and pointing signs used for predication correlates with a difference in form. We can thus distinguish pointing signs as pronouns and determiners from pointing signs as verbs.

The noncontrastive (singular) pronoun and the noncontrastive (singular) determiner[4] are made with a short movement in the direction of a locus or with a very short side-to-side movement with the index finger pointing in the direction of the locus. The index finger is lax and held horizontally unless the referent or the imagined referent is located above or below the level of the holder of the point of view or the pronoun or determiner is marked for proximity. The hand and arm are normally neither pronated nor supinated, but contrastive forms may be pronated.[5]

Some of the verb forms that are related to the pointing gesture are forms of two lexemes, GO-TO and BE-AT, that can be modified for loci. The lexeme GO-TO is made with an arclike or straight movement in the direction of the fingertip, the movement is longer than in the pronoun and the determiner, and the hand is pronated. The handform combined with the movement may give the impression that the locus is a specific point in space and that the finger touches the locus. BE-AT is the static form made with a shorter movement.

All sign languages include constructions that denote motion or location and are composed of many meaningful units. The hand in these constructions takes on a form that characterizes a particular entity such as it is involved in a specific motion event, for example, in Danish Sign Language, a flat hand for a car or an upright index hand for a human being approaching or passing someone. The handform must be supplemented with a meaningful movement, orientation, and so on to form a full sign denoting motion or location. The unit expressed by the handform has been compared with classifiers in spoken languages (Supalla, 1986), an analysis that has been criticized, however (Engberg-Pedersen, 1993). The term *classifier*

---

percentages of pointing signs in relation to the total number of signs: 19.6% and 30.8% in the dialogue, and 22.2% and 26.4% in the two monologues, making an average of 24.4% (88 pointing signs out of a total of 360 signs).

[4]Here I only talk about the pronoun and the determiner that are pointing signs. There are other pronouns that can be modified in space. The pronoun and the determiner derived from pointing gestures can be marked for various types of plurality (the hand moves sideward or makes a circle, for instance). A point to the signer is the first person pronoun transcribed 1.p; it can be analyzed as a different sign than nonfirst-person pronouns (Engberg-Pedersen, 1993, pp. 134–139).

[5]The orientation of the hand can assimilate to the hand orientation of a preceding sign, but the orientation may also vary in ways (palm sideward or downward) that are not due to other signs but may be significant (cf. later in this chapter and Kendon & Versante, chap. 6, this volume).

predicates is currently used in sign linguistics, although much debated by sign language researchers (Emmorey, in press). A pointing index hand can be used as a general classifier in verbs denoting motion of any entity; the index finger traces a stylized version of the entity's path of motion.

The forms of the pronoun and the determiner have less formal weight than the verb forms, but when they are contrastive, pronouns can occur with a number of the form features of the verb forms or their movement is repeated.

The Pronoun and the Determiner

The pronoun and the determiner are distinguished distributionally. A pronoun is used to refer by itself while a determiner occurs with a noun in a noun phrase. In (1), the two instances of pointing signs are determiners in the nominals meaning "my American father" (1.p AMERICA FATHER DET+fr) and "volleyball" (DET+m VOLLEYBALL).[6]

(1)   "My American father said to me, 'Why don't you sign up for volleyball.' "

V+   fr +   V+
1.p AMERICA FATHER DET+fr /   NOTIFY+1.p WHY NOT

DET+m VOLLEYBALL /[7]

In (2), the first pointing sign is a pronoun that constitutes the topic of UNDERSTAND PROBLEM; the last pointing sign is a resumptive pronoun separated from the preceding clause by nonmanual signals and often seen at major discourse boundaries.

(2)   "She understood the problem."

+   V +   fr V +
PRON+fr   UNDERSTAND PROBLEM   PRON+fr /

Only specific referents can be represented by a locus. A pronoun or a determiner modified for a locus thus always indicates that the referent is specific. But the determiner does not express definiteness, it can be used with a new referent as in (3).

---

[6] The transcription system is explained in the appendix.
[7] Danish Sign Language has a distinct possessive pronoun, but 1.p is often used with a possessive meaning as in (1).

(3)   "Fortunately, we got another flat."

FORTUNATELY OBTAIN SECOND DET+fl LIVE^FLAT /

Both the pronoun and the determiner have *undirected* variants (see also Zimmer & Patschke, 1990). In these the index hand is held without movement for a brief moment or it occurs in a transition movement and the direction in which the index finger points is irrelevant. As the undirected variants of the pronoun do not have a deictic element, they are referential without being indexical. It is not yet clear whether undirected determiners can occur in a nominal used to refer to a new referent. But determiners modified for a locus (directed determiners) occur in nominals with both an indefinite and a definite meaning (see examples (3) shown earlier and (6) later). That is, if undirectedness codes definite meaning, this coding is not obligatory.

The frequent occurrence of undirected pronouns and determiners in Danish Sign Language seems strong evidence of the integration of pointing gestures as signs with specific syntactic functions in a language.[8]

Verbs

The pointing signs that function as verbs can be classified as forms of the stative verb BE-AT, the dynamic verb GO-TO, or classifier predicates with General-entity.

The lexeme GO-TO is seen in Example (4).

(4)   "On Saturday night the deaf people there invited me to the deaf club in Bristol."

+   sl +   sl +
SATURDAY NIGHT /   DEAF DET+pl.+sl   INVITE

1.p c+GO-TO+fsl DEAF UNION / BRISTOL c+GO-TO+fsl /

---

[8]At The Max Planck Workshop on Pointing Gestures, June 1997, Oud-Turnhout, Belgium, Adam Kendon and Laura Versante presented a videotaped example of an Italian man using an undirected pointing gesture accompanying his speech. Formally, it was very different from the undirected pronouns and determiners in Danish Sign Language, however. The Italian man held his hand without movement for a period while speaking; the undirected forms of the pronoun and the determiner in Danish Sign Language, in contrast, occur between other signs and are often so brief that they are hard to perceive except in slow motion. The Italian gesture is reminiscent of another type in Danish Sign Language, namely, an undirected index hand (or other hand shape) held motionless in signer's nondominant hand while the signer articulate a number of other signs with the dominant hand (Engberg-Pedersen, 1994).

GO-TO is here modified indexically for two loci, one representing the moving individual's starting point, where "I" is, and one representing its end point, the Deaf club.

Some pointing signs made with an arc or a straight movement seem to function as a particle linking two nouns, but it is doubtful whether they can be distinguished from the verb forms:

(5) "Deaf people in Bristol feel offended."

$$\overline{\hspace{6cm}}^{\ \ t}$$

DET+sl DEAF PARTICLE(?)+sl Bristol(M) / OFFENDED /

The topicalized constituent in (5) includes two pointing signs, a determiner and possibly a particle. The second pointing sign, transcribed PARTICLE(?)+sl, is made with a downward movement, a rebound, and a hold, the hand is pronated, and the sign is accompanied by the mouthing of the Danish preposition *i* "in." It is not clear whether the topicalized constituent is clearly distinct from a clause. If it is not, the pointing sign between DEAF and Bristol(M) can be analyzed as a form of the stative verb BE-AT, the first part of (5) constituting what looks like a relative clause with an internal head. In that case it is not possible to maintain a distinction between a particle and the verb (see also the ambiguous example (8), later).

The Proform

One more type of pointing sign can be distinguished formally and functionally from the other types. This type is used as a carrier of information which is otherwise expressed in spatial modifications of manual signs; the form is usually made with the nondominant hand, that is, the signer's least active hand in articulating signs:

(6) "The leader, later she went to Jutland."

$$\overline{\hspace{4cm}}^{\ \ t}$$

fr +   V
DET+fr LEADER DET+fr / AFTER PRON+fr TRAVEL^GONE

JUTLAND   /
PROFORM+sr

The sign transcribed as PROFORM+sr consists of an index hand pointing in the direction of the locus sideward-right. It is made with the nondominant hand with a hold movement simultaneously with the sign JUTLAND. At first, the pointing sign might seem to be a determiner articulated simultaneously with the noun. But the proform can occur in contexts where it can be analyzed as neither a pronoun nor a determiner. Like JUTLAND, DEAF has a place of articulation on the body and cannot be modified in space, but the modification +group, which is expressed spatially by reduplication of the sign in a circular movement of the hand(s), can be transferred to the proform as in (7) where the sign DEAF is reduplicated at the ear and the circular movement is made by the nondominant hand:

(7)   "It seemed obvious since many members of our family are deaf."[9]

   THINK OF-COURSE / SINCE 1.p+pl. MANY FAMILY

   DEAF   /OF-COURSE /
   PROFORM+group

In (7), the pointing sign cannot be a determiner because it occurs simultaneously with the predicate, and it cannot be a pronoun because the nominal 1.p+pl. MANY FAMILY occupies the argument position in relation to the predicate. Instead, I propose to analyze the pointing sign occurring simultaneously with other signs as a proform that carries a spatial modification [in (7), a modification for distribution] either when the sign cannot be modified because it has a place of articulation on the body or head, or as an intensification of the spatial modification.[10] A proform may occur both with a referential nominal as in (6) and with a predicate as in (7).

   In (7), the proform is modified for distribution (+group), but not for a locus: The hand articulating PROFORM+group is moved in a circle in neutral space just outside the signer's chest. If PROFORM is also modified for a locus, the hand is moved out in the direction of the locus and makes a circle in that direction. The proform may thus be indexical as in (6), or it may be nonindexical as in (7).

---

[9]The proform in (7) is made with a loose hand with all fingers extended, either as a consequence of assimilation to the handshape of MANY and FAMILY or to indicate plurality.

[10]Friedman (1975) analyzed the use of an "index" made with the nondominant hand simultaneously with another sign made with the dominant hand in ASL as having an emphatic or contrastive function or serving to "establish or refer to the location of the NP" (when it is simultaneous with a nominal), to indicate "the location of the action" (when it is simultaneous with a verb), or to "incorporate the subject of the verb plus its location" (when it is simultaneous with a verb). In Danish Sign Language the proform can be simultaneous with a verb and carry modification for a timeline (e.g., an example meaning "I'll run into trouble again and again" where IN-TROUBLE cannot be modified spatially itself). In such cases it is only possible to talk about the location of an action in a very abstract sense.

An Ambiguous Case

Pointing signs sometimes occur after verbs where they seem to take over modifications from the verb sign. In (8), a pointing sign occurs after the verb SIT, indicating the locus of the balcony, whereas SIT is not modified:

(8) "We theatre people sat all the way up in the balcony. We were not allowed to sit down below [in the stalls]."

1.p+pl. THEATRE^PERSON+pl. SIT POINT+u

BALCONY / MUST-NOT POINT+d /
BALCONY - - - - - - - - - - - - - - - - - - -

SIT can be modified indexically, but as it is made with both hands, the signer of (8) may feel a certain reluctance to move her hands up in front of her face. The pointing sign after SIT is accompanied by the mouth pattern of the Danish adverb *op* "up," whereas the signer does not use any mouth pattern with the pointing sign after MUST-NOT. Both signs are made with a straight movement in the direction of the tip of the index finger. In the first sign, the arm is pronated and the palm faces outward as a consequence of the index finger pointing upward. In the second sign, the arm is also pronated. The first pointing sign can be analyzed as a form of the stative verb BE-AT in a serial verb construction (see also Bos, 1994; T. Supalla, 1990), as a particle or preposition linking the verb SIT and the nominal BALCONY, or as a contrastive form of the determiner with BALCONY as its head, and the second pointing sign can be analyzed as a form of BE-AT or a contrastive form of the pronoun referring to a location. In the first clause the predicational and the referential part of pointing gestures is split up between the lexical verb SIT and the pointing sign referring to the location; in the last clause POINT+d combines the predicational and the referential aspect. The linguistic ambiguity of the two pointing signs in (8) is, of course, evidence of the original multifunctionality of pointing gestures.

In summary, the pointing signs in Danish Sign Language demonstrate a major form division between, on the one hand, the pronoun and the determiner and, on the other, stative and dynamic verb forms and maybe a locative particle. The form distinction correlates with a functional distinction between signs that are used to refer and signs that function as predicates, that is, the basic distinction between nominals and verbs. In a study by McNeill, Cassell, and Levy (1993), one narrator was found to use a pointing gesture simultaneously with a (spoken) nominal to refer to a particular referent for the first time. In the narrator's next sentence, another pointing gesture was simultaneous with the predicate describing what the referent did (the brackets indicate the temporal position of the pointing gestures, in both cases points to the left: *and in fact, a few minutes later we see [the artist] and uh she [looks over] Frank's shoulder at him*—where the second gesture is simultaneous with mentioning the action of looking at the artist, that is, the new information about the newly introduced character). We thus see here in embryonic form the distinction between referential and predicational use of points, but it is not clear whether the two pointing gestures are different in form.

The pointing signs that can have a predicative function predicate an entity's being in a place or moving to, from, or about in a location; the two semantic aspects of the predicate, being or becoming located and the location, can be expressed in separate signs as in SIT followed by a pointing sign in (8), or they may be integrated in one verb form as in c+GO-TO+fsl in (4). The pronoun, the determiner, and the proform may be indexical or nonindexical, whereas the verbs are always indexical, with their main function being to relate a referent and a location.

Because the pronoun, determiner, and proform are normally made with a neutral hand orientation and the verb with the hand pronated, neutral hand orientation seems to indicate the referential aspect of the pointing signs, whereas pronation indicates the locational aspect. The referential aspect may be emphasized in a sign that functions predicationally, such as the predicate in a clause that sums up the signer's discussion of who was allowed to sit where after Example (8): She signed BE-AT+u in 1.p+pl. BE-AT+u ("We (should sit) there") with the hand orientation of the pronoun. Conversely, the signer of Example (4) made the determiner in the phrase DEAF DET+pl.+sl ("the deaf people there") with the hand halfway between neutral orientation and pronation as if to emphasize that she meant the deaf people located in Bristol.

EYEGAZE

Sender's Level and Characters' Level

In signed discourse, signers switch back and forth between, roughly speaking, two types or two levels of signing depending on whom the signer's locus represents. The signer may represent either the signer as the sender of the communication act or a character talked about. The latter phenomenon is traditionally called *role shifting* in sign-language research (Padden, 1986), and it is reminiscent of mime. Role shifting should, however, be broken down into different features with different distributions (Engberg-Pedersen, 1995; see also Liddell & Metzger, 1998). Signers may express a character's appearance or emotions by their facial expression and body posture (*shifted attribution of expressive elements*); for instance, the signer of (5) looks stern while signing OFFENDED. Signers may further use their own locus to represent an individual talked about (*shifted locus*); if the signer's locus represents the agent, verb signs such as GIVE or SEND-MAIL are made in such a way that the hand moves out from the signer's locus ("someone gave/sent ..."); if the signer's locus represents the recipient, the hand moves inward toward the signer ("someone got/was sent ..."). Shifted locus is also indicated by eyegaze direction and face and body orientation; the signer's eyegaze direction and/or head and body orientation may reflect the point of view of one of the characters talked about (discussed later). Finally, in quotations, signers may use the first person pronoun to refer to somebody other than themselves (*shifted reference*).

Blink, Eye Contact, and Imitative Eyegaze

Example (9) demonstrates several typical features of eyegaze behavior in signing.

(9) "One day when I had finished work, I went home and as I was walking along, I saw something that puzzled me."

+		V	fsl	V+		V
ONE DAY 1.p	WORK	FINISH	/ 1.p	HOME WALK[+]	/	

flu		V+
1.p WATCH HOW-STRANGE	/	

The signer has eye contact (indicated by +) with the person that she is talking to almost all the time. Eye contact is, of course, essential to the signer's checking the receiver's understanding, but here the signer breaks off eye contact by blinking at all major boundaries (V indicates eye blink) and while signing the predicate FINISH and the last part, where she looks in the direction of the loci *fsl* and *flu*, respectively. Simplifying the issue, we may say that signers have eye contact with their receiver when they sign nominals that establish referents, and they have mime-like eyegaze behavior when they explain what the referents do or how they react, that is, when they sign predicates. In this much too simplistic way, with the predicates the signer can be said to imitate the referent's body and head posture, eyegaze direction and facial expression, and in the case of some manual signs, also the referent's gestures in the sense that the predicate can be seen as a stylized reenactment of the action described (cf. the term *constructed action* used by, among others, Liddell & Metzger, 1998). The prolonged look to the left during the sign FINISH in (9), where the signer also rotates her head, imitates the signer's paying attention to her work, and her looking in the forward-left direction while signing WATCH HOW-STRANGE imitates her own eyegaze direction at the time when she was walking home from work and saw something that made her wonder. In (9), however, the predicates cannot be said to imitate anything the referent could have done with her hands when finishing work or discovering the strange sight. The sign WATCH is iconic (a fist with the index finger and the middle finger stretched out as a representation of the eyes), but not mimetic because people do not do anything with their hands to look at something.

The sign that I have transcribed as HOW-STRANGE is one of a group of signs that denote people's emotional reactions. They can occur with a preceding nominal or pronoun, but never with any sign following within the same clause. That is, it is impossible to indicate the reason for one's emotional reaction by a manual sign in the same syntactic unit. But the sign HOW-STRANGE must be accompanied by a look in the direction of the locus used to represent the item that causes the emotional reaction.

In (9), the eyegaze behavior imitates the agent or experiencer referent's eyegaze (the topics of FINISH, WATCH, HOW-STRANGE). But eyegaze behavior may also imitate what can best be described as a patient referent in relation to the verb. In a different monologue, a signer described a birthday party where two children started a fight but were stopped by an adult who grasped both children's shoulders. The signer first imitated the adult person while making what could either be described as a classifier construction or a gesture (Emmorey, 1999) meaning "grasped their shoulders": She rotated her head and body so that she faced left and looked downward left. Then she imitated one of the children: She shrank, rotated her head so that she faced right and looked upward right with a frightened expression while she grasped her own right shoulder. The last part demonstrates the child's reaction to the adult's interference—that is, the signer imitated the eyegaze direction of the inactive participant in the interaction.

As can be seen from (9), eyegaze behavior of the imitating type may be indexical. The signer looks in the direction of the loci used to represent her work and the thing that puzzled her. The eyegaze directions are the only indications of these referents' loci. The last locus, the locus of the signer's house, is used subsequently in manual signs, but is introduced here only by means of the signer's eyegaze. But imitative eyegaze is not necessarily indexical. Signers may imitate a person in deep thoughts, in which case the direction in which they look may be irrelevant. Or they may imitate people closing their eyes.

Eye contact with receivers as in the beginning of Example (9) can perhaps be said to index receivers. In certain contexts—for instance, at the end of topicalized constituents and questions—eye contact with receivers is normal, which is consonant with its function of checking the receivers' understanding and giving them a chance to respond (Baker, 1977). The direction of signers' eyegaze when they have eye contact with receivers depends, of course, on where the receivers are located, and in this sense eye contact can be said to be indexical.

The fact that imitative eyegaze resembles mime suggests that the eyegaze direction indicates not only the item looked at, but also the referent personified by the signer, that is, the holder of the point of view. When signers take a character's point of view, their eyegaze direction and the direction in which they face indicate, of course, the referent interacted with. Yet this direction does not indicate the character from whose point of view the interaction takes place. What happens when signers take a character's point of view, is that this character takes over the signer's locus in the center and views the other referents from this egocentric point. The configuration of loci does not change except that the locus of the referent that has taken over the center is suspended. This can be seen, for instance, when signers recount a dialogue between themselves and another individual: They look in the direction of the other person's locus, such as the locus forward-right, when they recount what they said to this person themselves, and they tend to look at the receiver when they quote the other person (an example of that can be seen in (1) [= (10) later]). If we imagine a situation where the signer explains that a third party joined the conversation, the signer may use the locus forward-left to represent this new person. When recounting things addressed to this new individual, the signer would look in the direction forward-left, but it would be impossible to guess only from the eyegaze direction who was the quoted person, the signer on the earlier occasion or the person represented by the locus forward-right. In such cases, signers can indicate who is being quoted, by means of a pronoun or other nominal before the quoted speech, but the direction of the signer's eyegaze only indicates who is being addressed.

As signers sometimes refer to themselves as senders or individuals with current ideas or desires and sometimes as characters in, for instance, a past course of events, it might be expected that they would distinguish these two functions by their eyegaze; that is, we might expect them to have eye contact with the receiver when referring to their current selves and to use imitative eyegaze when referring to themselves as characters in a past course of events. There does indeed seem to be a tendency for signers to break off eye contact with the receiver while signing sequences where they refer to themselves as characters, not only by looking in the direction of a locus, but also simply by avoiding eye contact without looking in any particular direction. Yet Example (9), where the signer talks about past events that she was involved in, demonstrates that signers may also maintain eye contact with receivers during such sequences.

Reference-Tracking Eyegaze

Loci contribute to keeping track of referents, and signers may look briefly
in the direction of a referent's locus to remind the receiver of the referent.
An example of that is seen in (1), repeated here as (10).

(10)   "My American father said to me, 'Why don't you sign up for volleyball.' "

V+   fr +   V+
1.p AMERICA FATHER DET+fr /   NOTIFY+1.p WHY NOT

DET+m VOLLEYBALL /

The signer establishes a referent in the discourse universe by means of the
first nominal accompanied by eye contact with the receiver. Then she looks
very briefly in the forward-right direction before the start of the predicate
NOTIFY and the quoted speech, "Why don't you sign up for volleyball."
Signers also often look briefly in the direction of a referent's locus before
or simultaneously with a resumptive pronoun at the end of a sentence [see
Example (2)]. This type of eyegaze behavior cannot be described as imitative of a character in the discourse. Looking very briefly in the direction of
the father's locus in (10) just before signing the utterance verb NOTIFY
does not imitate anyone's eyegaze behavior. It is rather the sender's way of
indicating the topic of the verb and contributing to keeping track of the referent. In (10) the signer uses the locus forward-right in the immediately
preceding determiner, but the reference-tracking eyegaze may be the first
link between a referent and a locus, as in Example (11), shown later.

     Eyegaze used for reference tracking is always indexical, and imitative
eyegaze behavior is often indexical, but there is an interesting difference
between the two in terms of indexicality. As imitative eyegaze behavior most
often imitates the agent or experiencer referent's eyegaze behavior as in
(9), the signer looks in the direction of a locus of someone or something
other than the topic of the predicate. In (9) she looks in the direction of
the locus that is used to represent what puzzles her, for example. But
eyegaze used for reference tracking is typically in the direction of the
topic's locus as in (10), where the signer looks in the direction of the locus
used to represent the person who does the notifying.

Configurational Eyegaze

Configurational eyegaze is seen with classifier predicates. One signer described how water was streaming down the walls of her bathroom. She used
a classifier predicate about the water: Her hands moved from above her

head alternately downward repeatedly. During this construction, she looked up, moving her head and her eyegaze from side to side as if looking at the wall, that is, an imaginary configuration in space.

Streeck (1993) described dialogues in German and Ilokano where speakers look at their hands. When a woman speaking German told her interlocutor about a theatre performance, she said *Und hat so zwei Mikrophone, so inner Hand, nich?* ("And she has like these two microphones, in her hand like this, right?") (Streeck, 1993, p. 283). While saying *zwei Mikrophone* ("two microphones"), she held up her fists outside her body and looked at them. Streeck described the function of this type of eyegaze as pointing, namely pointing to the speaker's gestures as the objects of attention: "by pointing to them with her eyes, the speaker demonstrates that the gestures are relevant to her talk at the moment" (1993, p. 286). This cannot be the function of the configurational eyegaze in sign languages because the "gestures" constitute the signer's "talk at the moment." Moreover, signers may look at their hands in these situations, but they may equally well look beyond their hands to the imaginary configuration in space, as in the example with the water where the signer's eyegaze moves over the imaginary wall. Still, the examples from signing and the examples from Streeck's dialogues share the element of complex configurations in space. Other examples described by Streeck are circular movements while describing actors going in circles and gestures describing the position of cement in a basin for rainwater.

The configurational type of eyegaze shares features with both the imitative type and the reference-tracking type. In the bathroom example, the signer perhaps imitates her own eyegaze behavior at the time when she saw the water damage, or she may be the narrator explaining what had happened and drawing attention to the water. We cannot decide. But the typical reference-tracking eyegaze is brief and occurs usually just before or simultaneously with a referential nominal or pronoun, whereas imitative eyegaze and configurational eyegaze accompany predicates and are usually more prolonged [see, however, Example (12) later].

With respect to indexing, classifier constructions such as the one about the water streaming down the wall are interesting because they iconically represent referents in states or dynamic events in a location. They combine representations of the three elements: the referent represented by the hand(s); the location where it is found, represented by the place of articulation; and the item's state or activity in that location, represented by the handform and the movement or lack of movement of the hand(s). Classifier constructions may constitute a full clause, but they may also be preceded by a nominal used to refer to the referent. That is, even though classifier constructions represent referents iconically and are indexical, they are not referential. The indexical aspect is emphasized by the signer's eyegaze direction.

Eyegaze at Major Boundaries

Eyegaze is also used to indicate major syntactic boundaries independently of the functions I have listed here. Signers change their eyegaze direction at major boundaries either as a result of switching between the types I have mentioned here [see, for example, the three boundaries in example (9)], or if there is no reason to switch between, for instance, imitative eyegaze and eye contact, they simply change the direction from eye contact to looking away at the boundary, and then back to eye contact at the beginning of the next sentence. At boundaries with less discourse weight they only blink.

Discussion

The five types of eyegaze behavior described here are:

- The *narrator's eye contact with the receiver*, which has the function of checking the receiver's understanding.
- *Reference-tracking eyegaze* in the direction of a locus just before a predicate or with a referential nominal or a pronoun; it is always indexical.
- *Imitative eyegaze* with predicates or quotations, imitates the holder of the point of view or the quoted person; imitative eyegaze may be indexical, but can also imitate thoughtful eyegaze in no particular direction or closed eyes.
- *Configurational eyegaze* with classifier constructions; draws attention to a configuration either at the narrator's level or at the characters' level; it is indexical.
- *Avoidance of eye contact at major boundaries* to indicate the boundary if there is no other change and the signer wants to continue.

Formally there are only three types of eyegaze behavior: Signers may have eye contact with the receiver, they may break off eye contact looking in some other direction, or they may break off eye contact by blinking or closing their eyes. How can we then justify an analysis of eyegaze behavior into five different types, especially when they are not exclusive—a configurational eyegaze may also be imitative, and being indexical it serves a reference-tracking purpose.

It is only by analyzing eyegaze behavior in the context of what signers express by manual signs that we can distinguish different functions of, in particular, eyegaze not directed at the receiver. The main distinctions here are between reference-tracking eyegaze, imitative eyegaze, and configurational eyegaze. Bahan and S. Supalla (1995) presented an analysis of eyegaze behavior in American Sign Language that differed slightly from the one I have presented here. They described three types corresponding to my narrator's eye contact with the receiver, imitative eyegaze, and configurational eyegaze[11]; that is, they do not single out the narrator's reference-tracking eyegaze. The difference between reference-tracking eyegaze and imitative eyegaze is brought out clearly by the following examples.

(11) "Earlier the dishwasher had broken down."

```
           t
———————————
+            fld V +                                         V
EARLIER /        DISHWASHER+fld BROKEN+fld / PRON+fld /
```

(12) "I walked there and opened the door."

```
+  flu +      rd    +
WALK  PRON OPEN-DOOR /
```

In (11), the signer looks in the direction of the locus of the dishwasher just before the sign DISHWASHER, which constitutes the topic of the predicate BREAK. This is the narrator's reference-tracking eyegaze, it could not possibly imitate any character's eyegaze. In (12), the signer looks briefly in the direction of the locus of the house at the end of the verb WALK, and anticipatorily, in the direction of the locus of what is inside the house at the beginning of the verb OPEN-DOOR. The topic of the predicates in (12) is the first-person pronoun of the preceding clause—that is, the eyegaze direction does not indicate the topic, but imitates the signer's eyegaze at the time when she was walking home and opened the door. Because it is not possible to attribute the eyegaze direction *fld* in (11) to any of the characters in the narration, and because the eyegaze direction of (12) does not trace the topic of the predicates, I find that we need to distinguish reference-tracking eyegaze from imitative eyegaze.

It might be claimed that the narrator's reference-tracking eyegaze is imitative eyegaze at the narrator's level: Narrators are masters of the narration, and they survey the "players" (reference-tracking eyegaze) before launching into descriptions of what they are doing (imitative eyegaze at the characters' level). But although it is possible to compare the narrator at the metalevel and the characters at the level of the narration, they are clearly distinct, a distinction that also appears from expressions of emotions. Emotions may be expressed manually by signs such as DAMN-IT or LUCKILY or

---

[11]With the last type they claim that signers look at their hands, but as I have pointed out, signers of Danish Sign Language may also look beyond their hands at an imaginary configuration in the air.

by facial expression and body posture, and such expressions should be attributed either to the narrator or to one of the characters represented by the narrator. In the story from which (13) is extracted, the signer represents the king's thoughts, his eyegaze directions (imitative eyegaze indicated by an asterisk),[12] and his manual and nonmanual expressions of emotions. The signs DAMN-IT and FINE express the king's emotions as do the mouth movements as parts of the emotional facial expressions, that is, *tight-lipped, adh* (part of a facial expression of exasperation), and *ahh* (part of an inspired facial expression).

(13)   "The king felt lost. Damn the two of them! He thought about it and got an idea. He would make a contest. That was it. That would be fine."

```
gaze:  +*        +              V *              V  +            V *
       KING gesture / TWO+pron. DAMN-IT TWO+pron. / THINK
mouth:           adh ----                  tight-lipped ------------------------
```

```
brow:  up --                     up -------
gaze:  +                            *      V *     V* +
       GET-IDEA MAKE   CONTEST   gesture FINE   /
mouth: ahh                        ahh
```

It is the basic distinction between the sender and characters talked about that justifies the distinction between reference-tracking and imitative eyegaze, with configurational eyegaze attributable to either the narrator or to one of the characters.[13]

HEAD AND BODY ORIENTATION

By *head* and *body orientation* I mean signers' orientation when their front is turned toward the receiver and all deviations from this orientation. Signers' head or body orientation changes when their head or body is rotated

---

[12]As Example (13) demonstrates, imitative eyegaze often starts already at the initial nominal establishing who should be held responsible for the quotation or representation of thoughts or actions. It has been demonstrated also for spoken languages that eyegaze shift occurs anticipatorily before the keyword (Streeck, 1993; see also Example (11) in this chapter where the signer looks in the direction of the dishwasher's locus just before signing DISH-WASHER), as do manual gestures in relation to speech (McNeill, 1992).

[13] The description of eyegaze behavior may give the impression that it is only relevant to storytelling, drawing on terms such as *narration, narrator,* and *character.* This is, however, not the case. What has been called *role shifting* is an integrated part of all types of signed discourse besides the merest requests for the time or the salt.

around its vertical axis. Orientation should be distinguished from *body posture*, which is used to cover differences such as straight or upright versus hunched body posture. Differences in body posture link with emotionally different facial expressions to signal sequences of discourse with shifted attribution of expressive elements; this signals the intended character, but is not indexical, as changes in body posture do not indicate a locus.

Body orientation and body posture should also be distinguished from sideways movement or movement backward or forward of the torso. Signers may move their torso slightly backward and sideward to signal, for instance, an earlier point in time. This is particularly clear in lecture style when the signer is standing (for an illuminating example from American Sign Language, see Winston, 1995).

Head movements may be linked with manual signs to signal specific types of meaning, such as head shake to negate a proposition; withdrawal of the head to indicate topicalized constituents in the beginning of a sentence (Engberg-Pedersen, 1990); a forward downward movement followed by a movement back to the neutral position (a distinct head nod) accompanying resumptive pronouns at the end of sentences; or shifts in tilting to the sides or very small changes in head rotation to indicate boundaries between closely related clauses in a sequence. Moreover, head rotation may accompany specific manual signs such as FUNNY, NICE, or DETEST to express intensity.

Here I want to focus on changes in *head* and *body orientation* where signers rotate to face the direction of a locus. There is a hierarchy such that the body is not rotated unless the head is rotated, and the head is not rotated unless the signer looks in the direction of the locus.[14] Moreover, configurational eyegaze and imitative eyegaze are more likely to be accompanied by head rotation than reference-tracking eyegaze. In (9) [repeated here as (14)] the signer faces left and looks left during the predicate WORK and again when she signs WATCH HOW-STRANGE.

(14)   "One day when I had finished work, I went home and as I was walking along, I saw something that puzzled me."

```
                        rot.fsl---
+               V    fsl     V+                    V
ONE DAY 1.p  WORK  FINISH  / 1.p HOME WALK[+]   /

rot.fl-----------------------------------
flu                          V+
1.p WATCH HOW-STRANGE     /
```

---

[14]Unless, of course, the signer imitates someone looking in one direction and facing another direction.

Example (11) [repeated here as (15)] represents one of the rare occasions where a signer rotates her head with reference-tracking eyegaze. After the topicalized constituent EARLIER, where she faces the receiver, the signer looks in the direction right and also faces this direction before turning to the receiver again and signing DISHWASHER+fld.

(15) "Earlier the dishwasher had broken down."

```
       rot.rec.      rot.fld rot.rec.                          nod
  _____t
  +            fld   V +                                        V
  EARLIER /          DISHWASHER+fld BROKEN+fld / PRON+fld /
```

One of the factors that influences whether the signer rotates her head seems to be how well established the referent represented by the locus is. Just before signing (15) the signer starts signing DISHWASHER in neutral space, but she hesitates and then signs (15), apparently because she realizes that she has not yet introduced the dishwasher or the fact that it was broken. Later in the monologue when she refers to a workman to whom she has referred several times, she uses a pronoun modified for his locus, but without facing the direction or even looking in the direction of the locus. There is no need to help the receiver with the reference at that point in the discourse.

Rotating one's face and maybe even the body and looking in the direction of a locus give the impression of reenactment. Head and body rotation is thus often, but not necessarily, seen with quotations and with shifted locus and shifted attribution of expressive elements. Thus there seem to be two factors that influence the use of head and body rotation: first, whatever makes signers choose the livelier style of "reenactment," and, second, the need for referent establishment and reference tracking.

CONCLUSIONS

Pointing signs, eyegaze behavior, and head and body orientation in sign languages originate in nonverbal communication, but the more mimetic uses of these expressions interact with their use as markers of such linguistic features as reference, predication, topicalization, specificity, and constituent boundaries.

The different aspects of a holophrastic pointing gesture are distinguished in pointing signs that differentiate reference to an entity from predication of an entity's being in a location or moving to, from, or about in a location, and the functional difference by and large correlates with differences in form. Although predicates in the form of pointing signs are always indexical, indicating the state or action of an item in its location, a referential pronoun or a determiner as part of a nominal may be indexical or nonindexical.

Eyegaze behavior and head and body rotation can only be interpreted in the light of the manual signs. Breaking off eye contact with the receiver can be interpreted in different ways depending on the manual signals. It may signal the characters' level in imitative eyegaze, or the narrator's level when used for reference tracking or to signal major syntactic boundaries, whereas configurational eyegaze is ambiguous between the characters' level and the narrator's level. Although there is a tendency for imitative eyegaze to be of longer duration than reference-tracking eyegaze and for the eyegaze in configurational eyegaze to move around rather than just being fixed in a single direction, these form differences are not absolute. In the same way, signers may reorient their head or their body for other purposes than to indicate a locus.

Research on gestures accompanying speech has found both examples of pointing gestures with nominals that establish referents and with predicates, but it is not clear whether there is a difference in form between these two types as in Danish Sign Language. Another question for future research is the significance of the orientation of the hand (palm sideward or downward) in pointing signs and any possible interaction between significant hand orientation and assimilation to the hand orientation of the preceding or the following sign.

APPENDIX

The examples from Danish Sign Language are simplified versions of transcriptions in a system where the individual lines indicate simultaneous actions by different articulators (hands, eyes, head, mouth, etc.). The central line indicates manual signs transcribed by glosses in capital letters. If the signer makes a sign with the nondominant hand, the gloss is placed in the line below the central line.

OBTAIN	English gloss for a manual sign.
MUST-NOT	A gloss consisting of more than one word, but standing for one sign only.
Bristol(M)	A name articulated by means of the mouth–hand system, a sort of manual alphabet.
gesture	A gesture that native signers do not consider a standard sign.

TRAVEL^GONE	A compound sign.
1.p	The first-person pronoun.
PRON	The non-first-person pronoun.
DET	The determiner.
POSS	The possessive pronoun.
PROFORM	A pointing sign made simultaneously with other signs (described in the text).
/	Boundary shown by visual "rhythm."

Modifications of signs are indicated by + followed by a label for the modification.

[+]	An unspecified modification.
+pl.	Plural (the hand moves sideways).
+group	Collective (the sign is repeated in a circular movement).
TWO+pron.	A dual pronoun derived from the number sign TWO.

Modifications for loci, that is, indexical modifications, are represented by letters or letter combinations for individual loci. The letter or letter combination before the gloss for a verb refers to the agent or experiencer's locus and the letter or letter combination after the gloss refers to the patient or receiver's locus: fr = forward right; fl = forward left; sr = sideward right; sld = sideward left downward; slu = sideward left upward; fsr = forward sideward right; c = the signer's locus; neu = a neutral marker, the direction forward from the signer.

Nonmanual signals are transcribed in the lines above and below the line with glosses for manual signs. An activity continues until a new symbol appears, or its duration is indicated by a dotted line. For eyegaze direction, letters corresponding to the letters for loci on glosses indicate that the signer looks in the direction of the locus.

+	Eye contact with the receiver.
V	Eye blink.
*	Imitative eyegaze in no particular direction.
-	The signer looks away from the receiver, but the direction is irrelevant.

Head and body orientation is transcribed as follows:

| rot.fr | The head (occasionally the body) is rotated so that the signer faces the direction forward right. |

rot.rec.

The head (occasionally the body) is rotated so that the signer faces the receiver.

____t

Topicalization expressed by a combination of nonmanual signals with the scope of the entire constituent (Engberg-Pedersen, 1990).

Mouth movements are transcribed underneath the glosses, either by means of a sequence of letters that approximates the signer's soundless mouth movements [*adh* and *ahh* in Example (13)] or by a description of the mouth movements [*tight-lipped* in Example (13)].

REFERENCES

Bahan, B. J., & Supalla, S. J. (1995). Line segmentation and narrative structure: A study of eyegaze behavior in American Sign Language. In K. Emmorey & J. S. Reilly (Eds.), *Language, gesture, and space* (pp. 171–191). Hillsdale, NJ: Lawrence Erlbaum Associates.

Baker, C. (1977). Regulators and turn-taking in American Sign Language discourse. In L. A. Friedman (Ed.), *On the other hand: New perspectives on American Sign Language* (pp. 215–236). New York: Academic Press.

Bos, H. F. (1994). An auxiliary verb in Sign Language of the Netherlands. In I. Ahlgren, B. Bergman, & M. Brennan (Eds.), *Perspectives on sign language structure: Papers from the Fifth International Symposium on Sign Language Research. Vol. 1* (pp. 37–53). Durham, England: University of Durham, International Sign Linguistics Association.

Butcher, C., Mylander, C., & Goldin-Meadow, S. (1991). Displaced communication in a self-styled gesture system: Pointing at the nonpresent. *Cognitive Development, 6,* 315–342.

Emmorey, K. (1999). Do signers gesture? In L. S. Messing & R. Campbell (Eds.), *Gesture, speech, and sign* (pp. 133–159). Oxford: Oxford University Press.

Emmorey, K. (Ed.). (in press). *Perspectives on classifier constructions in sign languages.* Mahwah, NJ: Lawrence Erlbaum Associates.

Engberg-Pedersen, E. (1990). Pragmatics of nonmanual behaviour in Danish Sign Language. In W. Edmondson & F. Karlsson (Eds.), *SLR '87: Papers from the Fourth International Symposium on Sign Language Research* (pp. 121–128). Hamburg: Signum.

Engberg-Pedersen, E. (1993). *Space in Danish Sign Language: The semantics and morphosyntax of the use of space in a visual language.* Hamburg: Signum.

Engberg-Pedersen, E. (1994). Some simultaneous constructions in Danish Sign Language. In M. Brennan & G. Turner (Eds.), *Word-order issues in sign language: Working papers* (pp. 73–87). Durham, England: University of Durham, International Sign Linguistics Association.

Engberg-Pedersen, E. (1995). Point of view expressed through shifters. In K. Emmorey & J. S. Reilly (Eds.), *Language, gesture, and space* (pp. 133–154). Hillsdale, NJ: Lawrence Erlbaum Associates.

Friedman, L. A. (1975). Space, time, and person reference in American Sign Language. *Language, 51*(4), 940–961.

Greenberg, J. H. (1985). Some iconic relationships among place, time, and discourse deixis. In J. Haiman (Ed.), *Iconicity in syntax* (pp. 271–287). Amsterdam: John Benjamins.

Gullberg, M. (1996). Deictic gesture and strategy in second language narrative. In L. S. Messing (Ed.), *Proceedings of the Workshop on the Integration of Gesture in Language and Speech* (pp. 155–164). Newark, DE: Applied Science and Engineering Laboratories.

Gullberg, M. (1998). *Gesture as a communication strategy in second language discourse: A study of learners of French and Swedish.* Travaux de l'Institut de Linguistique de Lund 35. Lund: Lund University Press.

Lakoff, G. (1987). *Women, fire, and dangerous things: What categories reveal about the mind.* Chicago: University of Chicago Press.

Liddell, S. K. (1990). Four functions of a locus: Reexamining the structure of space in the ASL lexicon. In C. Lucas (Ed.), *Sign language research: Theoretical issues* (pp. 176–198). Washington, DC: Gallaudet University Press.

Liddell, S. K. (1995). Real, surrogate, and token space: Grammatical consequences in ASL. In K. Emmorey & J. S. Reilly (Eds.), *Language, gesture, and space* (pp. 19–41). Hillsdale, NJ: Lawrence Erlbaum Associates.

Liddell, S. K. (1996). Spatial representations in discourse: Comparing spoken and signed language. *Lingua, 98,* 145–167.

Liddell, S. K., & Metzger, M. (1998). Gesture in sign language discourse. *Journal of Pragmatics, 30,* 657–697.

Lillo-Martin, D., & Klima, E. (1990). Pointing out differences: ASL pronouns in syntactic theory. In S. D. Fischer & P. Siple (Eds.), *Theoretical issues in sign language research: Vol. 1. Linguistics* (pp. 191–210). Chicago: University of Chicago Press.

Lyons, J. (1977). *Semantics* (Vol. 2). Cambridge: Cambridge University Press.

McNeill, D. (1992). *Hand and mind: What gestures reveal about thought.* Chicago: University of Chicago Press.

McNeill, D., Cassell, J., & Levy, E. T. (1993). Abstract deixis. *Semiotica, 95*(1/2), 5–19.

Padden, C. A. (1986). Verbs and role-shifting in American Sign Language. In C. A. Padden (Ed.), *Proceedings of the Fourth National Symposium on Sign Language Research and Teaching* (pp. 44–57). Silver Spring, MD: National Association of the Deaf.

Poizner, H., Klima, E. S., & Bellugi, U. (1987). *What the hands reveal about the brain.* Cambridge, MA: MIT Press.

Streeck, J. (1993). Gesture as communication: I. Its coordination with gaze and speech. *Communication Monographs, 60,* 275–299.

Supalla, T. (1986). The classifier system in American Sign Language. In C. Craig (Ed.), *Noun classes and categorization* (pp. 181–214). Amsterdam: John Benjamins.

Supalla, T. (1990). Serial verbs of motion in ASL. In S. Fischer & P. Siple (Eds.), *Theoretical issues in sign language research: Vol. 1. Linguistics* (pp. 127–152). Chicago: University of Chicago Press.

Winston, E. A. (1995). Spatial mapping in comparative discourse frames. In K. Emmorey & J. S. Reilly (Eds.), *Language, gesture, and space* (pp. 87–114). Hillsdale, NJ: Lawrence Erlbaum Associates.

Zimmer, J., & Patschke, C. (1990). A class of determiners in ASL. In C. Lucas (Ed.), *Sign language research: Theoretical issues* (pp. 201–210). Washington, DC: Gallaudet University Press.

Chapter 12

Pointing and Morality in Chicago

David McNeill
University of Chicago

Although pointing appears to be a simple matter of aiming the hand at some target, it is in fact a process with several components. There is the *pointing sign* itself, and also an *origo* and a *deictic field* (which includes the target, the addressee and the speaker). The target, moreover, is not always present. A target can be *created* through the act of pointing, and this is the case with the gestures described in this chapter.

All of the components of pointing fit into a single semiotic structure. Anything with this structure is considered to be pointing. In North American culture, the pointing sign is canonically an extended index finger, or G-hand.[1] The deictic field is the spatial domain of both the referent of the pointing and the pointing itself. It must be part of pointing in order to ensure the identifiability of the referent. The perspective within the deictic field is such that the object is presented in this field from the point of view of an origo—the zero point from which the pointing is oriented. The term *origo* is from Bühler (1982). The end result of pointing is a structuring of space in terms of a spatial location, regarded from the origo, with everything in a framework that includes the target, the speaker and the addressee (see Hanks, 1990; Levinson, 1983). For example, pointing to a cup

---

[1]Pointing is not limited to the classic extended index finger. To point requires only an extensible body part—hand, arm, and head are the most common—and it can also be accomplished with metaphorical body parts, such as imagined "eidola" beaming out from the eyes. The analysis in this chapter does not depend on the specific form of the gesture.

on the table in the next room organizes the space in terms of, not the room or space as laid out by a floor plan, but the object in a deictic field that shows the whereabouts of this object in relation to the origo.

The same process can map nonspatial content as well, doing this as if the content were spatial. A mapping of nonspace onto space creates a target object where none exists. This "abstract pointing" (McNeill et al., 1993) is a kind of gestural metaphor; something (space) is used to present something else that is inherently nonspatial. Bühler (1982) referred to such pointing as *deixis at phantasma*. In this chapter I analyze a case of *deixis at phantasma* and present evidence for its conversational functionality. In this example, the spatial construction that is achieved had a decisive effect on the course of the conversational interaction. A moral conflict arose over the meaning of the created space, and this conflict, and the responses to it, became a turning point of the conversation.

DISTRIBUTION OF POINTING IN A CONVERSATION

The conversation I examine was recorded in the mid-1970s by Starkey Duncan in the (then) Department of Behavioral Sciences at the University of Chicago. It features two previously unacquainted male graduate students. Following Michael Silverstein's notation (explained later), one student is called Mr. A and the other Mr. B. Mr. A was a law student and Mr. B a social work student. The experimenter had introduced the participants to each other and video recording began immediately. The instructions were simply to "hold a conversation" for 10 or 15 minutes. There were spontaneous (unprompted, un-called-for) gestures throughout. All cases of pointing were metaphoric in the preceding sense; all were creating abstract meanings in space, and none were indicating real entities in space.

From the point of view of the pointing gestures, the conversation naturally breaks into three unequal phases.[2] Pointing dominated the middle phase.

The first phase was taken up with brief remarks about a questionnaire that both Mr. A and Mr. B had completed and about two other subjects in the experiment with whom Mr. A and Mr. B had previously held separate conversations, also video recorded. Mr. A and Mr. B performed 14 gestures in this phase. Of these, 57% were nondeictic metaphoric gestures of the "conduit" type (e.g., saying about one of the other experimental subjects, "so I kinda know her," and appearing at the same time to hold a bounded

---

[2]The Mr. A–Mr. B conversation was transcribed by Starkey Duncan and was first used for analysis in the early 1980s by the Anaphora Workshop, at the University of Chicago. The Workshop included Starkey Duncan, Maya Hickmann, Elena Levy, Rebecca Passaneau, Michael Silverstein, and myself.

entity in the hand; see McNeill, 1992), 28% were points or deictics, and 14% were other types or were difficult to classify. The second phase was the initiation of an attempt on Mr. A's part to discover Mr. B's academic biography, part of an interactional game that Silverstein (1997) dubbed Getting to Know You. It took a form typical among students, the exchange of academic histories, although in this instance the game was strangely one-sided. Mr. A probed; Mr. B evaded. Mr. B never quite revealed his educational past and gave the impression of wanting to avoid the topic. Mr. A's pursuit of Mr. B during this middle phase climaxed in the snippet focused on in this chapter. Mr. A and Mr. B together produced 13 gestures in the Getting To Know You phase, of which 23% were metaphoric and 77% deictic (there were no others). Thus, there was a dramatic upsurge of pointing during this phase.

The third phase began immediately after the pointing phase with the following:

A: óh óh óh óh óh I'm an óld Jésuit Boy mysélf / / unfórtunately

This statement was the start of the actual conversation in the sense that, from this point on, Mr. A and Mr. B talked about a mutually accepted topic, the character of Jesuit education, how it is special and how it compares to experiences at the University of Chicago, with Mr. A's "unfórtunately" announcing the end of his until-then relentless pursuit of Mr. B and his past and his ushering in of a newfound fellow-student camaraderie. The gesture situation also changed dramatically, in that pointing virtually disappeared. Of 110 gestures from Mr. A and Mr. B in the third phase (by far the largest part of the interaction), fully 93% were various kinds of nondeictic conduit metaphoric gestures, and only 6% were pointing.

The near total disappearance of pointing in Phase 3 can be explained with the aid of the concepts of the origo and the deictic field, and the use of pointing to create new references. Pointing embodies the orientation of the speaker toward a topic by placing the topic at a location in the deictic field vis-à-vis the speaker as the origo (McNeill, Cassell, & Levy, 1993). The key to the second, pointing phase in the interaction was that the pointing by both speakers toward possible topics realized these topics as loci in space. Once Mr. A and Mr. B had found a topic, this motivation disappeared and with it the urge to point at empty space, and other forms of gestural metaphor took over.

THE POINTING PHASE

Table 12.1 gives the snippet of the Mr. A–Mr. B conversation that is the focus of this analysis. It picks up at the end of what has been Mr. A's already, by then, extended effort to uncover Mr. B's academic history. Mr. A had

TABLE 12.1
Selection From a Conversation Between
Two Male Students

Mr. A	Mr. B
QA6 how do you like Chicago compared to QA7 did you [go to school thére] or uh *points to shared space*	

	RB7.1 I did go to school [there]
	    points to shared space
	RB7.2 [I went to school hére]
	    points to left
	RB7.3 [álso]
	    circles to left

uh-huh	RB7.4 [I]
	    points to shared space
	RB7.5 [/ um]
	    points to left
	RB7.6 so I [came back]
	    points to shared space

oh, uh-huh	RB7.7 [kind of /] *points to right*
QA8 an' [you wént to undergraduate hére or -------- (A's gesture held) --------------]	
points to shared space	RB8 [in Chicágo] át, uh, Loyola *points to shared space*

pursued this line for a number of turns and had earlier asked "Where did you come from before?" and Mr. B had offered, "Mm, Iowa. I lived in Iowa." This led Mr. A down the garden path, however, because Mr. B proved reluctant to take up Iowa as a topic, but the Iowa theme is relevant since it led directly to the exchanges in Table 12.1. After Iowa petered out, Mr. A resumed his quest for Mr. B's biography (Q means a question, R means a reply, A or B means the speaker, and the number of the question or reply is the ordinal position of the item in the snippet; notation as in Silverstein, 1997).

Silverstein's Analysis of the Text in the Pointing Phase

Silverstein identifies "stretches of interactionally-effected denotational text." These are runs of local cohesion indexed via references to past or present locations. In QA7 "did you go to school thére or uh," Mr. A formulates his probe about Mr. B's past temporal location, "then**B**," with "go to school," although his goal was actually to elicit information about Mr. B's relationship to the past spatial location, "there**B**." This indexical probe, "go to school," carries a framework for coherence into the next step of the conversation. The most recent denotational frame before Q**A**7 was that of Iowa (either Iowa City and/or State). This would have been the default frame for the emphasized "thére" of Q**A**7. Mr. B in his reply at R**B**7.1 picks up this frame, when he says, "I did go to school there." Yet, ambiguity remains because Mr. A's "thére" can be a substitute for either "*in* Iowa" or "*at* Iowa" and which, "in" or "at," is left unsaid. In other words, it could equally designate "$^{C/S}$there**B**" ("in") or "^{U}there**B**" ("at") (C means City, S State, and U University).

Mr. B does nothing to disambiguate the frame in R**B**7.1, where he repeats the precise formulation of Mr. A's Q**A**7, using the same predicating phrase "go to school there." Mr. B however continues to clarify the temporal order of the paradigm that he has set up, but still not the institutional affiliation: He has gone to school "here**B**," he says in R**B**7.2, as well as "there**B**" in R**B**7.1. The result, as Silverstein pointed out, is a deictically organized progression of references that sketches Mr. B's academic biography ($\rightarrow$t means temporal succession):

$$in \text{ or } at \text{ }^{U/C}\text{Chicago} \rightarrow t \text{ } in \text{ or } at \text{ }^{U/S}\text{Iowa} \rightarrow t \text{ } in \text{ or } at \text{ }^{U/C}\text{Chicago}$$

This contains multiple ambiguities of deictic reference between "in" and "at," but the most important of these for the remainder of the snippet is, what "Chicago" is Mr. B speaking of: "The University of" ("at") or "the City of" ("in")? Mr. A pursues the topic once again and asks in Q**A**8 "an' you wént to undergraduate hére or" if Mr. B had been an undergraduate at the University of Chicago, using a noninverted, confirmatory question that preserves the exact predicate form of Mr. B's R**B**7, the "go to school."[3] Even this formulation by Mr. A is not without "denotational-textual wiggle-room," as Silverstein described it. It would have been possible for Mr. B to have replied as though Mr. A had been asking if he had been an undergraduate "^{C}hére," that is, in the City of Chicago, simply by saying "yes," for example.

Yet "for reasons unknown," Mr. B chooses to reveal that "most important of emblems of identity in professional- and upper-class America, the 'old school tie,' " and supplies the long-sought information in R**B**8 ("in Chicágo át, uh, Loyola"). Mr. B at last differentiates City and University—although

---

[3]"[Mr. A] seems to blend two simultaneous informational quests in his utterance, which makes for a rather strange discontinuous colloquial phrase with focal stress, 'wént . . . hére' superimposed upon the . . . repetition of [an] earlier construction. . . . The different focalization of these two blended constructions leaves no doubt to us analysts which is the more important piece of information being asked for; it is the undergraduate institution with which Mr. B's identity can be affiliated" (Silverstein, 1997, p. 293).

apparently with reluctance. The result is the following now clarified deictic structure in which the only ambiguity remaining is whether "Iowa" meant the University as well as the State:

in ^{C}Chicago, *at* ^{U}Loyola →t *in* or *at* $^{U/S}$Iowa →t *in* ^{C}Chicago, *at* ^{U}Chicago.

As it turned out, Mr. A also "went to undergraduate" at an (albeit different) Jesuit institution. The conversation thereupon took off and Mr. A's hard-won discovery led to many nonproblematic exchanges on the theme of Jesuit education.

Analysis of the Pointing

Not included in Silverstein's analysis of the A–B text is the creative use by both speakers of the gesture space via pointing. Analysis of the metaphoric deictic structures in the conversation will lead to an explanation of Mr. B's unexpected capitulation in **RB8**. In general, the patterns of pointing were:

Mr. A points only into the shared or landmark space.
Mr. B points into this space and also points to the left and, crucially, once to the right.

In the rest of this chapter, "left" and "right" refer to directions from the point of view of the speakers. Mr. A was seated to Mr. B's right and the shared space is the overlapping part of their personal spaces between them (Özyürek, 2000). This had the advantage that left, center, and right were the same for both speakers.

The shared space acquired meaning as the discourse topic, and this meaning and its shifting values and the contrasts of other gestures to it are the subject of the analysis to follow. The shared space initially had the meaning of Mr. B's academic past in Iowa, "Iowa-then." As noted previously, this reference is ambiguous between the State of Iowa and the University of Iowa, and which was meant was never spelled out. The meaning at **RB7.1** when Mr. B pointed to the shared space and said "I did go to school [there],"[4] thus could have been either the State or the University of Iowa.

A corresponding ambiguity exists during **RB7.2–3** when Mr. B continued, "[I went to school hére] [álso]," and pointed two times to the left, that is, away from the shared space. As with the verbal deixis, "hére," this left

---

[4]In describing gestures, square brackets show when the hands were in motion; / signifies an unfilled speech pause. All gestures are pointing, Mr. A's mostly with the classic G-hand shape, Mr. B's with a loose 5-hand shape (see Fig. 12.1 for typical gestures).

space could have meant either the *City* of Chicago or the *University* of Chicago, and following Silverstein is designated "$^{C/U}$Chicago-then."

The meaning of the deictic field clearly changed for Mr. B at RB7.6, when he said "so I [came back]" and pointed to the shared space that previously had meant "Iowa-then" (the status of the shared space at RB7.4–5 is unclear). This meaning shift could have hinged on temporal updating. Mr. B wanted to move the topic into the present and thus contrasted "now" to the "then" that had been the left space at RB7.2–3. This contrast put "now" into the shared space, and "Chicago" came along with it. However, once imported, "Chicago" too became part of the shared space for Mr. B. Thus, at RB7.6, the shared space meant "Chicago-now," and this became Mr. B's new thematic reference point. But which "Chicago"—the City or the University?

I argue that, at this moment, if not sooner (for we can't be sure about RB7.4–5), the shared space meant for Mr. B the *City*. The crucial indication is that Mr. B pointed to the *right* at RB7.7 and hedged the reference to coming back with "[kind of /]." He was evidently saying that he had come back to Chicago, but hadn't come back to *Chicago*, and placed this Chicago$_1$ versus Chicago$_2$ opposition on a new shared versus right space axis.

I claim that the shared and right spaces cannot have the same meaning: that one is the City and the other is the University (or at least is *not*-the-City), although we cannot say from the spatial contrast itself which space has which meaning. Subsequent pointing however soon makes this clear.

Mr. A now asks his fatal question (QA8): "an' [you wént to undergraduate hére or]" and points again to the shared space with an extended hold that is maintained during Mr. B's response. Mr. A's use is unambiguous: The space means for him the University (see note 3). Mr. B's response at RB8 also points to this space while saying, crucially, "[in Chicágo] at, uh, Loyola"—the unexpected capitulation after a career of evasion.

The preposition "in" shows that Mr. B was indicating the City as opposed to the University. Thus the shared topic space for Mr. B at this point meant the City, not the University. This in turn suggests that the *right* space at RB7.7 meant the University and not the City.

This meaning allocation moreover would explain the hedge "kind of." What Mr. B meant when he said "so I came back kind of," was that he had returned to one kind of Chicago (the City), but it was not the Chicago that might have been supposed in this conversation—the University where Mr. B and Mr. A were students and where the conversation was taking place (or alternatively, the "kind of" hedge flagged *not*-the-City).

That Mr. B hedged and introduced a new spatial contrast also suggests that he was aware of the "$^{C/U}$Chicago" ambiguity. Had he been thinking only of his own meaning of "^{C}Chicago" for the shared space, there would have been no motivation for introducing a new space for "^{U}Chicago" (or "*not*

^{C}Chicago") and the hedge. In other words, Mr. B, without realizing it, tipped his hand that his persistent "$^{C/U}$Chicago" ambiguity had been intentional.

That Mr. A and Mr. B had conflicting meanings for the shared topic space and that Mr. B was aware of this also explains why Mr. B gave up his resistance at this very moment. This is the puzzle that remains after Silverstein's analysis. As noted earlier, Mr. B easily could have continued dodging Mr. A by perpetuating the ambiguity, had he wished, merely by answering QA8 with "yes."

However, the shared space and "here" meant the City for Mr. B whereas they meant the University for Mr. A. This contradiction confronted Mr. B with an interactional problem on a new level: the need to cease being merely evasive and to start lying; apparently Mr. B did not make this choice.

Mr. B could not avoid his dilemma by not pointing: Mr. A had already pointed into the shared space with the unambiguous meaning of "^{U}Chicago" and Mr. B had previously pointed to it with the opposite meaning of "^{C}Chicago"; moreover, Mr. A was *continuing* to point at the shared space with the contradictory meaning; Mr. B's confrontation with morality was inescapable.

That Mr. A maintained his pointing gesture during the entirety of Mr. B's response suggests that for Mr. A, also, there was a sense that the central gesture space had become a field of confrontation.

Thus, the role of pointing into the gesture space was an active one in this stretch of conversation. Pointing contributed to the dynamics of the conversation and included such interpersonal factors as evasion, probing, and confession. Table 12.2 summarizes the meanings given to the right, shared, and left spaces in the snippet. Figure 12.1 shows the phases of the denouement—Mr. B's pointing both immediately before and during his hedge,

TABLE 12.2
Meanings Attributed to the Right, Center,
and Left Spaces by Mr. A and Mr. B

	Right	Shared	Left
QA7 did you go to . . .		$^{S/U}$Iowa-then	
RB7.1 I did go to . . .		$^{S/U}$Iowa-then	
RB7.2 I went here			$^{C/U}$Chicago-then
RB7.3 also			$^{C/U}$Chicago-then
RB7.4 I		??	
RB7.5 /um			??
RB7.6 so I came back		^{C}Chicago-now	
RB7.7 kind of	^{U}Chicago-now		
QA8 you went to under- graduate here		^{U}Chicago-now (held through the following)	
RB8 in Chicago at Loyola		^{C}Chicago-now	

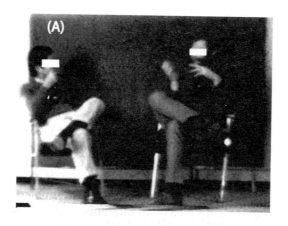

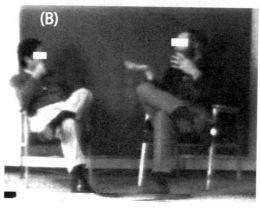

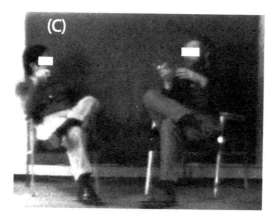

FIG. 12.1. (A) Mr. B's two-handed deixis in the shared space with "so I [came back]." (B) Mr. B's immediately following two-handed deixis in the right space with the hedge, "[kind of /]." (C) Mr. A's held deixis in the shared space as Mr. B also points in the shared space and answers the fatal question with "[in Chicago]." Reproduced with permission.

and Mr. A's held deixis in the shared space as Mr. B also pointed in the shared space and answered the fatal question.

ANALYSIS OF B'S GROWTH POINT AT RB8

Although Mr. B's utterance "[in Chicágo] át, uh, Loyola" displays minimal linguistic structure, it is interesting as a microcosm of the conditions under which utterances form in general. These conditions can be analyzed with the concept of a growth point (McNeill, 1992; McNeill & Duncan, 2000). Such an analysis will help generalize the growth point concept by exhibiting a case where the core idea of an utterance is abstract and moral rather than (as in most earlier examples) visual and spatial.

The growth point (GP) is the name we give to an analytic unit combining imagery and linguistic categorial content. GPs are inferred from the totality of communicative events with special focus on speech–gesture synchrony and coexpressivity. It is called a growth point because it is meant to be the initial form of a thought unit out of which a dynamic process of organization emerges. It is also called a GP because it is the theoretical unit in which the principles that explain mental growth—differentiation, internalization, dialectic, and reorganization—also apply to real-time utterance generation by adults (and children). A final reason for calling it a GP is that it addresses the concept that there is a specific starting point for a thought. Although an idea unit continues out of the preceding context and has ramifications in later speech, it does not exist at all times, and comes into being at some specific moment; the formation of a growth point is this moment, theoretically.

Growth Point and Background

In the view of the GP concept, thinking is carried out fundamentally in terms of *contrasts*. The gestalt principle of a figure differentiated from a ground applies. The background of thinking indexes and is constrained by external conditions, cognitive, social, and material, but the background is also under the control of the speaker; it is a *mental construction*; it is part of the speaker's effort to construct a meaningful context and a thought unit within it. The speaker shapes the background in a certain way, in order to give significance to the intended contrast, and the background and the contrast are constructed together. The joint product results in the differentiation of a new meaning from a background. Obviously, in this view, meaning and background are inseparable in their existence.

I use the terms *field of oppositions* and *significant (newsworthy) contrast* to refer to this constructed background and the differentiation of GPs. All of this is meant as a dynamic system in which new fields of oppositions are formed and new GPs or psychological predicates (Vygotsky, 1987) are differentiated.

Mr. B's GP

The concept of a GP elucidates Mr. B's thinking at the critical juncture when he confronted the moral crisis of lying or telling the truth. Under the prevailing imperative to orient himself to the proffered topic of his personal biography (itself a product of the pointing procedure), Mr. B's thinking was dominated by the distinction between ^{C}Chicago and ^{U}Chicago on which his biography turned, and his apparent wish to blanket this distinction under the ambiguous word "Chicago."

In the case of **RB**8, the field of opposition, as Mr. B construed it, was something like To Lie About Loyola versus To Tell The Truth About Loyola. Mr. B's chosen contrast in this field was the To-Tell-The-Truth pole. That is, Mr. B's meaning at this point was not just the denotational content of "in Chicago, at Loyola," but the moral content of coming out with the truth when the alternative was lying. This was a product of his current field of oppositions. This hidden content was, I believe, the core of his meaning at this moment, and the various parts of the meaning materialized in one or both of the modalities, speech and gesture (in other words, I claim, this utterance could not have significantly deviated from this form), to wit:

> Mr. B's contradiction with Mr. A materialized via pointing at the space that Mr. A had designated as "^{U}Chicago" but meaning by this space, "^{C}Chicago."
>
> The "in" lexical choice brought out ^{C}Chicago, which is the "Truth" alternative.
>
> The "in"–"at" succession arose from the "$^{C/U}$Chicago" ambiguity that Mr. B had been perpetuating. Having separated the City meaning with "in," Mr. B went on to lay out the University component with "at."
>
> The stress pattern, "in Chicágo–át," displays precisely this contrast within a consistent rhythmic and vocalic pattern (i.e., "ín Chicago–át," or "in Chicágo–at Loyóla"—the other possible combinations—twist the rhythm and poetics, and lose the contrast that splits out the University concept as something distinct from "^{C}Chicago").
>
> The "át," in turn, led to "Loyola" but with hesitancy as if completion of the City–University paradigm had taken on a life of its own and was unfolding somewhat against the will of the speaker or at least with lingering uncertainty.

The conditions leading to **RB**8 included: (a) Mr. A and Mr. B's joint orientation to the shared gesture space, (b) Mr. B's awareness of his contradiction with Mr. A over the meaning of the shared space, and (c) the role of this contradiction in creating the moral dilemma that Mr. B ultimately confronted. The contradiction with Mr. A was one pole of the utterance and the resulting moral dilemma for Mr. B was the other. The contradiction was highlighted by Mr. A's protracted pointing to the shared space while Mr. B invoked the "^{C}Chicago" meaning. Together, these poles were the direct determinants of the form of the utterance that we observe.

The GP thus incorporated information about the contradiction with Mr. A and Mr. B's awareness of it, plus Mr. B's sense that he was confronting a moral dilemma and his decision to resolve it. Mr. B's unpacking of the GP into "[in Chicágo] át, uh, Loyola" grew out of the contrasts built into it, despite Mr. B's squeamishness over the final revelation. Thus, according to this model, the utterance was a product of Mr. B's individual thinking at a particular moment in a specific pragmatic–discourse context, and encompassed interpersonal, moral, discourse, and historical-biographical dimensions.

Mapping Thinking Onto Space

The shared space (indicated only in gestures) thus had a compelling reality for Mr. A and Mr. B. Mr. B's immediate cognitive experience was mapped onto this space and its left and right alternates. Pointing worked like referential deixis, only in reverse. By pointing, Mr. A and Mr. B created and instantiated referents in the discourse. The critical "object" ($^{C/U}$Chicago) was located in the shared space that existed for both Mr. A and Mr. B, and became the focus of Mr. B's moral dilemma—what was he to say it *was?* By pointing at QA8 and holding the gesture, Mr. A made clear that he thought it was "U"; however, Mr. B knew that it was "C." The conflict was inseparable from the pointing procedure, without which there would have been no conflict, and no dilemma.

THE INTRAPSYCHIC/INTERPSYCHIC INTERFACE

I conclude with a brief statement of the implications of the Mr. A–Mr. B conversation for the relationship of the social context of a conversation to the individual thought processes of the participants in it. The dilemma that Mr. B confronted occurred at the interface of mind and the social context. We can regard it as at the interface of Vygotsky's (1987) two planes, the *interpsychic* and the *intrapsychic* (the interpsychic alone tends to be discussed in the conversation analytic literature where Vygotsky's theory often undergoes an "intraectomy"; cf. Duranti & Goodwin, 1992). The GP (awareness of the contradiction, the moral dilemma) is intrapsychic in the Vygotskian dichotomy and yet it interfaces with the interpsychic plane (the interactional game, evasiveness, confession). It is important to maintain the inter/intra distinction, lest the mind be regarded as nothing more than a passive sketchpad of the social interaction. The challenge, which was seen clearly by Vygotsky, is to figure out how the mind remains autonomous while it engages the social context. The GP presents a picture of how this can be done. The GP describes how individual thinking internalizes content from the "interactionally effected" frame to create idea units that support, indeed cannot help but generate, textual coherence. Although interactional content appears on the two planes, the content has different functions on each. This is the key to their interfacing and their distinctiveness. The most visible manifestation of functional differentiation occurred at **RB**8 when both Mr. B and Mr. A were simultaneously pointing at the shared space but had opposite intended meanings. *Inter*psychically, this was a tussle over the meaning of the space. *Intra*psychically, the tussling had the further meaning that it embodied Mr. B's dilemma, whether to lie or tell the truth. On this *intra* plane, the tussle was part of Mr. B's personal mental life and was subject to autochthonous forces of his own (his wish to camouflage his past, his rejection of lying), whereas on the *inter* plane it was subject to the social forces of the interaction between Mr. A and Mr. B (politeness constraints in particular; cf. Brown & Levinson, 1990). The point is, both planes are sources of representations running through Mr. B's mind at this moment, as evidenced in the precise form of the utterance at **RB**8. Moreover, the very construction of the meaning—his Chicago past—as a deictic field with entities, an origo, and a perspective is a model translated from the inter to the intra plane. The GP as a unit of thinking is the point where these various forces come together. Although the GP is itself on the *intra* plane, it ties together influences on thought and action that scatter over both the interpsychic and intrapsychic planes. Vygotsky said that everything appears in development twice, first on the social plane, then on the individual. The same logic and direction of influence applies to the GP. Vygotsky saw the necessity of a unit that encompasses this transformation, invoking the concepts of psychological predicates and inner speech to express this unity in the minds of socially embedded individuals. The growth point concept is meant to be heir to these insights.

ACKNOWLEDGMENTS

Preparation of this chapter was supported by grants from the Spencer Foundation and the National Science Foundation (STIMULATE and KDI Programs). I thank Michael Silverstein for commenting on an early draft.

Chapter 13

Interplay of Gaze, Hand, Torso Orientation, and Language in Pointing

Sotaro Kita
Max Planck Institute for Psycholinguistics

Any analytical inquiry is destined to compartmentalize different parts of a complex system. The study of body movements in a communicative situation is no exception. Traditional nonverbal communication studies dissociated speech and body movement; however, a new line of inquiry emerged around 1980, in which gestures spontaneously accompanying speech were considered to be a psycholinguistic phenomenon (e.g., Butterworth & Beattie, 1978; Kendon, 1980; McNeill & Levy, 1982). It brought speech and body movement together. However, it created a new compartmentalization by treating speech-related body movements and other types of body movements separately. This contrasts with the studies of gesture in the tradition of conversational analysis, in which gesture and other body movements (including facial expressions) have been taken to be integral cues that regulate the flow of face-to-face interaction (e.g., Goodwin, 1986; Goodwin & Goodwin, 1986; Streeck, 1993; also Goodwin, chap. 9, this volume).

The goal of this chapter is to bring some of the body movements that might otherwise be considered as nonspeech related (e.g., the orienting the torso to a particular direction, the movement of gaze) back into the psycholinguistic study of gesture. More specifically, I aim to demonstrate that orientation of torso and movement of gaze are partly regulated by demands for spatial processing that underlies the production of co-speech gesture.

Most of the body movements and speech discussed in this chapter were produced during naturalistic route directions, recorded in Tokyo, Japan (some additional data on gaze movement and pointing were collected in an experiment also in Tokyo). The analysis focuses on speech and body movements associated with pointing gestures that indicate the direction of turns on the routes described, or the direction of a distant invisible landmark.

This chapter discusses two types of interplay among torso orientation, gaze movement, pointing gesture, and speech. First, the pattern of coordination among torso orientation, pointing gesture, and speech suggests that pointing gestures influence the process of speech production. More specifically, pointing gestures help the speaker to zero in on the correct choice out of the notoriously confusing pair of concepts, LEFT or RIGHT, in the course of verbally expressing a direction. (See also Kita & Essegbey, 2001, in press, for further evidence.) Second, the coordination between gaze movement and pointing gesture to a distant invisible location suggests that a visual strategy is taken to fine-tune the estimate for the target direction of a pointing gesture. These two lines of coordination can be interwoven in the stream of behaviors during route direction. Movements of torso and gaze that are initiated for spatial processing surely have further interactional consequences, and such movements are sometimes initiated primarily for interactional reasons. I do not intend to underplay the significance of interactional factors that regulate torso, gaze, gesture, and speech in face-to-face interaction. Rather, the goal of this chapter is to illustrate that cognitive processes underlying torso orientation, gaze movement, pointing gesture, and speech can partly account for how these behaviors are coordinate in the expression of a direction. Let us start with the first line of coordination among torso orientation, pointing gesture, and speech.

THE INTERPLAY OF HAND, TORSO ORIENTATION, AND LANGUAGE

In this section, it is argued that people coordinate pointing gesture and torso orientation to facilitate a certain cognitive process underlying speaking. More specifically, how the direction of a turn is indicated by speech and body movements during route direction reveals that pointing gestures can facilitate the choice between the concepts LEFT and RIGHT as a part of preparation for verbally expressing the direction of a turn. Let me first explain how the route direction data were collected.

The Route Direction Data

The data consist of video-recorded naturalistic route directions. I approached pedestrians in front of the library of a university in Tokyo and asked how to get to the subway station near the campus. After the route to the subway station was described, I asked how to get to the university bookstore. The interaction was video-recorded in PAL format (25 frames per second) with a Hi-8 camcorder by a research assistant from a distance. The audio signal was radiotransmitted to the camcorder and also recorded. After giving the directions, the people were debriefed that it was part of research and were asked whether the audio and video recording could be used for the study. All of the 20 people approached except for one who did not have time for debriefing gave permission to use the recording. All the people were familiar with the campus and the two target locations. Because of technical difficulties, only 17 people's route directions to the subway station and 18 people's route directions to the university bookstore were recorded with a quality suitable for the analysis.

The two routes described by the participants are illustrated in Fig. 13.1. X indicates the location from where the route direction was given. From X, cars on Hongo Street were partially visible through trees and a fence. This street leads to the subway station. No landmark along the routes beyond the first turn was visible. Red Gate is a landmark well known to the general public because it is a symbol of the university.

Evidence for the interplay among pointing gesture, torso orientation, and speech comes from gestural and linguistic expressions for the four turns that are invisible from X. Three of them are on the way to the subway station: turns A2, A3, and A4. The other is on the way to the bookstore: turn

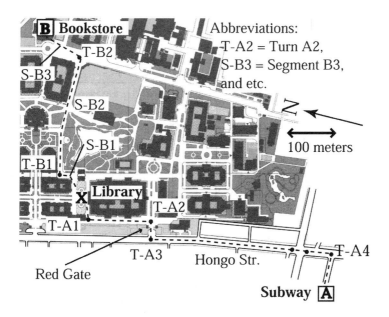

FIG. 13.1. The map of the two routes described.

B2. We focus on these turns in the following subsections. (For further information about the locale and more detailed description of the speech and gesture, see Kita, 1998.)

Linguistic and Gestural Means for Expressing Turn Direction

The direction of a turn was linguistically expressed in four ways. One way was to use *migi* "right" or *hidari* "left." Another was to specify the direction of the section of the path after a turn by means of a local landmark (e.g., "if you turn, there is a brick building, whose first floor is the bookstore," "If you go this way, there is Red Gate. Go out through the gate"; note that in the current context, one has to turn right in order to go through the gate). These two were the dominant ways of linguistically indicating the turn direction. For a given invisible turn, a majority of the people used one or both of the two means in their description of a given turn: turn A2, 100%; turn A3, 82%; turn A4, 75%; turn B2, 93%. There were two other less frequent ways to indicate turn direction. One was to perspectivize the target from the viewpoint of a person following the route (e.g., "it is on the other side of the intersection"). The other was to use a demonstrative word (e.g., *acchi* "that direction," *koo* "like this"). For a given invisible turn, only a minority of people used one or both of these means in their description: turn A2, 0%; turn A3, 9%; turn A4, 17%; turn B2, 29%.[1]

Gestural expression of turn direction can be classified into three categories depending on the coordinate system (or frame of reference) under which the gesturally expressed vector can be interpreted (for a more general discussion about linguistic and nonlinguistic frames of reference see Levinson, 1996, in press; Pederson et al., 1998). Imagine a situation in which a person is facing away from a turn, and gesturally indicating the turn direction (person A in Fig. 13.2). One possibility is for the person to gesture to the left because the turn is a left turn for a person who is traveling the relevant part of the route. The coordinate system underlying this type of gesture is relative to the gesturer's body and the person's body orientation is not aligned to the route; thus, we call this type a *nonaligned relative gesture*. In the same situation, the gesture could be oriented to the geographically correct direction of the turn. We call this type a *nonaligned absolute gesture*. The third type of gestural expression of the turn direction is veridical under both relative and absolute coordinate systems. This happens when the

---

[1]Note that for a given turn the numbers from this set and the earlier mentioned set do not add up to 100% because some people use multiple means to indicate turn direction, whereas others did not linguistically specify turn direction at all. See Table 3 in Kita (1998) for more details.

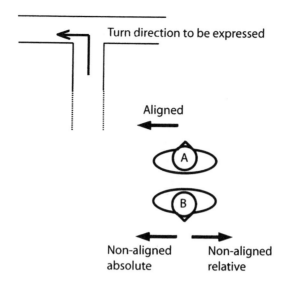

FIG. 13.2.   Three types of gestural indication of the turn direction.

gesturer's body is aligned to the section of the route that leads up to the turn (person B in Fig. 13.2). In this case, the two coordinate systems are aligned, and a gesture to the left is correct in terms of both relative and absolute coordinate systems. We call this type an *aligned gesture.*

The Mechanism of Gestural Facilitation of Conceptual Planning for Speaking

Now we are ready to formulate the thesis of this section: Some of the aligned gestures were produced to facilitate the choice between the concepts LEFT and RIGHT, in the course of linguistically expressing the direction of an invisible turn. I propose that such gestural facilitation takes place through the following steps.

Step 1. A decision is made that one of the left/right terms will be used in speech to express the turn direction, as opposed to other linguistic means (e.g., by referring to a landmark).

Step 2. The torso is rotated so that the absolute and relative coordinate systems are aligned.

Step 3. The direction of the turn is calculated and gestured on the basis of an absolute coordinate system.

Step 4. The gestural body movement heightens the "awareness" of the relevant half of the body.

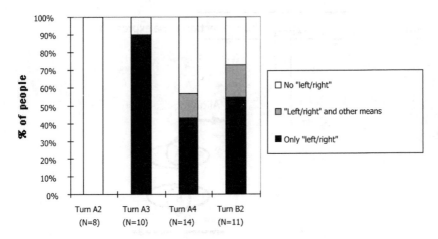

FIG. 13.3. Linguistic expression of turn direction that is concurrent with the gestural indication of the turn direction. (N refers to the total number of people who gesturally indicated the direction of a given turn.)

Step 5. This "awareness" facilitates the choice between LEFT and RIGHT.

Aligned Gestures and the Linguistic Expression of the Turn Direction

First, I provide the evidence for the first two steps of the proposal for gestural facilitation of conceptual planning for speaking: People get into the aligned position in preparation for saying *hidari* "left" or *migi* "right." The evidence for this claim in a nutshell is that aligned gestures are selectively produced in the turns for which *hidari* "left" and *migi* "right" are more likely to be used in the speech concurrent with the gesture.

Turn A2 is unique among the turns in the choice of linguistic means to indicate the turn direction. The left–right terms were never used for this turn. Everybody used the "Red Gate," which refers to a prominent and famous landmark, to indicate the direction of turn A2. Figure 13.3 summarizes uses of the left–right terms that were concurrent with gestural indication of turn direction (the concurrent speech of a gesture is defined as the clause that overlaps with the stroke or hold phase of the gesture).[2] The four

---

[2]An excursion of a hand for a gesture can be broken down into distinct phases (Kendon, 1980). In the hold phase, the hand stays still in the air. In the stroke phase, the hand makes more forceful movement than the surrounding phases. See McNeill (1992) and Kita, van Gijn, and van der Hulst (1998) for further discussion.

turns differ as to whether or not the left–right terms are used for at least one concurrent turn-indicating gesture (the sum of the black and grey bars in Fig. 13.3) (chi square = 16.25, df = 3, $p < .00$). More specifically, the left–right terms are less likely to be used in turn A2 compared to turn A3 (Fisher's exact test, two-tailed, $p < .00$), turn A4 (Fisher's exact test, two-tailed, $p = .04$), and turn B2 (Fisher's exact test, two-tailed, $p = .01$).

If some of the aligned gestures are preparations for the utterance including the left–right terms, then it is predicted that aligned gestures are less likely to be produced for turn A2 than other turns since no left–right terms are used. Figure 13.4 shows exactly this tendency. There is evidence that fewer people chose aligned gestures (as opposed to nonaligned relative or absolute gestures) for turn A2 compared to turn A3 (Fisher's exact test, one-tailed, $p = .01$), turn A4 (Fisher's exact test, one-tailed, $p = .04$), and turn B2 (Fisher's exact test, one-tailed, $p = .07$).

The analysis of semantic coordination of speech and gesture at the gesture token level also provides converging evidence (Fig. 13.5). Nonaligned relative gestures and nonaligned absolute gestures differ very much in how the concurrent speech expressed the turn direction: nonaligned relative gestures' concurrent speech contains the left–right terms as opposed to other linguistic means (a local landmark, a demonstrative, a perspectivizing expression such as "on the other side of the intersection") much more often than concurrent speech with nonaligned absolute gestures (Fisher's exact test, two-tailed, $p = .01$). If some of the aligned gestures are produced in association with the choice between the concepts LEFT and RIGHT, then it is predicted that the data for aligned gestures should lie somewhere between those for nonaligned absolute gestures and nonaligned relative ges-

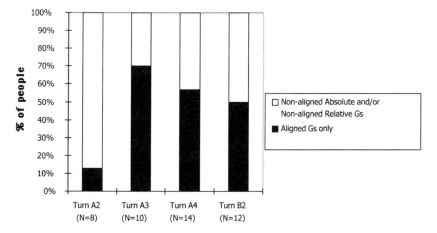

FIG. 13.4.   Gestural expression of turn direction. (N refers to the total number of people who gesturally indicated the direction of a given turn.)

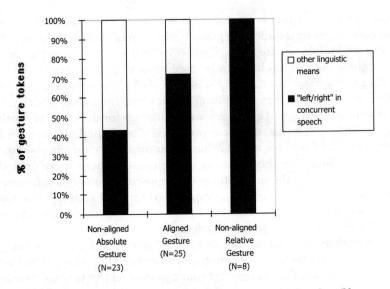

FIG. 13.5. Gesture types and linguistic expressions of turn direction. (N refers to the number of tokens of a given gesture type that have linguistic indication of turn direction in the concurrent speech. The tokens are aggre-
gated over all the participants.)

tures. This prediction is born out, as shown in Fig. 13.5. With regard to the
likelihood of using the left–right terms to indicate turn direction in the
concurrent speech, aligned gestures differ from nonaligned absolute gestures (Fisher's exact test, one-tailed, $p = .04$), and marginally from
nonaligned relative gestures (Fisher's exact test, one-tailed, $p = .08$).

These results suggest the following. First, people make a decision as to
the type of linguistic expression to be used for direction indication: a
left–right term or some other linguistic means. When people decide to use
a left–right term, at least some of the time, they turn their torso to get into
the position for aligned gestures.

The Shape Features of Aligned Gestures

Now we move to Step 3 of the gestural facilitation of conceptual planning
for speaking. Supporting evidence for this step is provided by shape features of the three gesture types. Aligned gestures are shaped more like
nonaligned absolute gestures than nonaligned relative gestures. More specifically, in nonaligned absolute gestures and aligned gestures, the elbow is
more likely to be fully extended during the stroke or hold phase than in
nonaligned relative gestures (Fig. 13.6). The entire hand (from the wrist

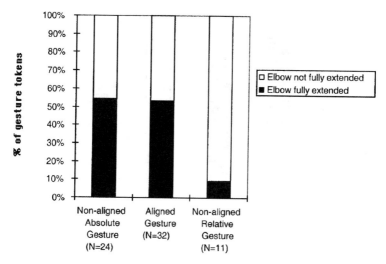

FIG. 13.6. Gesture types and elbow extension. (N refers to the number of tokens of a given gesture type from all the participants.)

up) is raised above the shoulders more often during the stroke or hold phase than in nonaligned relative gestures (Fig. 13.7).

There is virtually no difference in the likelihood of elbow extension between the nonaligned absolute gestures and aligned gestures, whereas there is a significant difference between nonaligned relative gestures and aligned gestures (Fisher's exact test, two-tailed, $p < .00$). Similarly, the difference in the highest hand level between nonaligned absolute gestures and aligned gestures is not statistically significant (Fisher's exact test, two-tailed, $p = .28$), whereas there is a significant difference between the nonaligned relative gestures and aligned gestures (Fisher's exact test, two-tailed, $p < .00$).

This pattern of shape features suggests that nonaligned absolute gestures and aligned gestures share an underlying production mechanism, which is distinct from the one for nonaligned relative gestures. More specifically, the results just described suggest that, like nonaligned absolute gestures, aligned gestures are produced on the basis of some calculation of the absolute direction.

The Gesturing Hand Heightens Awareness of the Relevant Half of the Body in Preparation for Uttering "Left" or "Right"

Step 4 in the facilitation process is the crucial step toward gestural facilitation of the choice between the concepts LEFT and RIGHT, in which the absolute coordinate system is translated into the relative coordinate system. Sup-

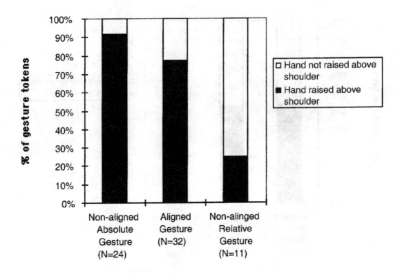

FIG. 13.7. Gesture types and the highest hand level. (N refers to the number of tokens of a given gesture type from all the participants.)

porting evidence for this step comes from the observations that (a) the over-whelming majority of the direction-indicating gestures are performed in the ipsilateral gesture space (not crossing the body midline to the other side), and (b) when the word *right* is uttered, there is a preference for a right-hand gesture, and when the word *left* is uttered, there is a preference for a left-hand gesture. Among the total 42 right-hand gestures produced by the people who participated in the study, 40 are performed in ipsilateral gesture space. Among the total 27 left-hand gestures, 25 are performed in ipsilateral gesture space. Figure 13.8 shows the choice between left and right hands for direction-indicating gestures in different linguistic contexts.

When neither *right* nor *left* is used in speech (i.e., the clause that is syn-chronized with a direction-indicating gesture does not contain either of these two words), then there is a slight preference for a right-hand gesture (61%), which we can take as a baseline. There is a tendency that when the word "right" is used, right-hand gestures are more frequent than in the baseline, and when the word "left" is used, left-hand gestures are more fre-quent than in the baseline (however, these differences do not reach statisti-cal significance). Concurring with earlier reports on synchronization of coexpressive gesture and speech (McNeill, 1992; Morrel-Samuels & Krauss, 1992), the onset of the preparation phase of a direction-indicating gesture always precedes the word *left* and *right*.

Data on the choice of hand summarized in Fig. 13.8 are, however, com-promised by the fact that most of the people (14 out of 19) were holding

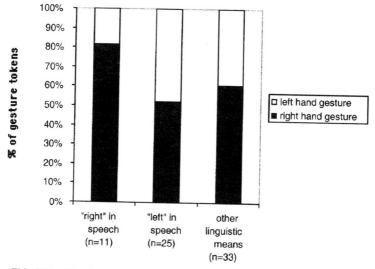

FIG. 13.8.   The hand choice in direction indicating gestures in three linguistic contexts.

something (a wallet, a bag, etc.) in one of their hands, and they could not freely choose the hand to gesture. This is presumably the reason that the data summarized in Fig. 13.8 do not show a strong enough tendency to reach statistical significance. Holding an object in a hand, however, sometimes creates a situation that in fact strongly indicates a left-hand preference when the word *left* is about to be uttered, and a right-hand preference when the word *right* is about to be uttered. Three of the participants passed an object from one hand to the other hand before the word *left* or *right* was uttered, as if to make the appropriate hand (the left hand for *left* and the right hand for *right*) free. The hand that became free indeed then indicated direction when the left-right term was about to be uttered.

The following example is such a case. In this example, the speaker linguistically described the direction of turn B2 twice in a short succession: first with *mae* "front," and then with a complex expression, *hidari naname mae* "left diagonal front," which included one of the left-right terms.

Example 1

Speech–gesture synchronization is indicated in the following way. Square brackets ([ ]) indicate the onset and offset of a gestural excursion of hands (a gesture unit in Kendon, 1980, a movement unit in Kita et al., 1998). The bold-faced portion of the speech is synchronized with the stroke phase of a gesture (the phase that is more forcefully performed than neighboring phases), and the underlined portion of the speech with a hold phase.[3] The stroke and hold phases potentially bear meaning. An excursion can contain more than one stroke or hold with preparation phases in between; in that case, the vertical bar (|) indicates that the onset of the preparation for the next gesture.

A, B, C, D, E, F, and G refer to the frames in Fig. 13.9. They are aligned with respect to speech to show the relative synchrony (e.g., E occurred between *aso* and *ko*). Numbers 1, 2, and 3 indicate the beginning of gesture 1, gesture 2, and gesture 3, respectively.

$$\hphantom{xxxxxxxxxxxxxxxxxxxxxxxxxxxxxxxxxxxxxxxxxxxx} \text{A}$$

|1 mawa-rer-u   yoo-<u>ni   koo   maruku nat-te-ru   n</u>
   turn.around-can-Pres in.order.that like.this round   become-Resl Noml

|2 des-u   yo
   Polite:be-Pres PrgPrt
"in order that (a bus) can turn around, (it) is round like this."

$$\hphantom{xxxxxxxxxxxx} \text{BC   D}$$

sore-no   **ma<u>e</u>**-ni   nari   mas-u]
Pronoun-Gen front-Dat become be:Polite-Pres
"(the bookstore) is on the other side of it."

$$\hphantom{xxx} \text{E   F   G}$$

[3 aso   **ko-cchi-kara**<u>   ik-u   to hidari nana</u>]me mae no
   the(re) ProxD-way-side-from go-Pres if left   diagonal front-Gen

hookoo-ni (unintelligible)
direction-Dat
"if (one) goes from the(re), here, (it is) at the direction of left-diagonal-front."

The speaker's body is in the orientation for aligned gestures throughout. The first linguistic expression of turn direction is accompanied by a right-hand gesture, which points across the torso to the left (gesture 2 in Example 1; see also frame C in Fig. 13.9). The torso orientation (Fig. 13.10) and the direction of the gesture make this gesture an aligned gesture. Up to this point, the right hand alone has been performing a series of gestures (except for gesture 1, where both hands are used to represent roundness), and the left hand is holding a purse. After gesture 2, the speaker passes the purse from the left hand to the right hand, and then an aligned gesture by

---

[3]See Kita et al. (1998) for more detailed definitions of different gesture phases and the coding criteria.

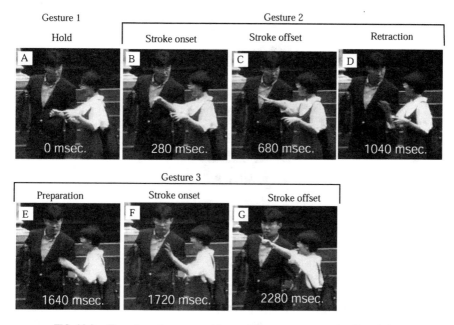

FIG. 13.9. Two aligned gestures with two different accompanying linguistic expressions for the direction of turn B2. See Fig. 13.10 for the orientation of the speaker's torso. The building in the background is the library.

the left hand indicates the same direction (gesture 3). While the left hand is being held after the stroke of gesture 3, the speaker starts to utter the word *left*.

Making the left hand free by passing the purse to the other hand indicates that there is an urge to perform the gesture with the left hand at that moment. It is reasonable to assume that step 4 in the facilitation process is more effective when the left hand points to the left than when the right hand points to the left. The three cases like this example in the data suggest that the people, at some level, "know" that a certain body movement would heighten awareness of the relevant side of the body, which is helpful for choosing the appropriate concept: LEFT or RIGHT. Otherwise it is difficult to explain why they bother to switch hands by passing an object from one hand to the other when they are about to utter a left–right term.[4] I pro-

---

[4]One could argue that this is due to a "recipient design": namely, pointing left with the left hand is more helpful for the addressee than pointing left with the right hand. However, this depends on the relative orientation of the speaker and the addressee; when they are facing, then the speaker's left is the addressee's right. In the three cases of passing an object from one hand to the other, the speaker and the addressee are in roughly the 90 degree angle as in Fig. 13.9. Thus, the recipient design explanation is not straightforward, although it cannot be ruled out.

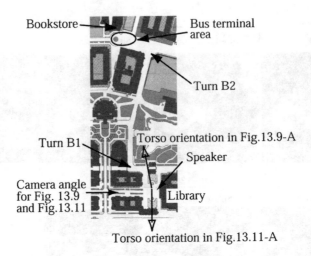

FIG. 13.10.   Detailed map of the route to the bookstore for Fig. 13.9 and Fig. 13.11.

posed that this tacit knowledge people have leads to the preference for a left-hand gesture when the direction is to the left, and a right-hand gesture when the direction is to the right.

Facilitating the Choice between the Concepts LEFT and RIGHT

In step 5 of the facilitation process, I conjecture that the locus of facilitation is at the level of conceptualization, rather than at other levels of speech production. In the literature, there have been different proposals as to exactly which stage of the speech production process gesturing facilitates. One view is that gesture facilitates conceptual planning (e.g., Alibali, Kita, & Young, 2000; Kita, 2000). Another view maintains that gesture facilitates lexical retrieval either from the morphosyntactic lexicon or from the phonological lexicon (e.g., Krauss, Chen, & Chawla, 1996). Although the present data do not clearly differentiate the two views, I argue that it is at the conceptual level, not at the lexical level, that direction-indicating gestures facilitate production of an utterance containing the words *left* or *right*. There are two reasons for this. First, "left" and "right" are confusing at the conceptual level, but not at any lexical levels. This pair of words is confusing neither morphosyntactically nor phonologically (in any case, this pair is no more confusing than pairs such as "up" and "down"). Second, it is not clear how body movement can affect access to the mental lexicon (especially the phonological lexicon). In contrast, it is plausible that the concepts LEFT and RIGHT have an embodied component as a part of their mental representation, and that the embodied component of these concepts is activated by relevant body movement (Kita & Essegbey, 2001). Kita (2000) presented further arguments for the conceptual planning view as opposed to the lexical retrieval view.

In summary, I have argued that pointing gesture plays a role in facilitating the choice between the concepts, LEFT or RIGHT, in the course of linguistically expressing a turn direction. When people decide to express a turn direction with a left–right term, they orient their torso for an aligned gesture. The aligned gesture is produced on the basis of absolute sense of direction. This gestural body movement activates the appropriate concept, LEFT or RIGHT, because both the absolute and relative coordinate systems are aligned.

THE INTERPLAY OF THE GAZE AND THE HAND

Visual Probing Prior to Pointing to an Invisible Target

In the preceding section, I discussed the interplay of torso orientation, gestural movement, and speech. In this section, I discuss how gaze is woven into the orchestration of body movements in the course of pointing. When one points to a visible target with a hand, the gaze first seeks the target. The question arises as to what the gaze does when the target is invisible. I argue that a visual strategy is employed even for invisible targets to fine-tune the estimate for the target direction. Gaze movement during pointing to an invisible target is at least partially governed by this strategy (Of course, gaze movement is also governed by interactional factors). Evidence comes from the route directions analyzed in the previous section and an additional experiment.

In the route directions already analyzed, the transition between the route direction to the subway station and that to the bookstore provides clear cases of visual probing before pointing to an invisible target. Many people are standing with their back to the bookstore after describing the route to the subway station. (One indication of this is that eight people were in the aligned position when gesturally indicating the direction of turn A4 [Fig. 13.4].) Seven out of the 19 people gesturally indicate the direction of the bookstore at the beginning of their answer to my question how to get to the bookstore. The bookstore is about 400 m away and invisible. All of the seven people look at the area around turn B1, which is the only visible part of the route to the bookstore, before the stroke of the pointing gesture (the pulsive movement that leads to the apex of pointing).

The following is an example of visual probing of the area around turn B1.

Preparation onset   Stroke onset   Stroke   Stroke offset

FIG. 13.11.   Visual probing during pointing to the bookstore, which is invisible for the speaker. See Fig. 13.10 for the speaker's torso orientation. The
building in the backgroun is the library. The gaze is on the direction of turn
B1 from 800 ms. till 1640 ms. The hand shape in B, C, and D is a fist with the
thumb extended and separated from other fingers, as in the "thumb-up" emblem in Morris et al. (1979).

Example 2

A, B, C, and D refer to the frames in Fig. 13.11. The sequence of plus
signs (+) indicates the period when the gaze was locked on to the direction
of turn B1. Square brackets, a vertical bar, boldface, and underlining indicate when the gesture occurred with respect to speech (see preceding example for the explanation of the conventions). A, B, C, D, +, and the speech
transcript are aligned to represent relative synchrony (e.g., B and C occurred sometime between the first *desu-ne* and *ko-cchi-gawa* and when the
gaze was on the direction of turn B1; the gaze continued to be on the direction of turn B1 till *ko* was uttered).

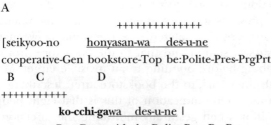

A

            +++++++++++++++
[seikyoo-no   honyasan-wa   des-u-ne
cooperative-Gen bookstore-Top   be:Polite-Pres-PrgPrt
  B   C   D
+++++++++++
          ko-cchi-gawa   des-u-ne |
          ProxD-way-side be:Polite-Pres-PrgPrt
"As for the cooperative bookstore, it is this way."

I propose that people fine tune the target direction by extrapolating
from the visible part of a path that leads to the target. In other words, people imagine how the invisible part of a path to the target (segment B2 and
segment B3 in Fig. 13.1) would look if there were nothing to obstruct the
view, and the visible part of the path is examined to increase the accuracy of
the imagination.

There are a couple of problems with this interpretation of the speakers' gaze movement. First, it is not clear whether the people look at the area around turn B1 to fine-tune their estimate for the target direction, or whether they have already calculated the target direction and use the gaze to establish joint attention on the target direction with the interlocutor (cf. the interlocutor's gaze direction in A and B in Fig. 13.11). This lack of clarity stems from the fact that turn B1 and the bookstore are in roughly the same direction from where the speaker is. Another possibility is that the speaker looks at the area around turn B1 in order to prepare for following utterances about the new route.

To rule out these alternatives, an experiment was conducted in which the direction of the target and the direction of the visible part of the route to the target were dissociated. Furthermore, pointing was performed outside the context of route direction. The participants of the experiment were asked to point to a certain location without saying anything; thus, the participants did not have to prepare for the description of the route to the target.

Experiment on Gaze in Pointing to an Invisible Target

This experiment was carried out in the same university campus as in the route direction study. Twenty participants were recruited on the street next to the library and tested individually. They were asked to point to the location of Red Gate and Main Gate, which were both invisible (Fig. 13.12). Before pointing, they were asked to align their bodies along a line drawn on the ground. This surreptitiously oriented their bodies directly toward the target. A video camera was placed directly in front of the participant, 2 m away. Participants were told to look at the camera and were then instructed

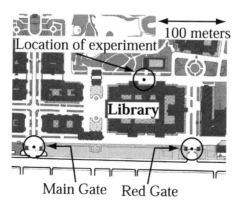

FIG. 13.12. The location of the experiment and the two targets for pointing.

TABLE 13.1
Errors in the Pointing Direction (Degrees)

	Mean	Median	SD	Minimum	Maximum
Red Gate (n = 20)	7.5	12.5	12.5	-19.0	22
Main Gate (n = 20)	10.7	7.5	15.9	-16	43

Note. A positive number indicates a bias to the counterclockwise direction in Fig. 13.12.

to point at one of the two target locations: for example, "please point to the following location: Red Gate." The experimenter stood behind the participant and out of sight from her/him. The order of the two targets was counterbalanced. The direction of pointing was measured by aligning the side of an orienteering compass (a compass built into a rectangular plastic plate) along the index finger after the participant's hand became still.

The results are summarized in Table 13.1. It indicates that the participants are reasonably accurate in their pointing;[5] the majority of the participants are within ±20 degrees of error or less (18 participants for Red Gate, 14 participants for Main Gate).

The participants were able to make a reasonable estimate for the direction of the invisible targets.[6] The question is whether there is evidence that gaze movement was used for calculation of target direction. If a participant visually imagines a path to the target to fine-tune the target direction, then the shortest path will provide the most accurate estimate. Thus, it is predicted that the participant visually examines the direction that leads to the shortest path. Thus, the predicted gaze movement pattern is the following. The gaze shifts to the right prior to the pointing to Main Gate. It shifts to the left prior to the pointing to Red Gate. In the postexperiment interview, all the participants said that they would go to the right in order to go to Main Gate, and to the left in order to go to Red Gate. This confirms that they know what the shortest paths to the targets are.

Gaze shift during gestural hand movement for pointing (from the end of the instruction till the pointing hand became still) was coded. The results are summarized in Table 13.2. There is a significant relationship between the target locations and the gaze movement patterns (chi square = 27.14, *df*

---

[5] The errors for the two targets do not differ (paired *t*-test, t = 0.79, df = 19, not significant), but they are significantly different from zero (Red gate: t = 2.67, df = 19, p = .02; Main gate: t = 3.00, df = 19, p = .01). The positive shifts in the error may be due to the measuring method. The vector between the eyes and the tip of the pointing finger may be the measurement that is more faithful to what the participant tries to gesturally express. Because most of the participants pointed with the right hand, the alternative measurement would shift the measurement clockwise on Fig. 13.12. This might bring the mean error closer to zero.

[6] See Lewis (1976), Baker (1989), and Levinson (1997, in press) for data from other cultures. Lewis and Levinson investigated Australian Aborigines, and Baker English.

TABLE 13.2
Number of Participants for the Three Gaze
Movement Patterns and the Two Target Locations

	Main Gate (Shortest Path, to the Right)	Red Gate (Shortest Path, to the Left)
Gaze to the right	15	0
Gaze to left	0	10
No gaze shift	5	9
Unclear	0	1

$= 3$, $p < .00$). The pattern of gaze movement suggests that participants fine-tuned the target direction by imagining the invisible section of the path to the target by extrapolating from the visible part of the path. I argue that this is why gaze movement to the visible part of the path precedes the stroke phase of a pointing gesture to an invisible target.

Gaze movement, torso orientation, and pointing can be orchestrated to facilitate the conceptual choice between LEFT and RIGHT. Prior to launching the stroke of an aligned gesture that indicates turn direction, gaze starts to probe the visible part of the route. Gesture 3 in Fig. 13.9 is such an example. This is presumably to fine-tune the computation of gesture direction.

CROSS-CULTURAL ISSUES

The specific orchestration of gaze, torso movement, and pointing, as described in this chapter, is not expected to be universal across cultures. This is because it involves (a) a convention of using left-right terms to express directions, and (b) fine-tuning of the estimated direction to an invisible target. There are reports that the former is not universal, and that the latter varies enormously across cultures.

Some languages do not have words equivalent to *left* and *right* (Danziger, 1997; Levinson, 1997, in press; Levinson & Brown, 1994; Pedersen et al., 1998). An example of such a language is Guugu Yimithirr, an Australian Aboriginal language (Haviland, 1993; Levinson, 1997). In this language, the cardinal direction terms (roughly equivalent to "north," "south," "east," "west") are used extensively (e.g., it is common to say things such as "there is a fly on your east shoulder"). Because Guugu Yimithirr speakers never have to say "left" or "right," it is predicted by the argument presented in this chapter that they do not bother to get into the torso orientation for an aligned gesture. Reports by Haviland (1993) and Levinson (in press) are consistent with this prediction. The vast majority of gestures in Guugu

Yimithirr narratives are absolute in orientation, and speakers do not rotate their torso to get into position for aligned gestures.

The way the direction of an invisible target is estimated also varies cross-culturally. Levinson (1997, in press) reported that speakers of Guugu Yimithirr can quite accurately estimate the direction of distant locations (from a few kilometers up to several hundred kilometers), where the visualization of a path would not help. Levinson (in press) reported that in Guugu Yimithirr discourse, "gaze is released from orientational functions." There is also a converging report about speakers of Arrernte, another Aboriginal group (Wilkins, 1996). In these cultural groups, gaze is coordinated with pointing in more diverse ways. Because Guugu Yimithirr and Arrernte speakers estimate the direction of distant locations apparently without the help of vision, gaze is free to take on other interactional functions.

There is cross-cultural supporting evidence for gestural facilitation of the conceptual choice between LEFT and RIGHT. In Ghana, there is a taboo on left-hand pointing. However, Kita and Essegbey (2001, in press) reported that the taboo does not lead to the total inhibition of direction-indicating gestures by the left hand. When the speaker is about to utter the word "left," the left hand becomes gesturally active despite the fact that such a gesture can be socially inappropriate. Similarly to the passing of a purse to the right hand to make the left hand free in Example 2, Ghanaian left-hand pointing just prior to uttering the word "left" indicates that there is a cognitive urge to gesture with the left hand when the speaker faces a confusing choice between the concepts LEFT and RIGHT.

SUMMARY

I have argued that the orchestration of pointing gesture, torso orientation, gaze movement, and speech can be partly accounted for by the interaction of the underlying cognitive processes. More specifically, I have discussed two kinds of interplay among these components of communicative behavior. First, pointing gestures in coordination with torso rotation facilitate the choice between the concepts LEFT and RIGHT. Second, gaze movement is used to visually fine-tune an estimate for the direction of an invisible target for pointing.

This study has brought together components of communicative behavior that are typically treated separately in psycholinguistically oriented studies of gesture. It has demonstrated that body movements such as torso rotation and gaze movement have close processing ties with pointing gestures, which in turn are interlinked with the speech production process. The coordination of gaze, torso movement, gesture, and speech is surely motivated by communicative factors, as scholars in the tradition of conversational analysis have demonstrated. However, it is also partially motivated by the interlinkage among various cognitive processes. Both interactional and cognitive sides of the story need to be taken into account in order to reach a full understanding of various body movements and speech as a unified system of communication.

ACKNOWLEDGMENTS

I would like to acknowledge helpful comments from the members of Gesture Project at Max Planck Institute and participants of the Pointing Workshop. I thank Mandana Seyfeddinipur and Nick Enfield for detailed comments on the chapter. I also thank Fuyuko Aoki for helping with the data collection.

REFERENCES

Alibali, M. W., Kita, S., & Young, A. J. (2000). Gesture and the process of speech production: We think, therefore we gesture. *Language and Cognitive Processes, 15,* 593–613.

Baker, R. R. (1989). *Human navigation and magnetoreception.* Manchester, England: Manchester University Press.

Butterworth, B., & Beattie, G. (1978). Gesture and silence as indicators of planning in speech. In R. N. C. & P. T. Smith (Eds.), *Recent advances in the psychology of language: formal and experimental approaches* (pp. 347–360). New York: Plenum.

Danziger, E. (1997). La variation interlangues dans l'encodage sémantique et cognitif des relations spatiales: quelques réflexions sur les données du Maya Mopan. In C. Fuchs & S. Robert (Eds.), *Diversité des langues et Représentations cognitives* (pp. 58–80). Paris: Editions Ophrys.

Goodwin, C. (1986). Gestures as a resource for the organization of mutual orientation. *Semiotica, 62*(1/2), 29–49.

Goodwin, M. H., & Goodwin, C. (1986). Gesture and coparticipation in the activity of searching for a word. *Semiotica, 62*(1/2), 51–75.

Haviland, J. B. (1993). Anchoring, iconicity, and orientation in Guugu Yimithirr pointing gestures. *Journal of Linguistic Anthropology, 3,* 3–45.

Kendon, A. (1980). Gesticulation and speech: Two aspects of the process of utterance. In M. R. Key (Ed.), *The relation between verbal and nonverbal communication* (pp. 207–227). The Hague: Mouton.

Kita, S. (1998). Expressing turns at an invisible location in route direction: The interplay of speech and body movement. In E. W. B. Hess-Lüttich, J. E. Müller, & A. van Zoest (Eds.), *Sign & space—Raum & Zeichen* (pp. 160–172). Tübingen: Gunter Narr.

Kita, S. (2000). How representational gestures help speaking. In D. McNeill (Ed.), *Language and gesture* (pp. 162–185). Cambridge: Cambridge University Press.

Kita, S., & Essegbey, J. (2001). Pointing left in Ghana: How a taboo on the use of the left hand influences gestural practice. *Gesture, 1,* 73–94.

Kita, S., & Essegbey, J. (in press). Left-hand taboo on direction-indicating gestures in Ghana: When and why people still use left-hand gestures. In M. Rector (Ed.), *Gesture: Meaning and use.*

Kita, S., van Gijn, I., & van der Hulst, H. (1998). Movement phases in signs and co-speech gestures, and their transcription by human coders. In I. Wachsmuth & M. Fröhlich (Eds.), *Gesture and sign language in human-computer interaction, International Gesture Workshop Bielefeld, Germany, September 17–19, 1997, Proceedings* (pp. 23–35). Lecture Notes in Artificial Intelligence, Vol. 1371. Berlin: Springer-Verlag.

Krauss, R. M., Chen, Y., & Chawla, P. (1996). Nonverbal behavior and nonverbal communication: what do conversational hand gestures tell us? In M. Zanna (Ed.), *Advances in experimental social psychology* (Vol. 28, pp. 389–450). Tampa, FL: Academic Press.

Levinson, S. C. (1996). Frames of reference and Molyneux's question: Cross-linguistic evidence. In P. Bloom, M. A. Peterson, L. Nadel, & M. Garrett (Eds.), *Language and space* (pp. 109–170). Cambridge, MA: MIT Press.

Levinson, S. C. (1997). Language and cognition: The cognitive consequences of spatial description in Guugu Yimithirr. *Journal of Linguistic Anthropology, 7,* 98–131.

Levinson, S. C. (in press). *Space in language and cognition: Explorations in cognitive diversity.* Cambridge: Cambridge University Press.

Levinson, S. C., & Brown, P. (1994). Immanuel Kant among the Tenejapans: Anthropology as empirical philosophy. *Ethos, 22,* 3–41.

Lewis, (1976). Route finding by desert aborigines of Australia. *Journal of Navigation, 29,* 21–38.

McNeill, D. (1992). *Hand and mind.* Chicago: University of Chicago Press.

McNeill, D., & Levy, E. (1982). Conceptual representations in language activity and gesture. In R. J. Jarvella & W. Klein (Eds.), *Speech, place, and action* (pp. 271–285). Chichester, England: Wiley.

Morrel-Samuels, P., & Krauss, R. M. (1992). Word familiarity predicts temporal asynchrony of hand gestures and speech. *Journal of Experimental Psychology: Learning, Memory, and Cognition, 18,* 615–622.

Morris, D., Collett, P., Marsh, P., & O'Shaughnessy, M. (1979). *Gestures: Their origins and distribution.* New York: Stein & Day.

Pederson, E., Danziger, E., Wilkins, D., Levinson, S., Kita, S., & Senft, G. (1998). Semantic typology and spatial conceptualization. *Language, 74,* 557–589.

Streeck, J. (1993). Gesture as communication: I. Its coordination with gaze and speech. *Communication Monographs, 60,* 275–299.

Wilkins, D. (1996). *Turning heads and making points: A case study of the Arrernte deployment of deictic gestures in relation to speech.* Unpublished manuscript, Cognitive Anthropology Research Group at Max Planck Institute for Psycholinguistics.

Author Index

Subject Index